Randolph Macon College
in the Early Years

Randolph Macon College in the Early Years

Making Preachers, Teachers and Confederate Officers, 1830–1868

JOHN CAKNIPE, JR.

McFarland & Company, Inc., Publishers
Jefferson, North Carolina

LIBRARY OF CONGRESS CATALOGUING-IN-PUBLICATION DATA

Caknipe, John.
    Randolph Macon College in the early years : making preachers, teachers and Confederate officers, 1830–1868 / John Caknipe, Jr.
        p.   cm.
    Includes bibliographical references and index.

    ISBN 978-0-7864-7946-7 (softcover : acid free paper) ∞
    ISBN 978-1-4766-1602-5 (ebook)

    1. Randolph-Macon College—History. I. Title.
    LD4701.R42C35   2015
    378.755'462—dc23   2014045858

BRITISH LIBRARY CATALOGUING DATA ARE AVAILABLE

© 2015 John Caknipe, Jr. All rights reserved

No part of this book may be reproduced or transmitted in any form or by any means, electronic or mechanical, including photocopying or recording, or by any information storage and retrieval system, without permission in writing from the publisher.

Front cover: Randolph Macon College main building (scrapbook of Mary McKinney, courtesy of Lisa A. Gillispie)

Printed in the United States of America

*McFarland & Company, Inc., Publishers
    Box 611, Jefferson, North Carolina 28640
    www.mcfarlandpub.com*

Table of Contents

Preface and Acknowledgments   1
Prologue   5

1. The Building of a Community   7
2. The Auxiliary Programs of a Country College: Involving the Community   41
3. A House Is Only as Good as the Foundation   68
4. The 25th Anniversary Reunion   86
5. Go Forth and Sow the Fruits of Thy Labor   101
6. Pranksters to Professors—The New Regime   130
7. The Military Institute and Those War Years   157
8. A Broader View of Some of the Faculty   173
9. The War Years   186
10. A Procrustean Analysis   203
11. Boydton Has a Voice   219

Epilogue   230
Appendix A: Salute to the Class of 1861   231
Appendix B: Roll of Honor   244
Appendix C: Faculty and Graduates of Randolph Macon College, Boydton, Virginia   276
Appendix D: Randolph Macon Cemetery   287
Chapter Notes   291
Bibliography   304
Index   315

Preface and Acknowledgments

Ever since I can remember, the old college at Boydton was a fascinating sight, although I hasten to admit I knew very little about it. When I was a child, my father would drive past it on our way to the lake fishing and my mother would have to make a quick stop to dig up a flower bulb to transfer to our home. For almost forty-five years, I drove or rode by the college and knew almost nothing about it. In doing research for books, articles and a couple of television shows, including *Who Do You Think You Are?* I drove by the college three or so times a week for about five years, and finally, one day I stopped and went in—that was 2006. Since then the magnificent building has rapidly deteriorated. After standing there for over one hundred and eighty years, the roof and walls have finally given up.

In 2007, I was writing a series of stories about the college for a local newspaper. I delivered copies to some local people, who I knew had a knowledge of the college, for proofreading. They suggested I do the research and not rely so much on handed down county folklore, and my journey began. I knew I needed a foundation resource from which I could gain a rudimentary understanding of the college and develop a working design. Jodee Showalter, assistant research librarian with the McGraw-Page Library of Randolph-Macon College (R-MC), Ashland, Virginia, informed me that most of the records of Randolph-Macon were absent, for a variety of reasons, and she suggested two books: *A History of Randolph-Macon College* (1898) by Richard Irby and *Randolph-Macon College: A Southern History 1825 to 1967* by Professor James Edward Scanlon (1983, University of Virginia Press). She also sent me a copy of a four part series on the history of Randolph Macon College by Jack Trammell with James Scanlon, written for the fall 2004 and 2005 issues of *R-MC* alumni magazine.

Irby's book provided a chronological listing of most of the graduates of the college, with some brief student and college history interspersed throughout. References were made to many of the Randolph Macon College Board of Trustees meetings and to some of the Methodist Conference records. Scanlon's book provided a more in-depth survey of the trustees and conference records with some reliance on archival documents at R-MC in Ashland. Both writers included the history of Randolph Macon College in Boydton, Virginia, and Randolph-Macon College in Ashland, Virginia. Deciding where to begin the monstrous task of doing research on a college, I knew that I was only interested in the part that was local—but what part? I was convinced that once I began the research, the story would evolve, and it did—five years and this manuscript later. It began as a research project for some history stories, then it became a story much bigger than just the town of Boydton or the county of Mecklenburg. It became a jigsaw puzzle that begged to be put together. At times, doing the research, I felt like a private investigator or detective, other times as my training dictated as a forensic psychologist—but it was never boring.

Researching Randolph Macon College in Boydton began with how, why, and when the college was located there. I felt it was important to develop a mental picture of college life at the time, especially since it was a farm environment and not referred to as a campus. As with any college, it was important to find a gauge to determine the level of success achieved by the students and faculty. I believe their collective accomplishments speak volumes of success.

The research began locally and then spread across the United States. Locally, I am truly indebted to Walter Beales III, attorney, who was not only encouraging, supportive, and helpful with resources, but who also served as a proofreader and editor for part of this manuscript, and to his paralegal, Kimberly Fuller. Thanks to Gene Coleman, clerk of the court for Mecklenburg County and his staff; Jack Hite and the staff of Boyd Tavern Foundation; Leigh Lambert, director of Southside Regional Libraries; Cassie Boyd, librarian, and Wanda Brooks, historian, at Boydton Public Library; and Gloria Taylor, librarian of the R.T. Arnold Library in South Hill. Other staff and libraries include the Crewe Public Library, Blackstone Public Library, Stovall (North Carolina) Public Library, Burkeville Public Library, Halifax County (Virginia) Public Library, Georgetown (South Carolina) Public Library, and North Myrtle Beach (South Carolina) Public Library. To Mark Pace, historian and librarian, the North Carolina Room, Granville County Public Library, for his assistance in going the extra mile with research, support, and suggestions, thank you.

Thanks goes to Bob Flippin, Southside Virginia Historical Press of Prince Edward County; James Bernie of the South Boston Library, Military History

Room (former instructor of military history for Penn State University); Gerald Gilliam, Dr. Harold Crowder, James and Louise Sheppard (local historians), and Beth Coates, director of the South Boston Museum; and Dr. William Shelton, Sr., and Mrs. Roberta Shelton of the former Southern Virginia Historical Society and owners of Steward Hall. I'm also grateful to Panthea Reid, professor emerita, Louisiana State University (an undergraduate of Randolph-Macon Women's College), Lynchburg, Virginia, for her family histories and encouragement early on in the process. Also, Rubinette Niemann, the historian of the Rose family who has a copy of the "Index for Church Book for the Mecklenburg Circuit Commencing in 1833 at Randolph Macon College," and Virginia Minnich for her help with research and the family histories of the Puryear families in the United States. Thank you to Lisa and Glen Gillispie for sharing their scrapbooks compiled by Mary McKinney.

My grateful appreciation extends to Larry Smith of Boydton, who provided me with a copy of some of the estate records from his collection of John and Alfred Boyd; Virginia Dare Wright, who graciously shared her scrapbooks, home, and family history with me about the Wright, Wootton and Carter families; and CWO-3 (U.S. Army, Retired) Ronnie Bugg for sharing his family history and research and family documents, and for his support, friendship, and encouragement, which included, following my experiencing some health issues, chauffeuring me to Randolph-Macon College–Ashland, the Lynchburg Public Library and to the Virginia Methodist Conference archives in Glen Allen, Virginia. My thanks also go to Stephanie Davis, archivist for the Methodist Conference of Virginia and the staffs of the Nottoway County Courthouse and Lunenburg County Courthouse.

My appreciation goes to Fred Anderson, director, Commonwealth of Virginia, Virginia Baptist Historical Society and Archives at the University of Richmond; Guy Hobb, archivist, Birmingham-Southern University, Birmingham, Alabama; Dr. Phillip Stone, archivist and historian, Wofford University, Spartanburg, South Carolina; Anne M. Veerkamp-Anderson, Smith Library Center, Southwestern University, Special Collections, Georgetown, Texas; also from the same library, Kathryn Stallard, head of Special Collections, Senator John F. Tower Archivist; Paul Crutchers, general manager 1610 XLR, broadcast and emerging media specialist, Lander University, Greenwood, South Carolina; and Dr. Dewitt Stone, Jr., special assistant to the president (and great grandson of Samuel Lander, Jr.); Shelley Wallace, temporary reference archivist, Special Collections and University Archives, University of Oregon, Eugene, Oregon; Bruce Tabb, associate professor, Special Collections Librarian, who went the extra mile to assist in my research; Lyle Lankford, in-house historian, Vanderbilt University, Nashville, Tennessee; Jackie

Wood, archivist, University of Memphis, Special Collections Acquisitions, Jackson, Tennessee; Valerie Gillispie, university archivist, and the staff of David M. Rubenstein Rare Book and Manuscript Library of Duke University, Durham, North Carolina; Jodee Showalter, assistant director, McGraw-Page Library, Archives and Special Collections, Randolph-Macon College–Ashland, and Laurie A. Preston, associate professor and head of research at that same college; and lastly, to Robert Rackley, research assistant, Central Missouri University, Fayette, Missouri, for his support, encouragement, research assistance and friendship. To Matt Fisher and Glenda G. Wootton, for their proofreading and editorial assistance, and to all the operators and administrative staff who helped me get to the right department and people, and to those I may have overlooked—thank you.

Last, but certainly not the least, is a special thanks to my family and to God's gift and blessing to me, my wife, Betty Mckinney Caknipe. These past three years have been filled with personal tragedies, but each time I would open my eyes, Betty was there. Each time there was a need or even with the silence, a family member would arrive with a smile and cheer. They endured and helped to make this manuscript become a reality, especially Ann McKinney Shelton and the late Arlene McKinney Wootton.

Prologue

Dr. Moses D. Hoge delivered the commencement address to the Washington and Franklin Literary Societies at Randolph Macon College in Boydton, Virginia, preceding the commencement exercises of 1867.[1] Part of that address follows.

The Dangers of the Hour

Henceforth mind will be the master, and Education the true signet of publicity. In the past, but few of our Virginia men have devoted themselves to letters, but have rather shown in the political arena. Virginia has produced some of the greatest orators, statesmen, and divines, that the world ever saw, but they have written but little, and their fame will pass away while that of inferior men in the North will live in their books. There is now greater danger than ever that this shall be so, since the young men of the South are so absorbed in efforts to attend to material interests and rebuild their fallen fortunes. But there is no real conflict between material and intellectual wealth. After all, it is the theorist who gives direction to the practicalities of life. Theory is to practice what cause is to effect. To the theorist we are indebted for all the great discoveries and inventions which have blessed mankind. And those who have added most to the glories of the lands in which they lived have been those who devoted themselves to literary pursuits. We pass by the heroes of old to admire Horace, Virgil, Homer, and Herodotus; and the visitor to Westminster Abbey will pass by the tombs of kings and mighty men to linger in dreamy sadness in "the poet's corner."

In our stricken land to-day we need ripe scholars, and our colleges must furnish them. But they cannot be produced in a day. Genius is of priceless value, but its lamp will go out unless it is fed by the beatten oil of patient labor.

Chapter 1

The Building of a Community

Randolph Macon College is the oldest continuous Methodist College in the United States, opened for the first term on October 9, 1832. It took four years for the process to come to fruition. The idea began, was formed into a motion, and was adopted by the Virginia Annual Methodist Conference held in Oxford, North Carolina, on February 24, 1825. The college was created in part by a $10,000 donation raised by concerned citizens of Mecklenburg County. Just as they had done in creating the William and Mary Seminary in 1817, they poured out their generosity again. The delegation before the Virginia General Assembly was led by Delegate William O. Goode, author of the legislation, who introduced the bill in the House of Delegates. It was sponsored by George Coke Dromgoole in the Senate. It was presented on January 15, 1830, with support from Colonel William Townes (the school's best friend and largest benefactor, owner of the Boyd Hotel and Tavern), Honorable Nathaniel Alexander (who had served both in Virginia's House of Delegates and Senate), Captain Beverly Sydnor (a War of 1812 veteran who was a Boydton merchant and gentry planter), and Howell Taylor of Bellegrade Plantation (which was originally built for William Randolph of the Virginia legislature).

William Randolph was an influential member of a pioneer Methodist family who owned a sizable plantation about three miles southeast of the town of Boydton, and nearby was Taylor's Ferry. The plantation was purchased by Colonel William Townes in 1837 as a wedding gift for his daughter, Isabella Townes, and Francis W. Boyd. The Taylor family was the eponym for Taylor's Meeting House, which was established before 1810 and was located on former property of David Brame. It became known as Poplar Springs Meeting House and later became Rehobeth Church. According to the church secretary in 1933, Virginia Haskins Bugg, the church is "located in a community of large landed estates, the church roll has always been small, but has ever been considered an active, dependable, well beloved church."[1]

On February 3, 1830, when the Randolph Macon College charter was approved by the Virginia General Assembly, Section 3 addressed,

> And be it further enacted, that [list of 30 names] be and are hereby constituted and appointed trustees of said college, who, and their successors, shall be a body politic and corporate by the name of "The Trustees of Randolph Macon College," who shall have a perpetual succession and a common seal, and by the names aforesaid, they and their successors shall be capable in law to possess, purchase, receive and retain to them and their successors forever, any lands, tenements, rents, goods, chattels or interest of any kind whatsoever, which may already have been given, or may hereafter be given, or by them purchased for the use of said college; to dispose of the same in any way whatsoever they shall adjudge most useful to the interests and legal purposes of the institution; and by the same name, to sue and implead, be sued and impleaded.[2]

In February 1830, the Virginia General Assembly approved the construction of the "Henry-Macon College." There had been extensive debates, especially over a college of theology, since they were considering chartering the Baptist College of Richmond at the very same time. During the debates, Senator Alexander changed the name to Randolph Macon College in honor of John Randolph of the Roanoke Plantation near present day Saxe, Virginia, and Nathaniel Macon of North Carolina—neither of whom were Methodist. But, because the Virginia Methodist Conference comprised most of the southeastern and Piedmont counties of Virginia along with the Piedmont counties of North Carolina, the choices seemed logical at the time.

John Randolph was the Virginia Congressman for the region, and he was also a close cousin of President Thomas Jefferson and Chief Justice John Marshall. Born in 1773, he studied at the College of New Jersey (Princeton today) and Columbia College in New York City. "Randolph was considered a great orator despite the handicaps of a sickly body, effeminate manner, and high speaking voice."[3] At the time the college was named, he was serving in the U.S. Senate. Before the college was consecrated, Randolph died in 1833, and in his will he made provisions for his slaves to be freed. Some historians regarded him as the premier authority in the United States on thoroughbred horse racing and breeding.

Randolph Macon College came as an afterthought. The Methodist Episcopal (M.E.) Conference had originally begun its quest for a school of theology much earlier in its history. Not unlike the other denominations in the "New World," the Methodists desired to have a school in each of their circuits, if not at each of their churches. According to James Becker in his article on Randolph Macon, "John Wesley and Francis Asbury had reservations about Methodist involvement in higher education."[4] Wesley had an Oxford education, but because of poverty he had been a scholarship student and his

1. The Building of a Community

"emphasis was on development of preparatory education for poor children."[5] After a continuous flow of unsuccessful attempts at establishing schools and as a result of the Revolutionary War, education was set aside as a priority until the latter 18th century (and because "no American Methodist suggests a need for higher education as an arm of the church"[6] until after Asbury's death in 1816). In 1820, 1824 and 1828 at the Methodist General Conferences, proposals were sent forth to establish "literary institutions." "By 1828, Methodists had begun to move toward a new social reality.... [They] desired social advancement for themselves and their children to support the culture of their substantial gains in status. But American colleges in that era were committed to the 'classical curriculum' which had evolved in increments from the Middle Ages."[7]

According to Dr. Stephen Bradley, in his article "Canaan" at the Christmas Conference of 1784 in Baltimore, "The colonial Methodists broke with the tenets of the Methodist Church of England and ordained their own bishop, Francis Asbury."[8] Wesley appointed Bishop Francis Asbury the first general superintendent of education on September 18, 1784. He began the groundwork to establish a Methodist school in Brunswick County ("halfway between Boydton and Petersburg," Virginia) that was subsequently chartered on December 6, 1792.[9]

The school was Ebenezer Academy (referred to by some as the "old Ebenezer School"), which has some controversy surrounding just when it was built—most likely, either 1780 or 1784, and it had operated for almost ten years before being chartered as a Methodist school. It was referenced as the first (successful) Methodist school in the United States, and is certainly the first in the South. The building, situated on a 51 acre farm, was 20 by 40 feet and constructed of rough stone, two stories high, with a Dutch roof and old-fashioned dormer windows. Teachers' cabins and two student boardinghouses were built near the schoolhouse around 1800. All that remains are a two foot high stone wall outlining the foundation and a historical marker, which were accomplished by the Methodists of the Petersburg District in the 1920s.[10]

The academy was about thirty miles south of Petersburg, Virginia, in Brunswick County, which borders the North Carolina state line. By 1798 the school was having difficulties. Asbury wrote, "Ebenezer Academy is under poor regulations; and what is more than all, some of the gentlemen of Brunswick County had the confidence and want of propriety to wish to wrest it wholly out of our hands." Shortly thereafter, the school was no longer under the charge of the Methodists.[11] But residents still called it "Edward Dromgoole's House." Sometime before 1830, the school was being referred to as

"Canaan" (the name of Dromgoole's plantation). Canaan, according to some county lore, was presumed by many to become the name for the new college that was being proposed. Ebenezer continued in operation as a respected academy until sometime around 1837, when it became known as the Brunswick Academy, which stayed in operation until sometime after 1856.[12] When it appeared certain the South was going to war with its sister states, many of the counties in Virginia, and elsewhere, began to reorganize their militias. In Brunswick County, Ebenezer Academy served as a recruitment center for what became known as the Brunswick Grays. When this organization went to Richmond to become part of the Confederate States of America (CSA), it was established as Company E, 56th Virginia Infantry.

Edward Dromgoole was born in Sligo, Ireland, and raised as a Roman Catholic. Attending a meeting being held by John Wesley (the founder of Methodism), Dromgoole chose his new path of faith and worship. His family was very upset with his choice, so in 1766, he left Ireland and came to the United States, settling in Maryland. In 1768, he moved to Baltimore, and after

Sketch of Ebenezer Academy, drawn by V.S. Mason for the Old Brunswick Circuit Foundation, August 30, 2001 (www.oldbrunswick.org).

years of contemplation, he approached the Methodist Conference for a trial appointment. In 1776, he was assigned to the Brunswick Circuit of Virginia which had been established in 1774 by Robert Williams of England and included 14 Virginia counties and two North Carolina counties. It became known as "the cradle of Methodism in the South."

Dromgoole married Rebecca "Mary" Walton of Brunswick County in 1777 (much to the displeasure of Asbury, who referred to marriage as "family entanglements"),[13] purchased land, and built a manor house, naming the plantation "Canaan." Rebecca's father was John Walton, a signer of the Declaration of Independence, who had come to the area in 1732 as a record keeper even before it was Brunswick County, and had amassed a sizable estate.

Dromgoole stopped traveling the circuit in 1786, but his home became a centerpiece of the Methodist Conference. It served not only as an ordinary for Asbury and others of the faith, but also for the school, and in 1803, Asbury wrote that the Virginia Conference met at his home. Asbury died on March 31, 1816, in Spotsylvania County, Virginia. Dromgoole served as a member of the board of trustees for Ebenezer Academy along with John Easter, Jesse Lee and other leaders of Brunswick County and the circuit. He died in 1835.

Recorded family history states that when U.S. mail service was begun, carriers would simply leave local mail at Canaan. In 1800, a post office was established in the community known as Gholsonville, Virginia. Around 1850, the post office was renamed South Gaston, North Carolina. Since 1887, the post office and community have been recognized as Valentines, Virginia. Dromgoole and his wife had thirteen surviving children. Edward Dromgoole, Jr., attended William and Mary, then medical school, becoming a successful physician, preacher, merchant, and planter by 1800.[14] In November 1828 he was a delegate, along with his father, to a "Conference of Reformers" held in Baltimore, Maryland.

On September 17, 1783, the elder Dromgoole was assigned to the Mecklenburg Circuit after several other preaching assignments, and in 1785, he returned to the Brunswick Circuit. In 1786, he retired as a circuit rider, having established at least seven meeting houses in his territory—one of which was named Dromgoole's Chapel, which later became Olive Branch. Returning to Canaan, he established a successful sawmill and operated a mercantile business which he named Sligo after his Irish birthplace. (His records from the mercantile and his journal and other papers while a circuit preacher are on file with the Southern Historical Collection, Chapel Hill, North Carolina.[15]) Following his conversion in Ireland, he and John Wesley continued their friendship. Also in the historical records are letters from John Wesley to Dromgoole while he was living in Petersburg. The tenth born child, George, became a successful physician and Virginia legislator. Another son, Thomas, served as a Methodist elder for many years in Brunswick County and was still in that capacity in 1834.

Nathaniel Macon (December 17, 1758–June 29, 1837) attended New Jersey College for a while but had his education cut short in 1776 by the American Revolution. For a short time, he served in the New Jersey militia before returning to North Carolina. He and his brother established the Warrenton Male Academy in 1788, in the newly created community of Warrenton, North Carolina. He served in the Colonial military on several occasions during the Revolutionary War, but refused to accept any rank except that of private. He was elected and served in the North Carolina House of Commons. Macon was elected to the United States House of Representatives, where he served from 1791 to 1815. From 1801 to 1807, he was speaker of the House. From 1815 to 1828, he served as a U.S. Senator from North Carolina (he also ran unsuccessfully for vice-president of the United States in 1825), and in 1835, he represented North Carolina at the Constitutional Convention in Washington, D.C. Macon was proud of the fact that he had never campaigned for any election or office held. He served North Carolina from age 33 until he voluntarily retired at age 70, always being truthful and frugal. He always accepted reimbursement of his actual expenses but never took his allotted "maximum allowance." He lived as a role model for "Classical Republicanism" of the day, rigid in his philosophy. Almost no reliable likenesses are found of him and he reportedly destroyed his own accumulated papers out of his distaste for pomp and the idolatry that attacked the grave of George Washington. He did not want a tombstone nor an autobiography done of his life. In making his will, John Randolph wrote that aside from the Virginian executor, Mr. Macon was the wisest man he had ever known.[16]

The first board of trustees of Randolph Macon College included Hezekiah G. Leigh, presiding Methodist elder who also became an agent of the college, John Early, also a presiding elder of fame, and William A. Smith, plus nine others. Before passage, the bill was amended. One of the original twelve trustees was not accepted and seventeen additional trustees were added. The board of trustees was now twenty-nine strong with three representing Mecklenburg County—William Goode, Nathaniel Alexander, and Howell Taylor. The amendments by the General Assembly also included a section prohibiting the college from becoming a school of theology,[17] but "An Act to Incorporate the Trustees of Randolph Macon College" that was passed by the legislature February 3, 1830, reads, "#2—And be it further enacted, That the said seminary shall be known and called by the name of 'Randolph Macon College.'"[18]

It was decided that it would be located in Mecklenburg County.[19] By 1844, the trustees included William Townes and Beverly Sydnor (1834). Other prominent names that appear throughout Randolph Macon's history are original 1830 board of trustee members William I. Waller, Joel Blackwell (whose son, William T. Blackwell [b. 1823] attended RMC from 1842 to 1843), and James Garland.

William Osborne Goode was born September 16, 1798, to John Chesterfield and Lucy Claiborne Goode of Inglewood Plantation. He graduated from the College of William and Mary in 1819, studied law, and was licensed to practice in 1821. On January 22, 1820, he and Sarah Bolling Tazewell, daughter of Governor Littleton and Catherine Tazewell of Williamsburg, were married in Goochland County. They built their home, Cedar Crest, in Boydton in 1820.[20] His wife died on June 8, 1825, at age 25. All four of their children died in early childhood.

Goode married a second time in September 1829, to Sarah Maria Massie, daughter of Dr. Thomas and Lucy Waller Massie of Blue Rock Plantation, Nelson County, Virginia. A few years later, they purchased land on both sides of Butcher's Creek from Thomas M. Nelson and built their new home, Wheatland Plantation. They had eight children. Sarah Goode died on April 14, 1844, at age 32.

Goode served as a delegate to the Virginia House of Delegates from 1822 to 1833 and 1839 to 1841. He then served in the U.S. Congress from 1841 to 1843. Then, he returned to serve in the House of Delegates in 1845–1847 and 1852–1853. He was re-elected to the U.S. Congress, where he served from 1853 until his death on July 3, 1859. On three separate occasions he was speaker of the House while in Congress.

Nathaniel Alexander served terms in the House in 1823–1825 and 1828–1830, then as a state senator from 1830 to 1832 and as state senator to the Peace Convention during Reconstruction from 1865 to 1867. William Townes served as a delegate to the House under Reconstruction for the Peace Convention from 1865 to 1867.

One of the more powerful and supportive original members of the board of trustees, representing North Carolina, was James Wyche from Ford Creek, Granville County. Born December 25, 1785, in Granville County, he served as a North Carolina congressman from 1828 to 1833, and as a North Carolina state senator 1834 to 1835. He and his wife had fourteen children, one having died young. The remaining thirteen all attended college, and most all the sons attended Randolph Macon for a time. He died March 28, 1845. One of his sons was George E. Wyche (b. 1822; A.B. 1841 and A.M. 1845, RMC). Another was Cyril C. Wyche (b. 1825), who attended in 1842 and 1843, at least, but did not take a degree.

Nestled in a farm community about one mile west of Boydton, the new college, like a typical plantation during the antebellum period, created a community unto itself. The land for the college proper was acquired, in part, from Colonel Townes and included the site of the former "Newmarket Race Track" with, presumably, its support works built by Townes in 1820. The racetrack was located near the Boydton to Clarksville Courthouse Road and had closed to horse racing in 1828. In 1856, when the Boydton Plank Toll Road was completed, Courthouse Road became known as the Old Boydton Dirt Road and sometimes as the Boydton Mud Road.

The original college property consisted of 86 acres and 84 poles, purchased for $432.70 from Colonel Townes, and 50 acres and 12 poles purchased from Beverly Sydnor. Additional tracts were added later to include: Beverly Sydnor and James Maclin, 104 acres and 55 poles for $573; James Bruce, 24 acres 34 poles, and a second parcel (for the president's house) of 2 acres 119 poles for $20 per acre; and Nathaniel and Elizabeth Maclin, 17 acres for $102. The campus now totaled over 284 acres. By 1850 the college properties were over 400 acres. And more parcels would be added in the 1850s and 1860s.

South of the college properties, Hezekiah G. Leigh (1795 to 1853) of Perquimans County, North Carolina, purchased a 500 acre farm on April 18, 1832, from Edmund and Elizabeth Taylor (called the Green Plantation[21]) where he lived the remainder of his life. He supported the college as an agent, farmer (purchasing two more parcels of land in 1839 and 1840) and member of the board of trustees. Leigh had a deep rooted Methodist history and had been living in Petersburg. With permission of the Methodist conference, Leigh, as a presiding elder, moved to Boydton. Leigh had a long established relationship with the influential gentry planter John Brame, who was a sizable landowner in Virginia, including Mecklenburg County. In the will of John T. Brame (his grandson) in New Bern, Craven County, North Carolina, October 1819, Hezekiah G. Leigh was referenced as a friend and a friend of his grandfather of Virginia. He left to Leigh "all my manuscripts written on Divinity and all my books immediately pertaining to that study." In 1845, when Brame's wife, Sarah P., died, she left Leigh $40 in her will.[22]

Five months after Randolph Macon College opened for instruction, Leigh and his wife had a new son, Hezekiah G. Leigh, Jr., born March 12, 1833. He attended the college, receiving in 1851 an A.B. (*artium baccalaureatus*, or bachelor of arts), and most likely the Medical Department, receiving his A.M. (*artium magister*, or master's degree) in 1854. He received his medical degree from the New York School of Medicine. He and his family lived in Petersburg until his death in 1896 (see Appendix B).

The college's main building was a brick structure of four stories, 187 feet

1. The Building of a Community

Randolph Macon College's main building (courtesy Mary McKinney).

long, nearly 80,000 square feet with a reported 70 rooms. The complex was also to include 10 support buildings. Tuition for the first year (10 months) was $30, but with room, board, laundry, wood, and fuel for the lamps, it rose to $115. The construction met with many delays due to weather, shortage of help, multiple projects, and other stumbling blocks. The first project completed was a four room framed structure for the Preparatory Department. It began operation in January 1832, and by April it had thirty-two students paying $10 to $15 per session, depending on what they were studying. While awaiting the new principal, Hugh Garland, a local lawyer, ran the school for a short time.

Garland and his wife, Ann Powell Burwell Garland (daughter of the wealthy Armistead Burwell, who had relocated from Mecklenburg County to Petersburg), purchased and ran the failing Boydton Academy for Girls in Boydton in 1831. The academy was organized and chartered in 1820. Depending upon the economy, it was either a male or a female academy. The first board of trustees was "a board of prominent men in the county ... the Reverend Mr. Cowan (Episcopal) was president; John W. Lewis, Boydton attorney was secretary; Alexander Boyd (Jr.), treasurer; and the others were Capt. Beverly Sydnor, Dr. Howell L. Jeffries, Dr. Tingnal Jones, Edward Tarry, Charles Baskervill, the Rev. John S. Ravenscroft, Dr. William Pattillo, Dr. Thomas Goode, John W. Jones, John Nelson, Jr., Samuel L. Lockett and Dr. Alexander S. Field."[23] It seems that Garland was anticipating being hired as the first president. He was elected to the Virginia House of Delegates (1833 to 1839) and had served as a professor of Greek at Hampden-Sydney College from 1826 to 1830. Beginning in 1835, he served on the Randolph Macon Board of Trustees.

Formal instruction began at Randolph Macon College in October 1832, although only one wing of the main building had been completed. With the main building being located on the former race track site, the stables, carriage houses, privies, pasture, and other support buildings, presumably built there in the 1820s, would have been welcome assets. For all of the brick structures within the college complex, the brick was hand-made on the college land from local red clay. A new street opened to the town of Boydton which traversed one mile due east, named College Avenue.[24] The college and town were in sight of each other. An 1861 lithograph on Benjamin Hawthorne's A.M. degree shows a fence surrounding the buildings with a gymnastics area and apparatus on the front lawn.[25]

In those days, fencing was quite common to keep animals out of a location, rather than pasturing like today, to prevent them from causing damage to the premises. (Today the fence is referred to as a split-rail fence, which was probably, in part, the fencing for the old racetrack.) The Boydton Courthouse was also fenced after completion.

In 1833, the college added another brick structure named Steward Hall, near the president's house, which wasn't completed until 1834. It served as the refectory and social center for the campus, similar to today's student union. Since the internal walls were movable, most of the first floor could be opened into one large area capable of accommodating about 200 people. Dancing was not allowed at the college, so the students would host promenading events. (To demonstrate the size of the building, when it was remodeled later it contained eight large rooms, two large bathrooms, and two kitchens. Though privately occupied at present, it still has one movable wall.)

Experiencing unanticipated student enrollment, the board of trustees met in June 1834 and voted to add buildings. The first would be a four story brick structure about sixty to one hundred feet west and perpendicular to the main building to serve as a dormitory. During the Mexican War, the students dubbed it "Texas Hall," although it had been completed in 1837. In front of the chapel, in the main building center section, an avenue was installed

1. *The Building of a Community* 17

Steward Hall, 1833 (photograph by Betty McKinney Caknipe; courtesy Dr. William and Roberta Shelton).

which ran due north for 300 yards. The end of this avenue was a designated college cemetery.

Also, a brick, 15 room "hotel" for visitors, trustees, and parents of preparatory students was built about one quarter mile south of the main building near the intersection of the Clarksville Road and Taylor's Ferry Road. The trustees directed hiring of a steward for the hotel, and furnishing the steward with a home nearby. A steward was also employed for the main building and the west building.

John Early was born in Bedford County, Virginia, and began to serve the Virginia Conference as a circuit rider around 1800. He was later a presiding elder, secretary to the Virginia Conference, and then bishop in 1854. In 1810 he was assigned to the Mecklenburg Circuit, and he, like many of the circuit riders, kept a journal of his travels and services. Often preaching two and three services per day, he could be in a church, meeting house, or someone's home. On one occasion, there was a camp meeting that began on a Thursday and "didn't end until Tuesday of the following week; but with many souls brought to the kingdom." Information about where he preached in homes or spent the night, and the elders of the churches where he preached, contains the same surnames as student rosters of that era.[26]

Bishop Early was chairman of the board of trustees throughout the college's operation in Boydton. In 1834, so much was developing in Boydton, he accepted charge of Calvary Church south of Lombardy Grove. He and his wife, Elizabeth B. Early, purchased a 21 acre, 14 poles parcel of land from James Bruce on September 12, 1834, that bordered the Randolph Macon College site. A new frame home had already been built there by Bruce. Bishop Early's family, from Lynchburg and Bedford County, was very prominent, and he would have been an uncle to Jubal Early (who became a Confederate lieutenant general) of Franklin County. He also was a cousin by marriage to the Episcopal Bishop Right Rev. John Stark Ravenscroft of the North Carolina Diocese (1823 to 1831).

Under the leadership of Bishop Early, the Calvary Church congregation secured the finances and a donation of land to build a new sanctuary in 1836, between St. Tammany and Lombardy Grove. Upon completion, the church was consecrated and renamed for those who donated the land and materials—Kingswood United Methodist Church, for the King and Wood families. Bishop Early served as president of the board of trustees for Randolph Macon College from 1830 until his death in 1874 in Lynchburg. He was described as a man "of distinction [who] left a lasting mark upon the church as he helped blaze the itinerant trail in those pioneer days. He was a preacher of spiritual fire and set the people aflame wherever he went assaulting sin and every foe of Methodism. He stands out as one of the great lights of those times."[27] Bishop Early's son or nephew, Thomas H., was born in Lynchburg, Virginia, in 1827 and attended RMC for at least a year from 1845 to 1846.

As a legacy, his great nephew L.L. Hunter Early became pastor of Jamieson Memorial M.E. Church, South, in 1925. While there, his son (great-great nephew of Bishop Early) William Ashby (1905 to 1977) met and later married a local woman, Glenna Jones. Choosing to pursue education over religion, William left the Clarksville area and went on to become president of the National Education Association in Washington, D.C., until his retirement. Following his death, his widow donated two hymn books to Jamieson Church —both had once belonged to Bishop Early. One book is an 1850 edition, and the second is an 1860.

A school was begun near Kingswood in 1859, with Jesse Gee (b. 1822) as headmaster. Jesse had married Mary Susan Smith on December 21, 1846, and they had five surviving children, with two never marrying. When the war began, Jesse left the school after closing the 1862–1863 school year. He enlisted, at age 40, into Company B, 38th Virginia Infantry, in Mecklenburg County. He was wounded in action on June 15, 1863, during the siege of Petersburg, taken to Petersburg CSA Hospital, and died there on June 17,

1864. His wife, Mary, took a wagon from St. Tammany to Petersburg and brought his body home to be buried in their farm cemetery plot. She never remarried and in 1904 when she died, she was buried beside him.[28] Jesse was related to Randolph Macon graduates Jessee Q. Gee (A.B. 1837) and Virginious Gee (A.M. 1861).

In 1833, the Earlys' good friend's son James L. Brown attended Randolph Macon, but it appears for two, possibly three years only. It also seems he lived in the home of the Earlys because even today the deed in the courthouse describes the home as the "Brown House" of the college. On September 4, 1833, he was elected as the first president of the newly established Franklin Literary Society at the college.[29] Later history discloses that James L. Brown became John Early's son-in-law. In 1859, Brown was invited to attend the 25th anniversary of the college but declined, indicating that business matters in Washington, D.C., were too pressing. On September 15, 1836, John and Elizabeth sold their property to the college for $2,500. The college used the home for the language professor's residence until 1868. The home is currently being remodeled by the new owners. It has served as a private residence since the 1870s.

From the same family, Edward S. Brown (b. 1818) received his A.B. degree

Language professor's house, 1832 (photograph by the author; courtesy Joe and Martha Ware).

in 1843. He was from Cartersville in Cumberland County and the son of Daniel Brown. According to Irby's book, Brown completed law school and became a prominent Virginia lawyer and legislator. He was still in the practice of law in 1897. No Civil War service record could be identified for either Brown.

As the college grew, so did the town of Boydton, as did the town of Clarksville and the nearby Buffalo Springs Resort. Visitors, tourists, and travelers frequented the college campus in awe, as it was a spectacular sight in those days. The hotel was built at the distant end of the college lands near the intersection of the Taylor's Ferry Road and Clarksville Road, a half mile south of the main building. The Randolph Macon Preparatory School building was a quarter mile west of the hotel, and the first principal of the school was Lorenzo Dow Lea, A.M., University of North Carolina, who arrived and began his tenure in March 1832. He was assisted at the school by the Rev. Robert G. Loving, A.B., University of North Carolina.

Lea was one of three brothers to graduate from college with their master's degrees, become Methodist ministers, and come to the Preparatory Department at RMC after first teaching for a year at the Warrenton Academy. His brothers were Solomon and Addison. Solomon and Lorenzo received their degrees from the University of North Carolina, and Addison received his degrees from Randolph Macon College (A.B. 1836 and A.M. 1851). They were the children of William and Sarah McNeil Lea of Leasburg, North Carolina.[30] William was a merchant in Leasburg and a county sheriff. Lorenzo Lea was born in Leasburg, Person County, N.C., on January 1, 1806. He was converted at a camp meeting when he was sixteen years old. His family home had been visited by Bishop Francis Asbury, but there is no record of the relationship.

Lorenzo graduated from the University of North Carolina on June 28, 1827. He tutored from 1827 to 1829, and in March 1831 he was assigned to the Mecklenburg County Circuit along with another preacher. Then he decided to attend medical school, according to an 1834 letter from RMC. In that letter, it was stated that he was also a minister in Charlottesville from 1830 to 1832, and then he was ordained a deacon.[31] He served as principal of the preparatory school in Boydton from 1832 to 1835. A letter from the University of North Carolina states he received two honorary degrees and was then ordained an elder in 1834 at Randolph Macon College. He purchased a 20 acre parcel of land with a home and outbuildings from Jacob and Nancy Venable bordering the college and James Maclin's properties on March 15, 1834. In 1835, he was married to Mary Ann Medley (b. 1812) of Halifax County, Virginia. In 1836, their son William F. was born, followed soon by a daughter, Georgina Hunt. In 1837, he founded Leesburg Academy near Danville, Virginia, and taught there until 1841. His son Lorenzo Jr. was born in North Carolina that year.

In 1843, Lorenzo Lea was principal of the Farmville Female Seminary, but a year later, he and his family traveled to Jackson, Tennessee, where he joined the Memphis Conference. In 1845, he became the first president of the Memphis Conference Female Institute. In 1846, his daughter Mary A. was born. He served as president of institute until 1853, when he sold his interest in the school to another Randolph Macon graduate, Amos W. Jones. Lorenzo left the school and served as professor of math at West Tennessee College from 1854 through 1857, when he was appointed by the conference to the Jackson Circuit. In 1857, he was also a supernumerary and appointed to the institute's board of trustees. He then went to Soule Female College, Murfreesboro, Tennessee, where he taught until 1870. In 1867, Miss A. Lea (possibly his daughter) was a member of the faculty serving as assistant in music at the same college.[32]

In 1871, the family moved south to Mississippi, where Lorenzo became president of the Corinth Female Academy in Corinth, Mississippi. He died there on October 7, 1876, at the age of 72. He is buried in the city cemetery.

In 1836, the tiny community of Boydton (formerly Mecklenburg Courthouse) boasted four stores, a tavern, two hotels, a coach factory and Randolph Macon College. *Martin's Gazetteer* of 1836 described it: "The college edifice stands on a beautiful eminence, from the summit of which a commanding view of the surrounding country may be seen: while from its base, springs of pure and living water constantly gush."[33] On December 30, 1836, Colonel George Rogers (1793–1856) purchased the Boyd Hotel and Tavern (established by Alexander Boyd in 1790, but after the Boyd family sold out, it was referred to as the Boydton Hotel) from Colonel Townes for $8,000, which included the dwelling houses, 5 acres, two slaves, out houses, and stables. Students and professors of Randolph Macon were added to its list of patrons. The hotel had been extensively remodeled by Colonel Townes and now offered special college dinners, balls, and parties.

In March 1837, Rogers purchased a 52-plus acre parcel from Townes and his wife, Lucy, which bordered the northwest boundary of the town of Boydton with home and out buildings included in the sale for $4,000. This became home for Rogers and his family. There is some town folklore that suggests this parcel of land was the one dug for the making of red clay bricks for Randolph Macon College's buildings and other structures built by James Whitice in Boydton.

Originally the Boyd Ordinary and Tavern was licensed in 1790, to provide accommodation for travelers coming to Mecklenburg Courthouse for court days. The court was a wing attached to the north end of the ordinary.

Boydton Hotel, 1790 (photograph by the author; courtesy Historic Boyd Foundation, Inc.).

Underneath the courthouse was a cellar with cells, used as the jailhouse for many years. Following the death of Justice Alexander Boyd in 1800 and the charter of Boydton as a town, approved in 1812, a new courthouse was built on "courthouse square" about 1813. Next door, a log jailhouse was constructed. In the fall of 1837, "By some accident, the log jail ... was set ablaze. Captain James L. Scoggins rushed to the fire and extinguished it before the flames could do extensive damage. The Justices acted in their December, 1837 session to repay Capt. Scoggins for his services." Two individuals "were directed to purchase a 'complete suit of fine clothes' for Scoggins," a War of 1812 veteran, as a "gesture to show their regard for Scoggins's 'extra ordinary exertions in preserving the said jail.'"[34]

Partnering with Townes, Rogers hosted many public events and celebratory dinners at the hotel. Probably the most significant was the Roanoke Colt Show on June 20, 1839, with attendance of participants from as far away as New York. This was the first notable thoroughbred colt auction sale in Southside Virginia since the Newmarket Track closed in 1828. It is reported to have continued as an annual event for several years.[35]

By 1840, plans were underway for a bank in Clarksville and a new coach-carriage factory (H.D. Gordon of Baltimore). A new tobacco warehouse and a tobacco stemming factory were opened in Clarksville, along with the first steam powered sawmill-foundry operation in the county. During this time, Clarksville began to see the first steamships coming upstream (water level dependent) from Weldon, North Carolina, and trains were in progress for town but not arriving until the 1850s, also coming from that same North Carolina neighborhood.

Construction of the present courthouse began in 1838 and, continuing for four years, drew considerable attention to Boydton. This imposing structure, closely modeled on Thomas Jefferson's Monticello, was the only courthouse built in antebellum Virginia with a hex-a-style (6 column) portico that employed the Roman Ionic order. The contractors, William Howard and James Whitice, were two of the four Randolph Macon contractors, and the town and surrounding community were hosts to numerous workers, sightseers, and civic leaders.

The construction crews were also contracted to build a new jailhouse. It "was described as a four room structure 38 × 20 feet. Quarters for the jailor occupied the larger first floor room. The other room was described as having 'a double wall of logs with puncheons (a vertical sheath of wood) between, weather boarded on the outside and sealed within.'" Once it was completed, an order was issued, and "by the Circuit Superior Court of Law and Chancery,

Boydton Courthouse, 1840 (courtesy William Gregory).

three commissioners were instructed to inspect the [new] Mecklenburg jail and file a report before the bench. The three inspectors were Robert C. Nelson, Warren Du Pre, and James H. Gholson. Security and safety were the main concerns." A comprehensive inspection report was filed with the court on May 15, 1840, and can be found among Mecklenburg Loose Papers, Virginia State Library, Box 42, Packet May term 1842 #2 H-Y.[36] The jailhouse burned later, and Jacob Holt was contracted to build a new one in 1870. The courthouse has undergone refurbishing in 2008–2011, and there is a historic marker on "Courthouse Square."

The board of trustees of Randolph Macon College was a "who's who" of prominent citizens from Virginia, North Carolina, South Carolina, and Georgia, and they certainly served as role models and mentors for the students and community. In the 1830s, when the Randolph Macon College Board of Trustees held its meetings in Boydton to acquire land, hire staff, approve construction, and handle other business, the Boydton Hotel was the meeting place. Many of the visiting trustees also stayed there. An emergency meeting was held there in April 1832 when the president selected by the board declined the offer. As school was soon to start, a new candidate had to be selected and hired. Meetings were also, on occasion, held in Trustee Beverly Sydnor's store.

Colonel Rogers was a man of ambition and motivation. Rogers was formerly from the "Tanner House" of eastern Mecklenburg County, where he had amassed a considerable estate from purchasing and selling real state. At one time, he owned several farms, a store, St. Tammany's Ferry, and other investments. The Tanner House was occupied by Rogers from 1807, and he also owned and operated the old community store with blacksmith shop nearby at Marengo on St. Tammany Road. He served in the 1st Regiment of the 98th Virginia Militia as an ensign with Captain Green Blandon's company from August 30 to November 30, 1814, in the war of 1812. In 1834, he was elected as the Southside representative to the Virginia House of Delegates and held that post until 1838. He was serving there when he purchased the hotel, and he certainly exerted some influence in Richmond to promote visitors to Boydton, especially for special events and college happenings. In 1837, he was also serving as a county commissioner, and in that year began a legal partnership with the Wright brothers, as Wright and Rogers, Ltd., to process and administrate estates for widows. He was high sheriff of the county from 1840 to 1842.

When the new courthouse was completed in 1842, there is speculation that the old frame courthouse was moved and became a ballroom addition to the hotel.[37] The original tavern-ordinary containing 14 rooms had been expanded and enlarged by Colonel Townes in 1820 when he purchased it.

But before the "old" courthouse was moved, a basement was dug, and the courthouse placed on top. This basement served as a storehouse, and in the former jail cells was stored the finest liquors from Africa, Europe, and the islands—under lock and key. Some historians have written the courthouse was built there and was part of the hotel with the jail cells in the basement.[38] In either event, Rogers did not get re-elected as sheriff in 1842 but served as a deputy sheriff (1842 to 1852) and was appointed to the Randolph Macon Board of Trustees that year.

Having built the business to a growing success, he sold out in 1846, to Francis Boyd for $10,000, when the college was at its lowest ebb. Boyd hired John W. Baskervill, son of William R., on January 1, 1850, as the hotel manager. John Baskervill's brother, Charles (b. 1821), had been a student at RMC in 1837. When Francis Boyd died, his widow, Isabella, sold the hotel at auction on February 17, 1854, to Richard H. Baptiste (with a group of investors) for $6,066.48, which included five acres, the hotel, household and kitchen furniture, two wagons, tools, implements, shop utensils, a stock of cattle and hogs, five horses, and three slaves.

Baptiste was from Christiansville and became superintendent of schools. His sons Samuel G. (b. 1819 in Christiansville) and Richard H. Baptiste, Jr. (b. 1829), attended RMC for a year in the early stages of development, 1837 and 1846. Colonel Rogers' sons, George O. (b.1827) and Thomas H. (b. 1824), also attended Randolph Macon and the Medical Department.

Colonel Rogers purchased West Hill, a fine home on Madison Street, from Colonel William Townes in 1846. As there was insufficient housing for the preparatory students, one to four would board with Colonel Rogers and his family. Following his death in early 1856, his widow (his second wife, as his first had died), Rebecca S.B. Rogers, and two sons sold the property and appear to have left the community. The April 22, 1860, *Tobacco Plant* said, "Dr. Thomas H. Rogers found dead along the roadside near Bethlehem Church 3 miles from Christiansville on Sunday [April 27] at 2:00 pm. A coroner's inquest was conducted."[39] The cause of death was not listed. Thomas's home and land were purchased by Dr. Richard R. Puryear, son of Richard C. Puryear.

The home and land holdings of Colonel Rogers were purchased in 1856 and 1857 by Professor Oliver Hagen Percy Corprew. By 1858, Corprew had acquired over 1,015 acres with a large number of slaves, was appointed a member of the board of trustees for Randolph Macon College and later became treasurer, and was a prominent farmer in town. He was also serving as an administrator for the estates of some widows. He continued to board students when he was joined by his new bride, Adeline (Ada) F. Rogers Corprew, daughter of Colonel Rogers. Following the Civil War, their home was sold on September 1, 1866, to Thomas Corprew (his brother from Norfolk) and mortgaged through the Boydton Savings Bank (established on March 24, 1851).

With news spreading of the college being established, John Fields and Alexander Jones purchased Buffalo Mineral Springs in late 1830. Their first task was to build a new hotel with a ballroom and dining hall. When completed, the ballroom and dining hall could accommodate 300 guests. They offered jousting tournaments, grand balls, and huge feasts. Although the operation was seasonal (June 1 to September 15), it is fairly certain that some of the students, families, and faculty of Randolph Macon visited or even worked there (many of the students were local and some were musicians). Around 1836, Jones and Fields announced the opening of their newest addition, Solomon's Temple, next to Spring No. 2. It was advertised as having "excellent cuisine, liquor and entertainment." They added "the finest bands have been employed," and the place could accommodate 150 overnight guests.[40]

Bear in mind that in those days an average family would travel by coach, carriage, surrey, or buggy about 9 to 15 miles per day, weather and road conditions dependent. By horseback, the distance could be more than doubled, but this mode of travel was unacceptable to the affluent. There were no trains or stagecoaches in the county until later. Thus when people traveled, the weather, temperature, and terrain made travel an arduous task requiring frequent stopovers for respite. The final destination was home for several weeks upon arrival. Thus when a family arrived in Boydton, from elsewhere, going to or from Buffalo Springs, they spent two or three days before going on to their next destination for the same.

As the college grew and expanded, so did Boydton, Clarksville, and Buffalo Springs. "The opening of the college coincided with the building of the Petersburg Railroad.... A stage line was begun from the new station at Belfield (Emporia) to Boydton by way of Lawrenceville and Lombardy Grove, and thence to Clarksville and to Halifax (by way of Buffalo Springs). The next year the same line was extended to Milton, N.C., where it intersected with a line to Danville. For the first time the people of Mecklenburg were connected by public conveyance with the outside world."[41] In the late 1840s, Boydton could boast of the Exchange Hotel of Boydton, modeled after the Exchange Hotel of Petersburg. Within a year, there was the Exchange Hotel of Clarksville. With the hotels came tailor shops in Boydton and in Clarksville, along with a wagon factory in both towns and a bank in Clarksville.

When Virginia citizens voted to secede, Dr. David Shelton, the owner of the Buffalo Springs Resort at that time, advertised in newspapers from Clarksville to Norfolk. The ad read, "Leave Norfolk, Richmond, Petersburg, Wilmington you'll reach Buffalo Springs by 5 p.m. same day. If you're wishing to be removed from the war. David Shelton."[42] Dr. Shelton had originally leased the springs resort from 1824 to 1828 but then purchased them in the 1840s. He was also treasurer of the Plank Toll Road from Boydton to Clarksville, had a practice and home in Clarksville, and had sponsored students to the college. He sold the springs in 1863 and died in 1864. His son, J. Harper Shelton (b. 1826),[43] attended Randolph Macon in 1845.

A president had not been hired by the time school began. Professors Garland and Sims suggested their colleague be appointed as acting president. The first president of Randolph Macon College, and professor of moral philosophy, was Martin T. Parks (acting). Parks was the son of N.P. Parks, a leader in the South Carolina Methodist Conference. Martin Parks had graduated from the United States Military Academy at West Point, New York, in 1826 and served for two years as an artillery officer. In 1828, he resigned from the army and became an M.E. minister, being admitted to the Virginia Conference. He had preached in churches in Lynchburg and Richmond before coming to Randolph Macon College.

He was considered a great man in many respects and a good preacher and teacher, but he was also described as suspicious, envious, unapproachable and an intemperate eater with bouts of melancholy. The college began operations on October 9, 1832, even though only one wing of the main building had been completed and none of the professors' homes were livable. When the new president arrived in March 1834, Professor Parks resumed his chair as professor of math.[44]

In 1836 he resigned, left the area and became affiliated with the Protestant Episcopal Church. He served as chaplain of the United States Military Academy from December 1840 until December 1846. He also served as professor of ethics and began a West Point choir. He left West Point to become the minister of Trinity Episcopal Church in New York City; part of his ministry was helping the poor. He resigned in 1853 due to poor health and died on July 21, 1853.

The first president was Dr. Stephen P. Olin (b. March 3, 1797) of Vermont, a graduate of Middlebury College in 1820. He was the son of Henry and Louisa Richardson Olin. Henry was a self-educated man, but had been elected as a congressman and was eventually selected as a judge in Vermont. Following graduation from college, Stephen P. Olin moved to South Carolina, where he began a teaching career with Tabernacle Academy from 1820 to 1824. While there, he felt called to preach, which he did for two years. He was described

Math professor's house, 1833 (photograph by the author; courtesy Dr. Bonnie J. Dattet).

as large in stature (over 6 feet tall) and well read; he had published numerous articles.[45] With his health continuing to decline, he returned to teaching, serving as a professor of ethics and belles-lettres at Franklin College (today the University of Georgia) in Athens, Georgia, from 1826 to 1833. On April 10, 1827, he married Mary Ann Aliza Bostick, but it appears she did not live long thereafter. In 1832, he received an honorary D.D. (*divinitatis doctor*, or doctor of divinity) degree from Middlebury College.[46]

He was recruited for Randolph Macon College, and his response was one of arrogance, but negotiable, and he stalled the board for over a year. He finally agreed to accept the position but only if furnished a suitable home and a salary of $1,500. The president's house had been completed in 1834.[47]

When he arrived in Boydton in March 1834, his keynote address was so stirring it was published by several sources.[48] Although in ill health, he was reported to have had a "big heart" and was popular with students and faculty. His splendid writings, preaching, and teaching made an impact upon Methodism. In 1834, he was awarded honorary D.D. degrees by Wesleyan College and the University of Alabama.

In 1836, Olin submitted his resignation due to his health. Professors Parks and Sims also submitted their resignations. Because of the other resignations, Olin was induced into staying with the college, but was granted a

President's house, 1834 (photograph by the author; courtesy V. Norvel Hansard Evans).

leave of absence until March 1837, at which time he left the campus. Olin left Virginia, having accepted the position as the second president of Wesleyan College in Connecticut. Upon arrival, he apologized, offering that ill health would prevent him from assuming the post at that time. He was scheduled for a medicinal trip to Europe and left the United States in 1839. He was joined in Europe in 1840 by a former student, Theophilus S. Stewart (RMC, A.B. in 1836 and A.M. in 1840) of Marietta, Georgia.

Stewart went on to attend medical school in Paris, where he graduated and returned to the United States, settling in Spartanburg, South Carolina, in 1843. When he first arrived there to begin his medical practice, he lived with the Rev. James Francis Smith of that town. The Reverend Smith was a Randolph Macon College graduate (A.B. in 1839 and A.M. in 1843) and sometime later married Juliana Forster. Smith moved to Cokesbury, Abbeville County, South Carolina, and during the war served in the ministry of the area.[49] His son James Perrin Smith became a paleontologist, geologist, and teacher. He received his A.B. from Wofford, M.A. from Vanderbilt and then his doctorate from the University of Gottingham in Europe. Another son, Charles Forster Smith, became a professor at Wofford College.

Olin spent three years traveling Europe and the Near East, returning to the United States in 1842. He accepted the position as the third president of

Connecticut Wesleyan College. Upon doing so, he was informed of the great financial and disciplinary problems the school faced. He immediately set about fundraising and getting the school's business in order. On October 18, 1843, he married Julia Matilda ("Hannah") Lynch and they had one child, Stephen Henry Olin. In 1845, Olin was awarded an honorary LL.D. (*legum doctor*, or doctor of laws) degree from Yale University. In 1850, the family was living in nearby New York State. Stephen P. Olin died on August 16, 1851.

In 1851, the Virginia M.E. Conference, South, built a new college atop a hill in the mountains of Virginia. The college faced and overlooked the town of Blacksburg, Virginia, looking down Main Street. The conference named the new college in the mountains in his honor: Olin and Preston Institute of Blacksburg, Virginia. Soon thereafter, the North Carolina Conference of the M.E., South, led by Professor Charles F. Deems, named their new high school in Randolph County, North Carolina, Olin High School, in 1858. Olin's son, Stephen Henry Olin, graduated from Wesleyan College in 1866.

Following the Civil War, the new president of the Olin and Preston Institute was Thomas Conrad, former headmaster of Georgetown Institute (the oldest Catholic school in the United States, established in 1789), Washington, D.C. He petitioned the Virginia General Assembly to change the name to Preston and Olin Institute, which was granted in 1869. Conrad had developed quite a reputation in Virginia during the war. For graduation exercises at Georgetown in 1861, he ordered the band to play "Dixie." He was promptly arrested and imprisoned. When released in 1862, he attempted to launch a single-handed campaign to defeat the North. He enlisted into the 3rd Virginia Cavalry with a number of Randolph Macon graduates and was established a chaplain with George Ray. Using his chaplain's robe and Washington, D.C., contacts, he developed and headed up the Confederate spy ring in southern Maryland and northern Virginia along the Potomac River. When the North began to close in on his capture, he returned to Richmond and took charge of the "Torpedo Bureau" for counterintelligence.[50]

The president's salary was set by the trustees at $1,000 per year and professors at $800, though for a suitable president, the salary could be flexible. In addition, each had to be provided with a furnished house with a yard and garden spot. In 1835, the salaries were raised by $200 each annually but not raised again until 1858, and then only by $200 annually. (With the financial crisis of 1844, the salaries were reduced to their original level.) Faculty houses were under construction in 1833, but in the interim, the faculty lived in Steward Hall. When the college began to struggle, the first item unpaid was the salaries, and by 1846, some of the faculty and tutors were over a year behind in pay.

The board of trustees made some early bold moves to shore up the success of the college. During 1832, members approached N.P. Parks of the South Carolina Methodist Conference and offered his group six seats on the board of trustees in return for their support. The conference readily accepted. In 1833 they made a similar offer to Georgia for four seats on the board and they accepted. Between 1837 and 1845, 42 students arrived from Georgia, comprising 12 percent of the student body. South Carolina furnished nine students in 1838, and five in 1843. One of the South Carolinians appointed to the board was (Bishop) the Rev. William Capers (b. January 26, 1790; d. January 29, 1855, of a long term heart disease).

The Reverend Capers was a bulwark of the Methodist Episcopal movement in South Carolina as charge of the conference, and later of the M.E. Church, South. He was described as "defined with a good tempered exponent." He resided at Bull-Head Swamp Plantation, a land grant in St. Thomas Parish his father had received for his gallantry during the Revolutionary War. During the war, his father served as a captain with Major General Francis Marion, the "Swamp Fox." The Reverend Capers was educated at Georgetown and Roberts Academies in South Carolina and entered South Carolina College in 1805. In 1808, he left college to read law, and the same year he attended a Methodist camp meeting. One year later, he was admitted to the South Carolina Conference for a one year trial. On January 13, 1813, he married Anna White Dirtson, but she died on December 15, 1815. He remarried to Susan Gill on December 31, 1816.[51]

Capers founded Asbury Mission for the Creek Indians in 1821 in Alabama and served as superintendent until 1824. From 1825 to 1827, he was editor of the *Wesleyan Journal*, and in 1828, he went to England as the South Carolina representative to the British Methodist Conference. Returning to the United States, he began a missionary program for slaves in South Carolina.

"Charles C. Pinckney was the first rice planter to introduce systematic religious instruction among Negroes on the Santee [River], influenced by Bishop Capers. He subscribed to the Methodist Episcopal Mission for them, and a minister came every week." With the help of his neighbors, Pinckney established fifty chapels on the Eastern Seaboard. "In the Methodist churchyard in Columbia, South Carolina, a modest monument marks the grave of Bishop Capers." Eliza Puryear of Christiansville heard Capers speak when she was a young teenager in the 1840s. She later described him as "the old man with such a vivid imagination and eloquence."[52]

In 1834, Landon Garland nominated Capers for the position of president of RMC, but it was not acted upon. Instead he was appointed to the board of trustees in 1834. Later, he was selected editor of the *Southern Christian Advocate* and served from 1837 to 1840. By 1844, his missionary program consisted of 80 missionaries serving over 22,000 slaves. His son and grandson became bishops in the M.E. Church, South.

In 1839, the student body had grown to 131. To bolster confidence in the institution, a United States senator, John Tyler of Virginia, delivered a keynote address in 1838. The audience had over 1,200 people, many in the chapel, which also included a balcony.[53] The balcony and ceiling of the chapel were supported by "solid heart pine marble grained wooden pillars."[54] The chapel was in the center of the main building and had large windows in the front and back for crowds to gather outside and still view and hear the presentations inside. Later, in 1841, then U.S. President John Tyler returned for an encore speech. He suggested that slavery may be a proposition that had run its course and might best be discontinued. He believed that the issue of slavery was to become most significant in the future.

Later, following the hanging of John Brown at Harpers Ferry, from his Virginia plantation President Tyler dispatched a letter to be read in open Congress when it reconvened on Monday, December 5, 1859: "To the 36th Congress, Virginia is arming to the teeth. More than 50,000 stand arms already distributed, and the demand for more increasing. Party is silent and has no voice. But one sentiment pervades the country; security in the Union or separation. An indiscreet move in any direction may produce results deeply to be deplored. I fear the debates in Congress and above all, the speaker's election. If excitement prevails in Congress, it will add fuel to the flame."[55]

When the college began, the Virginia Conference included 121 preachers with 60 assigned to North Carolina and 61 to Virginia. There were six presiding elders with three assigned in each state. The Virginia Methodist Conference split in 1837 as the North Carolinians sought to establish their independence within the church. This actually seemed to strengthen the working relationship of the two conferences. There were several members of the board of trustees and a steady flow of students from North Carolina. In 1838, an M.E.–Quaker School was organized in North Carolina, Union Institute in Randolph County, though not chartered through the North Carolina Conference. The first principal was Brantley York (1805 to 1891), a self-taught M.E. minister. York hired Braxton Craven (August 26, 1822–November 7, 1882) as his assistant. Craven had no formal education, but while teaching, he was also in attendance at the new Garden School (present day Guilford College) for the better part of two years and actually attended Union Institute at York's insistence in 1841–1842.

In 1842, York resigned, and Professor Braxton Craven became the only professor and president of the school. York was going blind but successfully began five more schools by 1870, when he lost his vision completely. Craven was granted an honorary A.B. degree by Randolph Macon College in 1849, and in 1851, Craven sought and won state recognition for the school for training teachers for the state's common schools. His school was not readily endorsed by the North Carolina Conference, had a poor reputation, and demonstrated slow progress. In 1851, Randolph Macon College and University of North Carolina awarded Professor Craven honorary A.M. degrees as president of the Normal College, and by his hiring of two new staff, the school began to turn around. In 1859, the North Carolina conference took over funding of the school and renamed it Trinity College. In 1892, it was moved to Durham, North Carolina.

When the Civil War began and North Carolina seceded, the Trinity class of 1860–1861 had 215 students. "In May, 1861, President Craven organized a student based military unit called the Trinity Guard that assisted in quieting local disturbances."[56] In November 1861, he took the guard to the new Salisbury prison, where he had accepted the position of commandant. Due to differences of opinion between Craven, who was also a minister of the M.E. Church, South, and the M.E. Conference, in 1863 he resigned from the college. The college did not close during the war, but in April 1865, a division of General Joseph E. Johnston's Confederate soldiers arrived on campus and used it as its headquarters. Due to "the presence of the soldiers, the excitement of the students, the anxiety and consternation of the people rendered further college exercises useless,"[57] said of President Pro Tempore William T. Gannaway. The school was closed until the fall 1865 term when the board of trustees met and voted to invite Craven to return as president in January 1866. Following the war, Craven resumed normal operations at the college in 1866 and soon thereafter received an honorary D.D. degree from Andrew College in Tennessee and an LL.D. degree from the University of Missouri.

Randolph Macon had several problems, and enrollment began to drop in the early 1840s. One problem was a young student body; 20 to 30 percent of the students were under age 18, with some as young as 14. For most, it was their first time away from home. Another was the old British style of education. This meant, as described by student Samuel Lander in 1850, a lot of reading, debates, isolation, no free time nor activities and this for almost 10 consecutive months without a break, except for one day of "intermission" December 25.[58] The first two years were the most grueling for the students and required intense dedication to their studies. Their courses of instruction included[59]:

Freshman Studies

First Term

	Text
Xenophon's Cryopedia (commenced)	Owens or Leipsie
Livy	Folsom
Virgil (the Georgics)	Gould
Algebra (through Quadratics)	Bourdon
Antiquities	Eschenburg
Latin Exercises	Andrews

Second Term

Herodotus	Leipie Ed.
Tacitus	"
Algebra (completed)	Bourdon
Geometry (commenced)	Legendre
Ancient Geography and Mythology	Eschenburg
Latin Exercises	Andrews

Sophomore Year

First Term

Homer	Leipie Ed.
Horace (begun)	Anthon
Geometry (completed)	Legendre
Trigonometry (Plane)	Garland
Mensuration	"
Classical Literature	Eschenburg
Latin and Greek Exercises	Andrews and Sophocles

Second Term

Demosthenes or Aeschines (two Orations)	Leipie Ed.
Horace (Satires, Epistles and Art of Poetry)	
Navigation and Surveying	Davies
Trigonometry (Spherical)	Garland
Analytical Geometry	Young
Classical Literature	Eschenburg
Terrence (one play)	
Logic	Hedge
Greek Exercises	Sophocles

In addition, financial concerns of a depression caused only about one of every five students who attended Randolph Macon to stay through the program and graduate. Many more attended one or two years only. Coupled with the fact that the Georgia Conference had established Emory College in 1837 and Wesleyan Female College in 1836, the Virginia Conference had established Emory and Henry College in 1838, and the South Carolina Conference was trying to create its own college, a dismal future appeared evident for RMC.

The first graduate was John Chapman Blackwell of Lunenburg County in June 1835. Over the next two years, 22 more graduated. Blackwell was formerly a student at Washington College and transferred to Randolph Macon in 1832 as a sophomore. He stayed at the school as a tutor while completing his A.M. degree and served as a local pastor for support. In March 1836, he was placed as temporary principal of the Preparatory School, replacing Lorenzo Lea, but soon became ill and was away from school for over five weeks. In 1839, he was replaced by Solomon Lea. With two professors not replaced and Blackwell sick, "the school was in great disorder."[60]

Solomon Lea had followed in the footsteps of his brother Lorenzo, who was later followed by another brother, Addison. Solomon was born November 21, 1807 (d. April 30, 1897), and graduated from the University of North Carolina (A.B. in 1833 and A.M. in 1838). He taught for a year at Warrenton Academy, where he met and married Sophia Ainger (1810–1866) of England. She was a music teacher at the school in 1837. They moved to Boydton and purchased the Boydton Academy and four acres from Hugh Garland on December 22, 1837, for $2,500. He was at Randolph Macon School from 1837 until 1841, when he accepted the post as president of the Farmville Female School in Virginia.

On February 1, 1846, Solomon Lea became the first president of the newly established Greensboro Female College in North Carolina. He and his wife both served as faculty. This was just the second such facility begun in the South. In December 1847, he resigned and returned to Leasburg. Later they traveled to Shelby, Tennessee, for two academic years but returned to Leasburg, where they began Somerville Female Institute. It was a preparatory school with a wide reputation, and at its height it employed four teachers with seventy-five students from several states. The Leas raised seven surviving children, but Sophia died in 1866 and Solomon did not remarry. He operated the school for 44 years until, due to ill health, he was forced to close in 1892 at the age of 85.[61]

During this time, Blackwell met and married Bertonia Letcher, the daughter of Virginia's future Civil War governor, John B. Letcher. On July 14, 1836, they were married on the grounds of the college. He and Bertonia established Hinton Hall Academy in 1839. They had at least one child, John D. Blackwell (c. 1838). John C. received his A.M. in June 1840 and a D.D. in 1860. In 1844, he was licensed to perform marriages in Mecklenburg County, and in 1848 John Chapman Blackwell became president of Buckingham Female Institute, a position he held until the school closed during the Civil War. He did not serve in the military, as his health was too poor. Instead, he became president of Petersburg Female College from 1863 to 1864, replacing Williams T. Davis. Following his son's death, Davis left Petersburg and took the position of president of Danville Female College until 1866.

After the war, Blackwell returned to Randolph Macon, where he served as interim president and professor of natural and moral philosophy (until a president was hired) and professor of chemistry from January 1867 until July 31, 1868. Following the closing of Randolph Macon College, in 1868, he was elected to serve as president of Danville Female College, replacing Wesley Childs Vaden. He held this position until 1870, at which time he retired. He died on February 1, 1885.

As an aside, Governor Letcher's youngest son, John D. Letcher (b. 1853), graduated from Virginia Military Institute in Lexington, where their family home was located before the war. During the war, John was literally hunted by the Union soldiers, particularly by the 23rd Ohio Infantry under General David Hunter. He was to be used for ransom. When the Union soldiers burned the family home in Lexington and the college, V.M.I., he was rescued by Miss Baxter, his teacher, and stayed in her home. He graduated from V.M.I. in 1873 with fourth place honors in a class of 51 graduates. With a degree in engineering, he alternated between teaching mathematics in small colleges and working in the field. For a time he served as chief engineer for the Ohio and Northwestern Railroad. In 1888, he was a professor of mathematics at Oregon Agricultural College. At that time the president of the college was Benjamin Arnold (see Appendix A). In 1892, when Arnold died, Letcher was appointed as president pro tem until the board could decide on Arnold's replacement. Letcher was selected as one of the final three, but not as president. (His friend and mentor at V.M.I. was president of the college, General Scott Shipp.)[62]

The Rev. John Davenport Blackwell (b. 1822) of Buckingham County was the brother of John C. Following his attendance at Randolph Macon (A.B. 1848), he became a Methodist minister and was licensed to perform marriages in 1849. He also became the chaplain for the college (1848 to 1849). When the Civil War began, he enlisted in the 18th Virginia Infantry Regiment on March 1, 1864 (age 42). He was placed in the field and staff (F&S) of the 18th, where he served as a chaplain (captain) until being paroled at Appomattox on April 9, 1865. He died in 1887.

John Davidson Blackwell was the son of John C. Blackwell and graduated from Randolph Macon in 1859 with an A.B. degree and in 1866 an A.M. When the Civil War began he enlisted into Company D, 4th Virginia Cavalry, as a private at Powhatan. He was later transferred to the newly formed Company K as a first lieutenant. Following the Battle of Gettysburg, he was captured on July 5, 1863, at Greencastle, Pennsylvania, made a prisoner of war and sent to Fort Delaware. He was transferred to Point Lookout Prison, Maryland, on September 2, 1863. On April 27, 1864, he was exchanged and paroled. On

May 1, 1864, he was admitted to Chimborazo Hospital for chronic diarrhea. He returned to his company and was paroled at Appomattox on April 9, 1865.

The main building of the college was begun by Dabney Cosby as contractor with his partner, William Howard, his son Dabney Cosby, Jr., and James Whitice, stonemason. Whitice had arrived from Prince Edward County with his building crew, including an apprentice, Jacob Holt (1811–1880). With the completion of the main building and the president's house in 1834, Cosby and son left town. Whitice and Howard (partners in their new contractor's firm), along with the Holt brothers, remained in Boydton for several years building most of the structures on the college farm and elsewhere in town, including the courthouse. Determining that an abundance of work existed in Boydton, Whitice purchased property in the area next to the college and moved his family from Farmville, Virginia. He even had his crew build homes for one another. One such home was that of Samuel Bugg (April 9, 1809–1844), an apprenticed carpenter, built around 1836 on a three and one-half acre pie shaped tract owned by Whitice. The property was nestled between the president's house and Steward Hall. Samuel's wife, Francis Hatsell Bugg, was an accomplished tailor-seamstress and offered this profession to the citizens of Boydton, along with college staff, faculty, and students.

Whitice came to Boydton with a reputation as a stonemason. Aside from building homes for some of his crew, he also hired a number of local craftsmen to join his seasoned crew. One such individual was a stonemason from Union Level, Chesley Curtis. Curtis (1805–1848) was the son of Zachariah Curtis (1775–1851) and Sally Ann Powers Curtis (1780–1851). He had just married Faithy Hubbard Lett (1810–May 13, 1886), also of Union Level and the daughter of Hardiway Lett, and was an accomplished stonemason from that community.

Another home was that of Elizabeth Yancey, which was also built around 1836, on a 65 acre parcel of land across the old Courthouse Road from the college's main building. Thomas Yancey, her brother, and their father, John, must have been carpenters for Howard and Whitice. John had purchased the 65 acre property, and two homes were built. He died around July 1840 and left the home and 35 acres to Elizabeth.[63] The remaining 30 acres he left to his son Thomas, who had already built his home on the land. In 1840, Elizabeth's son, William (b. 1826), was a student at Randolph Macon. By 1850, Thomas was also deceased, and Elizabeth inherited the home and land. Census records[64] show Elizabeth was steward for a college boarding house with her two adult daughters in July 1850. Bugg and Yancey both died on the job.

The second president of the college was Landon Cabell Garland (b. March 24, 1810) of Amherst County, Virginia. His father, Meredith (of Scottish descent), had been the Amherst County clerk of the court for 27 years. Landon's older brother, Hugh A. Garland, having completed his law studies at University of Virginia, moved to Boydton in 1831. In 1831, Hugh and his wife assumed operation of and taught at the Boydton Female Academy, which was also their home (privately occupied today on Jefferson Street). Tuition for the school was $130 for a ten month school year, and courses included French, Italian, music, piano, water color painting, drawing, and penmanship taught by Ann, and English taught by Hugh. In 1831, they were joined by Landon, who taught mathematics, science, and astronomy for a short period of time. Hugh later applied for the position of president of Randolph Macon. For some reason he was not considered for the position. Coinciding with the building of Randolph Macon, Hugh Garland was elected to the Virginia House of Representatives in 1833.

Landon was a graduate of Hampden-Sydney College (A.B. 1829) and had served as professor of chemistry at Washington College. He moved to Boydton on December 16, 1831, and lived with his brother and sister-in-law. On October 27, 1831, he and his sister-in-law, Mary Cole Burwell, were married in Boydton. Mary took over some of the teaching assignments from her sister, Ann. Landon joined the staff of Randolph Macon in 1832 as professor of natural philosophy and chemistry at age 21. In June 1836, he assumed the post as president of the college. He was described as a modest man who was well liked by students and faculty. In 1841, he published a treatise titled *Trigonometry, Plane and Spherical* through a company in Philadelphia.[65]

The board hired Robert Tolefree (Tolfree), M.D., to fill the chair of professor of natural science. Dr. Tolefree was born August 12, 1805, to Robert and Catherine Brand Tolefree in New York. He arrived at the college with his wife, Amelia Marks "Emily" Meriweather, in 1836, but they only stayed in Boydton for one year. Robert and Amelia had four children, and the family moved to Monticello, Georgia. Dr. Tolefree died there on February 1, 1850, and is buried in the local Presbyterian Cemetery.[66]

In addition to the Tolefree family, some of the Randolph Macon College students and other faculty had come to Boydton with a religious preference of Presbyterian. The Presbyterian Church of Boydton was the first church recorded as being built in the community. It was built in 1820 on land donated by the town's founder, Alexander Boyd, Jr., in 1819, and located across the lawn from the Boyd Hotel and Tavern. The church was opened to serve all faiths. The Episcopalians used the church until their sanctuary could be built. This church sanctuary was built by Whitice and his crew on its present location and completed in 1842. The Presbyterian Church maintained a good working relationship with the college throughout its history in Boydton. The pulpit Bible of the church was presented at a Temperance Society meeting held at RMC in 1861. Carved graffiti on the two rear pew rows is historically attributed to the students. Many of the RMC community members rest in the church cemetery.

Although Randolph Macon was regarded as a Methodist College, the religious practices were parenthetical to the overall mission. Students were not required to change their religious beliefs or affiliations. Neither were faculty. Within the chapel there were chaplains for the college, but most came from circuit appointments and not the student body nor alumni. The chapel served as a church, and the students and faculty were just that.

Many faculty were exceptional and continued their studies during the summers. One example is that of Professor Edward Dromgoole Sims, grandson of the Rev. Edward Dromgoole of Brunswick County, Virginia. Professor Sims was born March 24, 1805, in Brunswick County and was a graduate of the University of North Carolina (A.B. 1824 and A.M. 1827). He had tutored at UNC for three years and was a professor of math and natural philosophy at LaGrange College in Alabama from 1828 to 1832. He was selected as professor of math in 1832. During the summer of 1834, he went to Massachusetts to study Hebrew with a scholar there. Then, in the summer of 1836, he took a leave to go to Germany and England to study Gothic and Anglo-Saxon.

While studying in Genoa, Sims developed and wrote the first course recognized in the United States in Modern English grammar. He introduced the course at Randolph Macon College when he returned to teach for the fall term in 1838 as professor of English literature and history and Oriental language. In 1842, he resigned to accept a position with the University of Alabama as professor of English. His wife had died, and he wished to marry her sister, but legally was unable to do so in Virginia, so they moved to Alabama and were married. He died at Blount, Alabama, on April 12, 1845.

An interesting anecdote among the professors of Randolph Macon is a story concerning Dr. John William Draper.[67] A Quaker from England, he came to Mecklenburg County, Virginia, in 1832, with his new bride, Antonia Coetannas de Parva Pereia Gardner of Portugal. He came to the area to begin teaching at Randolph Macon, but his ship left England later than expected and his travel was lengthy. He arrived too late to begin instruction, according to family records. He joined his mother and sisters in Mecklenburg County, as they were teachers. He and his family began Draper Boarding School for girls in 1833, which was located near the Concord Meeting House about seven miles east of Christiansville. (The community became known in 1880 as Draperville.) He also did visiting lectures for Captain David Bigger, veteran of the War of 1812 and principal and teacher at nearby Christiansville Academy.

The academy had begun operation in the early 1820s but was not state accredited until 1829.

In the basement of the family home, Draper conducted research, particularly on uses of glass.[68] It is believed that in this home he developed the prototype of the first camera. In 1835, suffering from a bout of melancholy following a smallpox epidemic, he left Mecklenburg County to attend the University of Pennsylvania Medical School. In 1836, following graduation, he accepted a position with Hampden-Sydney College. He was professor of chemistry and natural philosophy. He formed and was the first president of the Mineralogical Society of the college. In 1839, he accepted a position with City University of New York. He published extensively, and in 1851, published his first textbook on chemistry. His position at Hampden-Sydney College was filled by Dr. Francis Mettauer.

CHAPTER 2

The Auxiliary Programs of a Country College: Involving the Community

In 1842, to coincide with the new courthouse, the college petitioned for a law school, and this was granted. A prominent attorney, Edward R. Chambers (May 23, 1795–1872), was selected as the new law professor. He became a prominent fixture in the college until 1869. Chambers was born in Lunenburg County and educated at the University of North Carolina. He was licensed to practice law in 1829. In 1842, he married Lucy Goode Tucker (February 11, 1824–1854), and they had six children. (Chambers and his wife are buried in the Boydton Presbyterian Cemetery.) Professor Chambers was a representative to the Virginia Methodist Conferences in 1851 and in 1861.

The law students lived in college buildings and could take classes at no charge, but the law studies took place in the new Boydton Courthouse and in the law offices of Chambers and selected associates. The Boydton community served as their classroom. Following the death of Chambers' first wife in 1854, he married for a second time to Virginia Betts (1825–1863), but apparently no children came from this marriage. With all the students in law studies conscripted in 1862, the law school apparently closed.

Chambers became a member of the board of trustees and a staunch advocate for not relocating the college from Boydton. Before, during, and following the war, he was a circuit court judge for the county. He spoke against the move of the college at every board of trustees meeting. On March 13, 1868, he was appointed to a committee to meet with Jefferson Davis, former president of the Confederate States of America. The committee's purpose was to secure the services of Davis as college president, but Davis declined since he was under house arrest by the federal government. Chambers resigned from the board when the lawsuit to block Randolph Macon College's relocation began. The case was scheduled to be heard in nearby Prince Edward County. The reason for the change in venue was that William Townes, Sr., E.R. Chambers and Charles S. Hutcheson were all justices of the Mecklenburg County Circuit Court.[1]

For an A.M. degree, students were required to complete at least three years of professional study beyond the A.B. degree. Graduates from the law or medical departments qualified in each department for one year toward their A.M. One such graduate of the law program was Langston Easley Finch, who graduated from the law department in 1849. Another was Thomas F. Goode, an 1848 graduate who documented in his Confederate service record[2] that he had completed his law studies and received an A.M. degree from Randolph Macon.

Students paid $30 per session to Chambers. The law school was part of the college and came under the scrutiny of the board of trustees, and Chambers was a staff professor. The trustees required that the law students write compositions, deliver public speeches, and study philosophy, logic, and rhetoric. The students were also required to stand for a public examination at the end of each semester. The law school appears to have reopened following the war, possibly in September 1865, but only continued through 1866. Chambers stepped down as judge on January 24, 1867, and entered into a partnership law practice with his son, Harvey H. Chambers, a graduate of the program at RMC. There is no known listing of students who completed the law training program.[3]

The college began offering French in 1842, along with ancient and modern languages, chemistry, natural philosophy/physics, math, political economy, and domestic slavery. The college and faculty owned several slaves, referred to as servants. Most of the faculty had quarters built for them with their families near their primary residence. When the college opened, a slave was hired from a local farmer for $75 per year. In 1835, Bishop Early, president of the board of trustees, purchased a slave, John Evans, for the college for $500. In 1837, Lewis was purchased for $250. By 1847, Lewis had become "so confirmed a drunkard as to be unfit for residence within the walls of the college" and was sold.[4]

On the other hand, John was so diligent he remained a trusted and loyal servant until 1851. In that year, it was determined that the college owed John so much money for his work performance that they would not be able to pay him. Instead, on September 20, 1851, at the age of 50, he was granted his freedom. It was recorded in a deed book by the county clerk.[5] The same year, Landon C. Garland freed three of his slaves: Elizabeth Evans, age 30, John

Evans, Jr., age 15, and Lucy Evans, age 13. John and his family stayed in Boydton and may have continued working for the college. From that point until the war, the college hired slaves from the landowners in the surrounding community.

The first instructor of French was Ezekiel A. Blanch (b. 1816; A.B. 1838, RMC), who was a college tutor of French, 1838 to 1840 and 1842 to 1843, toward his A.M. degree. He was sponsored by Robert Cook of White Plains, Brunswick County, Virginia. Receiving his A.M. in 1845, he tutored from 1845 to 1846, and in 1846, he became professor of math and astronomy. He purchased a small farm near the college and served as professor until he resigned in June 1850 due to ill health. Blanch was born in 1814 in Brunswick County and did not marry until 1854, when he wed Mary Alexander G. Strachan of Dinwiddie County. That year he also secured a position with the Roanoke Valley Railroad as chief engineer. He was responsible for surveying many of the railroad lines in Southside Virginia from Petersburg south and west to Danville. In 1859, the Blanches sold their small farm, and with their three small children moved to Texas. There Blanch became chief engineer for the Union Pacific Railroad. He worked in this position until his death on November 9, 1877, at Harrison County, Texas. He was replaced at the college in 1850 by Professor John C. Wills.

In 1842, the new Mecklenburg County Courthouse was completed. But even with changes in curriculum by adding a new law department, the college was experiencing financial hardships, costs were high, and it was feared the institution would only survive another one or two years. A regional drought, smallpox epidemic, and fewer than 50 students portrayed a bleak picture to the board of trustees. Financial support came almost entirely from the Southside and Piedmont regions. Preachers were expected to raise funds for the college from its earliest days. The Virginia Conference established a newspaper specifically to raise money and called it the *Richmond Christian Sentinel*. Much later it became *The Virginia Methodist Advocate*.

But with the continuously low ebb of funding, a committee was established of Chambers, Rogers, Alexander, Leigh, and the president of the board of trustees, Early, to raise funds for the survival of the college. Leigh, Rogers, and Chambers each, along with Dr. Archibald A. Campbell (board of trustees, 1840) and D'Arcy Paul pledged $500, with the Rev. H.B. Cowles (board of trustees, 1842) and Landon C. Garland (board of trustees, 1840) pledging $250 each. Also, to help offset costs, a committee was appointed to look into the possibility of establishing a medical program. In June 1845, the trustees voted to board up part of the new college building to save on costs. Likewise, the hotel and preparatory department were closed, and students were consolidated.

D'Arcy Paul (1793–1874), an Irish immigrant and successful merchant in Petersburg, was named to the board of trustees in 1839. Paul had served the college for several years as a trustee, financial investing agent, and a generous benefactor. On April 29, 1845, Paul and Mary J. Rainey of Mecklenburg County were married in the college chapel. She was given in marriage by her father, Phillip Rainey, the proprietor of the Exchange Hotel in Boydton. Rainey's son, A.F. Rainey (b. 1825), was a student at RMC.

This must have been Paul's second marriage because his son D'Arcy Paul (Jr.) (b. 1824) had been a student at Randolph Macon for a period of time beginning in 1839, and his son Samuel B. Paul (b. 1826) was a student, beginning in 1842, for a while as well. Neither took a degree. Aside from being a merchant, Paul was noted as an actor. Accolades were written of his performance as the "Bridegroom" in the play *Mistletoe Bough* around 1866.[6] He continued to own and operate a furniture and Steinway piano music store in Petersburg throughout the war and until his death in 1874.

Following the 1868 meeting with President Davis, Paul was appointed to a committee to apply to the proper authorities for permission to remove Randolph Macon from Boydton. The committee was formed June 25, 1868, and consisted of Paul, R.M. Smith, and the Rev. Leroy M. Lee. In 1869, when RMC was in financial distress, Paul again secured a loan to assist with the remodeling and expansion in Ashland, Virginia.

In 1842, Ira Irving Crenshaw of Blacks and Whites, Nottoway County, Virginia, received an A.B. degree with honors. He stayed with RMC as a tutor, receiving his A.M. in 1845. He left the college and was admitted into the Virginia Conference of the M.E. Church, serving Lunenburg and Buckingham Counties. He married Martha Jane Gregg of Brunswick County on November 23, 1848, and they had seven children.[7] "In 1852 ... Mecklenburg (Circuit) has as pastors two men, John W. Howard (b. 1823), son of W.A. Howard of Boydton, and Ira I. Crenshaw.... Mecklenburg had 682 members."[8] Both men were graduates of RMC (John W. Howard, A.B. 1844, A.M. 1847). In 1853, Crenshaw accepted a position as professor at the Buckingham Female Academy, but he was still conducting marriages throughout the 1850s, and during the Civil War he returned to Mecklenburg County, residing in Boydton. Born on January 5, 1819, to Allen and Mary Cabiness Crenshaw, he died on July 9, 1887, in Dyer County, Tennessee, and was buried at Church Grove Cemetery there.

Another graduate in 1845 was Turner M. Jones (A.B.). Turner (b. 1819) was the son of the Rev. Amos Jones of Lewisburg, Franklin County, North Carolina. He was also the brother of Henry F. Jones (b. 1818; A.M. 1844, RMC) and Amos W. Jones (b. 1816; A.B. 1839, A.M. 1842, RMC). He became a tutor at Randolph Macon and received his A.M. in 1848 and later a D.D. there. He was elected president of the Greensboro Female College in North Carolina, replacing Solomon Lea. He was president there during the Civil War. During this time, the students were continuously conducting stage plays, musical performances and other efforts to raise funds for support of the soldiers in the Confederate Army.

In 1846, there was disharmony among students and faculty. (One writer said the students were referred to as "inmates."[9]) Private conduct of the students was constantly supervised; they were not allowed to leave their residences to visit other classmates or go to town without permission. They were not allowed to play games, as this "would produce idle habits." They were forbidden from "attending circuses or any other demoralizing exhibits."[10] Their only outlet had been the debating and literary societies, but now these sanctuaries were being violated. The students began to riot over consecutive weekends and displayed a blatant disregard for the college rules. Garland was not a disciplinarian. Instead he delivered his speeches and sermons as chastisement. This only seemed to create more dissatisfaction among students and faculty.

The riots were outside the professors' homes, and the tutors had no control. It seems to have begun when a student, David R. Duncan, son of Professor David S. Duncan, complained to his father of his tutor. Professor Duncan in turn accused a tutor of being ineffective. President Garland became ineffective in handling the matter, which seemed to only ignite the situation. Several students went to Clarksville and returned after midnight. The second weekend, there were drunken riots on campus after midnight. The third weekend, there were more riots, and "the students burned an effigy of Garland in protest."[11]

At the board of trustees meeting in July 1846, Honorable Richard L. Baptist was appointed to the board (serving with little notoriety). Later he would also serve as secretary. Baptist served in the Virginia Senate from 1835 to 1848. In 1851, he was one of the organizers of the Bank of Boydton and later was one of the first clerks of Mecklenburg County, a position in which he served for several years.

Garland and faculty, being several months in arrears in their pay, appear to have simply run out of morale and energy. In November 1846, Landon Garland, professors Doggett and Duncan, with tutor Thomas Rogers, in disgust, resigned—but the board of trustees only accepted the resignation of the Reverend Doggett. Shortly thereafter, Landon Garland again resigned as president to accept another appointment. He was still owed $2,100 in back pay, the other professors were owed over $1,800 each, and the tutors $350. Landon and Mary left Boydton with heavy hearts. Aside from the turmoil of the college, their youngest son, Spotswood (July 19, 1845–July 28, 1846), had just died. He was buried in the college cemetery, only about 200 yards from their front door.

The Rev. David Seth Doggett was born to John and Mary Smith Doggett of Lancaster County, Virginia, on January 26, 1810. His first teaching position was for a private school in Orange County, Virginia, for one year, and he was accepted into the Virginia M.E. Conference in 1829. He was a pastor at churches in both Virginia and North Carolina. In 1834, he married Martha Ann Gwathney, and they had eight children. Doggett joined the faculty of Randolph Macon College in the fall of 1842 as professor of mental and moral philosophy. Two of the Doggett children met with disastrous deaths. Both had their clothes catch fire. One of these deaths took place while Seth Doggett was teaching at RMC.[12] It is believed that one of the unmarked graves is Doggett's son.

Professor Doggett was awarded an honorary A.M. degree by Randolph Macon in 1842, before he began teaching. Following his resignation in November 1846, he returned to the ministry. In April 1866, he was elected bishop of M.E. Church, South. He had a reputation of being an eloquent preacher. He was serving as bishop of the conference during the period of time that RMC was preparing to relocate. He was presiding bishop both in June 1868 and in June 1869. On December 8, 1869, the *Tobacco Plant* ran a story that Bishop Doggett was attending the North Carolina Conference that was being held in New Bern. He arrived on Tuesday, December 1, at the M.E. parsonage. He went for a visit, and while gone, someone broke into his trunk and stole $200.[13] He died on October 27, 1880, at Richmond and is buried in Hollywood Cemetery.

One of the faculty who wanted no part in the students' activities was Professor James W. Hardy (A.B. 1837, RMC). He was a tutor for the college from 1837 to 1840 and received his A.M. in 1840. While working as a tutor, he married Harriett G. Jones on June 25, 1838. Hardy was the first alumnus to be hired by the college, and he served as professor of natural science from 1840 to 1847. His college nickname was "Old Jim," although he was not much older than senior students. He left in 1847 and moved with his family to Alabama, where he was chair and professor of natural science at LaGrange College. He died there before 1850.[14]

Professor Garland went on to become the president of the University of Alabama in 1855, having received his LL.D. from that school in 1847. The university was burned during the Civil War, and rebuilding was slow. Garland accepted the chair of philosophy and astronomy at the University of Mississippi in 1867. In 1868, Randolph Macon contacted him to return to Virginia as president of the newly located college in Ashland. Garland declined, as he had been offered and accepted the position of president of the University of Mississippi. While at Mississippi, he wrote a series of articles for the *Nashville Advocate* on an educated ministry.

Over the years Professor Garland published numerous essays in Christian journals and church publications on the same topic.[15] Garland continued to serve on the board of trustees of RMC for several years and maintained contact with his Virginia colleagues. Some years later, one of his former students, editor and Methodist Bishop Holland Nimmons McTyeire (honor graduate, RMC class of 1844), traveled from Nashville, Tennessee, to Mississippi to ask his former professor for assistance in establishing a new Methodist college with financial support from Commodore Cornelius Vanderbilt (McTyeire's wife, Amelia Townsend ,and Vanderbilt's wife, "Frank" Crawford, were first cousins; also, Vanderbilt was a member of the Rev. Charles F. Deems' congregation in New York). Vanderbilt University was funded, organized, chartered, and began operation in 1873, later expanding and offering four programs: biblical studies and literature; science and philosophy; law; and medicine.

Bishop McTyeire traveled to New York to collect the money from Vanderbilt and was selected as the first president of the board of trustees upon returning to Nashville. The trustees selected Landon C. Garland as the first chancellor, and McTyeire was given the assignment of traveling to Mississippi to persuade him to accept. Garland did accept, came to Nashville in the fall of 1873, and continued to lead the college until he retired in 1893. Garland died February 13, 1895. He was buried at Vanderbilt with the three Bishops: McTyeire, Soule and McKendree.

Garland's cousin, Samuel Garland, also attended RMC, but for only one year, and then transferred to the Virginia Military Institute, where he graduated with an A.B. in 1846. Samuel was the son of Maurice Garland (an attorney in Lynchburg) and Caroline M. Garland. He graduated from the University of Virginia Law School and returned to Lynchburg to practice. In 1856, he married Elizabeth Campbell Meem. They had one child, Samuel. Following the capture of John Brown in 1859, Samuel (Sr.) was responsible for organizing the Lynchburg Home Guard.[16] Another Garland who attended RMC but did not take a degree was John R. Garland (b. 1821), son of David S., a member of the board of trustees.

In May 1861, Samuel was selected as colonel of the 11th Virginia Infantry, but tragedy struck. On June 12, 1861, his wife died, and he returned home for her service. He returned to the battlefield but had to go home again to bury his son, Samuel, who died in August. Again returning to the battlefield, he was wounded at the Battle of Williamsburg but refused to leave the field. He was promoted to brigadier general in May 1862 and put in command of the 3rd Virginia Brigade on July 14, 1862. He led this brigade into the battles of Seven Pines, Gaines Mill, and Malvern Hill. On September 14, 1862, he was severely wounded at the Battle of South Mountain and died of his wound.

Professor David S. Duncan (1791–1881) was born in Northern Ireland and educated at the Glasgow University, Scotland. He entered the British Navy as a midshipman on March 25, 1810, and served for three years. When the purser died on the ship, Duncan received the appointment and won the praise of his commander of the warship, *Helder*, on June 3, 1812. It is written that his trustworthiness, "exquisite handwriting and business ability fitted him."[17]

In 1817, a classical teacher in Norfolk wrote his former pastor in Northern Ireland for an assistant. The Irish Catholic pastor sent David Duncan for a one year assignment. He arrived in the United States with his new bride, Alice Amanda Needler Piedmont, and went to work at the school. In 1822, he became principal (the account book for his school from 1822 to 1828 is in the possession of the South Carolina Historical Society in Charleston).

In 1836, Duncan was hired as professor of ancient languages (Greek language and literature), a position he held until 1854. He served on the board of trustees, and for a time was the treasurer. He was later replaced as professor and treasurer by Corprew. In 1838, he was presented an honorary A.M. degree from Randolph Macon. Duncan was so impressed by the zeal and commitment of his fellow countryman that when his fourth son was born in 1845, he was named DeArcey Paul Duncan. He and his wife had five sons. They were David R., William Wallace, James A., DeArcey Paul, and Thomas C. The students referred to him as "Old Pad."[18] In 1854, he resigned to move south, where he became editor of the *Methodist Review*. In 1857, he was hired as professor at the newly established Wofford College. (Just outside Wofford College, "Duncan's Crossroads" [today Duncan, South Carolina] was established in the 1890s, but a local historian says there is no connection to the David Duncan family.[19]) He continued to teach until his death in October 1881. He is buried in Magnolia Cemetery in Spartanburg, South Carolina.

While he was teaching in Norfolk, his first son, James A. Duncan, was born in 1832. He was inspired to the church in 1847, licensed to preach in 1848 and graduated from Randolph Macon with an A.B. degree in 1849. The M.E., South, Conference established him into the ministry beginning in Alexandria, Virginia, in 1857, and later he was transferred to Richmond. In 1860, he served as editor of the Christian Advocate and served as pastor of the M.E. Church Petersburg from 1860 to 1866. On December 17, 1854, before leaving Boydton, he married Sallie Twitty of Warren County, North Carolina.[20] They were married in the Randolph Macon College chapel. The wedding was attended by Sallie's brother, Robert Cheek Twitty (January 6, 1838–July 2, 1903), who had graduated from RMC Ridgeway Preparatory Department. They were the children of James Turnbull Twitty (board of trustees, Ridgeway) and Caroline C. Cheek. Robert went on to marry Sara Fitzhenry Palmer (August 16, 1840–May 2, 1929) on May 30, 1860. They had nine children.

James's younger brother, David Robinson Duncan (b. 1836), moved with his father to South Carolina but first completed his A.B. in 1855 from RMC. In 1857, he received his A.M. degree from Wofford and began the practice of law in Spartanburg County, South Carolina. When the Civil War began, he was opposed to secession and the war, and did not want to serve the Confederacy. On September 26, 1864, he enlisted into Company C, 13th South Carolina Infantry, and was established as a major. (South Carolina historians were not kind in their portrayal of David.[21]) He left Spartanburg and went to the defense of Petersburg. He was captured on April 2, 1865, made a prisoner of war, and sent to Old Capitol Prison and then transferred to Johnson's Island, Ohio. He reportedly convinced his captors that he was pro–Union and had enlisted as a private into the Confederate Army only to avoid being conscripted into a unit of men he did not know. It appears that the Union soldiers believed him, as he was released on May 18, 1865, and sent to Richmond two months before any of his peers at Johnson's Island.

Following the war, he returned to Spartanburg and was elected solicitor (prosecuting attorney) for the 7th Judicial District of South Carolina. When the widow of Benjamin Wofford (the benefactor of Wofford College) was preparing to move from Spartanburg, David purchased the family clock. In the 1890s, he donated the clock to the college, and it is still there. He served on the board of trustees for Wofford College from 1877 to 1892 and again from 1898 to 1902.[22]

Professor Duncan's third son, William Wallace Duncan (b. December 30, 1839), was a student at Randolph Macon but moved with the family to South Carolina and graduated from Wofford College (A.B. 1858). In 1859, he was admitted to the Virginia Conference with his brother, James. When the war began, he returned home and enlisted into the 20th South Carolina Infantry and was established as an field and staff chaplain. Later he was assigned to the 7th South Carolina Reserves as chaplain. Following the war, the Rev. W.W. Duncan was a professor of natural and moral philosophy at Danville Female College.

He returned to Wofford College as a professor in 1875 and moved into the president's house. (The new president, James Carlisle, had his own home.) He was elected a bishop of the M.E., South, Conference (when it was stated, "He was the brother of the late president," referring to James, who had died in 1877[23]) but declined the appointment due to ill health. He served as chair of mental and moral science from 1875 until 1886 at Wofford. During his tenure, he received a D.D. degree from Emory College and from Central College. He also had built a fine Queen Anne style home which still stands and is on the National Historic Register of Historic Places. On one of his trips to Virginia, he took the time and made the effort of traveling to Clarksville, Virginia. On July 5, 1902, he dedicated the newly constructed Jamieson Memorial Methodist Church. In 1886, he was again elected as a bishop of the M.E., South, and this time he accepted. He served as president of the board of trustees and a financial agent for Wofford from 1889 until he died in 1908.

Professor David Duncan's oldest daughter, Mary Elizabeth Duncan, married Lucien Lomax of Abbeville County, South Carolina, on July 21, 1845. Lucien was from the same county as Tennent Lomax (A.B. 1844, RMC), and his older brother. Lucien (A.B. 1842, RMC) entered the ministry. Following his marriage, he returned to his home to take over the family farm, as his parents had died. In 1849, he received his A.M. from Randolph Macon and continued his ministry in western South Carolina. During the war, he was exempt due to age, but for the remainder of his life he served the M.E., South. Mary Elizabeth Duncan had frequent correspondence with her father,[24] and their letters are in the South Carolina Historical Society Archives in Charleston.

In 1846, a search committee was formed to hire a new college president for Randolph Macon. The Virginia Annual Methodist Conference was held there in 1846. Dr. William A. Smith, a noted debater and scholar, was offered the position. Dr. Smith was well known to the trustees, as he was one of the original board members, an alumnus who received his D.D. degree in 1843 and one of the first agents for the school. When Dr. Smith reluctantly accepted the presidency in 1846, he was well aware of the financial distress.

As a noted fundraiser, he immediately set out to begin an endowment drive. By 1859, $100,000 had been raised and invested in bonds believed to secure the future of the college for years. The monies had been invested by D'Arcy Paul, totaling $62,000. The investments were in 3 to 5 percent interest bearing bonds of Petersburg, Virginia, Southside Railroad, and Petersburg Railroad. (Colonel William Townes was chairman of the Southside Railroad board, having been elected into that position in December 1858. Also, Paul was on the Petersburg Railroad Board.) In 1861, the $45,000 in Petersburg

Railroad bonds was sold and the money invested in Confederate States of America bonds (which became worthless following the war). Last, in 1863, Paul transferred some of the railroad funds to 100 shares of stock in the Exchange Bank of Clarksville, which continued to operate throughout the war.

Student Residences

By 1849, under Dr. Smith's leadership, efforts were undertaken to regenerate utility of the college buildings. The hotel and the Preparatory Department had not been used in three years. It was determined that students should not live at the hotel unless a teacher or family lived there. Each hall was to be operated by a steward hired by the college. Due to financial constraints, instead of hiring stewards, the college leased the residential units to stewards for a fixed fee. The steward operation then became a "boarding house" operation. In Samuel Lander's diary[25] he refers to a visit from Dr. George Smith trying to persuade him to come back to his boarding house.

In 1847, Howard had retired from construction at the age of 60. He accepted the position of steward of the North Building, leased it, and moved into same with his wife, Rebecca W. (b. 1790), and a young woman, age 19, Frances Corprew, sister of O.H.P. Corprew. The November 1850 U.S. Census records list 23 students living in the North Building[26] and Professor Charles B. Stuart (b. 1824), son of John R. Stuart from Mangohick, King William County, Virginia.

Professor Stuart (A.B. 1845, RMC) became principal of the Preparatory Department at Garysburg, North Carolina. His teaching assistant in 1848 was Matthew S. Dance (b. 1826), son of the Rev. Matthew M. Dance from Sandy River Church, Prince Edward County, Virginia, who did not take a degree from RMC. Two of Dance's sons also attended RMC—William G. (b. 1820) and John Fletcher (b. March 21, 1828; A.B. 1850 and A.M. 1855), who also entered the ministry. Stuart received his A.M. degree at Randolph Macon in 1848, and that year a new course was to be offered by him, agricultural and natural chemistry. He was replacing James W. Hardy (A.B. 1838 and A.M. 1840, RMC), who had taught experimental sciences from 1838 to 1847.

In 1847, Professor Hardy resigned to accept the position of president of LaGrange College in Alabama. He died shortly thereafter. Stuart taught chemistry until 1857, when he resigned to accept another position in Louisiana. He was replaced by Professor N.P. Lupton. The college leased a farm of 65 acres and a home for Professor Hardy from Dr. John O'Brien, whose son,

Junius O'Brien (b. 1832), was a student at RMC. Dr. O'Brien was a friend and supporter of the college, but moved his family to Texas around 1853.

This became known as the chemistry professor's house and was the original home of the Rev. William and Julia Ann Crump Leigh, cousin and brother of the Rev. H. Gilbert Leigh, the next door neighbor. William Leigh and family moved to Mississippi in 1846, and he died there in 1852. (In 1858, this home was purchased by Nancy Venable, who appears to have built a new home next door because in 1852, she had sold the chemistry professor's home and 45 acres to Dr. Smith.)

Professor Stuart served as guardian for his younger brother, John W. (b. 1834), who also attended Randolph Macon. John was serving as principal of the preparatory school in Boydton in 1854. In the summer of 1857, as partners, they moved to Mansfield, Louisiana. Before leaving Boydton, on April 5, 1857, Charles Stuart's first child was born, Charles Bingley Stuart. In 1859 Charles became president of Mansfield Female College, and there is no further mention of his wife. John became principal of a boys' school. When the war began, the Rev. Charles Stuart (D.D., RMC) enlisted and was established as a first

Chemistry professor's house, 1849. It was purchased in 1934 and the deed is still registered to William Hughes of the Christian Missionary Alliance, Presbyterian Church, New Jersey. The home has been unoccupied for several years (photograph by the author).

lieutenant in the 1st Battalion, Louisiana Infantry. He was soon elected captain. The last communication the family had about Charles was that he had yellow fever. No further records exist of his service after May 19, 1863; he never came home and is presumed to have died of the fever.

Following the war, John and family (including Charles Bingley, for whom he was guardian) moved to Shreveport, Louisiana, and in 1873 on to Marshall, Texas. John Stuart sent his 16 year old nephew, Charles Bingley, to Ashland, Virginia, to attend R-MC. He appears to have attended for two or three years (1874–1876) before transferring to the University of Virginia law school and graduating about 1879. Following law school, Charles Bingley Stuart relocated near his family in Texas and began a law practice. He was appointed by President Grover Cleveland as judge for the First District, United States Court for the Indian Territory of Oklahoma, in 1893.[27]

The steward of the West Wing served a dual purpose—steward and campus physician. He was George J. Smith, M.D. (b. 1805), and was accompanied by his wife (Martha, b. 1810), and their three sons (ages 8 to 15) and four daughters (ages 3 to 17). Living with them in the West Wing in November 1850 were Professor Wills and family, tutor O.H.P. Corprew, Smith's father-in-law, Samuel Jefferson (age 70), and 28 students.

The students had a nickname for each hall and each wing of the buildings. The college advertised and published a North Building, West Wing, East Wing, the Centre Building, and the preparatory housing was Boarding House Hall. But in the local papers they were referred to as Dr. Smith's Boarding House, Mrs. Yancey's Boarding House, and like names. Several vignettes appear in the *Tobacco Plant*[28] of a wonderful dinner for the faculty or trustees being served at Mrs. Yancey's Boarding House. The stewardess of the East Wing of Randolph Macon was Mrs. Elizabeth Yancey (1795–1854) with her two daughters, Ellen (b. 1817) and Rosanna (b. 1819). Their home was located across the road from the main building. In November 1850, 36 students were living in the West Wing. On October 15, 1854, Mrs. Yancey died and was buried in the college cemetery. The home was subsequently referred to as the "Misses Yancey's Boarding House"[29] and continued in operation through 1863. It became the home of R.C. Covington on November 12, 1904. Covington came to Mecklenburg County from North Carolina and established a publishing and printing business in Boydton about 1900. He was later involved with a group of black merchants, clergy, and graduates of the Boydton Institute in purchasing the old Randolph Macon College campus for the use of the Boydton Training and Bible Institute in the late 1920s. He began printing the newsletters and other publications for the institute.

The Centre Building, which contained the chapel, some classrooms, and a post office, has a record of seven students living there in 1848; in 1850, the census records list the steward as Professor David Duncan from Ireland. Also listed as residents were his wife Alice (b. 1810), four children; with one son, aged 14, a student at Randolph Macon (David, A.B. 1855), and a 20 year old woman, Virginia N. Poemond (possibly Piedmont; she may have been a niece of Duncan).

Boarding House Hall was for the Preparatory Department. In November 1850, William S. Davis (b. 1817), teacher of the preparatory school (having replaced Solomon Lea, A.M. 1845, RMC), was the steward. His wife, Elizabeth (b.1817), and their six children were living there. Along with them were John D. Blackwell (college chaplain) and ten students. Even Dr. Smith's President's House included his wife, Elizabeth (b. 1808), and three daughters—Susan (b. 1829), Molly (b. 1836) and Laura (b. 1842), along with two students, two young women who were being tutored, ages 13 and 11, and a black slave (John Evans) as general laborer and groundskeeper.

All the professors had student boarders and one or two young women who were likely boarders receiving tutoring and helping out as nannies or servants, cooks, and housekeepers. These young women not only helped with household duties, but by being tutored by a professor, their parents were paying for part of their education, or it was bartered. Also, to supplement their income, many of the tutors and professors secured a license to perform marriages in Mecklenburg County. Some of those applying for and receiving a license to perform marriages included Dr. William A. Smith, John D. Blackwell, John C. Blackwell, Edward R. Chambers, James A. Duncan, H.G. Leigh, John Bagby, Hartwell Arnold, James McAdam, and S.G. Mason.

William S. Davis's first cousin William S. Davis (son of Joshua A. [1788–1845], of Warren Plains, North Carolina) graduated from Randolph Macon College with an A.B. in 1859 and was pursuing his A.M. William S. Davis the elder returned to North Carolina and began a ministry there. Completing his A.M. studies and having served as principal of the Preparatory Department, William (the younger, b. 1840) returned to Warren County, N.C., in 1861 and began a ministry there also. On April 30, 1862, he returned to Boydton and enlisted into Company D, 14th Virginia Infantry, as a private. He immediately requested a leave and returned to North Carolina. He was discharged on July 27, 1862. On December 29, 1863, he and Elizabeth Ann Jones of Warren County, North Carolina, were married. Shortly after their wedding, he was conscripted into military service but almost immediately was established by the Confederate Army as an M.E., South, chaplain with a rank of lieutenant colonel. Released in 1865, he returned to Warren Plains and served as a minister until retiring.

Jacob Holt (b. 1810) left the partnership and moved his crew of workmen to the rapidly growing Warrenton, North Carolina. Holt, son of David and Elizabeth McGehee Holt, became a Baptist in 1837. In 1838, he married Amelia Phillips, and they had six children. In 1842, following completion of the Mecklenburg County courthouse, Holt was contacted by citizens of Warrenton to bring his crew there, as the railroad was completed and the town and county were growing rapidly. Holt left Boydton with his crew of both black and white tradesmen and relocated his family near Warrenton, where he built a new home for them. His crew consisted of 18 young white men as skilled tradesmen and apprentices. He also owned 42 slaves who were mostly trained craftsmen. Like his building style in Boydton, his buildings were primarily of Greek Revival design. While in Warrenton, he was joined in 1849 by his younger brother Thomas, who had moved from Lunenburg County, Virginia. Thomas had studied to be an architect. They began to change to a more ornate Italianate style of building including "arched tracery windows and bracketed rooflines."[30]

He built the courthouse and many of the commercial buildings of Warrenton that still stand today. So famous was his building career from 1846 to 1868 that the town has erected a historic marker in his honor. There was one hiatus to his building in Warrenton. That came in 1857–1858 when he was persuaded to return to Boydton by William Baskervill, Sr., to remodel the Lombardy Grove Baptist Church. Holt not only remodeled the church for a small fee but he added a 20 room wing onto the ordinary at Lombardy Grove, for a cost of $1,560. This new wing was to accommodate the new stagecoach line. About twenty-five years later, the church was raised. While in the county in 1858, Holt and crew built a plantation home called Eureka for Dr. Robert Baskervill, son of William, which is still occupied today. Following the Civil War, Holt returned to the Boydton area. He built and remodeled several homes and commercial buildings in Boydton and nearby Christiansville.

In 1870, he was commissioned by Mecklenburg County to build a new jailhouse. Upon completion of the jail, the first jailor was James Bugg, brother of John W. Bugg. He served as the county jailor and lived in the jailhouse for several years. In March 1870 the *Tobacco Plant* newspaper said the new jailhouse was completed and James Bugg was the jailor. It was captioned "The Humbug Hotel."[31] In the 1890s Bugg was killed by a prisoner during an escape.

Holt's brother, Thomas, became the architect for the Raleigh to Gaston Railroad and was also the architect for Peace Institute (College) in Raleigh. Thomas came to Boydton in late 1871 to prepare a survey and plan for the college property and to make repairs on the buildings. Most were damaged during the Union soldiers' and freedmen's occupation of the buildings in

1865 and 1866. The repairs were initiated by Dr. Henry McGonegal, whose missionary group was purchasing them for a school for freedmen.

Another story appeared in the *Tobacco Plant* in an 1870[32] issue as an appeal by Jacob Holt to the Baptist of Mecklenburg County. He was seeking help with the fundraising for the new Methodist Church sanctuary following the close of Randolph Macon. It was stated that even though he was a Baptist, he was inclined to help such a worthy project. Holt did build the church and moved the chapel bell from Randolph Macon to the belfry of the new church. He then moved to the newly established community of Chase City and built and remodeled a number of homes and buildings there. In 1879, his son, William K. Holt, took over the business and established a lumber mill and building supplies store in Chase City. Jacob Holt is credited with being the first builder to accomplish the concept of prefabricated homes. He died in Chase City on September 21, 1880, and is buried in Woodland Cemetery. Thomas Holt also built several structures in Chase City, but when the railroad came to town, he spent much of his time designing and building in Newport News, Virginia, where he died in 1898.

The Chapel Boydton Methodist Church

The chapel at Randolph Macon College became the sanctuary for the Methodist of Boydton. For years they had met in the local Presbyterian Church. This continued even after RMC was completed. There would be occasions when the chapel was simply not available and the congregation would meet at the Presbyterian Church. With the completion of RMC, the Virginia Conference established a Randolph Macon Circuit referred to as the College Station (it later became the Boydton Circuit). The first quarterly meeting of the station was held at RMC Chapel in October 1835. Those attending included the Revs. H.G. Leigh, S. Olin, M.P. Parks, E.D. Sims, J. Boyd, W. Leigh, and I.I. Thomas, I.O. Wingfield, B. Clegg, I. Hardy, and A. Lea. George W. Bain, I. Carney and J.S. Clements (recording) were elected stewards.[33] H.C. Gregory recorded that "on the flyleaf of the record book, which has the minutes of quarterly conferences up to 1867, is inscribed, 'Records of the M.E. Church at Randolph Macon College.'"[34]

As quoted from L.E. Finch, recording steward, "To him in part we are indebted for putting into execution a long cherished wish of our people. In 1873 the church was made a station, and the Reverend Jamison, one of the pastors of college days, was appointed to this church."[35]

The Medical Department

In March 1847, a medical department was begun, but interestingly enough, it never gained in popularity. The reason I say "interestingly" is because of the international reputation and immense following of the instructors.

At Yorktown in the 1770s the chief physician for the French troops was Dr. Francis Joseph Mettauer. Once the Revolutionary War ended, Dr. Mettauer moved his family to the United States. His oldest son was John Peter Mettauer (b. 1785), who graduated college and went to the University of Pennsylvania. He graduated from the medical school there in 1809. His first position was professor of surgery at Washington Medical School in Baltimore, Maryland. John had a younger brother, Francis Joseph Mettauer, who graduated from William and Mary in 1837. Shortly after Francis was born, John married Mary Woodward and they had at least one son. Apparently Mary died, and sometime later, Dr. John married Margaret E. Carter. They had at least one son, Henry Archer Mettauer, born December 27, 1829, in Prince Edward County, Virginia.

In 1837, Dr. John Mettauer was serving as a surgeon's mate in the 63rd Virginia Militia. The same year, he began the Prince Edward Medical Institute for medicine and surgery near Hampden-Sydney College. He was assisted by his brother, Dr. Francis. In short order, the institute was accredited and became a one year training program in medicine.

Dr. John Mettauer negotiated with Randolph Macon College in 1842, but the matter was not seriously considered. In 1847, Dr. John Mettauer tried again, and this time he gained the acceptance of the board of trustees for RMC. The graduates of the institute could take their degrees to the Washington College of Medicine in Baltimore, Maryland, and be readily accepted as second year medical students.

One such student was William Travis Howard (January 12, 1821–July 31, 1907). He graduated from Hampden-Sydney, attended the RMC Medical Institute, and graduated from Washington Medical College in 1844. He returned to Warrenton, North Carolina, and practiced medicine there until 1866. During his practice years, he developed certain gynecological techniques and a number of instruments for medical practice. He was well published and recognized within the North Carolina Medical Society and its professional journal.[36] Following the Civil War he moved to Maryland and became professor of physiology at the University of Maryland. One year later he was selected to fill the chair of diseases of women and children—the first such position in any American medical school. He is buried in Richmond, Virginia.

Dr. Francis Mettauer had accepted the professor's chair of natural science and chemistry at Hampden-Sydney College which had recently been vacated by Dr. Draper. The institute became the Medical Department of Randolph Macon College in March 1847, but Dr. Mettauer had a dilemma. Hampden-Sydney (which already had a medical school in Richmond) agreed to allow him to keep his post at their school so long as he did not teach the same courses at Randolph Macon. He reluctantly agreed, but after two years he resigned to devote his full attention to Randolph Macon. He was professor of anatomy, physiology, chemico-pharmacy, medical jurisprudence, botany, and mineralogy. He died near Kingsville, Prince Edward County, Virginia, in 1882.[37]

For Randolph Macon, Dr. John Mettauer was the professor of the principles and practice of medicine, surgery and clinical practice. Dr. Francis Mettauer was the professor of anatomy, physiology and chemistry. In October 1849, they were searching for a professor to teach therapeutics and materia medica, chemico-pharmacy, midwifery, and diseases of women and infants. The fee for their course was $155, board was $100, and books $46 for the year with a $30 graduation fee. They were advertising in newspapers "get a doctorate for $350."[38] One graduate of the program was Dr. Charles B. Crute, who went on to establish a very respected practice in Farmville, Virginia (but does not appear as a soldier during the Civil War). His father was Judge J.M. Crute, who had graduated from the Randolph Macon law program earlier and was a respected judge in Buckingham County, Virginia.

Three of the first eleven students to complete the first program in 1848 were from Randolph Macon. They were: T.H. Rogers (A.B. 1844, a tutor at RMC, and A.M. in 1847) and George Rogers, Jr. (RMC 1841 to 1842). Both were from Boydton and sons of Colonel George Rogers. The third was J.A. Shelton of Pittsylvania County, Virginia, who had graduated from RMC with an A.B. 1845 and A.M. in 1848. The students came from all over. One was from St. Louis, Missouri, and one from Montreal, Canada. The school had such acclaim, even with the low enrollment, the Society of Medical Alumni began in 1849. These men were not found as Virginia soldiers during the Civil War.

Two other students in this class of 1848 were Hampden-Sydney College graduates—H.A. Mettauer and E.M. Mettauer. They were the sons of Dr. John Mettaur. The RMC Archives in Ashland has some of the catalogues for the 1850s which list the medical department students,[39] but no complete listing is known to exist. Similar to the law students, if a student left Randolph Macon and returned home in a short three or four year period of time or no record of a medical school is listed between 1850 and 1860, he most likely completed the medical program at RMC.

Henry Mettauer completed the medical program and was listed as an alumnus of RMC in 1853. He went on to graduate from medical school in Baltimore and returned to his father's home near Hampden-Sydney College. In 1850, he was on faculty of RMC in the Medical Department as professor of therapeutics materia, medica, midwifery and medical jurisprudence. In the later 1850s he relocated to Macon, Georgia, where he established a medical practice. With the outbreak of war, Henry A. Mettauer enlisted in 1861 in the 6th Georgia Infantry, A.H. Colquitt's Brigade. He was established as surgeon and assigned to a Confederate hospital in Atlanta for the duration of the war.[40]

Dr. John Mettauer was achieving an international reputation. He is credited with being the first known surgeon to successfully operate on and correct a cleft palate, the first to successfully amputate a shoulder, and he pioneered vesico-vaginal fistula surgery. He was the first to recognize and isolate typhoid fever from several other fevers[41] (which was extremely beneficial during the Civil War, as typhoid and bullets were the leading causes of death), and he was the first to use iodine in the treatment of scrofula. Medical students and doctors came from around the world to learn his procedures. The brothers also maintained a medical practice in Farmville, Virginia, and recruited students from that area to Randolph Macon.

Part of the lack of success for the program could have been that it took place at Prince Edward Medical Institute. At that time, the institute was located 55 miles north of Boydton. That would have been a considerable trip and would have required additional expenses of room and board for local students. The other part was that Dr. John Mettaeur had published a treatise on general surgeries and his practices that filled over 3,000 pages. The cost, should a student desire a copy, would have been prohibitive. Beginning in at least 1858, Dr. John discontinued making house calls in the heat of the summer (he was over 70 years old). This could have been the beginning of the closing of the medical program, but for certain, with the Conscription Act of the spring 1862 by the Confederate States of America, the school, lacking in students, certainly ceased operation. Dr. John died in Farmville on November 22, 1875.

William Hicks Bracey (b. 1829), son of Pascal Bracey of Tanner's Store, attended Randolph Macon and the Medical Department. He went on to Washington Medical School, Baltimore, Maryland, as an advanced student. He graduated as a dentist and returned to St. Tammany to establish his practice. When the Civil War began, he enlisted in Company F, 14th Virginia Infantry, as a private on August 12, 1861. He was sick and hospitalized at Williamsburg Hospital with typhoid fever on October 13, 1861, in Suffolk,

Virginia. He was furloughed home due to his illness on December 10, 1861. He was then given a medical certificate of discharge as disabled on April 12, 1862. He had come home to his wife, Bettie A. Simmons. They had wed on December 2, 1857, after his graduation from medical school. After the war, they moved to Florida. They lived out their lives in Gainesville.[42]

Hugh David Bracey (b. 1831) followed in his brother's footsteps. He graduated from Randolph Macon in 1852, attended the Medical Department, and went to Washington Medical School, also graduating as a dentist. Family lore is that William and Hugh's sister, Olivia, attended Hugh's graduation at RMC in 1852 (she was age 16). She became ill while at Randolph Macon, returned home, and died shortly thereafter.[43] Returning to St. Tammany to work with his brother, he purchased a home and farm called Loquacity. When the Civil War began, he enlisted as a private in Company F, 14th Virginia Infantry, on May 1, 1862, in Suffolk, Virginia. On October 31, 1862, he was transferred to the newly formed Company I. Following a Christmas furlough, apparently disappointed at not receiving a promotion, he furnished a substitute (John Kearney) and was discharged on January 10, 1863. He had married Francis O'Brien, but she apparently died during child birthing. His second wife was Mary Cornelia Dupuis-Yongue, and at the end of the war they sold their home and moved to Deland, Florida. He died there in 1914.

Flavious Joseph Gregory (February 21, 1826–February 13, 1910) was born at Woodburn, the family plantation in Lunenburg County near present day Fort Mitchell, to Zachariah Joseph Gregory, who was the great-grandson of Joseph Gregory and Mary Elizabeth Lee (niece of "Light Horse" Harry Lee). He had four brothers who received an education and became successful in their ventures as well as their military service during the Civil War. Flavious graduated from RMC in 1848, completed the medical program in 1849, but then attended Jefferson Medical Institute in Philadelphia. Completing his medical degree, he returned to Keysville, where he began a practice in medicine, serving Charlotte County and, as needed, northern Mecklenburg County.

When the Civil War began, Flavious Gregory quickly enlisted as a private in a Charlotte County volunteer infantry company, but upon arrival in Richmond, he was established as a junior first lieutenant with the Paris Artillery Company on September 18, 1861. During his service, he took only one furlough in late 1862 before being transferred to the Coastal Artillery Hospital, Wilmington, N.C. He came home to marry Mary Ellen "Etta" Walton Wootten (1844–May 10, 1911), daughter of Confederate surgeon Dr. Lucius T. Wootten and granddaughter of Honorable Taylor Wootten, who served in the House of Burgesses for several years and then served the newly formed United States government in a variety of responsible positions.[44]

2. The Auxiliary Programs of a Country College 61

Dr. Gregory became a sickly individual with a chronic condition diagnosed as phithisis pulmanaris. He was transferred from his hospital duties to Confederate headquarters in Richmond, Virginia, during late December 1864, just prior to the attempted siege of Fort Fisher, North Carolina, on January 4, 1865. He was transferred to Richmond to meet with a medical review board to prepare his medical discharge from the army. En route he made a short layover with his family in Keysville. Upon arrival in Richmond, he convinced the board to allow him to serve as a steward at a Confederate hospital in Richmond. He was reassigned to Company E, 22nd Virginia Infantry Battalion, and served as a hospital steward for the medical director's office in Richmond until discharged on April 21, 1865.

In 1848, two new members of the Randolph Macon College Board of Trustees were George D. Baskerville and Charles S. Hutcheson. Baskerville, of Warren County, North Carolina, was also a trustee of the newly established preparatory school in Ridgeway where his son, George Jr., was a student. He was a graduate of the University of North Carolina and was married to Lucy Herbert Waller Goode of Boydton. In 1851, he was one of the organizers of the Boydton Savings Bank.

Hutcheson, of Mecklenburg County, lived at Mount Airey Plantation. Hutcheson had served as a member of the Virginia House of Delegates in 1843–1844 and then was presiding justice of the county until 1865, when he was replaced by Professor Chambers. He also served as superintendent of schools for the county from 1850 to 1865. Hutcheson was born in 1804 (d. 1881) and was a steward of Easters Church on Old Cox Road just outside of Boydton to the north. His father, Joseph, had also served as steward for many years, as did his younger brother, Joseph C. (b. 1816). The church was named for the Rev. John Easter ("saddlebag companion of the Reverend Dromgoole")[45] and was established sometime before 1800, although the deed to the property was not completed until 1857 by Charles S. Hutcheson, along with John T. and W.M. Winckler as trustees.

Whitice, the college building mason, had purchased a 200 acre farm on Courthouse Road adjacent to the chemistry professor's house in the 1830s. The June 1850 Census[46] shows he was living on the farm with his wife. He was boarding seven students not living in school buildings, a new professor, and three boarders. The professor and boarders were Professor John C. Wiles (Wills), age 30, who became a licensed minister in the county in 1858 resigning from RMC in 1859; wife, Catherine, age 25; son Willie, age 2; and daughter Rosaline. His home and farm were near the farm and home of Hezekiah G. Leigh (D.D. 1853, RMC), who was operating his home as a boarding house for preparatory school students. His sons, Richard M. Leigh (b. 1820), who attended Randolph Macon for about a year in 1845, and Hezekiah Jr. (b. 1830), who graduated, were also living there. The farms of Leigh and Whitice must have been supportive of the college, at least for pasturing the horses.

Hezekiah G. Leigh, Jr., Dr. Leigh's son, graduated RMC 1853 and replaced Corprew as tutor. In 1854, Leigh received his A.M. degree (and continued on to the medical program and medical school). He was replaced as tutor by Thaddeus H.L. Young (A.B. 1854). Young tutored 1854 to 1857 for his A.M. degree, but in the 1860 Census he is listed as married with two children and farming in Mecklenburg County near the college. Following the war, Young and his family moved to Enfield, North Carolina, where he was a merchant and farmer in 1909.

Whitice sold his home and farm following his wife's death (in either September or October 1850). The new owner in 1851 was his neighbor, college supporter and gentleman farmer John W. Wootton. In the November 1850 census[47] Whitice was living in a smaller home next door to President Smith with property valued at $10,000. In the 1860 census,[48] he is listed as having land valued at $40,000 (he had purchased the adjoining farm) and personal property at $45,300. Whitice and Alexander Boyd, Jr. (treasurer for the RMC Board of Trustees), had been responsible for the financial backing of extending the Boydton Plank Road from Boydton to Clarksville. When the road failed in 1859, Whitice and Boyd purchased the Boydton to Petersburg Plank Toll Road at auction in Petersburg for $1,763.[49] Once the deeds were recorded, they began to sell sections of the road to communities along the road. One example was the Lombardy Grove to Boydton section, which they sold to Mecklenburg County for $1,500 in 1860. The section from Boydton to Clarksville was still in good condition, and they continued to operate it, even during the Civil War. (There is a replica of the Boydton-Petersburg Plank Road adjacent to Hull Street in Boydton with a historical marker indicating that it is on the original route.)

The road was an important asset to the college. There was a daily stagecoach between Petersburg and Boydton. This brought visitors, students, mail, and trustees, among others, to Boydton at 6 p.m. each day. The schedule was for a thirteen hour trip. A stagecoach would leave Petersburg for Boydton at 5 a.m. and a stagecoach would leave the Boydton Hotel for Petersburg at the same time. Weather and road conditions permitting, the stages were scheduled to arrive at 6 p.m. in their respective towns. There were also coaches leaving from the Boydton Hotel to Clarksville and Buffalo Springs, but these were short trips of about one-half hour each way. These stagecoaches only operated on Tuesdays, Thursdays, and Saturdays. Before, on the Old Mud Road (Clarksville Road), these segments could take three to four hours of very rough riding each way.

2. The Auxiliary Programs of a Country College   63

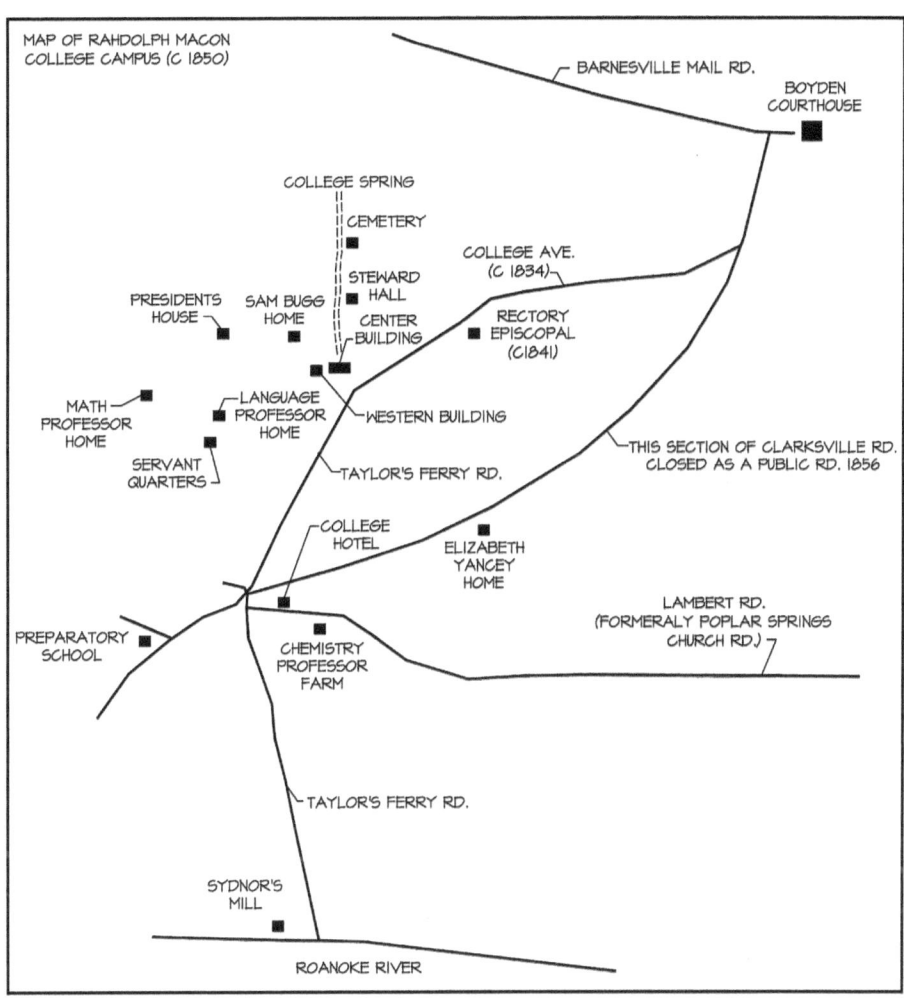

Map of college area (courtesy Sandy Wootton Herndon).

Prior to the road, Mecklenburg County was isolated and considered as part of the "western frontier." In 1821, the Roanoke River Navigation Company was begun using a fleet of bateaux, canoes, and the new 1817 pirogue canoes to ship freight, passengers, supplies, and slaves from Gaston, North Carolina, to as far west (with high water) as Danville, Virginia (using the Dan River) and to near Brookneal, Virginia (using the Roanoke [Stanton] River). In 1827, the company added keelboats which could carry twice the load, but were very hard to maneuver in the river and required a crew of 25 men. These boats also required a team of oxen to pull them through the canals. These boats rarely ever traveled farther west than Clarksville. In high water, if the oxen lost their footing or were unable to pull the boat across the canal, they would have to be cut loose, or they would be dragged into the current and drowned. Sometime before 1840, there were also steamships coming up river from North Carolina, operated by the Hamblets of Roanoke Mills,[50] but they depended on high water and were very unreliable for scheduled travel. This bateaux company was very important to Randolph Macon College for bringing supplies and goods into Taylor's Ferry, located about seven miles south of the college, from both the east and west.

By 1856, the locks and canals had fallen into disrepair and much of the shipping had ceased. Records do show, however, that the Roanoke River was used heavily during the war, and a Confederate commissary was at Taylor's Ferry. Clarksville and Boydton investors capitalized the Roanoke Valley Railroad Company, which followed the south side of the Roanoke River from Ridgeway-Manson to Clarksville, which was completed in 1854. This helped the county a great deal. But when the war began, the rails of the spur track were removed to the more strategic Confederate Virginia Central Railroad.

Next to the Whitice farm was the small farm of Alex Gillispie with his wife and son. In 1857, Alex's brother, George, moved into the home as the newly appointed postmaster for the U.S. Post Office at Randolph Macon (begun in January 1851 by David Duncan, postmaster and professor at Randolph Macon). On February 17, 1851, Richard A. Speed (b. 1827) from Richmond, a senior at RMC and a boarder with Professor Duncan, was appointed postmaster. Following his appointment Speed moved across the lawn from the Centre Building (the post office) and was living with Dr. Smith. He died in late 1853 or early 1854 and is buried in the college cemetery. According to the records of Irby, he did not take a degree.[51] The post office remained open throughout the Civil War, thus exempting the postmaster from military service.[52] It was closed by the United States postmaster general in September 1866.

Irby writes that the students were continually holding impromptu evangelical services. On the occasion of Speed's death in 1853 or 1854, within three days three mourners had arrived to pay respects. This was followed by more mourners arriving over the next two days. Thus, the students immediately organized an evangelical service for the benefit of the mourners.

To the southeast corner of the college lands was the farm of Captain (War of 1812, 6th Regiment, Virginia Militia) Thomas Reekes (b. 1771), which was being managed by his son, Thomas C. Reekes (b. 1814). Next door to the Reekes home was a small parcel of land owned by William J. Justice (b. 1813) of North Carolina with his wife and five children (all born in Virginia). His listed occupation was shoe and boot maker. Next door to Justice toward Boydton was the farm of George W. James (b. 1815) and his wife and three children. His listed occupation was miller. Among the next thirty households, four additional shoemakers were listed. South of the Reekes farm was a parcel owned by Trustee Beverly Sydnor[53] until his death in 1843. This parcel of 517 acres was in the low grounds and bordered on the Roanoke River near Taylor's Ferry. Sydnor operated the largest grinding mill, consisting of 100 acres, in the county. This also served a great need of the college.

This was a manufacturing area producing flour, grain, molasses, fodder, lumber, and much more. It was named Eagle Point Mills. It was sold at auction in 1843, but continued in operation and support of Randolph Macon College. Nearby was the small farm of William L. Harris. Harris served as a tutor of languages at the college in 1839–1840 but resigned without taking an A.M. degree. He chose to farm as his career. On December 9, 1843, he and Maria Speed were married in Mecklenburg County. They were still farming the same farm with their young family in 1850.

These and other farmers and tradesmen were of absolute necessity to the survival of Randolph Macon College. To put it into perspective, consider 130 students (some with families), five faculty and families with slaves and their families, five tutors and families, four stewards and families, 15-plus servants and families, a Preparatory Department and instructors with families—a total of over 300 individuals—and the amount of wood that would have been used in cooking every day nine months per year and heating for six to seven months per year. According to Scanlon (1983), 100 students would consume 200 cords of wood per an average season, just for heat.[54]

The wagon loads of grains, fruits, produce, dairy, preserved foods, condiments, and fresh meats to feed this body of people would have been nearly impossible for the college itself to have produced. There are no records of produce markets in Boydton or the neighborhood, so this was all most likely done by contractual arrangements. Add to that the amount of supplies needed for families arriving for a visit, special occasions, and graduation, plus the visits by the board of trustees and frequent guests staying at the hotel. Many farmers from the surrounding area were involved in the day to day survival of the college.

An illustration of how the need spread comes from the partial archives of the Wootton and Carter families which span 1850 through 1895.[55] From the many receipts of the Wootton family, it appears that John W. Wootton (1821 to 1887), grandson of John Wootton and Mary Christopher, who were married March 18, 1787, and son of John J. (C.) Wootton (1791 to 1857), was a hog farmer, at least on one 500 acre parcel he purchased in 1850. On this parcel he built a home for his new bride, Elizabeth A. Carter, following their marriage on June 25, 1845 (they had seven surviving children). She was given in marriage by her brother John T. Carter (she also had another brother, William N., who attended RMC), and they were the children of David Norfleet Carter, who was a veteran of the war of 1812. D.N. Carter (as he was known) owned a farm just west of the farm being purchased by Wootton and was also provider for the college. D.N. Carter's wife was Karen Happuch Brame, the daughter of Samuel and Elizabeth Brame of Boydton. Following the death of Whitice's wife, John W. Wootton purchased the Whitice farm, and one corner of this farm bordered that of his brother, John T. Wootton, who also supported the college. After purchasing the Whitice farm, John W. was raising tobacco and cattle.

Receipts from Wootton and Carter indicate they were involved in tanning cattle hides, selling bacon, in purchases of slaves and shipping, and in sales of hogsheads of tobacco. These receipts also include almost identical amounts on each transaction for the two individuals.[56] At least one check in the college's sole surviving check register[57] (which covers only part of 1862) shows a $600 payment to Wootton for bacon (about $1 per pound at the time). Many of the Wootton family married nearby members of the Brame family, as well as the Carters and Jeffress. Most all were married by Methodist ministers: Thomas Scott, William Richards, Jacob Manning, James McAden, and others. These farms provided not only food but wood, pasture, fodder, and plants for college and student use.

The check register from the Exchange Bank of Clarksville for Randolph Macon College in nine months of 1862 (in the archives at Ashland) has payments to Townes Jr. for bacon, Wootton for bushels, Baptiste for corn, James A. Duggar for a servant, and R.E. Butler, James Brooks, William Coleman, D.T. Hughes, and the Rev. William Carter for pasture.[58]

John Wootton's brother, Joseph L. (b. 1825, d. December 28, 1887), married Sally A. Daws on December 27, 1843, and the ceremony was consented to by Joseph's father, John Wootton. Sally's brother, Howell Wilkerson, stood on her behalf. Following the wedding, Joseph purchased the 500 acre farm south of D.N. Carter that bordered his father, John C. Wootton (who subsequently died in October 1857). His farm was divided and John T. received "240 acres and the homeplace."[59] John W. received 64 1/4 acres, and Joseph received 155 acres plus 120 pounds of tobacco. Joseph in turn sold his share to the neighbors, Overton and Wilkerson. He was already raising tobacco and food crops, which included sugar cane.

Before 1851, Joseph and Sally were attending members of the Zion Church; they are referenced in the "Index for Church Book for Mecklenburg Circuit Commencing 1833 at Randolph Macon College."[60] It is curious why they were members of Zion when their home was directly across the Boydton Dirt Road in front of Gilgal Church. In 1851, their names were listed in this index as "Wootten," and they are referenced again in 1854 and 1858 spelled "Wooten." There are no other Woottons listed in 1863. In 1870, John T. Wootton donated two acres of land across from his home for the construction of a new church and a parcel for the construction of a schoolhouse. The new church was the Fields United Methodist Church (which replaced Gilgal), and it still serves the community, but the nearby schoolhouse is gone.

CHAPTER 3

A House Is Only as Good as the Foundation

William Andrew Smith was born November 29, 1802, in Fredericksburg, Virginia, and as a child, when his parents died, he was adopted by Russell Hill, his father's friend. Hill was a merchant in Petersburg. Smith was provided a fair education but had established himself within the Methodist community and was admitted to membership in the Methodist Conference in 1825. He annually attended the Virginia–North Carolina Methodist General Conference, where he had gained significant influence. He displayed a "keenness of mind, warmth of person and an eloquence of speech" that "kept him in the very front rank of leadership in the church."[1]

Dr. Smith had been involved with Randolph Macon College for many years as one of its first agents and a member of the board of trustees. He was also an alumnus, receiving his D.D. degree from Randolph Macon in June 1843. On one occasion in 1833, as agent, his carriage overturned, breaking his right thigh and dislocating his left hip and leaving him lame.[2] When Dr. Smith became president of Randolph Macon College he was 43, his wife Elizabeth 39, and they had three daughters, Susan, age 14, Molly, age 10, and Laura, age 4. In 1853, son Thomas was born, 1854, a second son, John. For several years, their groundskeeper and resident handyman was John Bugg (b. 1835), son of neighbor and tailor Frances Bugg. John Bugg moved into the Smith home sometime after 1851 to ease some of the caretaking for his widowed mother.

Previous to Bugg, Dr. Smith had a black slave caretaker and handyman, Edward (John) Evans (b. 1827). When freed by the college in 1851, Evans was allowed to remain in Boydton with his family. There were still four other children in the Bugg home (three sons and a daughter, Mary Frances, who was learning the trade of seamstress from her mother), but the father had died in 1844 (accidental, per family history).[3] Thus, Frances Hatsel Bugg was the sole provider for the family.

Between Samuel Bugg's home and Steward Hall, a roadway had been graded which led to the back side of the Steward Hall property. This area was established as a cemetery for the college and church. Family lore[4] is that one of the first buried in the cemetery was Samuel Bugg, in 1844, followed by his mother-in-law, Betsey Hatsel, in the late 1850s. Frances, his wife, was buried there sometime after June 1865. When the college closed and the church was relocated, this continued to serve as the Methodist cemetery. Frances Bugg's daughter, Mary Frances Bugg (b. 1842), was living in the home at the close of the war and was an established seamstress. She married Hugh Weatherford, a veteran of the Civil War, in 1866 at the RMC Chapel. When she died in 1910, she was buried in the college cemetery. Also, when Hugh Weatherford (b. March 21, 1835) died on February 2, 1917, he was buried there. Sometime in the 1950s, the United Daughters of the Confederacy wanted to build an entrance to the Boydton Cemetery and reserve a section on Park Street, but there were no Civil War soldiers buried there. They sought the family's permission to move Hugh Weatherford and were granted same so long as they moved Mary Frances also. Both were moved.

James Whitice and Alexander Boyd, Jr., were the financial backers responsible for extending the new Boydton to Petersburg Plank Toll Road on to Clarksville, which was completed in 1856. In 1860, this was the only major portion of the road still safe to travel. One of the toll booths was located at Butchers Creek crossing to the west of the John T., John W., and Joseph Wootton farms. This location was important, as it allowed for the farmers east of Butchers Creek, who were supplying the college, to travel to and fro without paying a toll. The toll gatekeeper there was John Murray (b. 1810). Also around 1850 was the new Scoggins-Boyd Stage Line that provided travel from Hicks Ford (present day Emporia) west to Danville with numerous stops along the way. In Boydton, the coach stop was at the Boydton Hotel, but later it moved to the Washington Tavern (which still stands). One of the most popular stops was the Buffalo Mineral Springs Resort. The new stage coach driver in 1860 was David Inge (b. 1830) from the present day Buffalo Junction area.

To accommodate students' nightly needs in the dormitories, rooms were equipped with commode tables or chamber pots. Each day, these would be collected by the servants and dumped outside, near a stream for the contents to be washed away, or into an old privy. Another activity that Dr. Smith began around 1859 was that of Christmas break. As wonderful as this was for the students, it created quite a stir in neighboring towns and villages. A sign of the troubled times was that when people went to sleep at night, many feared insurrection by the slaves and for their lives. One young lady writes of her experience of a night in the 1850s in a letter to the editor published in the *Chase City Progress* in 1888[5]: "I was startled by a dozen whoops vociferated by senterian lungs ... my hair stood on end: perspiration started from every pore! My little sisters were sleeping by my side; oh my darling parents, our housekeeper, Miss Suky Stone, and three servants (were) below the stairs! ... I will be quiet ... I saw at a glance toward the time piece on the mantel, it was 4 o'clock A.M. Joyful explanation! The risters were the students from R-M Col., going home for the holidays, they had a relay of horses and were hallowing to awaken Uncle Patrick who gave the answering shouts."

The students of RMC seemed to have become widely well known. No longer confined to quarters, they would have required pasture, food and stables from nearby farmers. With this greater sense of mobility, students could now venture out farther than the previous short strolls, as written by Lander,[6] into downtown Boydton.

Bennett Puryear (July 23, 1826–March 30, 1914) was born in Mecklenburg County. He was the youngest son of Thomas and Elizabeth Marshall Puryear. His great-grandmother was a first cousin to Thomas Jefferson and his mother a cousin to Chief Justice John Marshall. Thomas was an elder first cousin to Richard Clausel Puryear. In 1804, Thomas married Elizabeth and purchased the eastern 600 acres of Robert Munford's Plantation—Occoneechee—on the Roanoke River. In 1820, Thomas sold the land to Colonel William Townes for a handsome profit and purchased another parcel on the banks of the Big Bluestone Creek, about four miles west. In 1838, Thomas died, leaving a widow and six children. Elizabeth received $320 per year support from the estate until it was settled in 1843. Bennett entered Randolph Macon College in the fall of 1844 and graduated in June 1847, with highest honors, first in his class. He continued his studies, completing his A.M. in June 1850, and became a professor of chemistry at Richmond College (which would become University of Richmond).

Bennett Puryear met his wife, Virginia Catherine Ragland (December 12, 1830–June 14, 1872), while teaching at Richmond College, and they were married on October 19, 1858, in Henrico County. They returned to Boydton, where Bennett had accepted and begun a position of professor and chair of the chemistry and geology department, also serving as student advisor at Randolph Macon. (He was a Greek and Latin scholar as well.) He replaced Professor Nathaniel T. Lupton, who resigned to accept a faculty position with another college, after having only taught one school year. Puryear became a pioneer in applying chemistry to farming. His friends Joseph L., John C., and John W. Wootton, who owned three large farms near the college, benefited from Puryear's research.

The Puryears' first child, Lewis, was born at RMC in July 1859. The family had settled into their new home—the Puryear House, originally Chemistry Professor's House—which was now owned by Dr. William Smith and consisted of 27 acres and 33 poles. Dr. Smith and his wife, Elizabeth V. Smith, sold the land and home to the college for $1,314 on December 15, 1862, with the notation that "Ben Puryear still resides there."[7] (The home is still occupied today.) In July 1859, a new professor arrived, Robert T. Massie, and boarded with the Puryears until his residence could be readied.[8] The farm next to Puryear on Taylor's Ferry Road in 1860 had a new overseer from Christiansville, Leroy W. Wiles and family.

The developing college community in 1859 included the Puryear House, math professor's house, the Brown House (languages), Preparatory Department, Steward Hall, and the hotel, which were separated and sold individually when the school closed. Another parcel owned by the college was next to the Corprew lands and consisted of 101 acres 120 poles, which was sold to William A. Homes for $685 in 1859. Additional properties were purchased from Professor Edward R. Chambers on August 31, 1858, consisting of two parcels. One was located on the Boydton Road near Old Cox Road about two miles from the college, and it contained 68 acres. The second was the small 35 acre farm of former professor and French tutor E.A. Blanch on the Boydton to Clarksville "Old Courthouse Road" near Butcher's Creek. They were purchased for a total of $625.

Next door to the chemistry professor's house was the large farm (apparently the former farm of Hezekiah Leigh who died in 1854) ($26,000 in 1860) and holdings ($10,000 in 1860[9]) purchased by Philmer W. Archer (b. 1820). Archer, the son of Allin Archer, esquire, of Petersburg, a member of the board of trustees, had moved back to Boydton after having spent a few years in North Carolina with his wife. They had six children (who included a set of 6 year old twins). The overseer of his farm was Henry Tallifarer (b. 1815). Although he did not take a degree, Archer had attended Randolph Macon College for at least one year in 1837.

Randolph Macon had laid the foundation for success. It was progressive and diversified in classical course offerings, along with establishing a resource base for continued growth. By 1840, RMC hosted preparatory schools in Boydton and a home school program. In addition, it had preparatory schools in Garysburg, Lowell and Richlands, North Carolina. To illustrate the reach of the college, the class of 1840 was composed primarily of students from Georgia and South Carolina. Then, in February 1848, an additional preparatory school was begun in Ridgeway, Warren County, North Carolina. This was a crucial location on the railroad between Gaston and Raleigh, North Carolina, for which construction had begun in 1836 and was completed in 1840. This was followed in the mid 1850s by a spur track from Ridgeway to Clarksville known as the Roanoke Valley Railroad.

The preparatory program was in fact college preparation. The program consisted of a series of studies that, when completed, would allow the student to enroll and be fairly certain of academic success. The course of studies was[10]:

Latin Grammar	Andrews and Stoddart
First Latin Lessons	Andrews
Caesar's Commentaries (five books)	"
Sallust (the whole)	"
Virgil (Bucolics and six books of the Aeneid)	Gould
Cicero's Orations (two Orations)	"
Greek Grammar	Sophocles
First Greek Lessons	"
Anabasis (six books)	Liepsie Ed., or Owens
Arithmetic	Davis or Smith
English Grammar	Murray
Modern Geography	Mitchell
Antiquities	Eschenburg
Anthon's Classical Dictionary	
Algebra (First Lessons)	

"It is recommended to Students preparing for College to purchase Leverett's Latin Lexicon, and Liddell and Scott's Greek Lexicon" (from the 1848 College catalogue).

The North Carolina community was supportive, and many of the leading citizens came forward to enter their children into the preparatory programs. The Rev. Henry Fitts (b. 1778 in Granville County) was a self-educated man. He married Sallie Duke in 1798. He was a farmer and lay Methodist preacher. In 1809, he was elected a North Carolina state senator, but with the War of 1812, he lost all. With his wife and seven children, he purchased a new farm and switched to growing tobacco. In 1840, he served as a delegate to the National Democratic Convention in Baltimore. Within a few years, he had acquired a vast estate and with his family, now being thirteen children, moved to Warrenton, North Carolina, for their education. Fitts served as one of the original members of the RMC Board of Trustees for several years until his death. His first born daughter was Mary Parham Fitts (b. January 31, 1799), who married Colonel George Rogers on March 13, 1823 in Boydton.

Fitts read all he could gather and took a special interest in medical books. His home in Warrenton served as host to the circuit Methodist ministers and dignitaries traveling through. He began to purchase medicines and visit the sick. He gave those he visited medicine at no charge. He became a member of the Court of Common Pleas and Quarter Sessions, serving as chairman for several years. His 10th born child, James M. Fitts, graduated from Randolph Macon with an A.B. degree in 1838. His 11th was Emily, who married Ezekiel Blanch, an RMC tutor and professor (A.B. 1838 and A.M. 1845), and his 12th child, Ann Elizabeth, married James L. Scoggins (co-owner of the stage line [1851] and owner of the temporary county jail house [1870]) on April 27, 1842, in Boydton).

Horace Palmer, Sr., a lawyer in Macon Depot, Warren County, North Carolina, was selected for the board of trustees in 1837. His son Horace Jr. was a student in 1850 at RMC and graduated with an A.B. in 1852, as did his cousin and brother, Reuben (A.B. 1851) and Jacob (A.B. 1851). On April 18, 1855, the younger Horace married Sarah Emily Milan. On May 4, 1861, he enlisted into Company C (Warrenton Rifles), 12th North Carolina Infantry Regiment, as a private under the command of Colonel Henry Coleman of Mecklenburg County, Virginia. In March 1862, he was promoted to corporal at Seven Pines. He was wounded in action on July 1, 1862, at the Battle of Malvern Hill. Upon medical release, he was detailed by the 12th North Carolina to an undisclosed location, possibly Weldon Ordnance Depot. He is reported to have been lame the rest of his life due to his wound. His wife died on July 19, 1870. His eighteen year old daughter died while a student at Greensboro Female College. Such a staunch supporter of the Confederacy, people in Drewry, North Carolina, still talk about Horace, who was notorious for his never ending exclamation, "Fergit! Hell!"[11] His second marriage was to Harriett Oliver on September 14, 1873. One of their sons was named Jeff Davis Palmer and another Malvern Hill Palmer. Harriett died on April 28, 1894. He had seven children with his first wife and five with his second. He died on December 22, 1902.

Another individual listed by Irby as having served on the board of trustees is Peter Doub, and a photograph of him is in the 1898 book.[12] Doub was not listed in the original board of trustees, nor in the 1848 catalogue, and in his own autobiography[13] he does not reference serving on the board. In any event, Doub (March 12, 1796–August 26, 1869) was a Methodist circuit rider born in Stokes County, North Carolina, as the youngest child of John Doub, a German immigrant, and Mary Spainhauer, a Swiss immigrant. Arriving in North Carolina in 1763, the elder family members became Methodists around 1780. The Doub children were home schooled with strict religious training supplemented with occasional attendance at a variety of old field schools in the neighborhood.

Peter's conversion was in 1817; in 1818, he became a candidate for the ministry in Norfolk, Virginia, with his first assignment being Culpeper. For 42 years he traveled the Methodist circuits and districts and served as a temperance lecturer. During 1823 and 1824, he lived with his new wife and their first born child (William) at the "northwest corner of Gilliam and High Streets in Oxford, North Carolina (unusual for a circuit rider)."[14] In 1832, he organized a group of laymen in Greensboro, North Carolina, to build the first church building in town on Market Street. Directly across the street, in 1832, a school was established for children of the members of the church. On December 28, 1838, that school received its state charter as Greensboro Female College, which became the employer of several of the Randolph Macon graduates. One of his sons, William C. Doub (b. 1823), attended RMC, receiving an A.B. in 1844 and an A.M. in 1847. Following graduation, he became a professor at Greensboro Female College for several years, and later was a professor at Trinity College.

In 1855, the Normal College of Randolph County, North Carolina, presented Peter Doub with an honorary D.D. degree. The Normal College, with President Braxton Craven, was taken over by the North Carolina M.E., South, Conference and renamed Trinity College in 1859,[15] with impetus from Deems and Doub. (The college was relocated from Randolph County east to Durham in 1892.) In 1866, when Trinity reopened after the war, Peter Doub (now age 70) was offered the position of professor of biblical literature. He taught until June 1869. William C. Doub taught until he died in the early 1870s. His papers are in the manuscript department, Library Archives, Duke University.[16]

Randolph Macon College had also accessed local preparatory schools to include the South Hill Academy begun in 1811 by the Rev. James Nolley (a graduate of the Brunswick Ebenezer Academy, d. 1857), whose son, the Rev. George W. Nolley, became a member of RMC Board of Trustees in 1855, and the Christiansville Academy. The Christiansville Academy was chartered in 1829 with the board of trustees being Peyton R. Burwell, Daniel Smith, Richard Russell, Richard Clausel Puryear (son of Samuel), William W. Smith, John Pettus, James May, Edward Dodson, Dabney Collier, and John F. Finch (many family names found among RMC students). The first instructor-principal was Captain David Bigger, followed by John Finch's nephew the Rev. Adam Finch around 1833, with his wife, Lucy, as his assistant. (This is the first recorded coeducational academy in Southside Virginia that this writer could find.[17])

Following Lucy's death in 1859, Adam Finch (June 23, 1800–October 4, 1874) married Martha W. Farrar (sister of RMC student Samuel G. Farrar from Cedaria, present day Baskerville) on January 4, 1860. Finch had become a licensed Methodist minister in 1848.

After remarrying, Finch left teaching at age 60 and was replaced by John T. Brame (d. 1888; A.B. 1838 and A.M. 1841, RMC), son of the widow Sarah

Brame of New Bern, North Carolina. Brame had purchased the Old Tabb Farm located on Little Bluestone Creek near Courthouse Branch in Christiansville in 1840. This farm was raided by Union soldiers during the Wilson-Kautz Raid on the Staunton River Bridge in June 1864. The thieves stole all the livestock and farm animals, as well as the family carriage. Later, Brame filed charges against the soldiers, but Grant simply dismissed the charges.[18] Following the war, the new principal of the Christiansville Academy was the Rev. J. Kirkpatrick. He assumed the post in 1868, as Brame had sold his farm and moved to Windsor, Missouri, that year.

Brame's wife and two sons, Dr. John Baker Brame (named for his grandfather in New Bern, North Carolina, who had died in 1828) and Robert Harper Brame traveled with him, but while in Missouri, he was not collecting payments on the property he had sold. He, his wife and Robert Harper returned to Christiansville, but John Baker Brame, M.D., stayed in Missouri. John T. was appointed Mecklenburg County commissioner of the poor for Christiansville in 1870. Family history reports that during the war, John T. and his son, Robert Harper, who was a sickly child, went to General G.W. Magruder and were assigned to the Confederate Army. But because of disability and age, they were sent to the commissary at Randolph Macon College to help with the collection of supplies. John Baker enlisted and served out the war as a sergeant in Company A, 3rd Virginia Cavalry.

As an aside story for the Christiansville Academy, the Rev. Adam Finch and his wife had several children. He also had a younger brother, Tyree, who served as the commissary agent for Randolph Macon College representing the county and the Confederacy during the war. Following the war, Tyree married, and his first born son was named Adam Tyree Finch. He went to medical college, served for a year as resident physician for Buffalo Mineral Springs, and returned to Christiansville (which had been renamed Chase City) in 1902. He began a pharmacy and medical practice in that year. In 1920, he built the Chase City Hospital on Boyd Street, which closed in 1932 due to the Great Depression. He died in 1933. He had married Elizabeth D. Morton of Charlotte County on July 7, 1899.

He and his wife had three girls and two boys, Adam T. Finch, Jr., and William Carrington Finch. Adam T. Jr. followed in his father's footsteps by attending the University of Virginia Medical College, returning to Chase City, and building a Chase City Hospital on Marshall Street in 1936, but in 1951 he moved to Farmville, Virginia. There he was part of the moving force to establish a community hospital.

William (b. December 21, 1909) was educated at Hampden-Sydney College, Union Theological Seminary, Richmond, Virginia, and Drew University.

Serving as a chaplain in the United States Navy during World War II, he settled in Oklahoma after the war and taught at Oklahoma City University. Then he went to Southwestern University in Georgetown, Texas, first as a professor, and then as president for twelve years. He then was hired (as a "troubleshooter") in 1961 as dean of Vanderbilt Divinity School.[19] In 1965 he was hired by Emory and Henry College as president. He served until he retired in 1971 at age 62. In 2000 he gave an extensive interview which has been included in the book by Dr. Jones on the history of Southwestern University. He died at Nashville on June 13, 2007, at age 97.

As for the South Hill Academy, little is known. The only documentation was for the meetinghouse and these records date to around 1811,[20] when John Early was the circuit preacher. Later came James McAden in 1819. Other preachers between 1820 and 1835 include Matthew Dance, Thomas R. Brame, John Thompson, James Smith, Phillip Anderson, John W. Childs, Rowland G. Bass, David Wood, Charles Ogburn, and Lorenzo Lea, among others. In the congregation, in addition to these names, were Nolly, Gee, Bugg, Bowers, and others. Early on, a Methodist minister was usually given an assignment for one year but could return after a respite. Later, with popularity, a congregation could request that a preacher stay for as much as five years.

As is true of all high points, there come the lows. Following a two year drought, poor crop prices, and a recession, there was "disharmony amongst faculty and students." In rebellion, the students pulled many pranks and partook of many "unwholesome suppers to their rooms brought by the negroes at night."[21] Students were known to fraternize with the black servants after hours, but when caught their behavior was punished. On one evening in 1851 two students were caught in a cabin with a young black woman and both were immediately expelled. They pleaded their case to the board and one was reinstated.[22]

With the new leadership of Dr. Smith, much of the unrest settled, and the school was again beginning to experience prosperity. The national political climate, fueled by the debates surrounding the Dred Scott cases' second trial, had already begun to fill the halls and was of much debate. After all, the lead counsel was well known to the students through the history of the college. In retrospect, Hugh Garland served as a delegate from 1833 to 1838, when he was not re-elected. His girls' school was failing, and he was passed over for president of RMC. He moved his family to Washington, D.C., where he became a clerk for the United States House of Representatives in 1839. Disenchanted, in 1841, he moved his family to his wife's family farm in Petersburg. Still dissatisfied, they moved to St. Louis, Missouri, around 1845, and he established a law practice. He also began to write and eventually had a book published, *The Life of John Randolph of Roanoke.* The book sold well, although poorly written, but his legal practice was struggling.²³

Garland witnessed the first trial of Dred Scott at St. Louis Circuit Court in 1847. The issue was that Dred Scott, a slave, had been taken by his owner into a non-slave state and Scott believed that that entitled him to his freedom. He lost in 1847, but with the continued help of abolitionists, he filed an appeal and was granted a new trial based on a legal mistake made during the first trial. A new trial was finally begun in January 1850. The lead counsel in the second trial was Hugh Garland representing the slave owner. Garland lost, and Scott and his family were set free. The case was not overturned by the Missouri Supreme Court in 1854, and Garland filed to have it heard by the United States Supreme Court the same year. He died in October 1854 and was not around for the Supreme Court decision in 1856.²⁴ Their final ruling was not only that Scott was still a slave and not free, but the Missouri Compromise was not legal and slavery was legal in all states and territories of the United States.

The school began a new magazine in 1851, *The Southern Literary Messenger*, with the first volume as a catalyst, 10 numbers (chapters) and over 300 pages with monthly reviews to follow. The diatribe for the magazine was, "It is at hand for us to throw off our dependence upon the North, and establish an independent Southern literature...."²⁵

So inspiring was the magazine that a local attorney began a newspaper, the Clarksville *Tobacco Plant*, in 1852. John G. Boyd (A.B. 1845 and A.M. 1848, RMC) had studied law with Professor Chambers and been licensed into the legal profession in Boydton in 1849. He later joined the practice of Henry Wood (who later became a noted judge) in Clarksville with an office on Virginia Avenue. The first page of the paper featured local sales ads and national and international news and stories. Page 2 was local news and stories with a few ads. Page 3 had statewide advertising, and Page 4 was more national advertising. Boyd was born November 23, 1827, and married Sallie Boyd on May 31, 1853, in Washington, D.C. By 1860 they had three children. The *Tobacco Plant* was being published throughout the Civil War until 1885 (with the exception of the Union Army ban from June 1865 through August 1866 (only a few issues are on microfilm). After the war, Boyd sold the newspaper to James M. Francisco before October 1866. He also sold his Clarksville legal practice to another graduate of RMC, Thomas C. Thackston (A.B. 1854 and A.M. 1857), formerly of Farmville.

Thackston continued the legal practice, and by March of 1867 had purchased the newspaper. After all, Thackston had been one of the agents for the Randolph Macon magazine in 1851 and was very interested in journalism.

Boyd was selected to serve on the RMC Board of Trustees in 1855. Following the sale of his practice and newspaper, John Boyd and family moved to Baltimore, Maryland. By 1872, Thackston had a new law partner, Samuel P. Thrower, and Boyd had returned to Mecklenburg County.

John Boyd's younger brother, Richard (b. February 9, 1835; A.B. 1854, RMC) went on to the medical program and medical school. When the war began, Richard enlisted and was established as a doctor. John wrote in his editorial in the *Tobacco Plant*,[26] August 9, 1861, "My brother Dr. Richard Boyd has been promoted to assistant surgeon of Charlottesville Hospital." This would have been equivalent to the rank of major. Military records[27] disclose that later he was again promoted to the Confederate general and staff (G&S) as a surgeon (lieutenant colonel). Following his military service, Richard married Pauline Rolfe of Mecklenburg County, Virginia, on May 19, 1869. He established a successful medical practice in Clarksville. On December 30, 1890, he died of pneumonia.

To further the school's success, a bold move was undertaken in 1852, following the closure of the preparatory school in Ridgeway. A new program was implemented as an "A.B. Degree in English Literature and Science." This was the first program offered that did not require any classical studies. It was favorably received by the students.[28]

The same year, the college began a new "demerit system." The first graduates receiving the BL&S degree in 1854 were Alexander Hogg of Virginia, J. Kirkpatrick and W.H. Shay. Of these three, Hogg (b. 1833) received an A.M. degree in 1858. He was originally listed as being from Virginia (son of Lewis Sr. of Yorktown), but for his master's, he was listed as being from Texas.

Samuel Lander (b. January 30, 1833) graduated with an A.B. in 1852 and studied with Professor Chambers. By testing, he received advanced standing to the sophomore class and was valedictorian of his class. In 1853, he became an instructor with Catawba College, and during the summer, he taught at the new Olin High School in northern Iredell County. In 1854, Lander became an assistant professor of ancient languages at Randolph Macon College. (His diary of student life in 1850–1851,[29] when he was 16 years old and a sophomore, is in R-MC-Ashland archives.) He left RMC in 1855 and moved to North Carolina, where he worked for Baxter Clegg, who was attempting to sell his academy. But just as Lander was about to purchase the school from Clegg he received a letter from Dr. Smith requesting that he return to RMC as a professor of language.[30] Lander again taught at RMC, from 1856 to 1857.

Samuel Lander, Jr., was born in Lincolnton, North Carolina, to Irish parents, the Rev. Samuel Lander and Elizabeth (Eliza) Ann Miller (d. December 29, 1875). Elizabeth's parents were friends with John Wesley, and on occasion

Wesley would visit the family home and conduct a prayer service. They immigrated to the United States in 1818. The Rev. Samuel Lander (Sr.) (d. December 17, 1864) was a lay Methodist preacher, founder of Lander's Chapel six miles south of Lincolnton, North Carolina, and a very successful coach maker in Lincolnton. The son Samuel began his education at age 4 with his uncle and sisters teaching him to play the piano and guitar.[31]

In 1853, Lander married Laura Ann McPherson (November 4, 1833– December 2, 1914) on December 20, 1853, and they had nine surviving children of eleven that were born. The second child was Martha (Mattie) McPherson Lander, who was born on October 4, 1856. She married January 24, 1878, and her husband went on to become the dean, School of Law, at the University of Southern California. The first son, John McPherson Lander, was born on December 17, 1858. He was married on January 14, 1886, while serving as a professor, with his father, at Williamston College. He and his wife traveled to Brazil as missionaries for the Methodist Church, and in 1889, they founded Granbery College in Minas, Gerais, Brazil.[32] The second son, William Tertius Lander, was born February 27, 1861. After completing his college education, he was married on February 25, 1889. In 1890, he became a professor of natural science and taught at Lander College until 1905. Resigning from the college, he entered the Medical College of South Carolina and later practiced medicine in Williamston until after World War II, when his health began to fail. He died in 1951. One of his brothers, Frank (b. December 17, 1872), also became a physician and practiced in Williamston from about 1905 to around 1935. A younger sister, Kathleen McPherson, was born on December 12, 1868. She married the Rev. John O. Wilson on August 27, 1897.

Lander resigned from Randolph Macon in 1857 to accept a position as professor of mathematics for Greensboro Female College. At age 26, he became president of High Point Female Normal School in 1859 and was licensed as a Methodist minister in 1861. He also practiced civil engineering and participated in surveying a new road from Lincolnton to Charlotte. He also acquired a habit of studying foreign languages. Not learning to speak them, but he could read German, French, Spanish, Italian, Hebrew, and Portuguese.

Samuel's oldest brother, William (May 9, 1817–1868), was born in County Tipperary, Ireland, and educated at Cokesbury College, South Carolina. He read law and was licensed to practice in 1839. He married Sarah Tillman Connor (d. April 1, 1863) on May 9, 1839. He was elected to the House of Commons for one term. He was then elected county solicitor, serving briefly before being appointed district solicitor. He held this position until 1862, when he was elected to the Confederate House of Representatives. While in Richmond, he also served with the Committees of Patents and the Quartermaster's and Commissary Departments.

When the war began, Samuel (Jr.) enlisted on October 1, 1861, into the 67th North Carolina Militia Regiment, Guilford County, as captain of the 10th Company of the 17th Brigade. On January 10, 1862, that regiment was thrown out by the Division Headquarters, and Lander was established as a second lieutenant. The new militia was established as Company K, 1st North Carolina Infantry, and he served for six months and resigned.[33] Returning home, he began to write. During the war years he wrote and had published a primary textbook on math, a higher version entitled *Our Own School Arithmetic*, and a textbook on English.[34]

He also began preaching and was accepted by the South Carolina M.E., South, Conference in 1864. After the war, he was a founder and professor at Lincolnton Female Seminary until he became president of Davenport College, Lenoir, North Carolina, in 1871. And in 1872, he was president of Spartanburg Female College in South Carolina. He was sent by the South Carolina Conference of M.E., South, to Williamston, South Carolina, in 1873 to establish Williamston Female College. In 1873, he purchased the old Williamston Hotel and converted it into the college, where he served as president and professor.

In 1878, he was granted a doctorate of divinity (honorary) by Trinity College, Durham, North Carolina. In 1903, he entered into negotiations with the South Carolina M.E., South, Conference to relocate the college to Greenwood, South Carolina. Before this was done, he died on July 14, 1904. The college was subsequently relocated to Greenwood and renamed Lander College in his honor. His son-in-law, the Rev. John O. Wilson, became the first president.

Following Lander's death, Dr. William Preston Few (1867–1940), president of Trinity College (1910–1924) and Duke University (1924–1940), wrote, "The female colleges under the guidance of Dr. Samuel Lander were pioneers among colleges for women in dispensing a solid Internal Conviction."[35]

Prosperity was brought to the United States and especially to the South in 1853 by the Crimean War. Property values in the South doubled, and wheat was selling at a record high of $2.35 per bushel. In the fall of 1855, the college board of trustees petitioned the legislature of the commonwealth to establish a school of military tactics (the persistent rumbles of North-South politics), but it appears the petition never made it out of committee.

One graduate of the class of 1854 was Adolphus Williamson Mangum (April 1, 1834–May 12, 1890). He was the youngest of eight surviving children born to Ellison Goodloe and Elizabeth Harris Mangum of Locust Grove on the Flat River at Deals Creek near Rougemont, Orange County, North Carolina. Mangum attended the South Lowell Academy, came to Randolph Macon College, and graduated with highest honors in his class. The Mangum Family Papers[36] "illustrates a pious and serious student with a strong inclination for the ministry."

In 1856, he became a junior minister and in 1860 was appointed pastor in the Roanoke Circuit. In 1861, he enlisted into the 6th North Carolina Infantry Regiment and was established as a chaplain. Following the Battle of First Manassas on July 21, 1861, he brought the body of his first cousin, William Preston Mangum, home for burial. He did not return to the military service. He began ministering to the Union prisoners of war being held at the Confederate Prison in Salisbury from 1861 to 1863 (an unpublished manuscript of this time is in his papers).[37] In 1863 he left to serve in the M.E., South, Church of Goldsboro. On February 24, 1864, he married Laura Jane Overman of Salisbury, and between 1865 and 1876 they had five children. Mangum had published over ten volumes of his works ranging from poetry, sermons and short stories to "The Introduction of Methodism into Raleigh, N.C."[38]

A July 1861 *Petersburg Express* story appeared about "Wylie" P. Mangum, Jr. (the first cousin), and it was reprinted in the *Tobacco Plant* on August 2, 1861.[39] "This young man was attached to Col. Fischer's Regiment, I believe, and owes the preservation of his life to a copy of a Bible presented to him by his sister. He had the good book in his left coat pocket. It was struck by a ball near the edge, but the book changed the direction of the bullet, and it glanced off, inflicting a severe, but not dangerous flesh wound. The book was saturated with blood, but the advice written on the fly leaf by his sister who gave it, was perfectly legible. It read this 'To my brother. He will read a portion of this blessed word every day, and remember his sister.'" It seems that the Reverend Mangum had reached his impasse. The reported flesh wound did, in fact, result in his cousin losing his life that day and Adolphus left the battlefield.

When the University of North Carolina reopened in 1875, he was appointed to the faculty as professor of mental and moral science, history, and English language and literature. In 1879, he received an honorary D.D. degree. He was described as a "man of warm and generous emotions, exceedingly kind to his students."[40] He suffered a stroke in 1889, forcing his retirement. In May 1890, he lapsed into a coma and died shortly thereafter. He is buried at the old Chapel Hill Cemetery.

Also in 1855, the famous trial of Deems versus Smith took place at the annual M.E. Conference, South, in Petersburg. Charles F. Deems was born on December 4, 1820, in Baltimore, Maryland. He was described as a precocious child, and attended and graduated from Dickinson College (established in 1783, but purchased and became an M.E. college in 1833) in Pennsylvania at the age of 19. From there he moved to New York City and in 1840 accepted a position with the M.E. Church of Asbury, New Jersey. In 1841, he became an agent for the American Bible Society, relocating to North Carolina. From 1842 to 1847, he was a professor of humanistic studies with the University of North Carolina. Shortly after accepting the position, he returned to New York to marry Annie Disoway, daughter of a prominent hardware merchant and RMC Board of Trustees member Gabriel Disoway, on June 30, 1843.

In January 1848, he accepted a position with Randolph Macon. Almost instantly, Smith and Deems did not get along. Deems resigned midway of the following spring (January 1849). Deems spent a good deal of time writing, and in 1853, Randolph Macon awarded Deems a doctorate of divinity degree. From 1850 to 1854, Deems was president of Greensboro Female College. In 1852, he purchased the Sylva Grove School property (which became Thomasville), renamed it Glenn Anna, and supervised it as a preparatory school for Greensboro under the auspices of the M.E., South.[41] In 1855, Deems accused Smith of "falsehood," "immorality" and "slander." This was as a result of Smith writing for the *Richmond Christian Advocate*. Smith in turn accused Deems of "writing an attack against another." This resulted in cause for the men to present their case before the M.E., South, Conference.[42] Having presented their diatribes for over five hours, the conference voted almost unanimously that Smith was innocent of any wrongdoing. Several members of the conference from North Carolina and RMC board of trustees members from North Carolina were supportive of Deems and resigned following the acquittal. As a result of this, Smith offered the board his resignation, but it was declined.

The trial established a precedent within the conference and received wide coverage and editorials within numerous publications. In 1858, a book was released by George F. Ford's (book dealer) of Richmond entitled *Speech of the Rev. Charles F. Deems*. The book was advertised in the *Tobacco Plant* as containing the "Trial of Rev. William Smith, D.D. for immorality, before the Virginia Conference, December, 1855,[43] with the most important documents connected with that trial, to which are appended historical sketches, together with other matter before published." With the embarrassment of this publicity, again Smith offered his resignation, but it was again declined.

Deems in 1858 became president of St. Augustine Institute (a nondenominational boarding school) in Wilson, North Carolina. He was in the midst of the North Carolina Conference taking over the normal school, attempting to move it from Randolph County and renaming it Trinity College. The conference was also building Olin High School in Iredell County, and Deems was serving as chairman of both boards of trustees. He served in this position until 1863. At that time he left St. Augustine and Trinity (which closed because of the war in 1863 and a conflict between Craven and the North Carolina Conference), and he taught at Olin High School until 1865. Opposed to secession, he did support the Confederacy, but his oldest son, Theodore Disoway Deems, was in the Confederate Army and was killed in action leading a charge at Gettysburg on July 3, 1863.[44]

Deems relocated to New York City in 1865, and he was the founder and editor of *The Watchman*. He served as minister at the New York University Chapel from 1866 to 1868. He was founder and minister of the Church of the Strangers, non-denominational, in New York City and served there until 1892. During this time, he became friends with Commodore Cornelius Vanderbilt and his wife, Frank. Some historians[45] record him as key to working with McTyeire and Garland in securing funding for Vanderbilt University. In 1877 he received an honorary LL.D. degree from the University of North Carolina.

Deems went on to become president of the American Institute of Christian Philosophy in 1881 and editor of *Christian Thought*. He published numerous books and journals. Throughout his life Deems was an earnest member of the Prohibition Party. The chapel at New York University was named in his honor. He died on November 18, 1893, and is buried in the city. Many of his works are found at Duke thanks to his two sons, Edward M. Deems, Ph.D., Presbyterian minister, and Francis M. Deems, Ph.D., who wrote a biography of their father.[46]

Following the resignations of the North Carolina board of trustees members, Professor Braxton Craven was able to persuade them, along with Deems, to support the school in Randolph County. The North Carolina Conference established in 1851 a board of trustees, and it became the normal school in 1856. Later they changed the name to Trinity College (which would become Duke University). When the war began, Craven enlisted into the 16th Brigade, Randolph County, "Trinity Guards" of the 53rd North Carolina Militia Regiment on July 29, 1861. He was elected the company's captain. When the militia was activated into Confederate duty he was released of his command but continued with a local defense unit of Trinity Guards (the students of the college).[47] In November 1863, Craven resigned under duress from Trinity due to a political dispute with several board members.

The "Trinity Guards" were activated for two years and sent to Salisbury Prison. There Captain Craven became commandant of the Confederate Prison until war's end. The reputation of the normal school was not good, and closing it gave an opportunity for new thought. When it reopened in 1865, Deems was an advisor, and two new faculty members were hired. Craven continued with Trinity for many years. During his tenure he received an honorary D.D. degree from Andrew College in Tennessee and later an LL.D. from the University of Missouri.[48]

Following the decision in the Dred Scott Case in 1856, Dr. Smith published a series of his essays, *Lectures on Domestic Slavery*.[49] He had delivered many of these lectures during his class on moral philosophy and political economy and slavery, both of which were very common courses offered by Southern colleges. Both southern and northern "college presidents used Paley's [Scots common sense philosopher William Paley] illustrations to demonstrate the defects of slavery" in New England colleges or "as an intellectual rationale to defend the same institution"[50] in Southern colleges. Later, Smith's essays were categorized as almost violent in tone, and Smith was committed to bringing the Northern Virginia Methodist under the Virginia Conference and removing it from Maryland. He was firmly convicted in his belief that slavery was of necessity. Even during the war, after the college closed to students in 1864, Smith embarked on a lecture circuit in the midst of battles. The January 19, 1865, issue of the *Tobacco Plant* noted that "the Rev. Dr. Wm. A. Smith delivered his celebrated lecture on 'Yankee Test Oath' in Lynchburg on Thurs., inst."[51]

In January 1856, 93 students were enrolled at RMC, and they were greeted by freezing temperatures and 15 inches of snow. It was the worst blizzard recorded in history, with constant temperatures below 10 degrees for an extended period of time.[52] Eight degrees were conferred in June. But January of 1857 proved to be even worse. The temperatures were the same but there were numerous days of snow with a large accumulation. On January 2, 1868,[53] the story in the newspaper stated that the snowfall in 1868 was the worst since the record amount in 1857. The college and preparatory department student population was 144. With the cold and snow many "college students [were] suffering for increased want of fuel." Fourteen students graduated in June 1858.[54]

The chaplain for the coldest recorded school year was the Rev. Alexander Gustavus Brown (b. February 22, 1833) from Frederick County, Virginia.[55] He was the son of Gustavas A.S. and Nancy Brown and was educated at Greenway, Hillsboro and New Lisbon Academies. He entered the M.E., South, Conference in 1853 and was assigned to RMC for the 1857–1858 academic year. He was appointed to the board of trustees but was inactive following his marriage to Fanny A. Cooksey on January 6, 1859. They had three surviving children. With the removal of RMC to Ashland, Brown became more involved by initiating much of the early transition. He served on the board for a total of twenty four years.

Another chaplain of note was Jacob Manning (b. 1816 in Baltimore). While he was an infant, his father died. His mother was a devout Christian and involved Jacob in the church to the fullest. When he was 15 he heard that the Virginia Conference was seeking some young ministers. He relocated, applied, and was accepted as a circuit preacher on trial in 1843. In 1844, he was assigned to Boydton as chaplain of RMC and minister of the Clarksville M.E. Church, South.[56] He chose to serve in the ministry for over 40 years with the first 15 years as a circuit rider.

A new member of the board from North Carolina was appointed in 1858, Dr. Thomas Palmer Jerman (1826–1905; A.B. 1846). Jerman was from Charleston, South Carolina, and the son of R.H. Jerman. He returned to Charleston and attended medical school. According to family history,[57] upon returning home he discovered his girlfriend, the beautiful, charming and musically talented Cornelia Klipstein, had married his older brother Edward. Following graduation from the Medical College of South Carolina, the school referred him to Dr. Henry L. Plummer of Ridgeway, North Carolina. In 1851, he moved to Ridgeway and became a partner with Dr. Plummer. That year he married Lucy Beverly Sydnor (1827–1883), daughter of Captain Beverly Sydnor of Mecklenburg County, whom he had met while attending Randolph Macon. They had eight children.

Edward and Cornelia moved to Winchester, Virginia, following their marriage. They had six children. In 1856, the "fever" took their lives, first Cornelia, then one month later, Edward. Dr. Jerman and Lucy became the guardians of the children and inherited the slave holdings of Edward. Dr. Plummer, his brother William (an attorney), and Dr. Jerman also controlled an active business as executors of estates in and around Warren County, North Carolina. In February 1869, Dr. Jerman and others were brought before the court to answer charges of mishandling the estate of John Vanlandingham (relative of the leader of the Knights of the Golden Circle, in 1859 renamed Sons of Liberty, with Clement L. Vanlandingham of Iowa becoming the new leader; he soon became a U.S. senator who was opposed to military movements against the seceded states). Jerman was found unintentionally negligent. A settlement was reached with the widow, Mary Ellen White Cawthorne, who was still residing in Warren Plains, North Carolina.[58]

CHAPTER 4

The 25th Anniversary Reunion

A 25th Anniversary commencement reunion was held in June 1859. Commencement was always a gala time for the college and town, as it was a week long process with a two day graduation event. The Sunday service at the chapel before graduation would have a guest speaker to start the process. The first day of graduation would begin around mid-morning with a speech by the college president and a guest celebrity speaker. After lunch, orations and debates would fill the afternoon followed by a grand ball in the evening (promenading of course, "unless at the Hotel").[1]

This 25th Anniversary event included a third day for the alumni featuring a speaker, business meeting, and social time. These events were heavily attended by not only college associated individuals but by all in the community for intellectual enlightenment, stimulation, and the social graces (for some, "The Enlightened Social Event of the Year"). Many romances and resultant marriages began at these gatherings. This event was so important to the families of and students, and the community, that the graduating students were dismissed from their classes four weeks early so they could devote their full attention and efforts to the preparation of their orations. The commencement announcement appeared in the *Tobacco Plant* on June 10, 1859:

> The annual commencement at this institution, will be held on Tuesday, Wednesday, Thursday the 21st, 22nd and 23rd instant. The first day Professor Warren Dupres, of Wofford College, South Carolina will deliver an address in commemoration of the completion of the endowment fund of Randolph Macon. In December last it was announced to the public, that this endowment fund had been raised to $100,000. This had been accomplished by the faithful, energetic and assisted labors of Rev. Henry B. Cowles, assisted by Dr. William A. Smith. For years upon years the friends at the institution had vainly striven to effect the same object, and when it was finally achieved the consummation was regarded of sufficient import to deserve some special celebration. The alumni accordingly determined to congregate on the next commencement occasion when one of

their number would be invited to deliver a suitable oration. The honor of performing this service has fallen to Professor Du Pre, whom we know to be eminently qualified for the task. The address will be delivered in the forenoon, and in the afternoon there will be a social meeting of the alumni at which 5 speeches will be expected from a number of them.

On Wednesday the annual address before the Washington and Franklin Literary Societies will be delivered by Mr. Jordan of North Carolina, and the regular annual address before the society of the alumni by President (E) S.E. Parham of Warrenton Female College, N.C.

On Thursday the usual orations will be delivered by the graduating class, which we understand is an unusually large one.

On the Sunday previous, Rev. Dr. Mc Tyeire, of Nashville, Tennessee is expected to deliver the annual sermon to the graduating class.

Among other facts, which conspire to render the occasion one of unusual interest, it is not amiss to mention that Hon. John Letcher, Governor, elect, of Virginia, has been invited to attend and has promised to do so.[2]

Professor Warren DuPre of the South Carolina Conference graduated from Randolph Macon College with an A.B. in 1837, became a tutor and received his A.M. in 1840. He stayed with RMC until 1844, when he was replaced by Holland McTyeire (A.B. 1844). In 1845, McTyeire received his A.M. and resigned to preach full time. He became the editor of the *Nashville Christian Advocate* in 1859. DuPre went on to become a professor of Wofford College in South Carolina. Later he became president of Martha Washington Female College of Virginia.

The following week another story appeared in the *Tobacco Plant* on June 17, 1859.

We have received a copy of the proceedings of the faculty of R.M. College, recommending to the trustees, important changes to the institution.

The prominent projects are:
1) A system of independent schools.
2) The supremacy of each professor in his own school.
3) The removal of all restrictions from the students as to the school they may choose to attend—provided they have employment—and as to the time of their stay at the college in order to graduate.
4) Special diplomas and certificates of each school.
5) The establishment of a chair of modern languages.

These are the leading features of the report, which, however, embraces other points of importance. The paper is drawn up with remarkable clearness, and the trustees can have no difficulty in promptly appreciating its suggestions.

We have not time for extended comment, but our own observations and our intercourse with gentlemen largely acquainted with educational enterprises, warrant us in giving our cordial sanction, to a plan so successfully illustrated in the University of Virginia, which removes so many unnecessary and antiquated restrictions alike, from professors and students, devolving upon each professor the entire responsibility of his own department, giving to the student credit for all he does, and allowing him to accomplish his objects as his industry and talents may enable him. In short, this plan lops off the senseless and frequently unjust restrictions, which embarrass collegiate education, and throws it open to the operation of the laws of political economy.

A chair of modern languages should by all means be established, and that at once. The monetary conditions of the college justifies it, and the public wants and expectations imperatively demand it. Arrangements for instruction in modern languages are made in most of our respectable academies, and shall Randolph Macon with her magnificent endowment longer neglect this matter.[3]

The proceedings of the faculty and the report to the board of trustees was prepared by Professor Bennett Puryear with the assistance of Professors Smith, Shepard, Wills and Carr.

In the same paper an advertisement was placed which reads: "We are requested to state to the public that a large and commodious arbor has been provided to accommodate the audience on the occasion of the commencement exercises at R M C which are to come off on Tuesday, Wednesday and Thursday next."

The next story appeared the following week, two days after graduation—Friday, June 24, 1859:

> Order of exercise at R.M. College on 22nd and 23rd instant. The addresses before the alumni, or before the Literary Society will occupy the morning of the 22nd. In the afternoon the following orations will be delivered by members of the graduating class:
>
> 1st "Best men on Sciences Rugged field, Have Spent their days before us"
>   Edwin S. Hardy, Lynchburg, Va.
> 2d "Republican Institutions as Effecting Individual Character"
>   Adam C. Bagby, Powhatan, Va.
> 3d "The Province of History"
>   William H. Davis, Petersburg, Va.
> 4th "Are we better than our Fathers"
>   Thos. W. Branch, Petersburg, Va.
> 5th "Literary Dietetics"
>   Leroy S. Edwards, Petersburg, Va.
> 6th "Tour in the Garden of Beauty—A Poem"
>   Jno. T. Humphreys, Lynchburg, Va.
> 7th "The Age of Pericles"
>   Jno. D. Blackwell, Buckingham, Va.
>
> The orations on Thursday will be as follows:
>
> In the forenoon,
>
> 1st "Give me the Writing of a Nations Songs, and I care not who makes its Laws"
>   Jno. W. Jones, Mecklenburg, Va.
> 2d "The finger of Glory shall point where they lie"
>   Jno. L. Johnson, Mecklenburg, Va.

3d   "Pitt and Fox—the Rival Statesmen"
         Aurelius T. Gill, Chesterfield, Va.
4th "The Triumphs of Learning"
         Jno. W. Hartsfield, Wake, N.C.
5th "Commerce"
         Christopher Thrower, Quachita, Ark.
6th "Powers of Imagination"
         Henry H. Cowles, Jr., Petersburg, Va.
7th "Conclusion of a Course of Lectures"
         A. Dibreld Crenshaw, Nottoway, Va.

           In the afternoon,

1st "Culture of Intellect"
         Thos. J. Overby, Granville, N.C.
2d   "Robert Emmett—The Irish Patriot"
         Luther Wright, Caroline, Va.
3d   "When Beggars lie, there are no comets seen"
         Jno. L. Chamberlain, Camden, N.C.
4th "The Triumph of Fame—A Poem"
         Wm. G. Starr, Petersburg, Va.
5th "The Valedictory"
         Wm. S. Davis, Warren, N.C.
     BENEDICTION.[4]

The board of trustees published the history of the college, including the changes, in several publications. One of those was the Clarksville *Tobacco Plant*. The report appeared, in its entirety, on the front page of the paper on September 23, 1859, and appears sufficiently important to include here in its entirety. (The newspaper was in poor condition when the Library of Virginia microfilmed it. The following is the best that could be gleaned. Faculty names in parentheses were added from Irby's book. Spellings are in the original. The ? indicates unreadable.)

           Randolph Macon College

The property ? the due to our possession will ? Of the ? of this institution, to ? Foundation to the present date. The obedient Methodist ministry and has flourished the type and ? Of the Methodist colleges, which have ? Arisen. It has set ? Been the "Mother of Southern Methodist Colleges."

? H.G. Leigh of the North Carolina

? Mr. Leigh brought the concept before the Virginia Conference in 1828, having previously secured subscriptions to a considerable extent, while Mr. Disosway operated largely on the public mind by timely and able appeals through the process.

The Act of incorporation was passed by the General Assembly of Virginia February 3, 1830, and the first meeting of the Board of Trustees was held in Boydton, the county seat of Mecklenburg, within one mile of which the college is situated, on the 9th day of the following April.

The institution went into operation on the 9th October, 1832, under the following organization:

Dr. Stephen Olin, D.D., President and Professor of Moral Philosophy
Landon C. Garland, Professor of Chemistry
Rev. Martin P. Parks, Professor of Ancient Languages

We give a list of the Presidents and Professors in the several departments, with the dates of service each:

Presidents

Dr. Stephen Olin, appt'd July, 1832   resigned 1836
Lannon C. Garland, appt'd 1837   resigned Nov., 1846
Dr. William A. Smith, appt'd Nov. 1846, is the present incumbent

Professors of the several departments

I. Ancient Languages

	Appointed	Resigned
Rev. Ed D. Sims	1832	1836
(Prof. David Duncan)	June, 1836	1854
Prof. O.H.P. Corphew	1854	1857
Wm. A. Carr	1856	to the pres.

II. Mathematics and Astronomy

Rev. Martin P. Parks	1832	June 1836
?	June 1836	Nov. 1846
[E.A. Branch]	Nov. 1846	June 1850
John C. Wills	June 1850	June 1859
R.T. Massie	June 1859	Present incumbent

III. Chemistry, i.e.

Professor L.C. Garland	1832	June 1836
R.C. Telefrue	June 1836	June 1837
Joseph W. Hardy	June 1837	June 1847
Rev. Charles F. Deems	served from Jany 1848 to Jany 1849	
Charles B. Stuart	June 1849	June 1857
N.T. Bupdon	June 1857	June 1858
Bennett Puryear	June 1858	is the incumbent

IV. Moral Philosophy

Professor Rev. Stephen Olin	1832	1837
Rev. W.M. Wightman	Mar. 1837	Sept 1838
Rev. Ed D. Sims	Sep 1838	May 1842
Rev. David S. Doggett	June 1842	Nov 1846
Rev. Wm. A. Smith	Nov 1846	is the present incumbent

A number of tutors and assistant professors have been connected with the several chairs.

Perhaps the period of the Presidency of the Reverend Garland was the most eventful in the history of the institution. At the opening of the college, an able faculty was appointed, and though, as might be expected, the tuition fees were insufficient to support, yet the fresh zeal of the friends of this institution afforded a ready subscription list from which they were promptly paid. The institution having an endowment, or at least, a very small one, the salaries of the officers and incidental expenses had to be discharged by the tuition fees and the annual subscriptions from the pupils. But, the public, of course, became weary of this constant drain on their charity, and the college, at the period to which we refer, was driven almost to absolute bankruptcy. The public confidence became weakened from a want of faith in the permanency of the institution, and the number of students rapidly declined. A suspension of operations, seemed inevitable. To crown this unhappy state of things, in the autumn of 1846, a violent disturbance occurred among the students, who, in their reckless frenzy, did not hesitate to ignore the obligation of courtesy to a distinguished and most valuable and esteemed member of the faculty. The result was the immediate resignation of the President and at the close of the session, the Professor of Chemistry.

As these things occurred during the Presidency, and indeed terminated his official connection with the institution, we must pause to protest against his responsibility for these disasters, and to pay a tribute, however feeble and unworthy, to his varied and profound scholarship, to his inestimable worth as a Professor, to his sterling qualities as a man. Twelve years have lapsed since we enjoyed the benefit of his instructions, and were admitted , to some extent, to his friendship and sympathy, but time has not abated the profound and affective admiration with we then regarded him; while our intercourse with society, somewhat extended and varied, has confirmed our early estimates of his abilities and attainments, and justifies us in asserting now after comparing him with many of the most Sanans of the country, that he is a peer among the greatest. Knowledge with him was not learned labor, but a living and practical reality, assimilated into the very texture of his mind, so that he could turn it at pleasure to his purposes. As a lecturer, he was admirable o what ? At first, the duller the materials, in passing through the glowing embers of his mind, became invested with intense interest, and the dry formulas of ? And science, as he explained their relations and connections, their importance and uses in industrial arts, were vitalized by his touch. He was so simple, so clear, he had so much collateral information with which he enriched his topics, that dullness itself could but listen and we may say of him what Johnson said of [the next three lines are torn out of the paper] irritable gratitude for his noble example.

In the darkest time of his peril, Wm. A. Smith, D.D. became President at the college. He accepted the office with great reluctance. It was pressed upon him, however, by considerations which were conclusive. The very salvation of the Institution was at stake, and he was appealed to as its friend. He was but little acquainted with college life, his modes of thought had been directed into another channel, his habits of mind had been formed by other pursuits. But he possessed qualities, which, as the result has shown, made him the man for the crisis. He was a thorough-going, practical man—bold, sanguine and on the basic ?. He had the ear of the Church and enjoyed the confidence of the public. A powerful and effective speaker, he could arouse, if anybody could, the dormant energies of the church and of the people at large. It was understood that his field of expectation would not be less abroad than at the College. Such were the considerations which suggested his appointment to the Presidency. The event has proved that they were well founded. He entered upon his duties in Nov. 1846 in the spring of 1847 he raised $7,000, which secured an additional $13,000 previously subscribed conditionally, the first Professorship was then endowed—since then he has made powerful addresses on the subject throughout most of eastern Virginia and a portion of North Carolina, which have thoroughly aroused the public mind. The endowment funded the college and now amounts to one hundred thousand dollars ($100,000) of which the interest only is available in defraying the expenses of the Institution, the conditions of which the principle was raised, requiring the whole of it to be invested as a fixed and permanent capital. Thus, unembarrassed by debt, and relieved of the pressure of contract means, the Institution with an enlarged corps of instruction has entered upon a higher and wider career of [cut from paper] to this country, and [cut from paper] nonombic to its friends

The average number of students from the foundation of the Institution has been about 120. The catalogue of the studies 1858–1859 shows an attendance of one hundred and forty one. We have been unable to ascertain the whole number of matriculates to date, two hundred and fifty-five have passed through the full course of study, and received the degree of Bachelor of Arts. Many of these are widely and honorably known, filling important and prominent positions in the Church and state. About one fourth is in the ministry.

Present Plan of Intentions

At the annual meeting of the Board of Trustees held in June last, a Chair of Modern Languages is created, and the old curriculum of studies fir four year courses was abolished, and a system of independent Schools established upon the principles of the University of Virginia. A confident conviction is entertained that valuable results will flow from this innovation. By this system:

1) Each Professor is made supreme and alone responsible for his school;
2) Diplomas are granted in each of the Schools separately, and the student is at liberty to graduate in any or all of the schools whenever he can show by actual examination that he is properly qualified, without reference to the period of residence at the institution.
3) The strongest stimulus is then afforded students to occupy themselves fully, becoming better scholars in a shorter time, thus saving time for themselves and money for their friends. [There was no number 4]
5) Students, who from want of time, capacity or means cannot take a full course, will find themselves accommodated in the privilege allowed them of studying the schools of their choice—credit being given then for all they accomplish by the diploma and certified [cut from paper] in the several schools.
6 [cut from paper] antiquated restrictions derived from the old English universities, and not in harmony with the spirit and tendency of our times, embarrassing alike Professors and students, are abolished, and education is thrown open, as it ought to be, to the operation of the laws of the political economy.

Government

Within the last few years, a change equally radical in the discipline of the Institution has been effected, which has been attended with the happiest results. Then nothing like espionage practiced; no faculty courts before which to arraign students as culprits. So that all unpleasant function between students and officers is removed. But the theory of discipline is based upon the hypothesis is that the student is a gentleman, that his work is fully accredited until he demonstrates to the contrary. Hence all the offenses and neglect of duty reported monthly to his parent or guardian against him, are only such as he has certified to be correct, knowing at the time, from a printed schedule in his possession, the number of demerits attached to each. When his demerits reach a certain number, he is remanded to his parent or guardian, where the responsibility naturally rests, to be treated as his judgment suggests. The continuance of the student at college is then left to the parent. As every student then furnishes the data, which make up his conduct roll, request as a gentleman strongly appealed be to deal honestly with himself.

But if this motive were not sufficient should be furnish incorrect replies to the reports publicly announced every week, his fellows who generally have access to facts, would frown him down and he would lose caste at once. In the very few cases in which the student abuses the generous confidence of the faculty, the President simply refuses to receive any reports against him, and his connection with the college is by his own act dissolved. This system of government, into the details of which we need not further go, the practical workings one must see to fully appreciate it has a degree of good order and good feeling which is without parallel. The College, under it, has become as quiet as a private facility.

We believe that the great disaster which befell the college in the autumn of 1846 arose from the strictly "police system," which then obtained. Students were naturally exasperated by the daily and nightly visits of the officers to their rooms; they felt insulted and degraded by the surveillance. Hence constant confrontations between students and professors with the absence of everything like frank, familiar and friendly intercourse. It afford, us sincere pleasure to record now in pleasing, and striking contrast the good feeling, the friendly and familiar, yet respectful intercourse which obtains. This not only good order secured, but the student not only progresses more rapidly and pleasantly in his studies, for it is certainly true that an instructor can render but little service to a class, in hope confidence and good feeling he does not enjoy.

In this connection we must submit a few remarks, which the truth of history demands. When Dr. W.A. Smith accepted office in 1846, not only many of his friends, but he himself, had great misgivings on the score of his imperfect acquaintenancure with the routine of college duties—with the interior of college life. But if he entered into office without experience, without special preparation, he came also without any educational bias. His mind was unlittered in applying strong common sense to college affairs.

The changes which have been introduced during his administration, originated, supported or approved by him, by which already signal benefits have been secured, with the promise in the fullness of time of still better things, are due to this freedom from all prejudices of education. It is strange, yet true as strange, that the very fact, which made him and characterized his appointment originally, has turned out to be the secret, which explains the eminent success of his administration. We have, then to congratulate the college upon having secured at the most trying point of its history, the services of a man who free from any wraping influence has had the good fortune to conceive and execute a system of measures, the value which is best attestedly the high prosperity they have already received for the institution. Entering upon the studies of the chair, with the enthusiasm which forms actually has turned out to be the secret, which explains ? of his administration. We ? how to congratulate the college ? occurred at the most trying period of its kind, the services of men who, free ? influence has had the good fortune to conceive and exceeds a system of language, the values of which is best attested by the high prosperity they have already secured for the institution. Ketering upon the studies of his chair with the enthusiasm, which forces so striking a trait of his character, he has given to his institution of interly valuable as a professor and executive officer.

The profound research and originality, display in his daily lectures to his class, have made the studies of his school as fascinating as important. His work of on Domestic Slavery, prepared for the benefit of his class, is a most masterly and luminous discussion of the principles of slavery and attests? while his devotion to duties, his untiring labor and powers of original investigator.

The faculty at present is composed as follows:

> Wm. A. Smith, D.D., President and Professor of Moral Philosophy
> Wm. B. Carr, A.M., Professor of Ancient Languages
> B. Puryear, A.M., Professor of Chemistry and Natural Philosophy
> R.T. Massie, Esq., Professor of Mathematics and Astronomy
> G. Staubly, Esq., Professor of Modern Languages
> W.A. Shepard, A.B., Asst. Professor of Languages & Mathematics
> E.S. Isbell, A.B., Principal Preparatory Department[5]

Following the graduation exercises on July 1, 1859, Professor John C. Wills (having received an honorary A.M. degree in 1858) submitted his resignation. Later, an article appeared in the *Tobacco Plant* dated October 14, 1859[6] announcing the first semester of Southern University had begun operation on October 8, 1859. The president was listed as Dr. William M. Wightman, and Professor J.C. Wills, formerly of RMC, was on the board of instructors. The same paper, in an earlier story, reported social news that Professor Wills had delivered the graduation speech for the Clarksville Academy and the editor was informed that he delivered "an excellent address."[7] He was replaced at Randolph Macon by Robert T. Massie, A.M., a recent graduate of the University of Virginia. Professor Massie also made the social news in November: "The new professor of Mathematics, Robert T. Massie, has made most favorable impressions upon the students and the surrounding community."[8]

The Rev. Dr. William M. Wightman (A.B. 1836, RMC) and was selected as professor of moral philosophy in January 1837. He held this position until June 1838 and received his A.M. degree. He returned to South Carolina to establish a ministry. Wightman was a member of the board of trustees beginning in 1834 and was secretary to the South Carolina M.E. Conference. He had been well known to the RMC student body, as he delivered a powerful inaugural address for the establishment of the first literary society, the Washington, at the college in February 1833. The address was published and widely distributed in 1837.[9] In 1837 he sponsored James W. Wightman (b. 1817 in South Carolina) as a student at RMC. He became editor of the South Carolina *Christian Advocate* and became one of the primary political forces in establishing a Methodist College in South Carolina. In 1846 he was awarded a doctorate of divinity by RMC. He was the first president of Wofford College, Spartanburg, South Carolina, in 1854.

The September 19, 1859, story now portrays him as the first president of the newly established Southern University in Greenville, Alabama[10] (present day Birmingham-Southern College, Birmingham, Alabama). In that position he taught biblical literature from 1859 until 1867. In 1867 he was elected bishop of the M.E. Church, South, a position he held until his death on February 15, 1882.

Professor Wills left RMC for Southern University in 1859. He had replaced E.A. Blanch as professor of math in 1849. With his wife, Catherine, and children, he settled into the college life in Alabama, but a short time later came the Civil War. Professor Wills enlisted into Company D, 15th Alabama Infantry, and was selected as first sergeant in 1863, and he served for one year. His wife having died, he was left with six children to care for: George M.D. Wills, age 14; Louisa Wills, age 12; Kate Wills, age 10; Rosine M.D. Wills, age 7; John H. Wills, age 6; and Edwin V. Wills, age 4. He married Martha Martin on January 12, 1864, and they moved to Missouri with their children, which now included the youngest, John C. Wills (Jr.), b. 1868. Professor Wills had been named the new president of Central (Methodist) College (established in 1854, chartered on March 15, 1855, adjacent to Howard-Payne Female Academy, established in 1849), Fayette, Missouri, in March 1872. He arrived seven months late for the position without any recorded explanation. He was elected president of the college by the board of curators in August 1871.[11]

There had been some concern about Randolph Macon being able to open in the fall of 1859. The newspaper article of September 30 reported that the county had experienced the worst floods in recorded history. There were torrential rains from September 10 to 25, which were so severe that "the mill dams of Richard Boyd and several others had been washed away."[12] The Roanoke River was several feet over its banks, making crossing from the south to the college impossible. The railroad spur track to Clarksville was also under water.

On September 24, 1858, the 98th Virginia Militia met to establish new officers and commands. The election results were to establish James T.

Alexander as colonel to replace the retiring Colonel John R. Chambliss. Also elected were William Townes, Jr., lieutenant colonel; Thomas H. Boyd, first major; and George W. Carter, second major.[13] (In 1860, George Waugh Carter was a professor at the University of Mississippi and then taught at Georgetown, Texas, at Soele College after the war.[14])

Of the rank and file, the 1st Division, 2nd Squad ("Butchers' Creek Squad"), consisted of John W. Wootton, sergeant, with John T. Wootton (second sergeant), Jos. Wootton (third sergeant), and privates Edwd. Overton, J.T. Carter, A.F. Davidson, D.N. Carter, Rich D. Jeffress, Jos. H. Jeffress, A.K. Adkins, E.W. Wootton, C.N. Wootton, and J.R. Stewart.[15] The later men were many of the primary sources of farm produce for the college from the west side of the college properties. (John C. Wootton died in 1857, and his sons—John W., John T. and Joseph L.—divided the farm.)

A November 25, 1859,[16] news article reported that 25 states had ratified November 24 as Thanksgiving, but several southern states, including Virginia and North Carolina, declined. The following week, December 2, 1859 (following the hanging of John Brown and anticipating a Northern aggression), a meeting was held in Clarksville at the Union Hall to organize a militia unit, and on December 19, 1859, the Boydton Cavalry was under command of Captain Thomas F. Goode (June 28, 1825–January 6, 1905; A.M. 1848, RMC), who was a delegate to the Virginia legislature at the time.

Before the graduation exercises in June 1860, Randolph Macon College was the host site for a retirement "Pic-Nic" for outgoing Colonel Chambliss of the militia. Since "a large and commodious arbor" had been completed for the 25th anniversary, it seemed to be the perfect location for a retirement function a year later. The invitations were printed and hand delivered by the militia to those invited to come to the retirement banquet (which was also a militia recruitment effort for the troubled times, especially in light of the forthcoming election). John W. Bugg received an invitation, as it is still in his historical documents.[17] The invitation read:

> Hosted by the Boydton Cavalry
> June 14, 1860
> Complimentary to Col. Jno. R. Chambliss, Jr.
> Sent May 10, 1860
>   Cavalry
>   President: E.R. Chambers
>   Vice-Presidents:
>   O.H.P. Corprew   Alex Sydnor
>   Dr. William H. Jones   John M. Tucker
>   Dr. R.P. Alexander   B.R. Williamson
>   Thomas L. Jones

Of these men, E.R. Chambers (d. March 20, 1872) was professor of law for Randolph Macon and serving on the board of trustees; his son, Harvey, graduated from the Law Department in 1860. O.H.P. Corprew, born in 1826 and sponsored by his widowed mother, Mary Corprew, of Norfolk to RMC, graduated with an A.B. degree in 1844. He had worked and served as a tutor (receiving an A.M. in 1848), professor of ancient languages from 1854 to 1857 (replaced by William B. Carr), a farmer and merchant, county trustee of widows and member of the RMC Board of Trustees, serving later in the capacity of treasurer for the college and for the board of trustees. He enlisted into the 3rd Virginia Cavalry, Company A, in Boydton on May 14, 1861, as a private and stated his occupation as farmer. He was age 33 (b. 1828) and described as 6 feet tall, blue eyes, dark hair, and dark complexion. He was transferred on November 18, 1861, to Mahone's Division, 6th Virginia Infantry, as assistant quartermaster sergeant and then promoted to captain. Throughout the war he spent most of his time in and around Petersburg. On file with R-MC Archives in Ashland is correspondence[18] between him and D'Arcy Paul outlining the death of a soldier in his company and the disposition of the soldier's property.

Alex Sydnor of Coldwater, son of late Captain Beverly Sydnor, like his father, was a noted merchant in Boydton, land owner, and member of the board of trustees. During the War Between the States, he served in Company B, 13th Battalion, Light Artillery. Following the war, he was sheriff for the county from 1868 to 1870 by military martial law appointment. In 1873 and 1874, he was elected and served as treasurer for Mecklenburg County.

Dr. William H. Jones and Dr. R.P. Alexander owned the Boydton Drug Store. They believed that the war would be fought to the death, so they sold their business in April 1861 to Dr. Miles M. Jordan (b. 1820; Jordan later became the resident physician for Buffalo Mineral Springs Resort). Jordan, son of Samuel P. Jordan of Smithfield, Virginia, had attended RMC at least for the school year 1837–1838, but there is no record that he applied for a degree. Dr. Jones enlisted into Company A, 3rd Virginia Cavalry, on May 14, 1861. He was established as the company surgeon. He was age 41 and described as being 5 feet, 7 inches tall, blue eyes, and fair complexion. He listed his occupation as that of farmer.

The *Tobacco Plant* published a story on August 23, 1861,[19] that "Major Thomas F. Goode resigned as commonwealth attorney but the court declined to accept. He and Dr. William Jones were in town for 'Court Day.'" In September 1861, Jones was elected as a captain and served in that rank until he resigned on October 21, 1864, due to ill health. He returned to Boydton and became partners in his old drugstore with Jordan. After the war, he was beginning to sell off his holdings. He sold a yoke of oxen to John W. Wootton for $40 on December 2, 1866. He died in the early 1880s.

His brother enlisted with him into Company A, 3rd Cavalry, on May 14, 1861. Thomas L. Jones was 43 years old and the Regimental Records describe him as 6 feet tall, black hair, black eyes, and a dark complexion. He enlisted as a private but was assigned as quartermaster sergeant on July 12, 1861. Then on December 24, 1861, he was discharged and sent home to resume his tanning business at Boydton, on Coleman's Creek, to aid in the war effort. This was the former 37 acre Brame's Tanning Yard, which had been acquired by Beverly Sydnor in the late 1820s. It was nearby to serve the tanning needs of the townspeople and tradesmen of Boydton. This prosperous business was sold at auction following Sydnor's death in the spring of 1843 and appears to have been subsequently purchased by Jones. This tanning yard was the third largest in the county with Goode's on Allen's Creek being about 39 acres and Puryear's on Bluestone Creek being 80 acres. The remaining four were much smaller.

R.P. Alexander had attended Randolph Macon Preparatory Department and College but took no degree. He was a student at the University of Virginia in the 1856–1857 school year. He was the nephew of board of trustees member and state Senator Nathaniel Alexander and the younger brother of militia Colonel James T. Alexander. James had also attended RMC (1849) but took no degree, as had his first cousin Mark Alexander III in 1840. They were the sons of Mark Alexander, Jr. (February 7, 1792–July 6, 1883), of Park Forest Plantation, who was a delegate to the Virginia House from 1845 to 1848, a lawyer and alumnus of the University of North Carolina. Robert P. enlisted into Company F, 14th Virginia Infantry, at Lombardy Grove. Regimental records list his age as 22 and occupation as planter. He was appointed a first lieutenant and assigned to courts-martial duty. He was promoted to captain on November 30, 1861. On May 5, 1862, he retired. But of interest, on January 22, 1864, he enlisted into Company A, 3rd Virginia Cavalry, and was detailed to the Signal Corps (of course no record follows that; the Signal Corps was the code name of the spy detachment under Thomas Conrad and others).

James T. Alexander (b. 1832) organized and enlisted into Company D, 2nd Virginia Artillery, at Lombardy Grove in April 1862. He was established and later elected as a captain of that unit when it joined the Confederate Army as Company D, 22nd Virginia Battalion of Infantry from Mecklenburg County. He was slated to serve one year from January 20, 1862, but according to the regimental records, he is listed on the rolls of prisoners of war paroled in Richmond on May 19, 1865. He was also required to file an application for a presidential pardon in August 1865.

Following the war, Robert Park was listed as single, and James was listed as widowed on the 1880 U.S. Census,[20] he being age 42 and James T. age 48. They were farming their father's plantation and other holdings in Flat Creek and taking care of their parents, Mark Alexander, age 88, and mother, Sallie P. Alexander, from North Carolina, age 65. Mark, like his brother and father, had served in the Virginia House of Delegates. In 1872, James was elected to serve as commissioner of revenue for Mecklenburg County. Due to many bad business decisions by Mark, the plantation was lost in 1882.

John M. Tucker enlisted into Company A, 3rd Cavalry, on May 14, 1861, as a private. On May 13, 1862, he transferred to Captain Bagby's Heavy Artillery. There is no further record of his military service.

Benjamin R. Williamson enlisted into Company A, 3rd Cavalry, on May 14, 1861, as a corporal. On October 19, 1861, he transferred to Company G, 59th Infantry, and was elected second lieutenant. He then transferred to Company C, 2nd Battalion, North Carolina Infantry, and is referenced in several miscellaneous regimental papers.[21] On September 26, 1862, he was reported to have died of a spider bite.

Lieutenant Colonel John R. Chambliss, Jr., enlisted into the 13th Virginia Cavalry and was appointed a colonel in 1861. In 1862, he was transferred to the Confederate General and Staff as a brigadier general in charge of the 41st Virginia Infantry. He was placed in charge of the 2nd Battalion, Virginia Infantry, and later to the 6th Battalion, where he served out the war until the surrender. As a general, following the surrender he was not paroled, but had to send a request for amnesty to President Andrew Johnson (on file in National Archives).[22] It was granted.

His father, John R. Chambliss, Sr., enlisted into Captain Scott's company, Greensville Local Defense. Following the war, the elder Chambliss was arrested and jailed for not having an "Oath of Allegiance" pass. A copy of his letter petitioning President Johnson for amnesty is on file in the National Archives.[23] His petition was witnessed and notarized by John Lyon (see Appendix B, 12th Infantry section). It too was granted.

Major Thomas H. Boyd (January 27, 1839–April 1, 1911) enlisted into Company G, 38th Infantry, at Boydton on May 18, 1861, for a period of one year. He was elected first lieutenant of his company but resigned on December 11, 1862, and came home. He opened a store in Boydton and in June 1864 he and his wife, Henrietta Waller Goode (February 3, 1842–July 2, 1876, the daughter of William O. Goode, Sr.), purchased a home on Madison Street and Plank Road from Elizabeth Rolfe. After the war he was managing the vast holdings of his father-in-law in the Ohio Valley and was making frequent trips to Baltimore for merchandise for his store. He is buried in the Boydton Presbyterian Cemetery along with his wife.

With the widespread publicity of the many changes to the college, in 1860 it boasted 149 students. However, due to the continuous low enrollment, the Boydton Preparatory Department was closed, as there were only 16 students.[24] The graduating class of 1860 had a surprise. The college's diplomas now contained a seal. The seal was an engraving of the main hall on the right and center with the Texas Hall on the left, and a gymnastics apparatus on the front lawn, all surrounded by a split-rail fence. The first diploma was presented to George B. Finch, master of arts, who took a teaching position in Clarksville. According to Irby, Finch received a cast reproduction of the engraving as an award and keepsake.[25] (Much the same seal style was in use until recently by Randolph-Macon College–Ashland.)

Not only was there a new college diploma, but there was also a new certificate of completion. This was awarded by the individual faculty member to students who had met the requisites for the one year study program as prescribed in the summer 1859. With the award of five prescribed certificates, the student could apply for a degree. The certificate was simple with "Randolph Macon College" arched over the center and Virginia in line with the R and e. This is followed by one sentence that the recipient has "been declared a Proficient in the class of...." followed by a date, signature and title of the professor.

The school year in 1860 began like any other at college, but now many lectures began to take a new format of preparing students for survival and warfare. Many of the professors and students had responded to the call for militia recruitment. They served and trained in Company D, Boydton Militia, alongside the townspeople with a common bond. They completed their share of militia patrols in town and the community without interruption of their studies. To some members of the M.E. Church, South, a call to military duty was a matter that the church looked upon most favorably. Some writers and preachers even went so far as to proclaim that failure to respond could be classified as heresy and the individual would be punished by the church.[26]

In 1840, the college petitioned for a normal school, but nothing happened with the petition. In 1854, it began a new BL&S program affording students an alternative format for a degree, but it wasn't until 1859 that they were granted recognition as a teacher preparatory program.

Chapter 5

Go Forth and Sow the Fruits of Thy Labor

In 1859, Randolph Macon College was granted recognition as a teacher preparatory program. Numerous graduates went on to become teachers or professors and many began academies. Several are discussed elsewhere in the text, but to enumerate further, Jesse Q. Gee, A.B. 1837, the son of Benjamin and Frances W. Harper Gee of Brunswick County, returned to Forksville in northeastern Mecklenburg County, Virginia, and began an academy in the Providence M.E. Church. On September 27, 1837, he married Martha Euphemia Clementine Rose (1820–1894), sister of Dr. L.I. Rose of Blackridge.[1] Ten surviving children were born of this union. In 1850, a new teacher on staff was James Northington (A.B. 1850, RMC), age 17. Subsequently Gee turned over operation of the academy to Northington. When the Civil War began, Northington enlisted on October 10, 1861, as a private in Company A, "Brunswick Guards," at Boydton. He was described as 5 feet, 10 inches tall, dark eyes, hair and complexion. On May 20, 1862, he was discharged for an "inability to render military duty."[2] He returned to Forksville and reopened the school in 1863.

During the war, Jesse Q. Gee (d. August 29, 1882) began a new school, Safe Retreat Academy, and provided boarding and taught from his home in Forksville. He was still teaching school in 1880. Another student was John Orgain (A.B. 1838, RMC), who organized and operated Flat Rock Seminary in eastern Mecklenburg County from about 1840 until his retirement in 1865, when the school was taken over by John Orgain, Jr. Nearby, Virginius O. (Oliver) Gee, son of Jesse, took over operation of the "Lombardy Grove Academy" after earning his A.M. from RMC in 1861. He married Rebecca Smiley of Canada, and they had no children.

Edward E. Parham became president of the Warrenton Female College after receiving from Randolph Macon College his A.B. in 1850 and A.M. in 1853, and appears to have served that school until after the war. Although not a graduate, the Rev. James A. Dean was a tutor at RMC 1850–1851. He was accepted into the North Carolina M.E., South, Conference in 1852 and served as principal of South Lowell Academy in the Raleigh District. In 1854 he was president of Danville Female College, but in 1855, he left the conference and the church. Of these men, except for Northington, none had any military service during the war.

Shortly after graduation, the Rev. Baxter Clegg (b. 1815, son of David Clegg from Pittsboro, Virginia; A.B. 1838), was serving as the M.E. preacher in Mocksville, North Carolina. Before leaving Boydton, he and Elizabeth Blanche, age 21, of Brunswick County, were married in 1837.[3] Along with another individual, Peter Stuart Ney, they began Mocksville Academy in 1840, across Depot Street from the church. Writers seemed to have been fostered by this academy. Students included Hardie Helper, journalist, who graduated in 1850, and his brother Hinton Helper, lecturer and abolitionist author who graduated in 1848.[4] Ney had a historical connection to Mecklenburg County, having served in the 1820s as a teacher for the Crowder children and the William Nelson family at Midway (sometimes called Riverview), about halfway between Abbeyville and the Prestwood Plantation. He replaced the former field school headmaster, John de Graffenreidt, when he had taken an assignment at White House with David Shelton (owner of Buffalo Mineral Springs). Later, Shelton, as guardian,[5] would sponsor de Graffenreidt's two sons: William (b. 1830) and Thomas (b.1833) as students at RMC. William graduated and attended the medical program (see Appendix B, Confederate G&S section), but Thomas only attended about two years.

Nelson family history states that Ney's student, Sally Nelson, discovered him painting a life-sized portrait of Napoleon. When it was completed, he hung it in the classroom along with a painting of the emperor's grave at St. Helena. Soon, another child was born to the Nelson family and Ney asked if he could name the child Catherine Isabella. Many believe that Peter Ney was in fact "Marshal Ney of France, a compatriot of Napoleon who was sentenced to die by a firing squad after the fall of the Napoleonic regime."[6] Marshal Ney's mother's name was Catherine Isabella. "On his death bed he is reported to have confessed to" being Marshal Ney. He died in 1846, was buried at Third Creek Presbyterian Church in Rowan County, and Clegg became the principal of the academy.

Edward Wadsworth of New Bern, North Carolina, received his A.B. in 1841, A.M. in 1844, D.D. in 1847, all from RMC, and a D.D. from Emory and Henry College later. He became president of LaGrange College, Greensborough, Alabama (1846–1852), professor at Nashville University (1853–1855), professor at Southern University (1859–1866) and acting president of Southern University from 1867 until 1870. He continued to teach at Southern and died in Greenville, Alabama, in 1883.[7]

Another professor of LaGrange College was James L. Pierce (A.B. 1840, RMC). He was the son of board of trustees member the Rev. Dr. Lovick Pierce of Georgia (D.D. 1843, RMC). James went on to complete his A.M. at RMC in 1851 and married the youngest sister of David Clopton.[8] Shortly after Wadsworth left LaGrange College, Pierce was selected and offered the position of president. He accepted.

The early graduates of RMC not only had the fortitude to stick out the four or seven years but continued in their behavior patterns throughout their lives. They studied and went to school together, married each other's sisters, and created jobs or positions for one another. Before 1855, if a Randolph Macon graduate had left a position, in most cases he was replaced by another RMC graduate.

William Flewellen Samford was born in 1818 in Wilkinson County, Georgia. He graduated from RMC with an A.B. degree 1837, A.M. in 1846 and LL.D. in 1867. Dr. Samford was hired as professor of belles-lettres, Emory College, Oxford, Georgia, in 1838, where he continued his studies in law. He was licensed to practice law in 1839. In 1844, he was a Georgia elector and in 1845 declined an appointment as ambassador to Italy. He married Susan Lewis Dowdell, sister of James F. Dowdell in 1842. In 1847, he moved his family to Macon County, where he acquired a large land holding near Auburn, but due to ill health withdrew from the political life. In 1856–1857 he was editor of a newspaper in Tuskegee and contributed several articles to New York newspapers under the pennames of "Zeno" and "Warwick." Just prior to the war he was selected as president of Oakbowery College. He and Susan had thirteen children. They named their eighth born child Randolph Macon Samford.

Their third born child was William James Samford, born September 16, 1844, in Merriweather County, Georgia. He attended college for two years, was the sergeant major of Company C, 46th Alabama, and later elected first lieutenant. He was captured and made a prisoner of war and sent to Johnson's Island, Ohio, in May 1863. One of his former professors (Slayton) was also a prisoner of war there, and for the next eighteen months he was tutored until his release in October 1864. In 1867, he was licensed to practice law. He was also a licensed M.E., South, minister. He served in several elected positions: alderman, state representative, state senator, and United States congressman. He was elected to the University of Alabama Board of Trustees in 1896 and in 1900 was elected governor of Alabama. His son, William Hodges Samford, became a lawyer and officer in artillery during World War I, following in his father's footsteps.[9]

There's a lot to be said for those early graduates of RMC. To try and put it into perspective, college students today think that the amount of work that is required for a doctorate is outrageous and should be modified. Then some are reminded that academic standards have been modified dramatically several times (at least) since 1970. When I completed my doctorate in 1978, the college had just substituted computer programming as fulfillment of the mandatory language requirement a year earlier.

The mid 1840s at the college were turbulent due to declining morale, and this spread among the students, who rebelled. After all, the second two years (like today) were more palatable and goal oriented than the first two, but were still very taxing, especially emotionally. To complete the requisites for an A.B. degree, the junior year required:

First Term	Text
Euripides or Sophocles (two plays)	Leipsie
Cicero de Officeiis, or De Oratore, or Brutus	
Diff. and Int. Calculus	Young
Chemistry (commenced)	Turner
Classical Literature	Eschenburg
Greek Exercises	Sophocles

Second Term

Aristophanes or Aeschylus (two plays)	Leipsie Ed.
Juvenal and Persius,	Boston Ed.
Mechanics (Statics)	Boucharlat
Chemistry (completed)	Turner
Rhetoric	Blair
Classical Literature	Eschenburg
Greek Exercises	Sophocles

Senior Studies

First Term

Moral Philosophy	Wayland
Political Economy (commenced)	"
Mechanics (Dynamics)	Boucharlat
Hydrostatics	"
Pneumatics	"
Optics	Brewster

Second Term

Mental Philosophy	Upham
Political Economy (completed)	Wayland
Astronomy	Gummere
Lectures on Mineralogy—Geology—Magnetism and Electro-Magnetism.	

Declamations, Compositions and Translations are required throughout the course; and the members of the Senior Class pronounce Orations of their own composition.
Lectures are delivered at stated times upon the most important subjects of the course.
Recitations of the Greek Testament every Monday morning.[10]

What appears consistently absent from histories of Randolph Macon College is the theological training. The people of Boydton and the surrounding area referred to RMC as a school of theology, and that begs the question "Where did they get that idea?" Aside from the chapel at RMC and the impromptu camp meetings initiated by the students (referenced elsewhere), it is recorded that the board of trustee members who were preachers in the nearby communities used senior students as substitutes when they were not scheduled for a particular church. Most of the churches even began to record in their minutes such as "the following have served Kingswood as pastors: ... Wm. Tucker (his assistant, a student of Randolph-Macon College)." This notation was found among a half-dozen churches under the Mecklenburg Circuit and others in Randolph Macon Circuit. The Rev. William Tucker appears as the principal trainer of students and was serving several churches that had been led by the Revs. R.G. Bass, T.A. Pierce and H.C. Bowles immediately before him.[11] Additionally, many local churches were hard pressed to afford a preacher and would use students. Some churches used students while they were awaiting the newly assigned circuit preacher, and some students were preaching to support themselves while attending college. At the end of three years in the ministry, following completion of A.B. degree requisites, a student could request and receive an A.M. degree.

Students who persevered and completed the four or seven years (the latter for an A.M. degree), we find a particular grouping of individuals. It appears that during the mid 1800s, there was an explosion of M.E. Conferences that were pursuing organizing and building colleges (over 200 between 1820 and 1860). The success of RMC became the seed pod for faculty and staff for many of these. Some colleges reportedly sent prospective faculty to RMC for training for a year or so before employing them in their home institution.[12] By 1860, institutions were operational for the M.E. South from Oregon and California to Indiana, Missouri and Louisiana. The following are some graduates with A.B. degrees from 1840 to 1851.

Woodson L. Ligon of South Carolina received his A.B. in 1840. When the war began he was established in the Confederate Army, Commissary Department of South Carolina. He was later transferred to the Engineering Department with no rank for either assignment being given. Irby writes that he was a colonel (but many gentlemen of the South, following the war, were referred to as "Colonel").[13]

David Clopton (A.B. 1840) was valedictorian of his class. He was born September 29, 1820, in Putnam County, Georgia, to Dr. Alford and Sarah Kendrick Clopton. His father was a physician, a legislator and president of the bank in Macon, Georgia. His grandfather, David, was a Virginia planter. At the age of 16, he entered Randolph Macon College. Upon graduation he returned to Macon, where he read law and was admitted to the bar in the fall 1841. His law partner was Robert Sampson Lanier (1819–1893), son of L.T. Lanier of Macon, Georgia, who had been his roommate at RMC in 1838–1840. The third member of the group was Burwell Kendrick Harrison (1818–1860), son of William Harrison of Macon, Georgia, one of David's cousins.[14]

Harrison was also a graduate of RMC, A.B., in 1840, and returned home to Georgia to read and study for the bar. The trouble was that his mind was just too preoccupied—he was in love. He met with Lanier and Clopton about returning to Virginia, but Clopton does not appear in the record later in Virginia. On October 27, 1840, a double ring ceremony took place in Crewe, Virginia, at the "Little Presbyterian Church." Harrison married Elizabeth Woodson Robertson (1820 to 1894), and Lanier married her niece, Mary Jane Anderson (1822 to 1865). Later, the Laniers became the parents of the esteemed author, teacher, and professor at Johns Hopkins University Sidney Clopton Lanier (February 3, 1842, Macon, GA to September 7, 1881, Lynn, NC), who was known as the poet laureate of the South).[15] The newlyweds returned to Georgia and a feast was held.

Joining them was another newlywed couple, Samuel Goode Jones (September 20, 1815–October 4, 1886) and his wife Martha Goode. Samuel was born in Boydton, educated at Ebenezer Academy in Brunswick County, and graduated from Williams College with honors in 1837. He worked as an engineer and gained great notoriety within the railroad industry. Jones was married on November 8, 1842, at his grandfather's (Dr. Thomas Goode) resort, Bath Springs (later renamed The Homestead) in Hot Springs, Virginia, to his cousin Martha Ward Goode. The newlyweds traveled to Griffin, Georgia, where they shared a home with Harrison and Lanier. He became a pioneer in the industrial development of central Alabama.[16]

His first surviving son was Thomas Goode Jones (b. 1844), who was born in Macon, Georgia (nephew of Colonel Thomas Goode) and eventually studied to become a lawyer. During the Civil War, he attained the rank of major and at Appomattox was a messenger from General Lee bearing a white flag of truce. Returning home to Georgia, he relocated his family to Alabama. There, he was elected to the Alabama House of Representatives and was selected later as speaker of the House. He ran for and was elected governor of Alabama twice and received a presidential appointment as a United States District Judge.

Soon the Clopton and Lanier Law Office added a third partner, Harrison. But this was moving away from goals that Clopton apparently had so in 1844, he left Georgia and moved to Alabama. Very soon he married Martha E. Ligon, daughter of the governor. In 1848, he established a law firm with his brother-in-law, Robert F. Ligon. In the spring of 1851, he joined as a private in Robert's militia unit, which had just returned from Mexico. He also received his A.M. from RMC in 1851. In 1859 Clopton was elected to Congress, but in December 1860, in protest, all Alabama delegates to Washington, D.C., returned home.[17]

When secession was announced by the state, Clopton's Militia Unit became the 12th Alabama Infantry; he was established as a captain, assistant quartermaster. His military career was short lived because in the fall of 1861 he was elected to the Confederate Congress, where he served until 1865. In 1866, he dissolved the law firm with his brother-in-law and moved his family to Montgomery, Alabama. He established a new practice, but his wife died in November 1867. At Columbus, Georgia, he married Mary F. Chambers (a widow) in 1871, but then she died in 1885. Clopton was one of the organizers of the First National Bank of Sheffield and the Sheffield Coal and Iron Company, and was director of each. He was also elected president of the board of trustees for East Alabama College.

In 1878, he was elected to the United States House of Representatives. He was then elected speaker of the House but chose not to run for reelection following that term. In 1884, Clopton was appointed by the governor as an associate justice of the State Supreme Court, and in 1886 he was elected without opposition by the Democratic Party to fill that position. He married a third time on November 29, 1887, to Virginia Clay (also a widow). He served as a justice until his death in 1892. He and his first wife had three children. There were no children from the other marriages.[18]

The Lanier and Harrison Law Firm continued to operate after 1844. Harrison, sometimes addressed as "Squire" and other times as "Colonel," became involved in federal law and went to Washington, D.C., to represent Georgia. He went there to plead the case for federal support to repair the damages the Creek Indians had inflicted upon the people of southwest Georgia. He had begun this campaign (according to Ancestor.com) in 1836, when he was eighteen and in his first year at RMC (logically, it would seem the correct date would be 1846). The letters he wrote home suggest he was in Washington, D.C., on at least three trips and at least for a month each. (While in

Washington, Harrison became extremely fond of French cooking and wrote home of gaining weight with each trip.) Sometime around 1855, these cases were lumped together as reparation cases and were approved by Congress, but the payments were never made. Harrison, the leader, died in 1860; and the cases were dismissed by a federal court on December 14, 1863.

Having attended Oglethorpe University, Georgia, and majoring in music (the flute), with the beginning of the Civil War, Sydney Lanier and his brother enlisted into the Confederate Signal Corps as spies. They worked undercover for about 18 months. Sydney then transferred to the Confederate Navy, where he served as a pilot for British ships for blockade running into southern ports for supplies and exports. After about 18 months, on one mission, the story in the regimental books is that the British captain of the ship told Lanier that the blockade was going to be tight and they may have to talk their way through. It was suggested that he put on a British uniform, which he refused to do. He was captured, made a prisoner of war, and transported to Point Lookout (they regarded him as an officer). While at Point Lookout, he acquired consumption (tuberculosis) and when discharged was in very ill health.[19]

He took a job for two years as a desk clerk in a hotel to try to recuperate, all the while writing as fast as he could to earn money. He published several books of poetry within about three years. In 1876 he married Mary Day, but with a wife and family on the way, he began to worry even more about finances. In 1878, he passed the Georgia bar and went to work in his father's law firm. Also at sometime around 1872 or 1873, he began teaching at Johns Hopkins University. Sidney must have become quite ill in 1880 or 1881; and Mary or other family members took him to a sanitarium because when he died in 1881, he was in North Carolina and was buried there. Mary Lanier and their son, Robert, died and are buried at Rose Hill, Macon, Georgia.

James Ferguson Dowdell (A.B. 1840, A.M. 1846, LL.D. 1867, RMC) was born November 26, 1818, in Jasper County, Georgia, son of Louis Dowdell of Virginia, who was residing at Waverly Hall, Harris County, Georgia. His mother, a Farley, was also from Virginia. In April 1841, he was admitted to the bar and established a law practice in Greenville, Georgia. In 1842, he married Sarah H. Render in Georgia. In 1846 he and his family moved to Chambers County, Alabama, where they pursued agriculture; and in 1848, he was ordained into the M.E., South, ministry. In 1853, he was elected to Congress. He was reelected and served three terms. He retired in 1859. He was also appointed to and elected to serve as secretary on the board of trustees for Oak Bowery Female College and represented Chambers County in the state's secession convention, voting to secede.

Dowdell returned home and organized the 37th Alabama Infantry and was elected colonel. "He led his regiment at Corinth and through the siege at Vicksburg, but the elements were too much for him. He refused to resign so his commanding officer referred him to a medical review board." He was given a medical discharge at age 55 and sent home. Following the war, Colonel Dowdell moved his family to Auburn, where he was president of East Alabama Female College until his death in 1871.

His oldest son, James Render Dowdell, was born on April 2, 1847, in Chambers County, Alabama. He attended the University of Alabama in 1864 and 1865 but when it was burned, he transferred to East Alabama in Auburn and graduated in 1867. He became licensed to practice law in 1870. He served as a solicitor from 1876 to 1880, when he was appointed judge for the 5th Circuit. In 1898 he was appointed associate justice of the Alabama State Supreme Court and in 1909 he was selected as chief justice. He resigned without a stated reason in January 1914.[20]

William McKendree Robbins (October 26, 1828–May 3, 1905) was born to Ahi and Mary Brown Robbins of Randolph County, North Carolina. His early education was at a local academy (most likely Mocksville); and then he entered RMC, graduating with an A.B. degree in 1851. He became a professor of mathematics at the normal college in Randolph County near High Point for the next two years. On September 7, 1854, he and Mary Montgomery of Montville, South Carolina, were married. In 1855, they moved to Glenville, Alabama, where Robbins began a female college. He soon abandoned teaching, studied law, and started a legal practice in Selma, Alabama, in 1858. That same year, in the fall, his young wife died, leaving him with two small children.

In January 1861, Robbins enlisted as a private into the Marion (Alabama) Rifles. Two months later, he helped organize the 4th Alabama Regiment, and he was elected as first lieutenant in Company G. His first action was in Virginia, where his unit participated in overtaking the arsenal at Harper's Ferry on April 18, 1861, even before Virginia had passed the vote to secede. He and his unit fought with General Longstreet all over Virginia and Tennessee and at Gettysburg. On May 5, 1864, he suffered a serious head wound at the Battle of the Wilderness.

While recuperating in North Carolina in December 1864, he married his first wife's sister, Martha Montgomery; they later had three children that survived. He had been promoted to field and staff major during his convalescence. Returning to his unit in Virginia, he was at Appomattox on April 9, 1865, for the South's surrender.[21]

He relocated his family and law practice from Alabama to Salisbury,

North Carolina, and was elected to the North Carolina Senate in 1868 and 1870. In 1872, 1874, and 1876, he was elected to the United States House of Representatives, and he moved to Statesville, North Carolina. In 1878, he returned to his law practice with his son-in-law, Judge Benjamin Franklin Long.

In 1894 President Grover Cleveland appointed him Confederate commissioner of the Gettysburg Battle Field Commission. He was characterized by a local newspaper as "truly a great orator," and his 1898 speech at Gettysburg in defense of secession was widely praised. Late in life, he switched from the M.E., South, to the Presbyterian denomination to protest the fact that the M.E., South, had procured a congressional appropriation for war losses. He died in Salisbury of an acute stomach illness and is buried at Oakwood Cemetery, Statesville.[22]

William G. Conner (A.B. 1842, A.M. 1846 and D.D. 1869, RMC) became president of Chapel Hill Female College and continued operation of same throughout the war. Another distinguished graduate of RMC was John Simmons Moore of Mecklenburg County, Virginia. He was born December 3, 1829, to Robert and Elizabeth Simmons Moore. He graduated with an A.B. in 1848 and taught in country schools for three years to earn enough money to attend the University of Virginia. He received his M.A. degree from there in 1854, and accepted a faculty position with Randolph Macon. He was professor of natural philosophy from September 1854 to January 1856, when he transferred to the Alabama Conference and began preaching. Due to ill health, he left the ministry in 1858, took a teaching position at Centenary Institute in Summerfield, Alabama, and in 1859 married Mary S. Porter. When the war began, he returned to preaching. He and his wife had six children. From 1871 to 1883, he served as professor of mathematics for Southern University, Greensboro, Alabama; from 1883 to 1898, he was professor of Latin at Emory College in Georgia. He continued to preach throughout the years until he died on March 28, 1909, at Oxford, Georgia.[23]

Olin M. Dantzler (b. 1826), son of Jacob M. Dantzler of Lewisville Depot, graduated with an A.B. in 1846 in that turbulent year of discontent but with no less pride in his education. He was from St. Matthews Parish, Orangeburg District, South Carolina. Believing that an attack by the North was inevitable, Olin joined Company D, Hagood's Regiment, the "Orangeburg Rifles," and was established as a lieutenant in 1859. With the northern moves on Fort Sumter taking place, Dantzler was established as a lieutenant colonel of the 20th South Carolina Militia, and he was also serving as a South Carolina state senator.

When he transferred to the 20th South Carolina Infantry, he was described as a "thorough disciplinarian," probably due to his RMC lifestyle.[24] He was established as a field and staff lieutenant colonel on January 11, 1862. On August 21, 1863, he was wounded in the breast but refused to leave the battlefield. The field report stated he was a "fine officer, good tactician and [had] a record of unswerving zeal and gallantry." He was promoted on April 29, 1864, to field and staff colonel "and the 20th grieved their loss" on his transfer.

Dantzler was reassigned to the 22nd South Carolina Infantry. On June 1, 1864, the governor of South Carolina received eight letters of endorsement from some of the most prominent men in South Carolina. All the letters recommended him as an "officer of the highest caliber, ability and efficiency" for a promotion to brigadier general. But before he could receive his "star" of confirmation, he was mortally wounded in action at Ware bottom church near Bermuda Hundred, Virginia, on June 1, 1864. He was captured and made a prisoner of war, but died of his wounds on June 2, 1864—"in the hands of his enemy."[25]

Of course, there were some students who could not undertake the long haul of four years of college and dropped out, and some who simply transferred closer home. One such student was John Willis Ellis (November 23, 1820—July 7, 1861). Ellis was from Rowan County, North Carolina, and the son of Anderson and Judith Bailey Ellis. They lived on a third generation plantation inherited from their grandfather Willis in 1806. John Ellis attended Randolph Macon College from 1837 to 1839 before transferring to the University of North Carolina, where he graduated with an A.B. in 1841. He studied law and began a practice in 1842 in Salisbury County. In 1844 he was elected to the state House of Representatives at the age of 23. On August 25, 1844, he and Mary White were married, but she died in October of typhoid. He was elected again in 1846 and 1848.

In 1848, he was chosen by Dorothea Dix to encourage an asylum in North Carolina. Dix (1825–1875) was the primary leader of the "Mental Hygiene Movement" with improved standards of care, and everyone was entitled to care if they needed it (this later more than doubled the number of patients, especially in the North). With little staff, facilities, and supplies, most asylums became modified pauper homes with the patients receiving meager custodial care. On December 21, 1848, the House passed a bill to establish a state hospital for the insane in North Carolina. In January 1849, the General Assembly elected Ellis to serve as a judge of the Superior Court of North Carolina. Having served for over ten years, he resigned on April 29, 1858.

Ellis was elected governor of North Carolina on August 5, 1858, and six days later he married Mary McKinley Daves. He was reelected on August 2, 1860. Following the fall of Fort Sumter, Ellis ordered the North Carolina Militia to seize the federal installations in that state. On April 17, 1861, he telegraphed President Jefferson Davis that he was in possession of the federal facilities in North Carolina and "we are ready to join you to a man." Ellis had been in poor health, and in June 1861, he traveled to Red Sulphur Springs, Virginia, for some curative treatments. A few days later he died at age forty-one. He is buried in Old English Cemetery, Salisbury.[26]

Another such student who went on to become a popular commencement speaker at a variety of colleges, including RMC, was Walter Leak Steele (April 18, 1823–October 16, 1891). He was the son of Thomas and Judith Moseley Cole Steele of Steele's Mill near Rockingham, North Carolina. He began his education at the preparatory academy of the Rev. Solomon Lea at Randolph Macon. He advanced to entering the freshman year but left at Christmas, entered Wake Forest in January 1840, and then transferred to the University of North Carolina in the fall 1840. He graduated from the University of North Carolina with an A.B. in 1844 and A.M. in 1847. After studying law, he won an election to the House of Representatives, where he served from 1846 to 1850, then was a state senator in 1852, went back to the House in 1854, and the Senate again in 1858.

At the state convention in 1861, he served as secretary and signed the ordinance to secede. His first wife died in 1863; he remarried to Mary J. Little, and they had six surviving children. In 1852, he had been appointed a member of the board of trustees for the University of North Carolina, and in 1891, he received an honorary LL.D. degree for over thirty years' service. In 1877, he was elected to serve a term in the United States House of Representatives and reelected in 1879. He chose not to seek reelection and in 1882 returned home to Richmond County. He replaced his brother as president of Pee Dee Manufacturing Company (textiles) until his death. As a college member of the Dialectic Society, he was a popular commencement speaker at RMC, UNC, Greensboro, and several other colleges.[27]

With alumnus John Boyd as editor of the local newspaper, the anniversary celebration of Randolph Macon was the subject of feature stories for several weeks in 1859. The celebration and commencement account prepared by Boyd and published on July 1, 1859, follows.

The Late Randolph Macon Commencement

The public exercises of the late commencement at Randolph Macon College, were deeply interesting—decidedly more so, in our opinion, than they have been on any occasion, during the acquaintance with the college, the past sixteen years. The alumni of the institution had determined to celebrate the completion of the endowment fund, and to that end had selected one of their number to deliver an appropriate address. This honor fell to the lot of Professor Warren Dupree, of Wofford College, South Carolina, and well did he perform his part.— This address, together with a beautiful poem from the Rev. Thomas B. Russell, another distinguished alumnus, also of the Palmetto State, constituted the public exercises of Tuesday morning, the 21st inst.

At 3 o'clock, according to previous announcement, the alumni, together with the faculty and trustees, who were their guests, met at the residence of the Misses Yancey, to partake of a magnificent dinner which had been specially prepared for them. The table was spread in a beautiful grove, and did credit to the ladies, who furnished it. It was a part of the arrangements of the occasion to pronounce at the table a series of sentiments prepared for the purpose. But a threatening cloud rendered it necessary that the company should adjourn to the College Chapel.

Here, Rev. John C. Blackwell, president of Buckingham Female College, the first graduate of Randolph Macon, assisted by Prof. Dupree and O.H.P. Corprew, Esq. presided over the adjourned meeting, and announced the regular toasts. To these the happiest responses were made. Thus was the whole evening spent most delightfully, so much so as to elicit from the president the remark that it was one of the happiest evenings of his life.—Long will the alumni remember their reunion of the afternoon of Tuesday, the 21st of June, 1859.

On Wednesday morning the regular address before the two literary societies was delivered by John Parker Jordan, Esq., of North Carolina, and the regular annual address before the Society of Alumni by Mr. E.E. Parham, president of Warrenton Female College. Immediately succeeding the delivery of these addresses, followed the interesting ceremony of a presentation of plate to Prof. J.C. Wills by the students of the college. One of the graduates, Mr. H.B. Cowles, Jr., of Petersburg, had been deputed by his associates to perform the office of presentation. This he did in one of the neatest and most admirable little speeches we ever heard. Professor Wills responded in a speech, brief, but in the highest degree appropriate and affecting.

The afternoon of Wednesday, and the whole of Thursday, were occupied in the delivery of speeches by the graduates. The publication of the program of exercises in our last issue supersedes the necessity of again furnishing the names of the speakers, and the subjects of their respective orations. It is enough to say, that of the sixteen commencements we have attended, this one was distinguished as being pre-eminently superior to any in the interest imparted to the exercises by the members of the graduating class. To diversify the entertainments of the occasion, two poems, each of singular excellence, were pronounced, one by Mr. John T. Humphreys of Lynchburg, on Wednesday afternoon, the other by Mr. Wm. G. Starr, of Petersburg, on Thursday afternoon.

In the absence of Dr. Smith, the president of the College, who was detained at home by indisposition, the baccalaureate address was delivered by H.N. McTyere, D.D. of Nashville, Tenn. And lastly, the exercises were closed with the valedictory address by Mr. Wm. S. Davis of Warren, N.C.

Added to the literary performances, which we have already detailed, we must not omit to mention the annual meetings of the two literary societies. These were held in public in the College Chapel contrary to former usage; that of the

Franklin Society on Tuesday night, and that of the Washington Society on Wednesday night.

At each of these meetings the debate continued until midnight, and afforded alike instruction and amusement to the audience.

Of the students' party on Thursday night, we can make no report, as we were necessarily detained at a meeting of the board of trustees, then in session. We doubt not, however, that the young people enjoyed themselves immensely.

The crowd of people in attendance upon this commencement was unusually large, and among them were prominent gentlemen from distant states. Among those we may name Mr. Disosway of Staten Island, New York, a gentleman of a high order of intelligence, and a liberal patron of education. Rev. Dr. Mc Tyere, of Nashville, Tenn., a distinguished alumnus of the college, for a series of years editor of the Southern Christian Advocate of New Orleans, and at present editor of the Nashville Christian Advocate; Thomas C. Johnson, Esq., of St. Louis, Missouri, also an alumnus, an eminent lawyer of his great city, and a member of the Missouri State Senate; Warren Du Pre, A.M., a distinguished member of the Board of Instruction of Wofford College, South Carolina; Rev. Mr. Baird, also of the Palmetto State; R.H. Powell, Esq. of Union Springs, Alabama; Dr. Reese of Georgia, Mr. Muse of Florida; Mr. Phillips of Washington City; Dr. Armistead of Mississippi, and others, whose names have escaped us.

Our guests from North Carolina, we claim as our own people, and therefore do not single them out by name. Indeed they were too numerous for this purpose. Of all these gentlemen present from a distance, we have every assurance that no one left for his home, without the most pleasing recollections of the scenes through which he had passed, and without the most decidedly favorable impression as to the character, value and importance of Randolph Macon College. We affirm, without the slightest hesitancy, that the institution never before in its history occupied such an eminence as it does in the public estimation. It is manifestly on the high road to unprecedented prosperity.

Among other important measures, the trustees adopted the Eclectic system of education, similar to the one used at the University of Virginia, instead of the system heretofore prevailing. So that hereafter, a student can take the studies of his own selection, and will not be forced to spend a tedious four years course in prosecuting studies unsuited to his taste or capacity. A chair of Modern Languages was established, and a professor in this department will be procured as soon as possible.

The chair of Mathematics, made vacant by the resignation of Professor Wills, was filled by the election of Mr. Robert T. Massie, of the University of Virginia, a gentleman of the highest distinction in his particular department. Indeed Professor Bledsoe, of the university, has paid him the high compliment to pronounce him "best mathematician of his age on the continent."[28]

Coincidentally, in the very next column of the paper is a sale ad listing a 950 acre plantation one mile south of town with an improved overseer's house, many outbuildings, several slave houses, granary, and much more to become available on January 1, 1860, belonging to O.H.P. Corprew.[29]

The Mr. Disosway of Staten Island referred to in the story was Gabriel

P. Disosway, one of the original founders of RMC. Disosway had come to Boydton from New York in 1828 to work with the planning and founding group. He was born December 6, 1799, and had graduated from Columbia (A.B. 1821). He left New York to begin a business enterprise in Petersburg, Virginia, and then returned to New York in 1828 but maintained constant contact and visited on occasion. Upon his return to New York, he was one of the founders of Wesleyan University, Connecticut, which was chartered in May 1831. In 1838, he was awarded an A.M. (honorary) by RMC. He died in 1868.

As part of the precursor to the 25th annual celebration, an announcement was made to the entire audience. Randolph Macon had graduated by "1859 a total of 255 A.B. degree students. Of those, fully one-third had entered into the ministry"[30] (at least 85 of the 255, and at least for a while).

The context of this new program and the liberalization in the early 1850s does not match with historical letters. The idea of a Christmas vacation, literary rooms off limits to faculty, a lesser restrictive environment and now the eclectic system such as the University of Virginia appear to be somewhat contradicted by the letters of George E. Butler (A.M. 1862). George Emory Butler was born on November 2, 1840, the son of Alexander Butler (August 8, 1807–December 7, 1881), a plantation overseer in Boydton, and Mary Wyche Reeves (1813–1890) (d. February 5, 1891). His parents were married in October 1832 and moved to Tulip, Arkansas, from Mecklenburg County shortly thereafter.[31]

The family acquired 562 acres of land, and Alexander became a merchant. In 1870, Henry A. Butler (former Confederate major in the Arkansas Infantry) joined his father as a merchant and partner. While visiting his sons, George and Charles in California, he died in December 1881.

Most of the family members made a vigil of contacting George's younger sister, Emma. She saved every letter, and in 1985 a descendant had them published. Butler appears to have attended Randolph Macon College from 1856 to 1862. As to college life, George writes to Emma on March 3, 1860: "Aunt Eliza is very kind to me.... I go over there oftener than any other place because it is nearer than any of the others." (This would have been Wheatland Plantation area, about two miles directly north of the college.)

In the same letter he addresses the chapel and chaplains. "We are now carrying on a protracted meeting, but there seems as yet to be but little feeling on the part of the ungodly. Members of the church are not generally warm. And I have heard here no such sermons as those we had at camp-meeting from brothers McKensie, Hunter, etc. I look back upon that meeting as the most pleasant and truly happy time I ever spent."[32]

The chaplain of RMC at this time was the Rev. Charles C. Pearson, who served from September 1859 through June 1860. He was a member of the North Carolina Conference. Following his service with Randolph Macon he was transferred to a church in Elizabeth City, North Carolina.

On December 28, 1860, Butler writes:

"It is Friday night. The Frank Society has just closed its weekly meeting, and I hasten to my room to answer your kind, sweet letter, which was handed me a few moments ago by a fellow Frank while the hall was in session. You may be sure I took the first opportunity to retire to my room, and reading the letter ... quickly did I return to the Hall to prevent being fined for staying over my time." He continues, "Christmas is nearly out. We had but one day given us here; but I took another.... I did so, with the consent of the president, Dr. Smith."

In a letter dated December 4, 1861, from Randolph Macon College, he writes: "I would like to have time this evening to write you a long letter as I have put it off so long, but the Sun is almost down and I have to walk two miles, you know, before I get supper. Besides it is quite cold; Snow on the ground, and it seems hardly to melt at all.... Oh, how hard it must be on our noble Soldiers who are encamped on the bleak and cheerless tops of the Allegheny Mountains. Tis almost enough to make a body shudder to think of it. God preserve our dear brothers."

He continues: "We have now in college thirty three students, a small number for a college, but the reason is plain. We drill every morning, near an hour. It is the very best kind of exercise, and a double quick for a few minutes is not disagreeable these cool evenings. We have no regular military instructor yet; but our Prof. in chemistry drills us.... I sometimes think the Virginia skies are bluer and clearer than ours in Ark."[33]

He graduated with his A.B. from RMC in June 1862. During the war he continued to write to his sister. Serving as a chaplain in the 3rd Arkansas Infantry Regiment, in January 1863 he wrote from Fredericksburg, Virginia, where he was sharing a winter cabin with his brother, Charles (a lieutenant), and was sitting by a "cheerful fire blazing in the fireplace and a board in my lap to write on." He said his officers are nice, but "like most of our officers, curses and swears when he gets vexed."[34]

In October 1863 he was near Henderson, North Carolina, and was planning to take a day and visit family in Mecklenburg County. He appears to have been sent to Weldon, North Carolina, after having been captured near Fredericksburg, made a prisoner of war and then exchanged. He referred to the ordeal in his letters as his "sojourn in Yankydom." Charles was also captured and made a prisoner of war. After two years, his older brother Lewis resigned his commission in January 1864 to return home after the Union Army had passed through Tulip and Princeton, Arkansas, in November 1863.

Following the war, George returned to Tulip, Arkansas, where he preached the Princeton Circuit and others. He married Julia Moores, sister of Thomas Moores, in 1868. In 1871, he and his family, along with Thomas and his family and brother Charles with family, moved to California. In the spring of 1872, he wrote his brother William, "Things grow in Cal. three or four times as fast as in Ark. Would you think of raising eight crops of hay on a piece of land in one year? ... Here I expect to live and die." By 1876, he appears to have returned to preaching a circuit but was also farming. That same year he writes from Abilene, Texas, that while visiting family he became ill and would have an extended stay. He died on February 5, 1891.[35]

A new textbook would be added to the college beginning in the fall of 1860—*Cutters Phisiology*.[36] The two copies for professor and library were ordered by Miss Hettie Farrar on April 25, 1860, from R.L. Hunt and Bros. The books cost $1 each, and with postage of 40 cents, the total bill was two dollars and forty cents. The bill was not paid until April 22, 1865, at which time a 44 cent interest charge was added.

"Phisiology" in those days would be the equivalent to first-aid today, less the CPR, which did not come into existence until much, much later. This course was most likely taught by Professor Puryear, as he had attended one year of medical school at the University of Virginia. Puryear's second son, Charles (Charlie), was born on campus (October 21, 1860) and his third son, Frank, was born in 1861. He and his wife Virginia also had Sallie (b. 1866) and Virginia (b. January 1870), both born in Richmond. His wife died from child birthing complications on June 14, 1870, in Richmond. Subsequently, Bennett Puryear married Ella Marion Wiles (1850–October 28, 1914) on September 14, 1871. She was the daughter of Leroy B. Wiles of Christiansville (which became Chase City in 1872), who had been the overseer of the farm next door to the Puryear home in the 1860s.

Most of the published formulas by Puryear, his lectures and experiments included phosphorus and potash. Many of his public recitations and school lectures focused on soils and "a seed to tree to seed." He was described as gifted and vigorous in his work, at times teaching math, Latin and Greek but always performing his own experiments so as not to endanger his students. One year of study toward his A.M. degree was spent in Monroe County, Alabama, where he met his first love, but it didn't seem to work out. While there he stayed with his widowed cousin, Polly Puryear.[37]

Polly was from the Greensborough Plantation, Mecklenburg County, Virginia, and had married Alexander Puryear, Bennett's cousin, in 1817. In Alabama, Polly was living on the family farm acquired in Burnt Corn, Monroe County, before her husband died in 1832. The administrator of the estate was established as Richard C. Puryear, his brother (son of Samuel) from Mecklenburg County, Virginia, who visited on a regular basis.

Following Bennett's stay with Polly he returned to Virginia and entered the University of Virginia in 1848. From there that year, he wrote her a letter which seems to describe his temperament. He closes with "P.S. I've been too familiar in using your name. Remember the license of poets I claim. But if you disdain to grant me the right, then henceforth I'll be more cold and polite."[38]

Following the 1860 graduation under the new program, George B. Finch (b. February 22, 1837) moved to Clarksville and accepted a teaching position. No records support which of the two schools hired him. The Clarksville Male Academy's principal was RMC graduate William T. Bailey (A.B. 1856). The Clarksville Female Academy was advertising on September 3, 1858. The principal and instructor of natural sciences and math, Edwin T. Finch, was his cousin, Edwin's wife was the music instructor, and staff included the Rev. and Mrs. J.E. McGowan. On May 14, 1861, when Company A, 3rd Virginia Cavalry, was recognized by the state, Finch enlisted as a private. Completing his school year, he became ill on July 8, 1861, and stayed home until January 2, 1862. He quickly caught up with his unit, which had already been in several battles and skirmishes. On October 24, 1862, he was elected second lieutenant.[39]

With many of his hometown friends and family, Finch was one of the leaders of Company A during Picket's Charge at the Battle of Gettysburg, and in his memoirs he reported that he was a brevet captain. He was severely wounded by a gunshot to the hip on July 3, 1863. Following hospitalizations and recuperation, a medical board retired him on October 24, 1864. He returned to his family home in Boydton. He read law at the University of Virginia in 1865, and was licensed to practice law in 1866. He became commonwealth's attorney for Mecklenburg County and served until 1870. He died in Boydton on September 13, 1900, and is buried at Zion Methodist Church Cemetery in Union Level.

Finch also served as a steward of the Boydton Methodist Church, along with board of trustees member Leroy M. Wilson (A.B. 1854); and they sent a petition to the Virginia M.E., South, Conference in 1867 suggesting that RMC was no longer supporting the church. The letter begins: "The stewards of the M.E. Church, South, at Boydton beg leave to report that in order to afford the preacher in charge a comfortable support there is urgent necessity that all the members and friends of the church should contribute as liberally as they may feel able to do." The letter continues that Clarksville will pay $150, $192 will be in board and the amount outstanding was $258, plus $19 for support of the presiding elder. Of the total they had only raised $36.[40]

Finch then became one of the principals in the Bank of Mecklenburg, which opened in Boydton in 1870, and soon opened a branch in Chase City.[41] In 1886, he married Alice Marrow (b. 1861) and as a wedding gift gave her $5,000 to remodel a family home he had inherited. She hired the son of Jacob Holt, William K. Holt, and the home "Twelve Oaks" or "On the Hill" was remodeled and expanded with a Victorian design (it still serves as a private residence today). This was a design Alice had seen while visiting a friend in Raleigh, N.C. She had the basic concept redesigned by William Holt's uncle Thomas.

In 1887, on behalf of the Bank of Mecklenburg, George seized his brother's (Langston Easley) Boydton Hotel, a property which had been tied up in a chancery suit and closed since February 1868. Langston had sold several lots and parcels of the hotel property but was still in financial trouble. The hotel was purchased at auction by their oldest brother Dr. Richard Henry Finch (April 24, 1827–1899), and he operated it until his death. Dr. Finch was the dentist who served the Boydton community from about 1855 until his death. He and George built an office building in Boydton for the two businesses.

During the war, Richard had served as a commissary agent for the Clarksville operation with Langston serving in the same capacity for Taylor's Ferry in Boydton. During the war many weary guests arrived at the hotel to escape the battles being fought on their lawns.

Another member of the class of 1860 was Thomas Jordan Jarvis (January 18, 1836–June 17, 1915; A.B. 1860 and A.M. 1867). Jarvis was born in Jarvisburg, Currituck County, North Carolina, to the Rev. (M.E.) Bannister Hardy and Elizabeth Daley Jarvis. Thomas spent most of his youth working on his father's 300 acre farm and attended nearby common schools on occasion. At age 19, he decided to attend RMC, but with limited funds, he taught during the summer months to pay his way through college. He graduated first in his class, returned home and began a school in nearby Pasquotank County.

When the war began, he enlisted into Company B, 8th North Carolina Infantry, on May 16, 1861, and was commissioned first lieutenant. On April 22, 1863, he was promoted to captain, and in May 1864, he was wounded in action at Drewery's Bluff that left him with a permanently disabled right arm. In May 1865, he was paroled while on sick furlough in Norfolk. Following the war, he and a partner began a merchant business, but he was also reading law. In 1867, he received his A.M. degree from Randolph Macon College and his license to practice law in North Carolina. In the spring of 1868, he won a seat in the new House of Representatives for North Carolina serving until 1872. He then moved to Greenville and in 1874 married Mary Woodson, the daughter of Judge John Woodson. They had no children.

In 1876, Jarvis was elected lieutenant governor of North Carolina. In 1878, when the governor was elected to the United States Senate, Jarvis took over that post on February 5, 1879. He won reelection to a full term in 1880. In July 1885, he was appointed by President Grover Cleveland as U.S. minister to Brazil. When President Cleveland died, Jarvis resigned and returned to North Carolina in 1889, beginning a law practice with Alexander L. Blow, and they handled many controversial cases and trials. In 1912, Jarvis's new partner was Frank Wooten. With numerous accomplishments in the legislature, education, and as a Methodist, Jarvis died June 17, 1915, and was buried at Cherry Hill Cemetery, Greenville. Jarvis Hall at East Carolina University and Jarvis Street in Greenville were named in his honor.[42]

William T. Bailey (A.B. 1856, RMC), upon graduation, accepted a position as principal of Clarksville Female Academy. When his school year ended in June 1861 he went home to Monterey, Virginia. He enlisted there on August 1, 1861, as a private into Company H, 44th Virginia Infantry. He was elected a second lieutenant on May 1, 1862, and ordered to arrest deserters. On January 22, 1863, he was established a first lieutenant following the Battle of Fredericksburg and appointed the regimental adjutant. On May 3, 1863, he was killed in action at Chancellorsville.[43]

Thomas T. Boswell (b. 1828) graduated from Randolph Macon with an A.B. in June 1851 and attended the law school. He became a successful planter-lawyer in the St. Tammany area. With the call for county militia, he went to Tanner's Store and tried to recruit a company. Unsuccessful, he went to Lombardy Grove, which again proved futile. When Virginia announced the decision to secede, he returned to Tanner's Store, where he was successful in recruiting a company of "rag-tag farmers and laborers." He called them the Mecklenburg Spartans but later changed it to the Mecklenburg Guards, as Spartans was being used by Captain Jones nearby.

He had all his men examined (and treated if necessary) by Dr. Latinus Irving Rose of Joyceville (Rosemont Farm). Dr. Rose later presented a bill for $108.85, which Boswell paid in November 1861. Boswell then ran an ad in the *Tobacco Plant* on June 21, 1861: "This is a notice to settle all debts before leaving for war."[44] He had his men fitted and ordered suitable uniforms for each and every one. He armed and drilled his men near Tanner's Store for weeks awaiting the uniforms. When the uniforms arrived, his company was attired, formed, and in June 1861, marched toward Camp Lee, Virginia. Captain Boswell paid for Dr. Rose's bill and the uniforms from his personal funds (although not paying for the uniforms until March 1863).

The unit became Company A, 56th Virginia Infantry Regiment, and mustered into the Confederate Army on July 6, 1861. Accompanying 1st Cap-

5. Go Forth and Sow the Fruits of Thy Labor

tain Boswell, and unwilling to be left home was his son, William Nelson Boswell, age 11. William had served during training as the company's drummer boy. When training and parading at Camp Lee, led by V.M.I. cadets, they were visited by the newly relocated President Jefferson Davis. He was so impressed with the young man that he gave him a little sword.

First Captain Boswell was dropped from the rolls on May 3, 1862, as being over age, and 2nd Captain George B. Davis was not reelected. Boswell applied for several positions to help the war effort in Richmond, but his offers were declined. He was sent home with his son against his wishes. Part of the reason he would not be allowed another position was that it was discovered he had a pulmonary disease.

Boswell and Davis were replaced by first lieutenant (1st Captain, May 3, 1862) John B. McPhail and 2nd Lieutenant F.W. Nelson. Captain McPhail, age 24, enlisted July 8, 1861. He was wounded at Boonesboro and reassigned to enforce the conscription law (draft) on May 8, 1864. He was promoted to major on June 17, 1864, then to lieutenant colonel on December 7, 1864. McPhail was an 1856 graduate of Hampden-Sydney College and was described as fair complexion, dark hair, hazel eyes and 5 feet, 10 inches in height. He was captured at Hatcher's Run on March 31, 1865, and sent to the Old Capitol Prison as a prisoner of war, then transferred to Johnson's Island and later paroled on July 15, 1865. He and his brother Paul inherited "Mulberry Hill" (the staging site of General Wilson's troops before their attacks on the Staunton River Bridge) in Charlotte County, where they resided after the war. He became president of the Richmond and Mecklenburg Railroad in 1882 (with a railroad depot in Five Forks, present day Skipwith, in 1884) but listed his occupation as farmer. He never married and died in 1904.[45]

Frank W. Nelson (son of William and Martha Lewis Walker Nelson of Midway, Mecklenburg County, educated by tutors) enlisted into Company A as a first sergeant on March 8, 1861. He was elected lieutenant on May 3, 1862. He was wounded at Chester Six on June 16, 1864, and admitted to Richmond General Hospital with a gunshot wound to the scrotum. He was later captured and made a prisoner of war. On May 10, 1865, he was paroled.

Following his release, he returned to Mecklenburg County and in 1866 was in partnership with Thomas T. Thackston, Esq. Nelson had attended RMC for a time and Thackston was an alumnus (A.B. 1854, A.M. 1856). They owned a processing and distributing center for concentrated lye and a retail ready-to-wear clothes store. Both were located in Clarksville. The businesses dissolved in January 1868. In 1936 (age 93) he was living in the Soldiers' Home in Richmond, the last survivor of Picket's Charge at Gettysburg. He died in 1936.[46]

Boswell was a determined individual. He became captain of Company A, 1st Virginia Reserves, when it was formed on April 20, 1864. Arriving to defend the Staunton River Bridge, he received a battlefield promotion to lieutenant colonel. For his conspicuous performance in defending the bridge against a far superior force, he was promoted to colonel on August 24, 1864. He was paroled on May 13, 1865, by the U.S. VI Corps. He had married Martha Nelson around 1850. He died in 1887.[47]

The Battle of Staunton River Bridge took place on June 24–25, 1864. Captain Benjamin F. Farinholt was in charge of the 1st Virginia Reserves even with four higher ranking officers on the battlefield. He put Lieutenant Colonel Boswell in charge of the Halifax County side of the defenses and Colonel Henry Eaton Coleman (Jr.) in charge of the Charlotte County defenses in the face of the enemy. In charge of the original fortifications was Lieutenant Jackson of North Carolina Infantry (wounded and in the Danville Hospital before the battle); he was accompanied by Lieutenant Colonel Flournoy, Captain Edmonds, 125 volunteers, disabled soldiers working at the Danville Arsenal, patients from the hospital and 59 soldiers who were awaiting transportation in Danville. They were soon joined by Captain Henry Pride's company of local defense troops (about 60), primarily from the Clarksville Ordnance Company. This later group included Charles Russell, a blacksmith, who suffered a gunshot wound to the head, and Robert F. Mason, who was a skilled saddler and had been released from the Confederate Army for the good of the service to work in Clarksville. He was the only one from the Clarksville shops who died (of a gunshot wound to the chest) at the bridge.

Mason's body and most all the Clarksville men were loaded onto bateaux and sent downstream to Clarksville on June 26, 1864. In 1910, Mason's widow (Virginia Puryear Mason Geoghegan) filed for her widow's pension based on his death in service. She had to secure a sworn affidavit from a Confederate soldier who had served with her husband and could verify that he was killed, because there were no records of the event nor his service.[48]

Coleman (Jr.) was from the North Bend Plantation south of Boydton, which had been given to him by his father as a wedding gift in 1858. The plantation was a compilation of farms his father (of Halifax County) had been buying at auction since his son's birth in 1833. His father had served in Congress 1843–1845 and 1847–1850. In total, the plantation consisted of over 1,200 acres with land from North Bend across the Roanoke River in Mecklenburg County and over 1,200 acres in Granville County, North Carolina. Coleman's Ferry connected the two parcels.

Coleman was an engineer and farmer and participated with his uncle in farm production for Randolph Macon College. When the war began, his uncle Charles Eaton (RMC Board of Trustees, 1848) of the large Eaton Plantation called Columbian Grove, with numerous slave holdings in Warren County, North Carolina, established, outfitted, equipped, and had begun training a company of men. Charles Eaton had success as a long time thoroughbred horse breeder in the 1790s and was the grandson of Colonel William Eaton, one of the original settlers to the old Franklin County, North Carolina. William served as an interpreter to the Indians from 1753 to 1758, and the first courthouse was in his home. During the Revolutionary War he had three sons to serve—Colonel William, Lieutenant Colonel Charles and General Thomas Eaton. Charles's son, Charles Eaton (Jr., b. 1816) was a student at RMC from 1837 to 1838.[49]

Colonel William (Jr.) of Warrenton, North Carolina, was one of the principals in securing Jacob Holt's crew from Boydton. In 1843, Holt and crew completed the new antebellum home for Eaton in Warrenton. Soon after, Holt purchased land just outside of town and built a fine home for himself, one for his brother and with three partners, donated a parcel of land and built Warrenton Baptist Church in 1847. Charles's brother James lived next door, and in 1848, James was approached to sell a small portion of his holdings in northeast Granville County, North Carolina (present day Vance County), to William Henry Boyd of Warren County.[50]

Boyd (June 6, 1819–July 17, 1892) was born in Warren County, attended the Randolph Macon Preparatory department and then entered RMC in Boydton but did not take a degree. Upon completion of his education, he became a merchant at St. Tammany's Ferry, Virginia. On February 16, 1848, he married Susan Swepson Davis of Mecklenburg County. They purchased 900 acres from James Eaton later that year and built their home, Belvadier. Susan died in 1854 at age 31 without children. William then married Sallie Virginia Daniel (December 13, 1833–October 22, 1915) on April 30, 1856. She was the daughter of Nathaniel Chesley and Ann Harriet Bullock Daniel of "Tranquility" in Granville County. They had thirteen children. All the children were born and lived at Belvadier, attending a one room school that had been built near the manor house. There is no record of any military service during the war. William and Sallie are buried at Tabernacle Methodist Church of Townsville, North Carolina, where they had attended for many years. Belvadier is still in family ownership.[51]

Colonel Eaton was told that he was too old and ill (b. 1809) to lead his company into combat, so he sent for his nephew, Henry, who had attended William and Mary College but was an engineer and graduate of Virginia Military Institute, and was living just a few miles away. When the war began, Henry Coleman, Jr., enlisted at Lombardy Grove in Chambliss Gray's militia and was established as first sergeant. Serving alongside of Captain Robert Dortch Baskerville and 1st Lieutenant Robert P. Alexander, they marched to Clarksville on Wednesday, May 8, 1861, where they spent the night. On May 9, they boarded the Roanoke Valley Railroad and arrived at Richmond that afternoon. There Sergeant Coleman was elected first lieutenant of the company, but he resigned in June to go to North Carolina, where he would become Captain Henry E. Coleman (Jr.) in command of the 12th North Carolina Infantry. His first assignment was to Norfolk, where he witnessed the Battle of the *Monitor* and the *Virginia* (*Merrimack*).

When the company was reorganized by the Confederate Army, Coleman was not reelected. But he was established as a lieutenant colonel of the 12th North Carolina Infantry Regiment by the Department of North Carolina. His regiment participated in several skirmishes and battles during the Peninsula Campaign, defense of Richmond and Petersburg and Battle of Chancellorsville. There he was wounded but also recommended for promotion to full colonel. From there, he led the 12th at the Wilderness Campaign and on to Gettysburg, where he was wounded again. From Gettysburg, he led his men to Chambersburg and to 2nd Manassas, where he was wounded for a third time. Later, Colonel Coleman was shot in the head at Spotsylvania Court House and lost a section of his skull. He was left on the battlefield for dead. When it was discovered the next day that he was alive, he was taken to Lynchburg Confederate Hospital, but they had no room for the seriously injured.

His wife was sent for at North Bend, and she went to her father for help, as he lived in northern Halifax County, not far from Lynchburg. A wagon and team was dispatched to Lynchburg and Colonel Coleman was transported to his father-in-law's (Richard Logan) home, called Oakville. He remained under the care of two doctors for several weeks with occasional loses of consciousness. On several occasions the doctors believed him to be "soon dead." He had been wounded on four occasions and refused to leave the battlefield for any of them.[52]

When the alarm sounded of the Union forces moving toward the bridge, against medical advice, Coleman was loaded into a carriage filled with pillows, comforters, and cold bandages, and cold bandages were strapped around his head to support his fragile life. He was taken to the battlefield. The trusted colored manservant, Murry, was the driver, and he was accompanied by Dr. John T. Sutphin (D.D; November 21, 1817–June 24, 1864), an Episcopal minister. Sutphin did not believe Coleman would survive the 25 mile trip. Upon arrival, Captain Farinholt placed Colonel Coleman in charge of the east side of the bridge, in the face of the enemy. Coleman was detailed 200 men, plus those already in the woods and trenches on the Charlotte County side. The entrenchments were improved and Coleman even got onto the train and ordered the engineer to head east so he could see the enemy firsthand. The battle began at 3:45 pm. During the fourth and final charge of the battle, Colonel Coleman was shot in the right knee but refused to leave the battlefield.[53]

While Dr. Sutphin was tending his wound, he was shot and killed. Dr. Sutphin left a widow (Martha Anne Singleton Sutphin, 1818–1894) and three children at home. Dr. Sutphin and his wife are buried in a small family cemetery on the Halifax-Mecklenburg County border near the battlefield.

They were both tended to in the field by Dr. Cabell Carrington. On June 29, 1864, Coleman received a message of commendation from General Robert E. Lee. He was physically unable to return home until the late spring of 1865. Following the war, Coleman Jr. served as superintendent of Mecklenburg County Public Schools from 1885 until 1890. Coleman died on the 26th anniversary of the Bridge Battle—June 25, 1890. Just before his death he told his son that he "had not known a waking moment since that day free from pain."[54]

Just prior to Professor Bennett Puryear's arrival, the college had become an exciting part of the community. Dr. Smith's debating skills had brought much notoriety to the school. Company D, Boydton militia, was organized in 1856, by G. Snead and L.E. Finch. It was referred to as the "Roanoke Guard" and had a balance of students and townspeople. This seemed to spur the students on to becoming more involved in community activities and politics. The county politics in 1856 took on a new driving force—the students.

Supported by the students, Charles Bruce defeated the incumbent and served in the Virginia Senate representing Southside from 1857 until the end of the war in 1865 (Bruce served on the RMC Board of Trustees and his nephew was a student there). Again in 1861 the hotly contested office of high sheriff became a priority for the students. A recent young graduate (who is not shown to have taken a degree) of Randolph Macon College was Samuel G. Farrar, whose campaign was run in part by William N. Jones, a senior at Randolph Macon. Farrar was running against former High Sheriff (1852–1856) Reuben A. Puryear, for a vacated seat by High Sheriff Charles R. Edmonson. (To the young student body, age was always an issue.[55])

"Colonel" Bruce, the senior, formed a company of 80 men in Charlotte County. He armed them and purchased uniforms and rations for them. They marched to Richmond, whereupon Bruce was relieved of his command and convinced to stay in the Senate. Charles Bruce (the younger) was born in 1842 to John Bruce. He was named after John's brother Charles, who was a bachelor and had become quite wealthy. Charles (Jr.) attended RMC for the year 1858 but then transferred to the University of North Carolina in 1859.

In 1861, he completed his education at North Carolina, formed a company of 70 men, Company K, "Halifax Volunteers," and continued to recruit his way to Richmond. He arrived there on June 2, 1861, and was established as Company K, 20th Virginia Infantry.[56]

The company, along with four others, was sent to Rich Mountain, Virginia (West Virginia today), to guard the pass against Union soldiers. Marching from the train depot in the mountains to the pass atop the mountain was a laborious process impeded by torrential rains "which kept the Yankees in their tents." The trip took twice as long as expected. Upon arrival on July 11, 1861, the four companies found themselves face to face with two regiments from Ohio and a regiment from Indiana. A skirmish ensued, but the companies stood no chance. Some were killed, a few escaped, and Captain Bruce and over 500 men were captured, stripped of their arms and rations and made prisoners of war.

No prisons were to be found in and around Randolph County, Virginia, so on July 17, 1861, they took an oath and were paroled. Returning to Richmond, Captain Bruce was placed in charge of Company K, 14th Virginia Infantry, on May 6, 1862. During the Battle of Malvern Hill, Bruce was wounded in action on July 1, 1862. He died of his wounds on July 3, 1862. His body was returned from the battlefield by train; and he is buried at Berry Hill Plantation, South Boston, Virginia.[57]

With the assistance, support, and votes of the students Farrar won the election. Some of Farrar's friends hosted a celebration in his honor at the Boydton Hotel. The event was described as the "biggest champagne supper ever had in Mecklenburg County." In honor of his victory, several Randolph Macon seniors were given honored seats at the banquet board.[58] The Boydton Hotel at that time was owned by Reuben Puryear, Richard C. Puryear, John Johnson, Henry Edmond, and Young Talley, purchased at auction in February 1854, from the widow of Francis Boyd. Professor Bennett Puryear and Richard C. Puryear were also investors in the Roanoke Valley Railroad starting in 1857.

The hotel company was reorganized into Johnson, Puryear and Company in 1858, with the new president being Henry Moss. The general manager was Benjamin D. Cogbill with his wife, Harriett Boyd Cogbill. They had moved back to Boydton from Petersburg in 1859, following the death of their three year old daughter, Lucy Boyd Cogbill, on June 15, 1859.

Company A, 3rd Virginia Cavalry, was organized; recruitment and registration were held at the Boydton Hotel. Once organized, outfitted, trained and ready for departure to Richmond, the men assembled in front of the hotel on May 9, 1861. It was reported that B.D. Cogbill, general manager, furnished them a most bountiful meal before their departure.

Following the meal, they paraded through town to Lombardy Grove, where they would spend their first night's bivouac. It was a sight to behold for the students and townspeople. The parade consisted of a mounted fife squad, over 120 horse mounted soldiers in uniform led by seven officers (including a surgeon and chaplain), followed by over 60 wagons (there was a wagon master and teamsters who were soldiers, but most of the handlers were slaves) of supplies and a few light artillery pieces, then wagons for blacksmithing, logging, building, cooking, soap making and other necessities. Wagons filled with the officers' tents, desks, chairs and trunks of clothing. These were followed by over 40 servants marching in precision as though a company of soldiers.

Richard Clausel Puryear (son of Samuel) was heavily involved in recruitment for the Confederate Army when the word "secession" was spoken. His focus was on the Christiansville area, but he was elected to represent the 6th District as a delegate to the first Confederate Congress held in Richmond, Virginia, on June 18, 1861. There he met with his first cousin Richard Clausel Puryear (son of John, born in Boydton), the North Carolina congressman for the Piedmont Region. Richard (son of Samuel) died in the fall of 1863, and was listed as one of the wealthiest men in Mecklenburg County. Richard (son of John) died in 1867, and was listed as one of the wealthiest men in Surry County, North Carolina.[59]

Shortly after the spring election, Reuben Puryear enlisted in the Boydton Cavalry as part of Company A, 3rd Virginia Cavalry, in 1861. Sergeant Puryear served in all 14 battles leading up to Gettysburg. On one occasion Reuben returned to Boydton, and his partners sold the Boydton Hotel to Langston Easley Finch on July 30, 1863. (Richard C. Puryear died a few weeks later.) At Gettysburg he, along with Company A, had been part of Picket's Charge. In early 1864, Puryear, with Company A, was in the Norfolk area. While there he required hospitalization on two separate occasions for gonorrhea. Later, after four more battles, Puryear succumbed to disease and died on August 8, 1864, following the battle at St. Mary's Church. At the battle of St. Mary's Church, Puryear's first cousin, John L. Puryear, also in Company A, 3rd Cavalry, and an orderly to General Raines, was shot and killed on June 24, 1864.

When Finch purchased the hotel, he paid $13,700, which included the hotel, three slaves, all furniture and stores, plus an additional 121 acre farm. Finch was no stranger to Boydton. He was born in Charlotte County, Virginia, on October 28, 1825, and was raised in Christiansville, Mecklenburg County. He was the oldest of eight boys. He was the son of the Rev. Adam Finch (and Lucy Goode Finch), who was also principal of the Christiansville Academy, where Dr. John Draper had lectured for brief periods in the early 1830s.[60]

Following his educational training at Christiansville, Langston Finch came to Boydton as a merchant and farmer and became a member of the Randolph Macon Chapel congregation. On September 4, 1851, he and Martha Emmett Boyd (August 18, 1829–June 12, 1859), daughter of Richard Boyd, who appeared and consented to the wedding, were married. They were married in the chapel of the college by Chaplain John D. Blackwell. They had seven children before she died.

He married a second time to her sister, Tabitha Walker Boyd (October 26, 1845–December 29, 1913) on December 10, 1865. They had nine children. Following the birth of their youngest daughter, Lucy Goode Finch, on June 12, 1859, Martha died of complications. Two days later, Lucy died. In 1861, Langston became president of the Roanoke River Railroad and invested heavily. When the railroad closed in late 1863, he lost most all his assets.

Langston was the elder brother of George B. Finch; and his youngest brother, Tyree Finch (b. April 27, 1840), was reported in family history to be a student at Randolph Macon College when the war began. Tyree enlisted as a private on May 14, 1861, into Company A, 3rd Cavalry, but was not assigned a unit. Instead, he was appointed to the field and staff service as quartermaster sergeant and returned to western Mecklenburg County until the war ended. Most of his service appears to have been in Boydton, establishing and operating a commissary for the Confederacy from RMC. But he is found at the ordnance and munitions company in Clarksville and at the ordnance company and commissary at Taylor's Ferry.[61]

Langston himself had studied with Chambers (1849) and had been licensed as a lawyer. On December 10, 1859, a board of organizers met in Boydton to begin preparations for a new bank. Members were Edward R. Chambers, presiding, Langston E. Finch, Esq., Wm. T. Atkins, and Alfred Boyd. Selected to be added to the board of trustees were William E. Blanch, Thomas F. Goode, J.J. Daley, S.P. Johnson, William T. Small and Leroy W. Wilson.[62]

After the war, Finch lost the hotel due to nonpayment of his note. It closed in February 1868 pending the outcome of the lawsuit. Sometime between March 1868 and July 1869 (there are no copies remaining of these newspapers), Langston purchased the *Tobacco Plant* from Thackston. He operated the paper until 1873, when the name was changed to *Southside Virginian*. It was then owned by L.E. Finch, J.A.H. St. Andrew of Wylliesburg and R.L. Baptist of Boydton. It was known as the newspaper for Boydton and Christiansville, owned and operated by Baptist, Finch and Company. Finch, a local Methodist preacher, was on a parsonage committee with the Clarksville Methodist Church and president of the Roanoke Valley Railroad reorganization group. He preached a published circuit in and around Mecklenburg County for over five years.

William H. Jones went on to enlist in Company F, 14th Virginia Infantry Regiment, "Chambliss Grays," in 1861, at Boydton, as a private. He was wounded at Gettysburg on July 3, 1863, and sent home. Later he was on the Mecklenburg County pension list. He ran for and was elected high sheriff in 1882. He served as a "most efficient and popular sheriff of the county" until 1891.[63]

Samuel Farrar served as high sheriff in the county from October 1861 through the war until September 1865. One of his deputies was S.G. Atkins (March 1839–April 1891) was the son of county attorney William T. Atkins, who was a noted slave breeder and trader. They were both buried in the Boydton Presbyterian cemetery. One of his duties during the war was to provide the Confederacy defenses with slaves to develop and maintain the fortifications of Petersburg and Richmond. In March 1863, he was ordered to deliver 300 (which was the wartime quota for Mecklenburg County) to Petersburg, which he did. In 1864, he was to deliver the same, but could not do so because torrential rains and high water conditions made the task of securing the slaves and making the trip impossible for several weeks. In 1865 he was only able to deliver 176 of the 300. He was reelected in September 1866 and served through 1867, then served as a deputy to the new sheriff in 1868.[64] He was also a gentleman farmer during the war and after and had married one of the Hutcheson girls (daughter of Charles S.), and thus was brother-in-law to John W., Joseph C. and Joseph V. In August 1881, he was elected Mecklenburg County treasurer, a position he held until October 1883.

CHAPTER 6

Pranksters to Professors— The New Regime

On one occasion, the students supposedly demonstrated their unified loyalty and that they had a signal for student distress. A popular student, William J. Carter, the son of trustee the Rev. William Carter (March 3, 1803–March 4, 1885), went in town to the local tavern (possibly Washington Tavern, built by James Bruce and his partner Captain Beverly Sydnor, in 1822). As the story goes, being drunk and creating a disturbance, he was arrested by county constable William F. Small.[1]

The news spread quickly to the college; and when the alarm was sounded, boys gathered from all directions in front of the main hall on the lawn. William A. Jamieson, son of the Rev. James Jamieson, a founder and trustee of the college, was described as the most popular and tactful student at the college for his time. Jamieson soon caught up to a farmer heading to town in his buggy. "Under whip and lash they went into town and young Jamieson" sprinted "into the courtroom." The sheriff was ordered to arrest him, whereupon Jamieson calmly announced, "Sir, I only entered so hurriedly to save the court. The boys are coming 150 strong and if Carter is not liberated before they get here I fear all of you who persist will be thrown out of the windows."[2]

The judge looked out, saw the boys coming over the fence instead of coming around to the gate, and ordered the courtroom vacated. The case against Carter, Commonwealth vs. Carter, was never finished.

Constable William F. Small was in the Boydton Militia, Company D. On May 14, 1861, at Boydton, he enlisted in Company A, 3rd Virginia Cavalry, and was elected first lieutenant. Just prior to the completion of his one year commitment, on April 25, 1862, he resigned his commission and returned home. He is buried at St. James Episcopal Church (which had been relocated to Boydton in 1842) cemetery in Boydton.

6. Pranksters to Professors—The New Regime

Washington Tavern, 1820 (photograph by the author; courtesy United Methodist Church of Boydton).

William J. Carter graduated from Randolph Macon (A.M., June 1861). He also received diplomas in mechanics and astronomy, political economy and slavery, mineralogy and geology, Spanish and moral philosophy. He enlisted on May 18, 1861, at age 21 as a third sergeant in Armistead's Brigade, "Mecklenburg Rifles," Company G, 38th Virginia Infantry Regiment, under the command of Captain William Townes, Jr., of the Cuscowilla plantation (c. 1858). Captain Townes, Jr., was given the plantation by his father as a wedding gift in 1858, but Colonel Townes never signed over the deed, something he celebrated following the war. As the next door neighbor of Henry Eaton Coleman's North Bend Plantation (Coleman had a reputation as a very progressive farmer, with advanced ideas and manicured fields), Townes also provided farm produce to the college. Carter was elected second lieutenant of the company on April 29, 1862, shortly after Captain Townes was admitted to Seminary Hospital in Williamsburg. Townes was transferred to Williamsburg General Hospital on April 23, 1862, for diphtheria and dropped from the rolls of the company on April 29.[3]

On November 15, 1863, Carter was promoted to first lieutenant (his 23rd birthday) and he was at Appomattox for the surrender on April 9, 1865. Upon his return to Boydton, he became a county land surveyor. On November 11, 1867, he was selected supervisor of the Randolph Macon district by the board of trustees. When the college properties were being sold, or parceled and sold, he completed most of the surveys on his alma mater through the 1870s. He is buried in Boydton Presbyterian Church cemetery.

Captain Townes, Jr., had attended Randolph Macon. Upon his return home he became a member of the board of trustees. He and his father were very adamant about not moving the college from Boydton. When the decision was finally made, they resigned from the board. Following the war and the move of RMC, Captain Townes became the editor of the *Roanoke Valley* in 1872. This was the new Boydton newspaper. In 1883 he was elected and served one term in the Virginia Senate.

With so many distinguished individuals serving on the board of trustees, Jamieson is often overshadowed in his role in representing Randolph Macon College as a board member and his contribution to the community. James Jamieson was born April 4, 1802, in Augusta County, Virginia, to Andrew Jamieson and his wife. Andrew was Scots-Irish and his wife is described as English; both were strict Presbyterians. They had a large family and a strong belief in education. All the children received an education from the Presbyterian Church school in Waynesboro. James attended a Methodist camp meeting and the conference in Oxford in 1825, when he decided Methodism was more to his desire.

He eventually married three times, with each wife dying within a few years after marriage. His wives were well educated, and all three had attended the noted Moravian College in Salem, North Carolina. Wives two and three were both widows. There were two children, but death took its toll there also. Jamieson became a trial Methodist preacher in 1829, an elder in 1833, and was assigned to Scottsville. He was one of the first chaplains of RMC, and became a member of the 1844 conference that divided the church into north and south. In 1848, he became an instructor with Greensboro Female College.[4]

In 1857, the Reverend Jamieson was elected president of Danville Female College, replacing Benjamin Watkins Ogburn (another alumnus from RMC). He left the farm he had purchased near White House and served as president for seven years. All the while, he continued preaching at the Clarksville M.E., South, Church part time and then full time in 1866 and 1867. Danville Female College struggled financially during the Civil War. In 1866, Wesley C. Vaiden (A.M. 1861, RMC) became president, but the college was not able to rebound from its financial hardships. In 1871 it ran out of money and was sold at auction. Jamieson borrowed $5,725 and purchased the college. He then turned the papers over to the board of trustees. It became Randolph Macon Institute, a female preparatory school for Randolph Macon Women's College. Later, it became Stratford Women's College but closed in 1974. The Reverend Jamieson is buried in Danville next to his second wife. Jamieson served on the board of trustees of RMC for many years beginning in 1837.[5]

Following the war, the Reverend Jamieson was selected by the board as charge of the Randolph Macon College (and chaplain). Following the move of the college in 1868, he helped the former congregation of Randolph Macon Chapel (the only Methodist church in Boydton) to establish their own church building in Boydton. Upon completion and dedication of the new church in 1872, he returned to his farm on Cherry Hill Church Road, near (present day) Buffalo Junction, to be closer to his son and family. In 1876, he became pastor of the Methodist-Episcopal Church, South, located in Clarksville. He died on June 25, 1880. When a new church home was erected in Clarksville sometime later, the church was named in his memory.

William A. Jamieson graduated from Randolph Macon College in 1860 and attended the law school. In 1861, he left the country for the city to establish a law practice. Before this could happen, secession had taken place and Virginia was readying for war. Instead of returning home, Jamieson enlisted in Company C, 5th Virginia Cavalry. He was elected second lieutenant in 1861 and was discharged at Appomattox with the same rank on April 9, 1865.

Upon discharge, he returned to Clarksville, where he established a law practice. He joined the local Methodist church and in 1867, married the daughter of his next door neighbor, Helen Yancey. He, along with Charles H. Russell, former welder at the munitions factory and foundry of Clarksville, and George N. Wells, began the Mechanics Building and Loan Association (the equivalent of a finance company today). Jamieson managed the company and the properties foreclosed on through its operations until 1888. On May 23, 1888, he was elected Mecklenburg County clerk of the court. He held this office until December 31, 1905.

Benjamin Ogburn (July 3, 1832–December 28, 1911), son of the Rev. Charles Ogburn of Whittle's Mill, Mecklenburg County, Virginia (A.B. 1852 and A.M. 1855, RMC), married Lucy Rebecca Harrison Harwell (January 28, 1835–December 18, 1869) on May 5, 1854. In 1852, he began teaching in John T. Claiborne's boarding school. The Ogburn family was instrumental in establishing two M.E. churches in the north central area of Mecklenburg County— Shiloh and Prospect. Another son of Charles Ogburn, John F. (b. 1830), also attended RMC in the 1840s but did not take a degree. Following his A.M. degree, he was offered the position of president of a failing Danville Female College. When he took over in 1855, there was an enrollment of 17 students. The following year, 1856, the enrollment was over 60 young women.[6]

When the Reverend Jamieson took over as president in 1857, Ogburn stayed as a professor. On July 1, 1860, he resigned due to ill health and returned to Mecklenburg County (the enrollment for 1860 at Danville Female College was 139 students). Due to his poor health he was exempt from military service. He and his wife had nine children, but with complications, she died in 1869. In May 1870, by a military tribunal court, Ogburn was selected as justice of the peace for Whittle's Mill District. On November 3, 1872, Ogburn married for the second time to Martha Rebecca "Queen" Walker (June 21, 1834–January 5, 1913). They had three children.

Also in 1857, William G. Connor completed his A.M. degree. When the war began he enlisted and served in the 34th North Carolina Infantry. Following the war, he went on to become president of Chapel Hill Female College and was awarded an honorary D.D. degree sometime around 1870 by R-MC–Ashland.

On May 12, 1861, Ogburn's younger brother, Charles Wesley Ogburn (Jr.) (b. July 4, 1834), enlisted into Company F, 14th Virginia Infantry, in Lombardy Grove as a private. He was serving with Captain Baskerville, but when established into the Confederate Army, Baskerville was not elected captain. Baskerville resigned and returned home. The Ogburn family furnished a suitable substitute in the person of James Knight, and Charles was discharged on May 17, 1862. Returning home, he married Flourney Gill. In 1865, he and his brother Benjamin began a country store and fertilizer distribution warehouse in North View, Virginia.

On January 17, 1868, Benjamin was appointed by the military tribunal of Mecklenburg County (martial law) to the county board of supervisors representing the Whittle's Mill District. In the early 1870s, he is reported to have begun the Grange Patrons of Husbandry in North View. In the 1880 census, it is noted that Benjamin and his wife were living in the Buckhorn District. They had a daughter and a son attending Buckhorn Academy, a son who was operating the farm, and a son working at Ogburn's Store. Also living in their home were three servants, a cook, a nurse, and two boarders.[7]

President Smith was a man of many talents and skills and displayed broad wisdom as a role model to students and faculty alike. But he was not without a sense of humor. Colleges throughout history have had their share of pranksters, and Randolph Macon was no exception. The back row of pews in the local Presbyterian church still displays the graffiti of some of the students.

Susan Bracey writes "their shenanigans included such things as cutting the bell rope, burying the bell, greasing the blackboards, putting a cow in a classroom overnight, nailing up classroom doors,"[8] etc. But Dr. Smith also

Presbyterian church, 1819 (photograph by the author; courtesy Town of Boydton).

experienced the direct brunt of some of their pranks. One story goes like this:

> On one occasion Dr. Smith learned of some boys in his chicken lot. Saturday nights the boys generally prepared an extra supper in their rooms. But being without meat, three of the boys decided to raid Dr. Smith's chicken lot. After dark they approached the lot and one of the boys climbed over the fence. As he would hand over the chickens the other two boys who would wring their necks. He named each chicken. Then they heard a disturbance from the hen house. The boys, leaving the chickens, ran.
>
> The following afternoon, three gentlemen were personally invited by Dr. Smith to join him and his family for Sunday supper. Unsuspecting when they arrived they discovered the table had three platters of prepared chicken—one placed next to each of the boys. Dr. Smith offered to serve them their choice of meat, and they gave him their preferences. Dr. Smith served them and in so doing—he said to Boy #1, this is a piece of the "plump Miss Susie." To boy #2, he said this is a piece of the "portly Mrs. Smith"; and to boy #3, he said, matter-of-factly, and this is a piece of the "fat old doctor." The table was quiet for the remainder of the meal.[9]

In the fall of 1860, the M.E., South, Virginia Convention met at Randolph Macon. On December 7, 1860, the *Tobacco Plant* carried the story. Among others, the following representatives were elected:

P.W. Archer, Presiding Elder
Geo. H. Ray, RM Col.
Wm. Carter, RM Circuit
Wm. A. Smith, RM Col. Pres.
Jas. Jamieson, Danville Female College, Pres.
J.D. Southall, Colored Missions[10]

The Rev. George Henry Ray was born in Delaware on October 21, 1832. His father, Enos, was from Maryland and his mother, Elizabeth, from Ireland. The family moved to Washington City (Washington, D.C.), and he attended Columbian College and later read law. Following his conversion, he was admitted to the Virginia M.E., South, Conference in 1853.[11] It appears in 1860 he moved with the Conrad family (with whom he was living) from Washington, D.C., to Harrisonburg, Rockingham County, Virginia. The family consisted of Susan, age 67, widowed, with her son, William, age 47, and his wife, Elizabeth, age 34, with child, Bear, age 6. Two other Conrads were listed in the home as Janetta and Virginia.[12] Ray arrived at Randolph Macon College in January 1861 for his assignment as chaplain. In June 1861, he graduated with diplomas in moral philosophy and political economy and slavery (both in the department of Dr. Smith).

On October 2, 1861, he traveled to York, Virginia, to enlist into Company A, 3rd Cavalry, as a minister. He was established with the Confederate Field and Staff, but resigned his commission on August 9, 1862.[13] On November 21, 1867, at the M.E. conference in Petersburg presided over by Bishop Doggett, Ray was appointed to the Burkeville district of Randolph Macon. He subsequently married Virginia Chambers Scott (b. 1843) of Lunenburg County and began to preach and teach. The 1880 Census records list him living near Richmond with his wife and their four children. His listed occupation was professor of gospel.[14] In 1893, he was awarded an honorary D.D. degree from Washington and Lee University. He served as a minister in Norfolk, Petersburg, Richmond, Lynchburg, and the eastern region of Virginia. His wife, Virginia, died in Baltimore in 1904. He died in Ashland on March 18, 1911, and is buried in Hollywood Cemetery, Richmond.

Also, during the fall 1860 meeting, William Thomas Sutherlin (also spelled "Sutherland") was nominated for, and accepted an appointment to, the RMC Board of Trustees. Sutherlin was born on April 7, 1822, to one of the wealthiest families of southern Pittsylvania County, Virginia (George S. and Polly S. Norman Sutherlin). He was home schooled for a few years, attended a male academy in Danville for three years, and then went to Joseph Godfrey's academy in Franklin County (near the Blue Ridge Mountain range).

He returned home, where he resided until age 21, at which time he moved to Danville and became a tobacco manufacturer. Soon, he was listed as the wealthiest man in Danville. In 1859, he had a modern mansion built which was and still is "considered to be one of the finest examples of Italianate architecture in the state."

On October 18, 1849, he married Jeanie (Jane) Erwin Patrick of Guilford County, North Carolina. At the time his personal holdings of farm land, slaves, and investments were already gaining on the family fortunes. In 1850, he was responsible for having a wooden bridge built across the Dan River at the lower end of Main Street in Danville, which allowed for easier access by individuals from the northern and eastern areas of the region. From 1855 to 1861, he was elected and served as mayor for the town of Danville. He was also county candidate to the state secession Congress in 1861. When the war began, due to poor health, he was unable to serve in a military capacity. He was, however, appointed commandant of the Danville Ordnance Company and served as relief assistant quartermaster when needed. At varying times throughout the war he served as the director of the public works for the Town of Danville.[15]

With the evacuation of Richmond in April 1865 signaling a close to the war, President Jefferson Davis's train stopped over in Danville en route south, and "Davis was met at the station by Commandant Major Sutherlin. He moved President Davis and members of his cabinet to his mansion, earning it the title of 'Last Capitol of the Confederacy.' In that hospitable home the table was set all the time for the coming and going. The board was spread with the best the bountiful host and hostess could supply. Mrs. Sutherlin brought out all her treasured reserves of pickles, sweetmeats and preserves. This might be her last opportunity for serving the Confederacy and its Chieftain. The Sutherlins knew ... their dwelling would be a marked spot."

The train was also met by Judge James Sangster (possible A.B. 1850, RMC, and the Law Department) of Danville, along with Admiral Raphael Semmes, Confederate commander of the James River Squadron of 400 sailors, Midshipman R.H. Fielding, and 50 to 60 cadets under the charge of Secretary Mallory.

When President Davis was leaving Danville, Mrs. Sutherlin "knew that he had no money in his pockets except Confederate notes—and these would buy next to nothing. We had some gold, and I offered it to him, pressed it upon him. He shook his head. Tears came into his eyes. 'No, no, my child,' he said, 'you and your husband are much younger than I am. You will need it. I will not. Mr. Davis did not expect to live long. He was sure he would be killed." While in Danville, "Mr. Davis told Mrs. Sutherlin that the songs of the mockingbirds refreshed him." Another thing that cheered him in Danville was the enthusiasm of the schoolgirls of the Southern Female College: "When these young ladies, in their best homespun gowns, went out on dress parade and beheld Mr. Davis riding by in Major Sutherlin's carriage, they drew themselves up in line, waved handkerchiefs and cheered to their hearts' content; he gave them his best bow and smile."[16]

Harwood Lockett, father of Phillip and Myrta, also had a ward who was attending the Danville Female College in 1865, when President Davis came to town. "Knowing that Danville might become a fighting center, Mr. Williams T. Davis [president of the college] wrote my father [Harwood] to send for Sue [the trusted and esteemed family servant]. The way to reach Danville was by private conveyance, seventy miles or more. Uncle Dick [the family coachman], mounted high on the carriage-box, a white-headed, black-faced knight-errant of chivalry, set forth.... In due time the carriage rolled into the yard [of the girls school], Uncle Dick proud and happy on his box, Sue inside wrapped in rugs, sound asleep, for it was midnight."[17]

A strong, compassionate relationship developed between President Davis and the Sutherlins. For some time after the president's party parted Danville, heading south, Major Sutherlin would receive word of a general, or other group, on the trail of the president. He would meet them and persuade them to come to his home for refreshments and a meal. If so inclined they could spend the night. The mansion is still occupied and since 1974 has been the home of the Danville Museum of Fine Arts and History.

Sutherlin, having served as a commandant, following the war he was referred to as "Major." In 1865, he was elected to serve from 1866 to 1868, as a delegate to the Virginia House of Delegates. With his acquired wealth and including some of his family's legacy, he was able to build Milton and Sutherlin Railroad and the Danville and New River Railroad. He also established the Danville Bank and was one of the organizers of the Border Grange Bank. He helped "to reorganize the Virginia State Agriculture Society, liberally aided the Danville Female College and Randolph Macon College."[18]

The 1870 U.S. Census Records list Sutherlin's age as 48 and his wife as age 38 (age 17 when they were married).[19] Living with them was their 18 year old daughter, Jannie L., and his mother-in-law, Martha Patrick, age 69. His holdings in Pittsylvania County were listed as $113,000 in real estate and personal property of $112,000. During the 1880's he is listed as a farmer and co-owner of Coal and Wood Co. at 600 Craighead Street, Danville. Also in the 1880s and 1890s he is listed as one of the principles of W.R. Fitzgerald and Co., at 953 Main Street, Danville. In the February 13, 1893, issue of the *Midland Express* (the Negro newspaper of Boydton, Virginia), W.T. Sutherlin is listed

Last Capital of the confederacy—Sutherlin Mansion, 1859 (photograph by the author; courtesy Danville Museum of Fine Arts and History, Danville, Virginia).

as president of the board of the World's Fair Managers of Virginia; unfortunately, he died in 1893 before the World's Fair was held.[20]

Following the secession of South Carolina, some of the students did not return from their Christmas break in January 1861. Secession, the elections and war were foremost on the minds of Boydton townspeople and the Randolph Macon College staff, faculty and students. This was a very serious time. Telegraph lines were busy. The only documented telegraph line in Mecklenburg County was at the train depot in Clarksville near the *Tobacco Plant* newspaper office, all of which were under the charge of John Boyd.[21] Militia volunteers were becoming very important as mail riders (like the pony express, which was still new out West, having begun in April 1860). These mail riders, sometimes called couriers, served throughout the war. Everyone was experiencing anxiety over when the North would invade—where and how? It was clear to all southerners that they definitely would.

For those students who had returned to school, the tension was mounting. On March 15, 1861, some students sent a "scathing letter of protest" to the board of trustees. The students had been granted use of the society rooms as a sanctuary from faculty. But some felt they had been violated by faculty interfering with their meetings. The letter was signed by four students (ages

19–21). They were David Doggett, son of a trustee, John W. Watts, Benjamin Jarratt and Phillip Lockett, the author of the letter. They were all expelled. All four students apologized, and Lockett withdrew his letter. Doggett and Lockett were allowed to withdraw, Jarratt received 20 demerits and Watts received 150 demerits.[22] (For more on Lockett and Watts see Appendix A.)

The society rooms and membership in the societies were of great importance to the students (closely resembling the fraternities of modern day). The first was the Washington Literary Society, which began in 1833. The first commencement address before this group was conducted by the Rev. William Wightman, RMC Board of Trustees and distinguished clergy, in July 1833, and became a keystone for future years of the society.[23] Each of the two societies had a library and belonged to the national society. Students paid dues and held offices. They received literary information from the national body and this encouraged the students to think not only intellectually but also abstractly and creatively—to sharpen their debating skills. In Lander's diary, he references the Franklin Literary (F.L.) Society, to which he belonged. He also wrote of the Thurmond brothers, R.J. and the treasurer P. Thurmond.[24] It does not appear that they took a degree, though an R.W. Thurmond (b. 1827) received an A.B. in 1853. But a history this family did make during the Civil War.

Benjamin Franklin Jarratt went on to leave a legacy for RMC. He did not record that he was an RMC student with the class of 1861, nor as a graduate of RMC, when he enlisted on May 24, 1861, at the Sussex Courthouse. He stated he was born August 18, 1839, and enlisted into Company A, 41st Infantry Battalion, and was selected a sergeant. On November 12, 1861, he was promoted to first sergeant. When his year was near completion, he reenlisted in March 1862 for a bounty of $50. On May 1, 1862, he was elected second lieutenant and was wounded in action in the leg at Second Manassas on August 30, 1862. Following complications, he was hospitalized for an extended period of time, starting in January 1863, and then reassigned to the light duty of conscription enrolling officer until August 1864. He was promoted to first lieutenant on May 3, 1863; when he returned to duty, he was promoted to company captain in September 1864. He was at Appomattox on April 9, 1865.[25]

He had become good friends with Major General William Mahone during the 1870s and 1880s, and was elected to the Virginia House of Delegates for the 1887–1888 term. Declining to run for re-election, he was elected Greensville County treasurer. He held that position until his death on August 1, 1913.

Plans for Wofford College, Spartanburg County, South Carolina, were begun in 1851 when the South Carolina M.E. Conference, South, received an endowment of $100,000 from Benjamin Wofford. The principal organizer was Dr. William Wightman (A.B. 1829, Charleston College; D.D. 1846, RMC). One half of the endowment was to be used for construction with the remainder for operating costs. The school became operational on August 1, 1854, with President Dr. William May Wightman (b. 1808). There was a college building, a president's house and four professor's homes. Faculty included Professor A. (Alfred) M. Shipp (b.c. 1795; D.D. 1858, RMC) professor of English literature formerly at the University of North Carolina; Professor David Duncan (b. 1791; D.D. 1847, RMC) professor of ancient languages; Professor Warren DuPre (A.B. 1838, A.M. 1840) as professor of chemistry and mineralogy; and Professor James Henry Carlisle (b. 1825; A.M.) formerly of Columbia Male Academy serving as professor of mathematics. Seven students attended for the first term. The first graduate was Samuel Dibble in 1856.[26]

Dr. Wightman resigned in 1859 to establish Southern University in Greenville, Alabama, which began the same year. In 1867, Wightman was elected to serve as bishop of M.E. Church, South. He held this position until his death on February 15, 1882.

All professors remained at their posts throughout the Civil War. Wightman was replaced as president of Wofford by Dr. Alfred Micajah Shipp (June 15, 1819–June 27, 1887). He was born in Stokes County, North Carolina, to John and Elizabeth Oglesby Shipp. He graduated with an A.B. in 1840 from the University of North Carolina, was licensed to preach in December 1840, and admitted to the South Carolina M.E. Conference. In 1848, due to a throat infection making his voice very weak, he left the ministry and was named president of Greensboro Female College. He married Mary Gillespie of Rose Hill Plantation in Marlboro County, South Carolina. They raised a large family. One of his descendants went on to become President of V.M.I. in the 1890s.[27]

In 1849, Wightman accepted a position as professor of history at the University of North Carolina, where he remained until 1858. In 1858, he was selected president of Wofford College, Spartanburg, South Carolina, where he remained until 1875. During his tenure he was awarded an honorary D.D. degree by Randolph Macon College in 1859, and later an honorary LL.D. degree from the University of North Carolina. In 1875, he was hired as chair of exegetical theology at Vanderbilt University. He served in that position until 1885. During that same period, he served for three years as dean of the Theology School and vice-chancellor of the university. His primary publication was the *History of Methodism in South Carolina* (a copy of which is located at the South Carolina Historical Society in Charleston). He came to Cleveland Springs, in North Carolina, for medicinal purposes but died there. He is buried at the Gillespie Family Cemetery near Wallace, South Carolina.

In 1875, Carlisle was selected as president of Wofford (1875 to 1902) and was the first president to conduct the commencement exercises in English instead of Latin. Professor Duncan stayed on the faculty until his death in 1881. (Duncan family photographs from 1842 to 1851 are housed by the South Carolina Historical Society in Charleston.)

After withdrawing from RMC, it would appear David Doggett (the son) enlisted into Company F, 35th Virginia Cavalry Battalion, on April 5, 1863, in Rockingham County. He was captured and made a prisoner of war on June 8, 1863, at Brandy Station, having been wounded in action in the arm. He was taken to Washington Hospital on June 10, 1863, with his arm being amputated, then released from the hospital and sent to prison at Point Lookout, Maryland, on August 25, 1863. He was hospitalized again on November 27, 1863, and exchanged and transferred to Chimborazo Hospital in Richmond on August 16, 1864. He served on detail until paroled on April 22, 1865.[28]

Most every exciting story of the Civil War in history has a reference to Major (Lieutenant Colonel) John Singleton Mosby ("The Gray Ghost"). References to Mosby's Raiders and Mosby's Rangers abound and even prompted a Walt Disney movie for television in the 1960s. Granted, Mosby had the largest unit (called a company, but with at times 3,000 soldiers, it was finally acknowledged as a regiment) of sanctioned partisan rangers. He was literally personally hunted by Union Army troops.

Adolphus E. Richards, of Loudoun County, graduated from Randolph Macon College with diplomas in mathematics and mineralogy and geology in June 1861. He was also a junior in chemistry and natural philosophy. He enlisted into Company B, 43rd Battalion Virginia Cavalry, Mosby's Regiment of Partisan Rangers. He transferred and was elected captain of Company C. For his bravery, gallant character and duty, he was promoted to major of the battalion on December 7, 1864.[29]

In fact, there were about twenty such sanctioned "ranger groups." Guerrilla units were common early in the war, but they were not recognized by the Confederacy until later in 1862. With Mosby in Northern Virginia, to his west in the Appalachian Mountains (part of Virginia that became West Virginia) was Thurmond's Partisan Rangers. They were under the command of Lieutenant Colonel William A. Witcher of the 34th Cavalry Battalion, and were sanctioned as three companies of men by Confederate Army, Department of Western Virginia and East Tennessee. By September 1862, they were reorganized into a battalion. Depending upon the origin of the history (Tennessee versus Virginia versus the North) it is referenced as "Morris's Battalion," "Houndshell's Battalion," and "Thurmond's Battalion." In late 1863, it was renamed the 44th Battalion, Virginia Cavalry. At war's end, Captain

6. Pranksters to Professors—The New Regime

William T. Thurmond was in command of nine companies of the battalion at the surrender.[30]

The original three companies were organized on May 2, 1862. Company A was established by Captain William Dabney Thurmond (November 11, 1820–1910) with his brother Richard C. Thurmond as his second lieutenant. Both were from Amherst County, Virginia. William enlisted on August 26, 1862, with his company of 55 men at Sulfur Springs. On November 24, 1864, his company still had only 58 men and horses. He was paroled on June 27, 1865, in Charleston, West Virginia, at the age of 44. He was described as 5 feet, 9 inches tall, dark hair and complexion, and blue eyes. Following the war, he became a land surveyor, land agent and coal operator. On November 1, 1906, he was president of the National Bank of Thurmond.

Lieutenant Richard Claiborne Thurmond (June 22, 1836–October 7, 1869) enlisted in Charleston, Virginia, on June 20, 1861. Described as 5 feet, 8 inches tall, light hair, fair complexion, and grey eyes, he enlisted into Company K, 22nd Virginia Infantry. When Thurmond's Rangers were established, he was detached to serve as a scout first for Phillip in July 1862, then later to William in November. Following the war, he moved to Fayette County, West Virginia, and soon afterward died.

Lieutenant Robert Given Thurmond (May 28, 1839–August 20, 1907) enlisted at Fayetteville into Company K, 22nd Virginia Infantry, on June 6, 1861. He was described as 5 feet, 11 inches tall, dark hair and complexion with blue eyes. On September 13, 1862, he was detached as a scout with his brothers. He was paroled on June 7, 1865. After the war, he became mayor of Mount Hope, Fayette County, West Virginia. He died while living in Thurmond, West Virginia, and is buried in a cemetery at Minden, West Virginia.[31]

Captain John W. Thurmond organized Company B, but there appears to be no additional records. Company C was begun by Captain Phillip (Peyton) James Thurmond (October 24, 1826–October 26, 1864) of Amherst County. Before the war he had married Sarah Pauline Jones, sister of Confederate Colonel Benhring Jones of the 60th Virginia Infantry. He enlisted at Red Sulfur Springs, Monroe County, on September 1, 1862. He was a skilled soldier, horseman and leader of men. In 1863, he was recommended by Lieutenant Colonel Witcher for a promotion to major. He was killed in action at Winfield, West Virginia, on October 26, 1864. Following the war Sarah moved to Indiana.

Following Phillip's death, John Dudley Thurmond was established as captain. John was described as 5 feet, 8 inches tall, light hair, dark complexion, with green eyes. He also enlisted with his brother on September 1, 1862, and established as a third lieutenant. He was paroled as a captain on June 27,

1865, at Charleston, West Virginia, at age 30. In 1916, he was still alive and listed as "in charge of the county."[32]

The youngest brother, Lieutenant Elias Thurmond (November 25, 1842–August 1, 1926) enlisted with his brothers on September 1, 1862. He was captured on October 26, 1864, and made a prisoner of war at Winfield, West Virginia. He was sent to Camp Chase, Ohio, until paroled in 1865.

The word finally came that on April 17, 1861, the Virginia Peace Convention went to meet "with Lincoln who gave them a letter for Governor Letcher of Virginia" setting forth a requisition "for troops to crush the rebellion of the South." In response to the letter, Letcher replied, "You have chosen to inaugurate civil war; and having done so, we will meet it in a spirit as determined as the administration has exhibited toward the South."[33] This, coupled with the news of President Lincoln's devastating (to the South) cabinet appointments and the fact that he had ordered 75,000 troops to prepare to move on those states of secession,[34] caused the convention to reconsider its vote of three days earlier, which was not to secede. Members met in a secret session and voted to recommend that Virginia secede, rather than "turn on our southern brothers and sisters." But it had to be voted on by the citizens of the Commonwealth. The vote was scheduled for May 23, 1861, and was nearly unanimous. On May 24, 1861, Virginia joined the other 10 of the Confederate states.

Following the announcement of secession, there was a great celebration at the college and in Boydton. According to the Rev. W.E. Edwards (D.D. 1862), who must have been present in Boydton when word of secession came, "Bonfires were kindled; a great torchlight procession formed; the different professors were visited, and, after the most approved style, called on for speeches. The march was continued to Boydton. Soon students in large numbers left for their homes to prepare for war."[35]

Many community meetings to elicit support, food, weapons, and clothing for the soldiers were held in Christiansville, Boydton and Clarksville. For several months, the Boydton tailor shop of Dugger and Gary had to have been operating above its peak abilities. Established in the late 1840s by prominent Boydton citizen, Richmond A. Dugger (b. 1821) (cousin of James B. Dugger, Jr., b. 1836; A.B. 1855, RMC), it was located around the corner from the Exchange Hotel of Boydton, which had opened in 1848. The first manager of the hotel was J. Phillip Rainey, whose son, A.F. Rainey, had been a student at Randolph Macon but did not take a degree. The tailor shop must have been a beehive of activity with all of the companies of soldiers organizing in and around the county. There was a need for thousands of uniforms and accessories of chevrons, stripes, insignias, etc., which would also have kept

6. Pranksters to Professors—The New Regime

Dugger and Gary tailor shop, 1842 (photograph by the author; courtesy Mecklenburg County).

RMC tailor-seamstress Mary Bugg and many others in the county extremely busy.

Around 1858, Richard Boyd of North Carolina died and his brother, John E., was appointed as administrator of the estate (taken over by Alfred Boyd around 1862). John took over operation of the store next to the Boydton Hotel and operated it for a short time and then, with a partner, he began a second store in Victoria, Lunenburg County, Virginia. By 1862, he had a partner in Boydton of M.A. Goode and the store became Boyd and Goode. In the records of the estate of Richard are a number of receipts that shed some light on the business acumen of Boydton during the war years. There is documentation of Alfred Boyd's store serving as the broker for fabric, yarn, and other items for the Boydton area and purchasing supplies in large quantity.[36] Although difficult to interpret the numbers presented for description, one receipt is for "200 (w) yarn on May 9, 1861 from William S. Battle of Rocky Mount, North Carolina for $40 plus shipping." There is a notation on the invoice "for cotton" and "only ½ of the above acct ... was for the benefit of ... Boyd."

Another receipt is for: "184 at $22.11 and 107 at $10.24." Additionally, there are receipts for Frances Bugg's fabric purchases from Boyd and Goode, and a large purchase by A. Dugger for $225. These are from 1862. Other significant receipts are from Petersburg:

May 10, 1861	9 yards of Alpaca extra	$6.75
	1 yard of heavy Alpaca	3.85
	1 yard extra plaids	9.20

Sales Receipt for Hamilton and Graham, importers and jobbers, 60 Sycamore Street.

and

September 12, 1861 172¾ ? by D. Osbornk of Davis, Abrams and Lyons, Wholesale and Retail, 13 Sycamore Street.

Alfred Boyd also owned about seventy slaves, and many of those were hired out to families in the community—some for child care, some for care of an aged widow, others for nursing care and still others for farm chores and servants for Randolph Macon College. He also owned a group of slaves that were masons, and in 1862 and 1863 they were being kept very busy with construction work. For some slave owners, the war began to have a direct negative impact to their operation as early as 1862. Boyd was kept very busy during the war; afterward, around 1870, his store was renamed "Boyd and Son."

With the conscription by the Confederacy of slaves and free blacks to work on the fortifications of Norfolk, Richmond and Petersburg, much of the able bodied labor of the plantations could not tend to the fields and chores. The files of D.N. Carter and John W. Wootton contain receipts for two of their slaves, each, conscripted to work on the fortifications in Petersburg for one year in 1862.[37] Farmers and free black families were unable to take care of their farming and community responsibilities. Thus, many of the plantation owners were relegated to the question of "what to do?"

For some slaves they had previously provided homage. Slaves that were productive and young were gone, which left the misfits and old. The few able bodied hands the Confederacy allowed each farmer to retain became shared property (as documented in Boyd's records) among family members and neighbors. Several receipts exist that document the movement of undesirable slaves from plantations to the county "poor farm" for a small fee. A few examples follow[38]:

- 1-1-1862, "For the care of old man Osborne and Lizzy" $200 Received of Jn E. Boyd and others, Warren, North Carolina
- 1-1-62, Received as payment in full for "3 idiot children (Susan, Elvira and Nanney)"
- 1-1-1862 Received of Jn. E. Boyd and others, "$1,300 Nannie for wife of Harrison Howell."
- 1-1-1862 "$150 for support and maintenance of old man Fed during his natural life."
- 1-1-1862 "$400 for maintenance of woman Becky and crippled Lizzy."

Slave sale records during 1861 and 1862 show a dramatic drop in price documented, among others, by John Wootton selling a slave to his brother Joseph in 1861 for $1,300; but by early 1864, the prices had rebounded. This is documented by John W. Wootton and D.N. Carter each purchasing a male slave on November 14, 1864, for $5,000 from slave breeder William Atkins, Esq. Wootton purchased Harry and Carter purchased Wyatt.[39]

Dr. Smith was a very busy man. A story about him appeared in the *Tobacco Plant* on May 10, 1861 (Friday):

Commendable Liberality

At Boydton, on Tuesday, after calling the roll of the company, a gentleman proposed to join the Boydton Cavalry, but said he had no horse, and was not in a circumstance to afford one. Dr. Wm A. Smith stepped forward and offered to furnish a horse, or at any rate to make himself responsible to raise the money to pay for one. Upon this the company called on the doctor for a speech. He responded briefly and eloquently. We are informed that the doctor's proposition was extended so as to raise the amount necessary to purchase three horses for the use of the cavalry, and that $450 was raised on the spot.

Dr. Smith has, on all occasions, shown himself to be a devoted champion of Southern rights, and his manifestation of this spirit when brought to the test on this occasion, is worthy of notice.[40]

Many companies were already organized and had left the county to serve in the Confederate Army before secession was even approved. The first two companies from the county left on May 14 followed by a third company on May 17, 1861. But for the students at Randolph Macon College who were not already committed, they chose to finish out the semester through June 22, 1861. For some that were committed, their professors allowed them the privilege of completing their studies early before marching off to war in April, May, and June. Many students, and a couple of professors, returned to their hometowns to serve. But others chose to stay and continue their chosen paths of teaching or learning. Some of the professors believed they could better serve the Confederacy by continuing to teach the students. Some of the students believed they could be of more help by completing their education, more so than simply adding another body with a rifle to a company of men.

After the first companies left the county in May followed by a second wave of companies in June, the student population was low. The board of trustees met. On a motion by Colonel Townes, it was voted to suspend the fanfare of the commencement exercises for 1861. There was a simple ceremony held for the remaining graduates. One graduate was Benjamin J. Arnold of Mecklenburg County, the son of Solomon and Phoebe Arnold, born in June 1834. He married Keziah Arnold in 1855 (she was three years his senior), and they moved to the mountains in Wirt, Virginia. He had apparently attended RMC off and on over several years, but with a wife and two children, completing his prerequisites was a challenge.

In June 1860, about the same time as the birth of his third child, he completed his A.M. degree requisites. Following the birth of their fourth child in 1862, the family, residing in the mountains of Virginia, found themselves in the midst of a national turmoil. Soon, some of the mountain counties seceded and became West Virginia. He and his wife had two more children over the next two years, and it does not appear he served in the military during the Civil War. The 1870 Census records list the family with seven children living in Wirt, West Virginia. There is no occupation listed. In 1920, he was living with his son-in-law, Jared J. Hainal, in Parkersburg, West Virginia. He died there soon afterward.[41]

The June 28, 1861, *Tobacco Plant* published the "Randolph Macon College, Virginia" commencement for "June 27th 1861."

I. Students distinguished at the intermediate and final examinations.

(**Note) The figure #1 denotes the intermediate, and #2 the final examination.

Latin

Junior Class.—W.D. Adams, 2. J.D. Carter, 1, 2. W.M. Chalmers, 1, 2. A.J.

6. Pranksters to Professors—The New Regime 149

Davis, 1, 2. W.S. Dibrell, 2. O.A. Glazebrook, 1, 2. C.W. Jarrett, 1. R. Mitchell, 1. T.A. Perkins, 1.

Intermediate Class.—J.R. Barr, 1. A.B. Coleman, 1. R.R. Cobb, 1, 2. R.E. Dunn, 1, 2. W.H. Farrar, 1. C.A. Hamner, 1, 2. W.F. Jordan, 1, 2. J.A. Mckinsey, 1. E. Mitchell, 1. G. Penn, 1. F.A. Pinckard, 1. A.E. Richards, 1. D.J. Waller, 1. W.A. Wheatley, 1. W.N. Holt, 2.

Senior Class.—J.C. Mundy, 1. W.K. Woodson, 1.

Greek

Junior Class—J.D. Carter, 1, 2. A.J. Davis, 1, 2. W.S. Dibrell, 2. O.A. Glazebrook, 2. C.W. Hill, 1. W.F. Jordan, 1. E. Mitchell, 1. G. Penn, 1. F.A. Pinckard, 1. T.S. West, 1.

Int. Class.—A.B. Coleman, 1. K.R. Cobb, 1, 2. C.A. Hamner, 1, 2. W.A. Wheatley, 1. G.E. Butler, 1, 2.

Senior Class.—K.R. Cobb, 2. J.C. Mundy, 1.

Mathematics

Junior Class—P.H. Arnold, 1, 2. N.P. Boyd, 1. J.D. Carter, 1, 2. W.M. Chalmers, 2. A.J. Davis, 1. E.H. Estes, 1. W.N. Holt, 1. J.A. Hughes, 2. C.W. Jarrett, 1. G. Penn, 1. T.A. Pinckard, 1. W.A. Shepherd, 1. A. Talbot, 1, 2.

Int. Class.—W.A. Archer, 1. J.R. Barr, 2. T.M. Beckman, 1, 2. N.P. Boyd, 2. J.T. Brown, 1. K.R. Cobb, 2. A.B. Coleman, 2. B.A. Compton, 2. C.A. Hamner, 1, 2. W.A. Hightower, 1. J.B. Jordan, 1. P. Lockett, 1. J.E. Maxey, 2. J.C. Mundy, 1. W. Myrick, 2. H.B. Phillips, 1. H.H. Sneed, 1. R. Stainback, 2. A. Talbot, 1, 2. R.D. Thackston, 1.

Senior Class.—C.W. Hill, 1.

Chemistry and Natural Philosophy

A.E. Richards, 1.

Moral Philosophy

Junior Class.—J.T. Brown, 2
Senior Class.—W.A. Wheatley, 1.

French

Junior Class.—A.B. Coleman, 1. W.H. Farrar, 1. W.F. Jordan, 1. G. Penn, 1. T.S. West, 1.

German

Junior Class.—W.E. Edwards, 2. O.A. Glazebrook, 2. J.T. Gray, 2. R. Stainback, 2.

II. Proficients.

I. The Latin Language

Butler, George E.	Dallas Co., Ark.

II. Mechanics and Astronomy

Carter, William J.	Mecklenburg,

III. Minerology and Geology

Arnold, Benj. L.	Mecklenburg, Va.
Bailey, Robert W.	Amelia, "

Carter, William J.   Mecklenburg, "
Hawthorne, Benj. J.   "   "
Hutcheson, Jos. C.   "   "
Jones, Caius J.   Dinwiddie, "
Jones, James W.   Brunswick, "
Judkins, William H.   Southampton, "
Richards, Adolphus E.   Loudon, "
Styron, Oscar M.   Princess Anne, "
Walker, Robert   Madison, "
Ware, Jordan P.   Caroline, "
Watts, Wesley J.   Amherst, "
White, William W.   Southampton "
Williams, William S.   Rocheport, Mo.

IV. Political Economy and Slavery

Arnold, Benj. L.   Mecklenburg, Va.
Butler, George E.   Dallas Co., Ark.
Carter, William J.   Mecklenburg, Va.
Coleman, Samuel F.   Cumberland, "
Cowles, James R.   Petersburg, "
Hamner, Clifton A.   Halifax, "
Hawthorne, Benj. J.   Mecklenburg, "
Hutcheson, Jos. C.   "   "
Jones, Caius J.   Dinwiddie, "
Jones, James W.   Brunswick, "
Judkins, William H.   Southampton, "
Ray, George H.   R.M. College, "
Sneed, Henry H.   Mecklenburg, "
Styron, Oscar M.   Princess Anne, "
Ware, Jordan P.   Caroline, "
Watts, J. Wesley   Amherst, "
Wheatley, William A.   Memphis, Tenn.
White, William W.   Southampton, Va.
Wynne, Arthur L.   Richmond, "

V. Modern Languages

FRENCH

Bagby, Bennett W.   Powhatan, "
Barr, John R.   Richmond, "
Boyd, Nath'l P.   New Orleans, La.
Boyd, Robert A.   Mecklenburg, Va.
Brown, J. Thompson   Richmond, "
Coleman, Samuel F.   Cumberland, "
Dibrell, Watson   Chesterfield, "
Gee, Virginius O.   Mecklenburg, "
Glazebrook, Otis A.   Richmond, "
Goode, William E.   Charlotte, "
Hightower, Wm. A.   Halifax, "
Hill, Chandler W.   Norfolk, "

6. Pranksters to Professors—The New Regime   151

Lockett, Phillip	Mecklenburg, "
Merritt, John B.	Brunswick, "
Myrick, Walter	Greensville, "
Reed, James C.	Bedford, "
Reynolds, J. Stanley	Cumberland, "
Richardson, Wm. C.	Mecklenburg, "
Styron, Oscar M.	Princess Anne, "
Talbott, Allen	Richmond, "
Vaden, Wesley C.	Chesterfield, "
Waller, Dabney J.	Caroline, "
Ware, Jordan P.	" "

GERMAN

Arnold, Benj. L.	Mecklenburg, Va.
Vaden, Wesley C.	Chesterfield, "
Watts, J. Wesley	Amherst, "

SPANISH

Archer, William A.	Mecklenburg, Va.
Carter, William J.	" "
Coleman, A. Buford	Lunenburg, "
Dunn, Robert E.	Louisa, "
Harrison, Benj. G.	Norfolk, "
Hawthorne, Benj. J.	Mecklenburg, "
Holstead, Robert N.	Richmond, "
Hutcheson, Jos. C.	Mecklenburg, "
Jones, James W.	Brunswick, "
Judkins, William H.	Southampton, "
Richardson, Wm. C.	Mecklenburg, "
Sneed, Henry H.	" "
Vaden, Wesley C.	Chesterfield, "
White, William W.	Southampton, "

ITALIAN

Jones, Caius J.	Dinwiddie, "
Judkins, William H.	Southampton, "
Wynne, Arthur L.	Richmond, "

III. Graduates.
I. Ancient Languages

Archer, William A.	Mecklenburg, "
Ayres, John G.	Buckingham, "
Bailey, Robert A.	Amelia, "
Boyd, Robert A.	Mecklenburg, "
Coleman, Samuel F.	Cumberland, "
Compton, Robert A.	Mecklenburg, "
Gee, Virginius O.	" "
Hawthorne, Benj. J.	" "
Holstead, Robert N.	Richmond, "
Maxey, Joseph E.	Powhatan, "
Reed, James C.	Bedford, "

Reynolds, J. Stanley   Cumberland,   "
Richardson, Wm. C.   Mecklenburg,   "
Stainback, Robert   Brunswick,   "
Williams, William S.   Rocheport, Mo.

II. Mathematics

Ayres, John G.   Buckingham, Va.
Bailey, Robert W.   Amelia,   "
Boyd, Robert A.   Mecklenburg,   "
Butler, George E.   Dallas, Ark
Cowles, James R.   Petersburg, Va.
Gee, Virginius O.   Mecklenburg,   "
Hawthorne, Benj. J.   "   "
Holstead, Robert N.   Richmond,   "
Hutcheson, Joseph C.   Mecklenburg,   "
Jones, Caius J.   Dinwiddie,   "
Judkins, William H.   Southampton,   "
Richards, Adolphus E.   Loudoun,   "
Vaden, Wesley C.   Chesterfield,   "
Walker, Robert   Madison,   "
Ware, Jordan P.   Caroline,   "
Williams, William S.   Rocheport, Mo.
Wynne, Arthur L.   Richmond, Va.

III. Chemistry and Natural Philosophy

Archer, Wm. A.   Mecklenburg, Va.
Ayres, John G.   Buckingham,   "
Bailey, Robert W.   Amelia,   "
Beckham, Thos. M.   Fauquier,   "
Cobb, Kenneth R.   Elizabeth City, N.C.
Coleman, Samuel F.   Cumberland, Va.
Gee, Virginius O.   Mecklenburg,   "
Hutcheson, Joseph C.   "   "
Jones, Caius J.   Dinwiddie,   "
Jones, James W.   Brunswick,   "
Maxey, Joseph E.   Powhatan,   "
Myrick, Walter   Greensville,   "
Styron, Oscar M.   Princess Anne,   "
Vaden, Wesley C.   Chesterfield,   "
Watts, J. Wesley   Amherst,   "
White, William W.   Southampton,   "
Williams, William S.   Rocheport, Mo.
Wynne, Arthur L.   Richmond, Va.

IV. Moral Philosophy

Arnold, Benj. J.   Mecklenburg, Va.
Carter, William J.   "   "
Compton, Robert A.   "   "
Edwards, William E.   Lynchburg,   "

Hamner, Clifton A.	Halifax,	"
Hawthorne, Benj. J.	Mecklenburg,	"
Hutcheson, Joseph C.	"	"
Jones, Caius J.	Dinwiddie,	"
Jones, James W.	Brunswick,	"
Judkins, William H.	Southampton,	"
Ray, Rev. Geo. H.	Virginia Conference	
Styron, Oscar M.	Princess Anne, Va.	
Ware, Jordan P.	Caroline,	"
Watts, J. Wesley	Amherst,	"
White, William W.	Southampton,	"
Wynne, Arthur L.	Richmond,	"

V. Masters of Arts

Arnold, Benj. J.	Mecklenburg,	Va.
Carter, William J.	"	"
Hawthorne, Benj. J.	"	"
Hutcheson, Joseph C.	"	"
Jones, Caius J.	Dinwiddie,	"
Jones, James W.	Brunswick,	"
Judkins, William H.	Southampton,	"
Styron, Oscar M.	Princess Anne,	"
Vaden, Wesley C.	Chesterfield,	"
Ware, Jordan P.	Caroline,	"
Watts, J. Wesley	Amherst,	"
White, William W.	Southampton,	"
Wynne, Arthur L.	Richmond,	"

With this publication, the 1860–1861 academic year came to a close. Thirteen A.M. degrees were presented. A total of 145 diplomas were awarded to 71 students.[42] The college had completely revamped its curriculum and graduation and certification requirements in the summer of 1859, effective the college year 1859–1860. A certificate for the professors' use had been developed and was available in June 1860 and again in June, 1861. But it seems that the 1861 supply was short, and many of the students received a simple letter from their professor attesting to their completion and status (attested to by the records of Hawthorne at Oregon).

Continuing school seemed to be the sentiment of the Confederate Army as well as many of the students. On July 14, 1861, Professor Godfrey Staubley (age 38) of Randolph Macon College enlisted along with two or three students as privates in Company A, 3rd Virginia Cavalry. He was described as 5 feet, 10 inches tall, blue eyes and light colored hair. But on September 26, 1861, he was released from the 3rd Virginia for the good of the service so he could return to Randolph Macon College in time to begin the fall semester. Staubly was a deeply religious man and a believer in the Roman Catholic faith. Behind his home was a slave quarters, and he owned at least three slaves.

As a professor of modern languages, he believed he was ill equipped to teach at a military institute (which RMC became in 1862). He resigned in October 1862, and accepted a position with the Petersburg Female College. After relocating, Petersburg was continually under siege by several Union Army regiments. Staubly became a member of Company D, 4th Infantry Battalion, Petersburg Home Guard, defending the city. In June 1864, preceding the Battle of Stanton River Bridge, Union General Kautz headed for Petersburg. Upon arrival, a well-orchestrated campaign was begun to capture the city. During this June 1864 campaign, Staubly and a graduate of RMC, George B. Jones (A.B. 1841, A.M. 1844) were killed.

Williams T. Davis (February 6, 1817–1880) served as principal of the Preparatory Department and received his A.M. degree from RMC in 1848 (honorary). He became president of Petersburg Female College and was quite familiar with Randolph Macon faculty, students and board of trustees. He married Elizabeth Tayloe Corbin Beale, and they had at least five children. She died on January 21, 1851, at the age of 36. Following the death of his son in 1863, Davis resigned from Petersburg and moved to Danville. In 1863, he was president of the Danville Female College, replacing the Reverend Jamieson. His faculty included Professor the Rev. Wesley Childs Vaden, who had received an A.M. from RMC in 1861. The January 30, 1865, Petersburg newspaper listed an ad by President William T. Davis for students to come to Danville for their education, but he did not return for the fall term that year.[43]

Wesley Childs Vaden (or Vaiden, on the Methodist church records in Clarksville[44]), of Chesterfield, was born on August 23, 1841. His parents were Michael and Catherine Rowlett Vaden. He received his diplomas in chemistry and natural philosophy, French, German, mathematics, and Spanish. He was also awarded his A.M. degree in June 1861. During the war, he served as minister of the Clarksville Methodist Church and taught modern languages at the Clarksville Female Collegiate Institute until 1865. He married Sallie F. Sadler (most likely a graduate of Danville Female College), and they lived in Danville, where he was a professor at the female college teaching mathematics and natural science. Sallie was also serving as a mathematics instructor. In 1867, Vaden took over as president of the college,[45] a position he held for two years. Upon leaving he and his family went first to Farmville and then returned to the Richmond area, where he was preaching and teaching. In the 1880 census records,[46] he was a minister in Richmond, and he and Sallie had six children. In 1888, he was back to preaching and teaching in Farmville, Virginia, and in 1890, the family had relocated to Norfolk.

In 1893, his son, Wesley Carroll Vaden, was in Georgetown, Texas. He was there to replace Samuel G. Sanders, the son of Samuel D. Sanders (A.B. 1842, A.M. 1859), who had recently died of typhoid. Vaden served as professor of modern languages for Southwestern University for forty-four years, only one of two professors to serve that long.

In the *History of Southwestern University* by Dr. William Jones, Wesley Carroll Vaden was educated with a B.A. and an M.A. in the 1880s at Randolph-Macon College–Ashland, and after teaching in Virginia for a short period of time moved to Texas to replace Sanders. In 1897, he married Kate Lockett, the daughter of M.B. Lockett, a prominent local merchant who had played a significant role in Southwestern affairs. Vaden went on to pursue continuing education by completing postgraduate studies at Cornell in 1901 and Yale in 1905. When his obituary was written in 1937, he was described by John C. Granbery: "It is difficult for us to understand how he dwelt not in the moment, but in the ages. A few of us are able to take a peep into the world of classic literature, but he dwelt there, feeling perfectly at home."[47]

Six companies of men were quickly raised in Mecklenburg County, with three departing in May for training, followed by the other three in June. A plea was sent out by the governor to the counties in Virginia to secure blacks, freemen or slaves, to work on the fortifications at Norfolk. D.B. Cogbill wrote to Governor Letcher on June 21 that he had "collected and will start tomorrow for Norfolk with about 20 free negroes and on Saturday with probably 50 more."[48]

The actions and methods used by Cogbill to collect the free Negroes "raised the ire of some citizens of Mecklenburg County." On June 26, John C. Blackwell, on behalf of the RMC board, reported to Governor Letcher that Cogbill was "pressing the free negroes of this vicinity into the service of the Commonwealth by the most violent means, under what he pretends to be an order from you through one of your aides, Col. Bassett French ... seizing and handcuffing or binding in some other way every free colored man who will not consent to go to Norfolk to labor for the state. Already about 150 have been sent off ... torn from their families, in the most violent way, leaving their crop without a cultivator and their families to charity or starvation."[49]

This was followed on July 11, 1861, by another letter to the governor from Professor William B. Carr. This letter contained a list of the free blacks at Norfolk that should be "reviewed with the consideration of perhaps letting them return home as they had left helpless families. It is reputed and believed here that they went away under the influence of threats on the part of Mr. Cogbill that he would carry either them or their heads or that if they did not go they would be sold as slaves or driven from the state."[50]

Following the war, Benjamin D. Cogbill (b. 1813), his wife, Harriett R. (b. 1825), and their five daughters and son (Mary F., b. 1857; Lilia C., b. 1858; Laura, b. 1860; Virginia, b. 1862; Bettie W., b. 1863; and Benjamin E., b. 1864), are listed in the 1870 Census records as having made their home in Boydton. Benjamin was working as a lawyer and was elected as a justice of the peace.

Hopefully, modeled in a similar fashion to that of Capers in South Carolina in the 1820s, the RMC Board of Trustees had seen fit to begin a segregated program of divinity for the blacks of the circuit. At the 1860 conference meeting, there are no minutes of discussion, nor of motions, but J.D. Southall was appointed in charge of colored missions. Although the archives of the Virginia M.E., South, and R-MC–Ashland are devoid of any descriptions of works undertaken, smatterings of references throughout the recorded histories indicate that the chapel at RMC, and many of the circuit churches, were constructed with galleries for the blacks. Virginia Haskins Bugg writes in 1934 that Rehoboth M.E., South, Church "is about five miles from the old Randolph-Macon College at Boydton, and during the time the college was located there the church was pastored largely by senior theological students, who preached to both whites and blacks, there being ample gallery space provided for the slaves."[51]

Chapter 7

The Military Institute and Those War Years

Professor Bennett Puryear (b. 1826) enlisted in Company A, 3rd Virginia Cavalry, as an experienced horseman in 1861. No rank is indicated, nor additional information provided. The next record is the surrender of General Robert E. Lee at Appomattox on April 9, 1865. Professor Private Bennett Puryear is listed as being in attendance with Company E, 14th Virginia Infantry Regiment, during the surrender, but no information is found on the discharge form. There are no other records of his involvement in the war, not even with the militia.[1] Fortunately for Professor Puryear, during the surrender at Appomattox, a printing press was brought in, and on April 10 and 11, 1865, thousands of passes were printed. "Under the surrender agreement, Confederate officers submitted muster rolls of their units and signed a parole before issuing the passes to their men." Following Appomattox, it was very important under military rule to have a surrender (prisoner of war oath of allegiance) "pass." If a man of military age or known military involvement did not have a pass in his possession, he could be arrested and imprisoned.[2]

The oath of allegiance was soon to become one of the most controversial components of the surrender. Soldiers were required to sign the oath or be arrested. Within a week, the oath had become required of anyone that any officer of the U.S. military thought might not be a loyal citizen. It became an issue of leverage to be used against those in politics favorable to the Confederacy. On May 5, 1865, a dispatch was sent from "General Hallock, from Richmond, to General Grant.... All classes are taking the Amnesty Oath; ... Lee's officers are taking the oath; even Lee himself is considering the propriety of doing so." The issue for Southerners was that they surrendered and admitted defeat. Why was a piece of paper necessary for them to make a pledge? And in many situations the piece of paper could be required multiple times by multiple people.[3]

Wootton oath (courtesy Virginia Woody Wright).

Referred to as the "oath," in actuality, it was General Order No. 4, April 29, 1865, signed by General Halleck. It basically outlined things that people could not do unless they signed the oath. Even with signing there was also a list of things that people could still not do. One of those was the "Button Order." No one could wear a Confederate button (put that in perspective of returning, defeated, and penniless southern Confederate soldiers). Another was the "Marriage Order," which stated that no one could marry until they signed an oath, even though many had been waiting for years for their fiancé to return home from the war. Other provisions included "no clergyman, magistrate or other party authorized by state laws to perform the marriage ceremony will officiate … until himself … shall have taken the prescribed oath, all under pains of imprisonment, etc."[4]

In addition to the oath, officers and plantation gentry were punished by having to make a second trip to the provost marshal assigned to the county seat and swear that they had, in fact, freed their slaves, whereupon they would then have to complete an application to be sent to President Johnson requesting that they receive a parole for their crimes.

The concept and utilization of an oath was not new in the United States. Oaths were a constitutional requirement in Missouri beginning in 1864. "No person shall practice law, be competent as bishop, priest, deacon, minister, elder or other clergyman of any persuasion, sect, or denomination, teach, preach or solemnise marriage until such person shall have taken, the oath required as to voters." Without signing the oath, southerners and those having southern sympathy were disenfranchised and excluded from public office. Preachers who did not sign the oath and continued to preach or perform marriages, "were condemned to work on the public roads and other degrading forms of expiation."[5] The Missouri law applied equally to blacks and whites, but not so of the federally mandated general order.

In the spring of 1862, Randolph Macon College was granted permission by the Virginia Legislature to establish a school of military tactics and ordnance. The board of trustees passed a resolution that established William A. Smith, colonel and commandant, moral science and philosophy; J.E. Blankenship, major, military tactics, math and history; Bennett Puryear, captain, professor of chemistry; William A. Carr, captain, professor of ancient languages; and G. Staubley, captain, professor of modern languages.[6]

In June 1862 Randolph Macon College had three A.B. graduates and six A.M. graduates. In June 1863 there were three A.M. graduates. According to Irby, the graduates of 1862 were[7] William E. Edwards, A.B. (later a D.D., after the war); B.L. Arnold, A.B. (who entered Epes Company, Heavy Artillery; this is most likely Benjamin W., A.M., 1860); R.A. Compton, A.B., of Virginia; William A. Archer, A.M., of Virginia; J. (George) E. Butler, A.M., of Arkansas; John D. Blackwell, A.M., of Virginia; William S. Williams, A.M., Rocheport, Missouri; Robert S. Isbell, A.M., of Virginia; and William G. Starr, A.M., of Virginia.

Following the war, Richmond College reopened in the fall of 1866. Professor Puryear accepted a position and relocated his family to Richmond. There, he was appointed chairman of the chemistry department until his retirement in 1895. He was also, at times, chairman of the faculty and the chief academic officer of the college (referred to today as dean). When there was no president of the college, he would be in charge of operations. He was described as "very tall and striking in appearance, possessed of a strong personality and a gift for teaching and administrative ability."[8] The August 2, 1878, *Roanoke Valley* published in the social column, "Mr. Bennett Puryear, LL.D., President of Richmond College and family are rusticating in town."[9]

The 1910 Census record shows Bennett Puryear as age 83, a farmer, and his wife, Ella M., age 60. Living with them is their oldest son, Frank, age 43, a college instructor, Virginia C. Puryear, daughter, age 39, and Lucy L. Wiles (Wyles), a sister-in-law. They no longer had the servants and it would appear Sallie had married and left home. (Of Charlie, well that's another story to come later.) The chemistry building at University of Richmond was named in his honor in 1944. He and his wife died at their home, Edgewood, in Madison County, Virginia. He is listed in the *Dictionary of American Biography*[10] as an educator and publicist who was a pioneer in applying chemistry to farming. (Several of his notes, journals and miscellaneous documents are located within the Virginia Baptist Historical Society Archives at the University of Richmond.)

Professor Robert T. Massie (b. 1826) stayed on at Randolph Macon College. But on May 6, 1862, Massie was commissioned captain, Company E, 14th Virginia Infantry. When the school year was over he resigned his commission and moved to Richmond. He was replaced at RMC by Professor Lewis Turner, but Turner resigned in December. In Richmond, Massie accepted a position with the Confederate government. He was appointed to the engineers as a first lieutenant, where he served until the end of the war.[11] Afterward he relocated to South Carolina and accepted the position of president of South Carolina College.

A story about him appeared in the *Roanoke Valley* by William Townes, Jr., on December 30, 1871. It seems that Massie had learned a great deal of temperament from Dr. Smith. When Massie assumed the presidency in South Carolina, some of the students decided to pull a prank on him. They planned to pull his carriage into the woods and hide it. Learning of the prank, Massie hid in his carriage, and the students came. It was a misty evening, but they pulled the carriage down the hill, across a creek, and into the woods. Being satisfied with their efforts, they were readying to remove the wheels, when President Massie emerged from the carriage floor. He thanked the young men for the ride but told them he really must be getting home, and they should return him and his carriage to the carriage house. Back at the carriage house, President Massie stated, "Thank you young gentlemen—good night."[12]

Professor Puryear's laboratory assistant, Professor William A. Shep-

Sketch of William G. Starr (sketch incorrectly identified him as William "R"), an 1862 graduate (illustrated for the author by the late Arlene McKinney Wootton, from an original sketch found in a scrapbook, dated 1899, of drawings from papers and magazines of famous persons, collected by Nannie Flannigan) (found in a trash dumpster by Posie Hugh Lankford and given to the author).

ard, was born in Dorchester, Massachusetts, in 1833. He attended Yale University in 1854, and then transferred to Randolph Macon. He graduated with his A.B. degree from RMC in June 1857, and his A.M. degree in June 1860. On September 3, 1858, he was appointed assistant professor of ancient languages, math and French. (Students had to pay an extra fee of $5 to take French.) He was appointed to the RMC Board of Trustees and was elected secretary to the board in 1859. Also in 1859, he was on the committee with Dr. Smith, Professor Wills, Carr and Puryear to write the new guidelines for the college.

When the war began he enlisted in Petersburg on July 22, 1861, into Company E, 12th Virginia Infantry, as a private. He was wounded in action at Chancellorsville on May 3, 1863. Following discharge from the hospital, he was detailed to the 12th Infantry Commissary Department. He was dropped from the rolls for disability and then appointed as a major in the Confederate quartermaster department.[13] He was assigned to the Commissary Department at Weldon, N.C., where the Roanoke River met the railroad, under the command of Brigadier General A.R. Lawton. This was the clearinghouse for quartermaster and commissaries along the Roanoke River, including the ones located at St. Tammany, RMC, Taylor's Ferry and Clarksville Ordnance.

He met and married Mattie (Martha Emma) Davis, daughter of Williams T. Davis, a former colleague from Randolph Macon College. Davis was in charge of the Boydton Preparatory Department in 1849, having received his honorary A.M. degree from RMC in 1848. Davis became president of Southern Female College in Petersburg but maintained contact with RMC, hiring two graduates as faculty and one former RMC professor. Following the death of his son in Petersburg, Davis resigned from the college and took the position as president of the Danville Female College, where he remained for two years. Following the attack on Petersburg, with two faculty killed, in 1864, the Southern Female College closed.

Following the war, Shepard accepted a faculty position with Southern Female College when it reopened and was serving as a Methodist lay leader and Sunday school superintendent. Subsequently, he was offered and accepted a position with Randolph-Macon College–Ashland. He served as professor of chemistry from 1870 to 1895.[14] He died June 3, 1895, and is buried in Blanford Cemetery, Ashland. Many of his notes and papers are in the R-MC-Ashland Archives.

Professor Captain William Brown Carr (b. February 4, 1820; A.M.) lived in the Language Professor's house. He was from northern Virginia, Leesburg, and began teaching at Warren Green Academy in Virginia in 1841. From there, he went to New Lisbon Institute in Virginia.[15] In 1854, he arrived at Randolph Macon College as professor of ancient languages with his new bride, Panthea (b. 1825). In 1858, their son, William Carr, Jr., was born on campus. They all seemed to have found a home until war's end. Behind his home were a smoke house, stable, store house and his slave quarters; he owned at least three slaves.

In 1862, he, along with Professor Puryear, rented the college hotel building from the board of trustees to operate a "Classical School." On September 14, 1864, a special board meeting was called at RMC to discuss requests from Puryear for supplies and the use of a blackboard.[16] The requests were granted by the local board of trustees members who were in attendance. On August 15, 1865, the RMC Board of Trustees met and passed a resolution declaring all professors' chairs were vacant. Four new professors were hired in 1866, with none of the existing being reinstated.

Carr accepted the position of president of the Petersburg Female College in 1866. After settling in to his new position, he sent a letter in 1867 to the RMC Board of Trustees requesting reimbursement for his personal expenses involved in building his servants' quarters.[17] From 1866 to 1879, he taught at Petersburg, Wesleyan Female College in North Carolina, and Madison Female College in Georgia. In 1880, he was teaching in Loudoun, Virginia, and as a widower was living with his daughter, her husband and two small children—the Saunders family. In 1900, the U.S. Census[18] has him listed as living with his son and family in Washington, D.C., and retired at the age of 80. His son was William P. Carr, M.D., age 42 (who had been born at RMC), and William's wife was Georgia R., age 34, from Texas. One of the grandchildren was William B. Carr, age 15.[19] His primary publications included two books: one an English textbook and the other a family genealogy.

The stage lines were still operational and the Clarksville to Boydton Plank Road still viable. In January 1862, the General Assembly approved Randolph Macon College as a military institute and ordnance location. A commissary was established there, and possibly some ordnance, but I did not find documentation for the latter. The college and lodge were very busy places. At least one company of Confederate cavalry stayed there for a short time in 1864, and another, in early 1865. They drew supplies while there.

Professor James Edwin Blankenship (b. January 1835) replaced Professor Turner and had been teaching math and history. But with the approval for a military department, he was selected for the position of professor of math and military tactics in 1862. Blankenship had graduated from the Virginia Military Institute "and said he was 1st in his class." Before the war began, he was working for Coastal Survey. On April 19, 1861, he enlisted as a captain into Company E, 11th Virginia Infantry. On August 25, 1861, he resigned from the military, citing ill health,[20] but moved to Boydton and began teaching at Randolph Macon. As the school continued to flounder during the war, in April 1863, Professor Blankenship petitioned the Confederate government for an appointment as a field service engineer. He attempted a second effort in February 1864, but both requests were denied. Following the war, Blankenship was principal, "with a full corps of teachers," of the Mecklenburg Female College. The college only lasted five years before closing due to financial and enrollment difficulties.

Blankenship then moved to Ansonville, North Carolina, where he became principal of another female academy in 1877. On March 21, 1878, he married Margaret "Maggie" Whitney and together they had four children. In 1885, he was principal of Belleville High School and examiner for the Danville District in Arkansas. In 1900, he was listed on the census records,[21] as a professor at the Chickasaw Nation Indian Territory and was still in Johnson County, Oklahoma, in 1910.[22]

At RMC, Blankenship owned four slaves. He established the military department which included uniforms. (This would have given Mary Bugg and her mother Frances work, as well as a fairly new business in town, Duggar and Gary Tailor Shop.) James B. Dugger (Jr., b. 1836; A.B. 1855, RMC) appears to have joined his older cousin's business. On November 16, 1861, he wrote a receipt to William N. Carter (b. 1834; A.B. 1855, RMC) for "alterations on a new suit, 3 yards of material, one roll of tape and a vest" for a total of $11.06.[23] Later, Dugger enlisted for a year at Richmond into the 1st Battalion Virginia Infantry, "Irish Battalion."

The uniform for a college cadet consisted of a frock coat of cadet gray cloth, white pantaloons, with white gloves, a white belt with brass buckle and a black stock. The cadets were served military rations just like the soldiers (when the soldiers got them) but many of the students were disgruntled.

The Rev. Major William Henry Wheelwright graduated from V.M.I. in 1845. He was born July 23, 1824, in Westmoreland County and, following his graduation, was working as a teacher and preacher. In 1858, he was serving as presiding elder of Providence Church, replacing James A. Riddick, who had served in that capacity since 1854. He married Margaret Kerfoot and they had several children. On July 1, 1861, he enlisted into the 26th Virginia Infantry Division, where he was established as a major in the Confederate field and staff. On May 13, 1862, he was relieved of his command. He came to Randolph Macon that fall as the new professor of military tactics (and most likely College chaplain, replacing Blackwell in March 1864). On October 29, 1864, he reenlisted into Company H, 9th Virginia Cavalry, and was appointed chaplain. He served in this capacity until paroled at Blacks and Whites on April 17, 1865. Following the war, the family went to Warren County to Margaret's family plantation, which they had apparently inherited. On February 19, 1866, their son, Thomas Stuart Wheelwright, was born and would later attend R-MC-Ashland. William died on December 17, 1879, in Warren County, Virginia.

In the fall of 1862, only twenty students arrived for school, but slowly the number grew to forty-four. With the Conscription Act of 1862, 22 students were drafted and had to leave college. The medical and law departments were vacated. Early in 1862, Joseph Wootton's wife died. They had no children. So distraught over her death, Joseph left the farm (and his farmers' exemption from military service) and enlisted into Company G, 2nd Regiment, Virginia Artillery, as a private for one year.[24] He returned home on leave in December and purchased "one negro man Isham and girl Elizabeth on 13 Dec 62" from his brother John W. for $2,680. He returned home again, and on July 1, 1863, Joseph L. Wootton and Martha Bedford Jeffress were married. She was "the girl next door" and had attended Hollis College.[25] She was the daughter of James Hamlet Jeffress and Nancey Bedford Mosely Jeffress, who owned the 1,500 acre plantation to the northwest adjoining Joseph (present day Finchley). They had five surviving children.

Receipts suggest life as normal: buggy repairs in Clarksville, banking at the Exchange Bank, etc., but there are also war receipts of "181 lbs. bacon for 1864 war tax" paid on "Feb. 3, 1865" to "Cpt A. Kinney, ACS," "July 2, 1865 Cpt. ACS E.A. Williams of Joseph L. Wootton 6 gal. molasses war tax," and on "Dec 31, 1865 Rec of Jos L. Wootton war tax 330 lbs of beef, 1st rate exemption as a farmer." Even though the war was over and the county was under military rule, the exempted farmers were still paying their ransomed share of taxes as much as eight months later. These receipts were for farming proceeds "December 22, 1865 tax on meat cattle to state for State Collections Dist. #17 of D.N. Carter $9.20."[26]

What is most interesting is that Kinney and Williams were Confederate officers of the Clarksville Ordnance and Munitions Company, not Union soldiers. For John W., Joseph L. and D.N. Carter, there are six more receipts for taxes imposed by the State or CSA over an eighteen month period following April 1865. In 1869, John W. Wootton was appointed road commissioner for the Boydton district by the presiding tribunal.

When the Union armies were in Boydton, many of the soldiers, stragglers, and "bummers" were constantly roaming the county to steal any and all contraband they could. Joseph and Martha's granddaughter wrote a story in the *Clarksville Times* during the 1970s that Martha had taken their valuables into the garden and buried them to keep them from being stolen. When Joseph died on December 28, 1887, Martha was described as "a sad widow, not old, who sat by the open fire and who told us bedtime stories and sang us wholesome ballads, such as 'Billy Boy,' 'Willie Blye,' 'I Give you a Dress All Red, Bound All Around in Golden Thread,' 'A Bright Gazelle with Silver Feet, I'll Give to You for a Playmate Sweet.'"[27]

On February 5, 1863, the board of trustees met and discussed suspending operation of the college. The school was in some form of operation during most of the war and subsequently hosted a scholarship fund supported by Colonel Charles Sterling Hutcheson. Colonel Hutcheson married Nancy J. Wootton, daughter of Samuel Wootton, Sr., and sister of John P. Wootton on February 18, 1818. Hutcheson served in the Virginia House of Delegates from 1843 to 1844, was presiding justice of the county through the war until 1865, and served on the RMC Board of Trustees for many years until the relocation to Ashland.

One of the students attending the college on Colonel Charles Sterling Hutcheson's scholarship (in honor of his son, Joseph Valentine Hutcheson, d. 1863) was Joseph Norfleet Wootton (b.1850), son of John W., who attended from 1866 to 1867, registered and paid his fee in February 1868, and was scheduled to begin RMC studies in October 1868. His first cousin, P.(owell) S.(wet) Wootton (b. 1849), son of John T. and Indiana E. Rogers, had also attended RMC from 1865 to 1866, with Dr. Smith, at the age of sixteen. But with the abrupt move to Ashland, Judge Hutcheson, P.S. Wootton and Joseph Wootton chose to stay in Boydton.

In the spring of 1869, John C. Wootton died, and his 577 acre estate was put up for public auction on November 10, 1869. Also, during the war, John W.'s oldest daughter, Annie N., had been attending Oxford Baptist Female Academy. John W. was paying for her education with bacon and other farm produce. In 1869, John W. built a two room schoolhouse in the front yard, next to Plank Road, and Annie began Lofty Oaks Academy.

In 1870, John T. Wootton donated two acres of land on the old Courthouse Road to build Fields Community Methodist Church. In 1884, Joseph N. Wootton and his younger brother, A.J. (Andrew Jackson) Wootton began *The Chase City Clipper* newspaper. Joseph also established an insurance agency. In 1886, they moved their newspaper and insurance agency to Clarksville. In 1890, N.J. was investing in a thoroughbred race horse.

Judge Hutcheson had two sons by his first wife before she died. Marrying for a second time, he and his wife, Mary Mitchell, had one son, Joseph Valentine Hutcheson. All three of his sons attended Randolph Macon College and served in the Confederate Army.

John Wootton farmhouse, slave quarters and Lofty Oaks, c. 1850. In the right bottom corner would have been the Lofty Oaks schoolhouse, followed by the servants' quarters, stable and barn, and to the center, the family home (courtesy Virginia Woody Wright).

Captain John William Hutcheson had attended RMC but transferred to the University of Virginia and graduated from law school there. In 1850, John had accused an RMC professor of favoring another student. With his father serving on the board of trustees, John offered a formal apology to the professor. In fact, the student that was allegedly being favored became the valedictorian. Following law school, John moved to Anderson, Texas, to establish a law practice. When Texas seceded, he formed a company of Texas volunteers. At his own expense he equipped the men, trained them, and then had them transported to Virginia to aid in the fighting. Captain Hutcheson's volunteers were established as Company G, 14th Texas Infantry. He was killed in action at Cold Harbor on June 2, 1864.[28]

Joseph Cabell Hutcheson completed his proficients in mineralogy and geology, political economy and slavery, Spanish, mathematics, chemistry and natural philosophy at RMC in 1861. He also completed a proficient in moral philosophy and completed his law studies, receiving his M.A. degree from RMC the same year. Following graduation, he married Mildred Carrington in Boydton on October 14, 1864, and then enlisted as a private into Company

C, 21st Virginia Infantry, that same day at Camp Lee, Virginia. He transferred to Company E, 14th Infantry, the Boydton Company, on October 22, 1864. He was elected a second lieutenant on November 8, 1864. For distinguished courage and fidelity he was promoted to first lieutenant following the Battle of Dinwiddie Court House. At Appomattox, he surrendered on April 9, 1865.[29]

Following the war, he and Mildred moved to Gaines County, Texas, and established a law practice in Houston. The August 20, 1878, *Roanoke Valley* reported that "Captain Hutcheson from Texas had visited town."[30] He and Mildred had eight children, but she died young in 1882. He then married Harriett Elizabeth Palmer Millby on August 11, 1886. He served in the Texas legislature from 1874, and in 1880, he became chairman of the State Democratic Convention. In 1890, he was elected to serve as a United States congressman for the 53rd and 54th Congresses, but declined to run again after the last term.

The third son, first by Charles' second marriage, was Joseph Valentine Hutcheson, a student at RMC. At the end of the school year, he enlisted into Company C, 21st Infantry, at Christiansville as a private.[31] He was born in either 1843 or 1844 (two records, two dates). At some point after May 6, 1862, he transferred to Company A, 3rd Virginia Cavalry. He was absent sick on September 10, 1862, but returned to duty.[32] The next record indicates he died of disease in 1863, and his mother filed an application with the Confederate government and received his last pay.[33]

Officially, the college closed to students on March 19, 1864, and there was already discussion among the board of trustees about relocating, but no action was taken. The college reopened in August 1865. The fall of 1865 semester had nearly 50 students. Dr. Smith persevered, alone, until June 1866, when many of the student body were "prep" students (ages 14 and 15), with most of them attending on scholarships. On July 11, 1866, in Mecklenburg County, Virginia, the Rev. Nelson Head of Forksville, Virginia, and the Rev. John C. Granbery of Richmond took an oath and were recorded as new trustees of Randolph Macon College.[34]

Dr. Smith felt himself too old to continue with college operations with such young men. He delivered his resignation, and it was accepted. His long time handyman, boarder and friend, John Wesley Bugg, had returned home from the war. Preparations were made and packing begun for Dr. Smith's long journey to move to Missouri. To show his friendship and gratitude to Bugg, Dr. Smith gave him his mantle clock. The clock remained in the Bugg family for over 100 years until his granddaughter, Sarah Leona (Bugg) Ingram donated it to R-MC–Ashland. It remains there in the president's office.

John Bugg was subsequently elected constable of Christiansville on May

14, 1870. He was known by family and friends to boast that he had attended Randolph Macon College longer than any student ever did, but he had no degree to show for it. He served for several years as constable and was then elected magistrate for the newly (1873) formed Chase City (formerly Christiansville). He served in this position and as a county coroner for twelve uninterrupted years. He was also a widely respected auctioneer. Bugg died on November 12, 1903, at age 67. He had suffered a severe stroke resulting in paralysis. The Tobacco Board of Trade adopted a resolution in his honor to be published in the local newspaper. He and his wife had five sons and three daughters.[35]

The board of trustees was having difficulty with hiring a new president. In the interim, Professor John C. Blackwell was appointed as acting president and professor of moral philosophy. Subsequently, the board hired Colonel Thomas Carter Johnson, the first A.B. alumnus of the college, as president. Johnson was born near Lynchburg, Virginia, on March 22, 1820. He received an A.B. degree (highest honors) from RMC in 1842, and that year married Martha R. Scott, daughter of H.B. Scott of Nelson County, Virginia. Johnson became professor of natural science and math at the Female Collegiate Institute in Buckingham County.

Following completion of his A.M. degree and law studies in 1847, Johnson and his family moved to Washington County, Missouri, around 1848 to be closer to his wife's family, who had recently relocated there from Virginia. There, he took a classical position in teaching until he could secure his license to practice law. In June 1849, there was a cholera epidemic and his wife, son and daughter died. In 1849, Johnson spearheaded a successful campaign to have legislation introduced that would establish the Iron Mountain Railroad. In 1850, he was then elected to the Missouri legislature and moved to St. Louis in 1851. There, he became a land agent and attorney for the Union Pacific Railroad and became very successful in representing the railroad's interests.

In 1853, he married Pattie B. Scott, daughter of the Rev. Robert Scott of the Virginia Conference, and they returned to St. Louis. In 1858, he was elected to serve in the Missouri Senate (serving on several committees, including the Committee on Federal Relations), a position he held until 1861. Also in 1858, the Rev. Thomas Johnson was appointed by the St. Louis M.E. Conference as a member of the board of curators for the Missouri Normal School (which became Central College following the war).[36] Due to Dr. William A. Smith's poor health when he accepted the presidency of Central College, he was guaranteed the full support of the board to assist with whatever he needed. It has been written by one historian, Becker (Virginia M.E.

Conference), that when Johnson left RMC after resigning in 1868, he was en route to Missouri to assume the presidency of Central.[37] This is plausible, as Johnson did make a fundraising trip to St. Louis in late spring of 1867 (at which time he could have met with his old acquaintances about their plans for Central—after all, he most likely was still on the board) on behalf of RMC. Dr. Smith left Central following the 1868–1869 school year, suggesting his health was rapidly declining, and went to Richmond where he died.

With the failure of the Peace Conference, the rejection of the Crittenden Compromise, and the secession of Virginia, Johnson resigned from the Senate and became an aide to General Sterling Price. In 1863, he brought to the attention of the Confederate government in Richmond that poor transportation was causing many difficulties. He was transferred to Columbus, Georgia, and established as a lieutenant colonel in the 19th Georgia Infantry with a special detachment to the Confederate General and Staff, Quartermaster Department, in charge of transportation. His primary mission was to build a railroad system to be used by the Confederacy and to insure it stayed in operation. He succeeded in establishing one of the best arranged, most extensive, and complete machine shops in the Confederacy.

After the war, he moved his family to Montgomery, Alabama, and began a new law practice, in part working with the regional railroad. To fill the position of president, replacing Dr. Smith, board members Bishop H.N. McTyeire (A.B. 1844) and J.F. Dowdell (A.B. 1840), both in Alabama at the time, nominated Johnson. He accepted and, in late 1866, moved his family to Boydton. He then had published, almost every week, from January 1867 through January 1868, an advertisement in the *Tobacco Plant* which read as follows (simply copied each week for over 8 months before being changed, primarily because Johnson was out of town fund-raising):

> RANDOLPH MACON COLLEGE, VA.,
> In full operation
> This TIME HONORED INSTITUTION IS once more in successful operation with a FULL CORPS OF PROFESSORS. The chairs of the several schools are filled by able and experienced men. There are five literary and scientific schools, vis: OF ANCIENT LANGUAGES, MATHEMATICS, CHEMISTRY AND NATURAL PHILOSOPHY, MORAL PHILOSOPHY AND MODERN Languages. In addition to the above, the Board of Trustees have established a school of COMMERCIAL SCIENCE, with the view of giving the young men of the country a BUSINESS EDUCATION.
> To graduates in all these schools, Diplomas are granted, and the Degrees of Bachelor of Arts and Master of Arts are conferred upon students who accomplish a certain course. The high grade of scholarship formerly required is still maintained. We are a full CHEMICAL and PHILOSOPHICAL APPARATUS for the illustrations of the subjects taught.
> The location of the College is unsurpassed for health and geniality. It is situ-

ated midway between the mountains and the seaboard; and during a career of thirty-three years, and with thousands of young men in attendance, there has never been a death arising from malaria or other local cause. We profess to educate young men not only mentally and morally but physically also.

BOARD IS SIXTEEN DOLLARS PER MONTH. Tuition is from $40 to $90, according to the number of schools attended. $250 will cover expenses of board, tickets for three schools, matriculation and contingent fees for ten months.

The location of the College is Boydton, the county seat of Mecklenburg County, Virginia.

Arrangements are made to transport students from Ridgeway Depot, on the Raleigh Railroad, whilst a train leaves the Roanoke Station, on the Richmond and Danville Railroad on Mondays, Wednesdays and Fridays and from the Wolf Trap Depot on the same line on Tuesdays, Thursdays and Saturdays.

We solicit a liberal patronage from Maryland, Virginia and North Carolina, from the West, South and Southwest.

Students will be received at any time. The second term will commence on the 6th February, next. Young men will be received and prepared for the College proper. For further particulars address the undersigned at Boydton, Mecklenburg County, Va.

Thomas C. Johnson
President R.M. College[38]

Following the war, medals were a new fad among college students in the U.S. and as part of the attraction to veterans organizations (similar to what happened following the Revolutionary War) that were beginning to organize. Johnson, as a fundraiser for the college, designed and had prototypes made for at least two different medals in the late spring of 1867. The day before the graduation exercises, on June 25, 1868, the Rev. John S. Long, of the Virginia Conference, returned the prototypes to President Johnson. (Could that have been the signal that his job was done?) All faculty submitted their letters of resignation.

With steps having been taken to remove the college from Boydton, on July 30, 1868, Johnson offered his letter of resignation and the board accepted it. Johnson was moving his family back to St. Louis, when on August 8, 1868, in Indiana, he fell between two train cars and his back and leg were crushed. He died some hours later of his injuries but not before he was able to dictate his legal argument to another passenger, to write down as a last rite. It was his position that the railroad was at fault and negligent, therefore, his family should be compensated.

Oh, yes—what about "Little" Charlie Puryear who was born on campus? Well, it seems Charles (October 21, 1860–July 13, 1940), the second born on campus to Bennett Puryear, received a master of arts degree from University of Richmond in 1888 and accepted a teaching position with the University of Michigan in the math department. In 1889, he was offered the position of associate professor of civil engineering and physics at the Agricultural and Mechanical College of Texas. From 1890 to 1930, he was professor of math at Texas A&M. He also served as the first dean of the college from 1907 to 1930 and on two occasions served as president pro tem. He was forced into retirement due to a stroke in 1930. In 1932, he was named dean emeritus by Texas A&M.

During college, Charles taught math in public school during the summers, and played football and baseball for the college. He attended workshops and continuing education through Harvard, Penn and Columbia. During his first year teaching at Texas, he began a tennis team. Like most Puryears he was also an accomplished horseman and was seen often riding about the Texas prairie. He was also an accomplished chess player. He became the Texas A&M football team manager in 1902. The same year, his first textbook, *The Elements of Plane and Spherical Trigonometry*, was published by Thomas V. Taylor. He became the first college dean in 1907, and a new student, all male, residence hall—Puryear Hall—was named in his honor (torn down in 1996). In addition to all his duties, in 1924, he organized and became the first dean of the graduate school. The pressures finally overtook him, and he suffered a stroke in 1930. He had built his own home on campus, and in 1930, sold it to a new professor, Paul C. Mangelsdorf and family, but continued to live there as a boarder until his death in 1940. He never married.[39]

In 1830, the population of Boydton was fewer than 200 people. A marketing ad in 1836 indicated the town had 76 dwellings with a population of nearly 400 with several establishments (two of the nine being part of the college). Richard Irby (b. 1825; A.B. 1844, RMC) was appointed to the board of trustees in 1858. Following his service in the war, he became recording treasurer and secretary, and was later declared historian for the board. In 1898 he published his book on the *History of Randolph Macon College* through 1897. On page 151, he writes, "In 1860 the college, perhaps, had attained the climax of its ante-bellum prosperity. It had met difficulties and conquered them. It had grown and developed into commanding importance."[40]

With this as a backdrop, in 1865, he was one of the leaders in suggesting the move to Ashland, and in 1868, one of the four investors in the new property at Ashland. The newspaper stories from 1868 to 1870 reveal a great sense of disdain and abandonment by the people of Boydton. There was a brief ray of hope when a letter to the editor in the *Tobacco Plant* stated in May 10, 1867, that the writer had it on good source that "Gen. Howard has ordered the damages done to the buildings, by the Yankees and the negroes, to be repaired, and I have no doubt the efforts that are being made to resuscitate the Old Institution will be successful."[41] But hope soon faded, as this did not happen.

Randolph Macon had been portrayed as a college with faculty and students, but even in Irby's words, it was much more. It served as the only Methodist Church in Boydton with sermons, studies and lectures given by some of the leading scholars of the time. The college graduated or entertained United States senators and congressmen along with a lecture visit from at least one president of the United States. To the community it served as a beacon and a role model, provided a philosophy to the citizens (Methodists and otherwise), unified the philosophy of the political environment in the community, and touched the lives of each individual in culture, morality, coexistence and humanity.

Of the great accomplishments of the college faculty and students (and there were many), were rooted in the local area which provided a hospitable and gracious acceptance. The Mecca had come to Mecklenburg County providing inspiration and meeting the scholarly needs of the gentry. Celebrations with dignity, pomp, and circumstance with orations and poetry recitals were welcomed as a culture of elegance and stature previously only found in the larger cities. It served to convert a community in the "wilderness" from thoroughbred horse racing, gaming, and parties to a community thirsting for intellectual stimulation and pursuits.

With so many role models as members of the board of trustees, the stage was set for graduates to enter politics, preaching, and teaching, along with farming—and most did. The text also describes that many of them did so with spouses having been met, lured and married from members of the college and Boydton community. This was the foundation for their professional future. I don't believe that there was one student who graduated and became doctor, lawyer, senator, governor, etc. who could say he did so, and not remember his life in Boydton. Then RMC turned its back and walked (galloped) away without as much as "have a nice day" or "see ya."

CHAPTER 8

A Broader View of Some of the Faculty

Most of the professors' stories are woven into the story of the college, but this section is for several of the success stories that might otherwise be lost through omission.

Bennett Puryear was born July 23, 1826, on the family farm near Abbeyville on the Big Bluestone Creek. He was home schooled by tutors (to include John DeGrafenreit and most likely Peter Ney), along with his five brothers and three sisters, until he entered Randolph Macon College. Following his graduation, he wrote numerous articles in opposition to public schooling—believing children should be taught at home—which is what he did with his children. He also prepared numerous articles and booklets on "The Atmosphere," "Vegetable Farming," and other agricultural and chemistry applications, but his one love was poetry.[1]

In his papers at Virginia Baptist Historical Society, the first entry in his journal in 1848 was a copy of a poem that had been published by *The Saturday Post* in Philadelphia that summer. His letters were written in prose, as were most of his notes. Following his A.B. in 1847, he went to Monroe County, Alabama, where he stayed with his cousin Pollie, who was living in Burnt Corn. He taught math, science, Greek, and Latin in a preparatory school until 1848. He made a decision—"I was influenced solely by the hope of gain, my heart was not in the matter. But law holds out tempting offers to ambition, and ambition has been the strong impulse, the actuating principle of my whole past life. But then it promises no immediate gain. I will interest my feelings as well as engage my mind in the study of medicine." He entered the University of Virginia Medical School in the fall of 1848.[2]

In the fall of 1849, he went to Richmond College, where he was hired as a tutor until 1850. Having completed the requisites, he received his A.M.

degree in 1850 from RMC. He was employed as a professor of natural science at Richmond College from 1850 to 1858 when he was hired by RMC. Following the war, he returned to Richmond College and was professor of the chemistry department from 1866 to 1873, when he was elected as chairman. He served in that position until he retired in 1895. He was also elected as chairman of the faculty, serving from 1869 until 1885 and again from 1889 to 1895. He seemed to have three habits: cigars, apples, and theater performances in New York. He was described as a gifted, popular and entertaining professor with a strong personality who conducted all his own lab experiments, and a gifted administrator.[3]

For many years, he served as associate editor of the *Religious Herald* and as the Dove's representative from Richmond College to attend the annual meetings of the Concord Baptist Association of Southside Virginia in 1870, 1875 and 1880. He was awarded honorary L.L.D. degrees by Georgetown College, Kentucky, and Howard College, Alabama. He died on March 30, 1914.

Bennett Puryear remarried "Ella" Wyles (Wiles) in Richmond and they had five children: Elizabeth Leroy Puryear (Mrs. Henry Wise Mayo of New York) b. 1874; William R. Puryear, b. 1879 and later moved to Baltimore; Alice P. Puryear (Mrs. Author Cobb of Raleigh); Bennett Puryear; Lucy Goode Puryear, b. 1886, moved to Radford for schooling and later married William Edward Garnett; and John Puryear, b. 1876, who later moved to Washington, D.C. Of his children born to his first wife, Lewis Puryear moved to North Carolina; Frank Puryear was living at Edgewood with a stated occupation of professor; Charlie is addressed previously; Sallie married Allan Christian Hill of Richmond, and Virginia lived at home in Madison County.[4]

Nathaniel Thomas Lupton was not a particularly remarkable professor of chemistry from June 1857 to June 1858, as I found nothing written about him in the RMC periodicals nor local newspapers. He was born on December 19, 1830, in Frederick County, Virginia. He attended Dickinson College (A.B. 1849), then went to Heidelberg, Germany, where he studied chemistry for over a year. Returning to the United States in late 1850, he accepted a position as professor of chemistry with Aberdeen Female College in Mississippi. In 1851, he was professor of chemistry at Petersburg Female College and, in 1852, selected as its president. He married Ella Virginia Allemong on September 26, 1854, in Newtown, Virginia. They had one daughter, Ellen, who became the first woman graduate of Vanderbilt University (A.M. 1879).[5]

He left RMC in 1858 after just one year to take a teaching position with Wightman and Wills at Southern University, Greensboro, Alabama. He was professor of chemistry and geology at Southern from 1859 to 1871. In 1871, he was selected as president of the University of Alabama and held that post until 1874. That year, he became professor of chemistry at Vanderbilt University and was later elected chairman of the faculty. In 1875, he was awarded an LL.D. degree from the University of Alabama. He was later awarded a D.D. degree by Vanderbilt and remained chairman of the faculty until he resigned in 1885. In 1880, he was elected chairman of the chemistry section of the American Association for Advancement of Science and vice-president of the American Chemical Society. In 1885, he was appointed as state chemist for Alabama and professor of chemistry at the Agricultural and Mechanical College in Auburn, Alabama, where he served until his death on June 11, 1893.

Another rather elusive and nondescript professor was Lewis Turner. He appears to have come from a long line of M.E. leaders during late the 1700s in Prince Edward and Halifax Counties; primarily William of Halifax. Turner, professor of mathematics and astronomy from September 1861 to January 1862, appears to have been born in 1822. In 1862, he enlisted and served in Hankin's Company of Light Artillery. Following the war, he is found in the U.S. Census living on a farm in Washington County, White River, Arkansas. The farm was owned by Dr. Samuel Bowles and family. Turner is listed as able to read and write (having attended school) and working as a farmhand. In the 1880 Census, he is back in Halifax County, Virginia, living on Black Walnut Plantation. He is living there with his two children, ages 8 and 10, and he is listed as a widower. The census was taken June 14, 1880,[6] and he was listed as living next door to the Dr. J.M. Craddock family, which included Elizabeth Craddock, age 21, schoolteacher. His occupation is also listed as schoolteacher.

Professor Warren DuPre, born January 24, 1816, in Mt. Pleasant, South Carolina, though never a professor for Randolph Macon College, was a tutor from 1838 to 1844, receiving his A.M. degree in 1840. He is the longest serving tutor recorded, although two years of this time he was tutoring at Charleston College. DuPre appears to have had some early interest in law. Following the death of board of trustees member and treasurer Beverly Sydnor in 1843, the administrators of the estate were Richard Russell, Warren DuPre, and soon to be Professor Edward Chambers. For a short time he became headmaster of the Newberry Female Academy in Newberry, Alabama, but then relocated to South Carolina.

In 1854, he was selected for the position of professor of chemistry and mineralogy at Wofford College, Spartanburg, South Carolina. He immediately requested a leave of absence so he could go north and purchase equipment for the lab. The leave was granted, and DuPre spent a year studying chemistry and geology with Professor Benjamin Silliman at Yale. DuPre was the board of trustees' choice because he was well known in South Carolina as a great teacher and was one of the original forty-one to organize the State Teachers Association in 1850.[7]

Unable to fill the chair of English in 1859, Professor DuPre and newly elected President A.W. Shipp divided the duties of the chair and continued to do so until war's end. Frequently, Professor DuPre returned to RMC to deliver addresses for the literary societies and commencements. On at least two occasions, he delivered keynote speeches. Around 1875, DuPre became president of Martha Washington College in Abingdon, Virginia.

Another distinguished individual who was not a professor at Randolph Macon but whose name appears frequently in its history is Holland Nimmons McTyeire (A.B. 1844, RMC). He was born on July 28, 1824, in Barnwell District, South Carolina, but his family relocated to Alabama in 1838. Before RMC, he had attended Collinswood and Cokesbury. Following his graduation from RMC, he entered the M.E., South, Virginia Conference in 1845, and was appointed to serve in Williamsburg. The following year, he was sent to Alabama, and on November 8, 1847, he married Amelia Townsend in Mobile. They had six children. In 1848, he was sent to Mississippi, and later in 1848, to New Orleans. He served as editor of the New Orleans *Christian Advocate* from 1848 to 1858. In 1861, he was returned to Montgomery, Alabama, where he served until elected bishop of M.E., South, in 1866. He authored five books, his last being *A History of Methodism* published in 1887. He died on February 15, 1887.[8]

Much has already been written in the text of William A. Smith, president of Randolph Macon College from 1846 to 1866, but there is more. Leaving RMC in late 1866, he traveled to St. Louis, Missouri, and changed his conference affiliation to Missouri. He was appointed to the pastorate of Centenary Church, St. Louis, and was named a curator to the board for the normal school conducted by H.A. Bourland in Fayette, Missouri. At the board of curators' meeting in 1868, it was determined that they should begin a $100,000 fundraising campaign for an endowment for the college. Dr. Smith accepted the position as director, and he was also nominated for president of Central College which was being formed. He accepted. The board changed the name to Central College Classical Seminary, Fayette, Missouri, and it was slated to reopen following repairs to the buildings in September 1868.[9]

In the summer of 1869, the board of curators met, and it was reported that they had secured $81,553.45 from Mr. Bourland and Dr. Smith. They also had, in hand, notes totaling $14,665 for a grand total of $96,218.45. In honor of Dr. Smith and his efforts for the college, the board of curators personally guaranteed the remaining $3,872.55. On December 1, 1870, it was announced by the board, in high tribute, that Dr. Smith had accomplished securing the endowment.[10]

One traveling companion with Dr. Smith for the trip to Missouri was Professor Frank (Francis) X. Forster (A.B. 1846, A.M. 1849, RMC), son of the Rev. R.M. Forster of the South Carolina Conference. Upon arrival in Missouri in 1867, Forster began a small private school in Jefferson City, but maintained contact with Dr. Smith. In 1868, when the new college was scheduled to open, Forster was nominated and selected principal of the seminary. Originally the school was located across the street from Howard-Payne Female Academy (established c. 1849). In 1854, construction began on what became known as the Provisional College (normal school), which began operation in 1859. The school was built originally as a minimal investment in one building designed for both male and female, which essentially made it a high school. The building had been occupied during the war (folklore history, by both the Union soldiers and Confederate soldiers at different times) and was now in serious disrepair.

The board of curators asked Bourland, the principal, to turn over management of the school to the new seminary, and he agreed. He also agreed to work with Dr. Smith on fundraising. An advertisement in the *St. Louis Christian Advocate* read:

> Central College Classical Seminary
> For Young Ladies and Young Gentlemen
> will open Sept. 7, 1868
> Wm. A. Smith, D.D.
> President of Central College.[11]

The school catalogue contained a note: "At present the school is composed of males and females. Thus far I am assured the presence of young ladies has been decidedly conservative. When the college shall go into full operation, a separate institution will, of course, be established for young ladies. The rules in regards to school diplomas will be observed in conferring the literary degree of Mistress of Liberal Arts and Sciences on young ladies [and] young men [will be] awarded the Bachelor's Degree."[12]

Smith immediately began an endowment campaign in early 1867 and within six months had raised $60,000. But this time the traveling, speaking, negotiating and fundraising proved too much for him. Following commencement in 1869, Dr. Smith was given a medical leave of absence. He returned to Virginia "literally broken in health." He seems to have taken residence near Richmond with former student the Rev. John C. Granbery. He died there on March 1, 1870. Following the funeral, "Mrs. Smith and their daughter, Mrs. Willie Fuller, returned to Fayette. Mrs. Smith became matron in Howard Female College and her daughter was head of the Music Department."[13]

Receiving word of Dr. Smith's death, Central needed a new president.

The board of curators elected principal of the seminary, Professor F.X. Forster (professor of English language and literature), as chairman of the faculty and appointed him to president pro tem. He had also worked closely with Dr. Smith in fundraising, but now he needed to focus on the selection of new faculty. "Under Forster's guidance a faculty was employed which became a legend in the history of the college."[14] The new fall 1870 faculty included Forster, O.H.P. Corprew, A.M., ancient languages, and John C. Wills, A.M., pure and applied mathematics. W.G. Miller, A.M., M.D., was professor of physical sciences.

Professor Wills had been enticed into leaving Southern University and joining the faculty at Central Methodist College. On August 18, 1870, the board of curators elected him as president and changed the name from Central College to Central Methodist College. At the opening ceremony on September 22, 1870, Bishop Holland N. McTyeire gave the address. Wills was not present for the ceremony and it seems that he did not arrive on campus until the spring of 1871 with no recorded explanation for the delay.

Before teaching at RMC, Wills had tutored at V.M.I. following his graduation and accepted an appointment as headmaster of Northumberland Academy. He was born and raised in Isle of Wright County, Virginia. While at V.M.I. as a tutor, he met and married Kate E. Duffy of Alexandria, Virginia. Following ten years with Randolph Macon College, he taught at Southern University until coming to Central. He was awarded D.D. degrees by both Emory College of Georgia and RMC. He was described as "of warm and vital piety; and of humility. His mind was clear and incisive, as be fit's a mathematician, broad in interests and sympathies. Faculty and students alike gave him their respect and admiration."[15]

As president, in organizing the school he harkened back to 1859 and introduced the "Virginia Scheme." After all, he was one of the committee to change Randolph Macon. The curriculum was composed of schools like that of the 1859–1860 RMC program. The first two graduates were in 1872. On February 11, 1878, Wills died, having suffered with a long term illness. He is buried at City Cemetery, Fayette, Missouri. Some years later a building appeared on campus for "messing and clubbing" and it was named "Wills Hall." This was a combination dormitory and recreation center. The dormitory had quarters for eight students that were selected based on a rigid criteria, including grade point average. It was an honor to be selected to live there. "Wills Hall" was removed in the 1950s.[16]

With the election of Wills to president, a professor of math had to be hired. Forster, still acting as president pro tem until Wills arrival, reached out to R.W. Jones (Richard W. Jones, A.B. 1857 and A.M. 1860, RMC, and professor of math, RMC, 1866 to 1868). Jones accepted the offer and arrived in time to begin the school year on September 22, 1870. He served as professor of math until 1876.

Professor Richard W. Jones (b. 1832) had returned to his alma mater following the war as professor of math. Soon, the tides were moving toward the removal of the college to Ashland, Petersburg or Richmond. With the progression of the movement and Jones' stand against it, he negotiated in June 1867, with the board of trustees "to rent the 'Old Prep Building' ... for $2.50 per month."[17] The board agreed, and it appears that Jones operated a "classical school" there along with teaching for RMC until selected as the new president of Petersburg Female College in 1868.

He held this post until June 1870, and left to accept the position of professor of math with Central. (The records at Central verify he was hired by Forster and the board, arrived in September for ceremonies on the 22^{nd,} but then his career is one of clandestine teaching, as there is no further record of him, nor is he mentioned in any of the school annual catalogues.) In 1876, he accepted a position as professor of chemistry for the Mississippi Industrial Institute (present day Mississippi Institute for Women).

He served in that position until 1885. In 1881, he was awarded an LL.D. degree by the college. From 1885 to 1888, he served as president of Mississippi Industrial Institute and from 1888 to 1890 as president of Emory and Henry College in Abingdon, Virginia. In 1890, he was hired as vice chancellor and professor of chemistry at the University of Mississippi. During his career, he published numerous articles. He died on December 18, 1918, and is buried at Laurel, Mississippi.[18] (See Appendix B, 12th Virginia Infantry section.)

Oliver Hagan Percy Corprew was born in 1828 in Norfolk and appears as a most interesting character in the history of Randolph Macon College and the community of Boydton. He received his A.B. 1846 and A.M. 1849, having tutored at RMC from 1846 to 1849. In 1854, he became professor of natural philosophy and in 1856 professor of Ancient Languages until resigning in 1857. He had acquired large land and slave holdings in the Boydton area. He served as a member of RMC Board of Trustees from 1859 and is listed as treasurer of the college in 1868. Following the war he accepted the position as professor of ancient languages from the fall of 1866 until July 30, 1868. Following the close of the college in Boydton, he briefly went to Ashland as treasurer for the board, but not as faculty.

Corprew enlisted into the 3rd Virginia Cavalry as a private on May 14, 1861, and at consolidation into the Confederate Army, he was transferred and assigned as a sergeant to the Quartermaster Department at an entrenched camp of the 6th Virginia Infantry. The 6th Infantry was begun as the 54th

Virginia Militia under the command of Colonel William A. Mahone. It was established on May 2, 1861, as Company S, 6th Infantry, and soon changed to 6th Infantry, field and staff, and on October 10, 1861, Mahone was promoted to brigadier general.[19] Fearing for the safety of his family, Brigadier General Mahone came to Clarksville, Virginia, purchased an elegant home near downtown and moved his family there. (It is curious that he knew in October 1861 Clarksville would be safe.)

On July 4, 1830, Thomas Jefferson Corprew, younger brother of O.H.P., was born in Norfolk. In 1860, he was serving as the county's high sheriff and that year was serving as a major in Company F, 3rd Battalion, 1st Norfolk Light Artillery Blues. When established with the Confederate Army, it became 6th Virginia Regiment, Corprew's Artillery Battery, and Major Corprew was promoted to colonel as part of the 6th Infantry, field and staff, serving under Brigadier General Mahone. On May 3, 1862, he was dropped from the rolls with no reason stated, and he returned to his job in Norfolk. Following the war, he purchased the lands of his brother, O.H.P., in Boydton in 1866, but died on July 24, 1873.

At some point in 1862, O.H.P. Corprew was elected or promoted to captain, field and staff, Quartermaster Department, but did not leave the field and staff assignment with Brigadier General Mahone until September 15, 1864. This following Mahone's promotion to major general on July 24, 1864. There is no record of his being detailed or where he went with the field and staff assignment. It is suspected that he returned to Boydton and took over the commissary and Ordnance operation at RMC.

The 1880 Census lists O.H.P. Corprew (age 52) as living in the town of Fayette, Howard County, Missouri, with wife, Ada, age 48, Julia Hicks, age 52, and three students age 18, two female and one male. Next door was Dr. James J. Watts (age 62) with a number of students and servants living in his home.[20] A photograph of Corprew's former home is contained in "Picturesque Fayette and Its People: A Review of Fayette, Howard County, Missouri." The home was actually the stately old bank building that had closed in 1876. It burned in May 1898.[21] On the census record, his occupation was listed as school teacher.

The 1900 Census records Corprew (age 72) with his new bride, Adeline (possibly Smith, widowed daughter of William A., who had returned to Fayette in 1871), age 46 (b. 1853 in Virginia). They were married in 1896 and had four servants living with them, along with a 16 year old black dressmaker. A photograph of his new home is listed in another edition of the pamphlet indicated previously. On this census his occupation is given as professor.[22] In June 1886, Corprew was elected chairman of the faculty and served as president pro tem of Central Methodist College from June 1886 to June 1888. Corprew Boulevard now skirts the east side and runs parallel to campus.

As the name Irby appears frequently in RMC records for many years, a little more information on this family may help put matters into perspective. The Irbys arrived in Virginia c. 1765 with the progenitor being William II from Sussex, England.

William arrived in the new world prepared to invest in substantial holdings, which he did. He and his wife had several children, but the only son who survived and remained in Virginia was Edmund (1781–1829). Edmund proved to be capable of following successfully in his father's footsteps. He served as the banker for several horse racing tracks in and around Nottoway County, acquiring substantial land and slave holdings in Nottoway, Lunenburg, Charlotte, and Halifax Counties. Edmund and his wife, Francis Briggs Lucas Irby (d. 1846), built and resided at Popular Hill Plantation in Nottoway County. Edmund was the only surviving child of William Irby of Sussex and his first wife, thus a bulk of the estate went to Edmund. In fact, William of Sussex purchased the land and had built Poplar Hill for his son and daughter-in-law in 1812. In short order, Edmund was considered the richest member of the Irby family in the United States.[23]

Richard (September 28, 1825) was the sixth born of the eight. He was apprenticed by his older brother William (1808–June, 1865). Edmund died in 1829, and Francis died in 1846, but she saw to it that Richard received a proper education. She sent him to Randolph Macon, and he received his A.B. degree in 1844.

William became very prominent in the community and even helped build an M.E. Church, South, in Blacks and Whites, called Crenshaw M.E. Church. In 1848, he was appointed to the RMC Board of Trustees. By 1850, the Irby family was getting "the call of the wild" and was moving south and west. William B. Irby (1st born son of William of Sussex by his second wife), along with four children of Edmund's, headed out on expedition. But it didn't last long and they went their own way—one or two to Alabama, one or two to Mississippi, same for Memphis and Tennessee. One of William of Sussex's children had already married and gone to Florida, where he and his wife had several children.[24]

Edmund was described as a good farmer, but his calling was as a thoroughbred race horse breeder. He was a personal friend of John Randolph, along with many other breeders. *The Virginia Aristocratic Book of Horse Breeders*, 1833 (although after his death) has him listed as a premier breeder. An anecdote was, John Randolph had written in his will that Edmund was to receive one of his championship thoroughbreds and a first pick colt at his death. Randolph died in 1832, but since Irby died in 1829, he didn't collect. Aside from being very skilled with horses and "lucky" at the track, he operated a personal banking and loan company based on registered notes (very common for the day).[25]

At his death in 1829, we know, per his will, that he had over $26,000 in notes still outstanding in 1832, and of slaves, he owned 51 in Nottoway, 41 in Halifax and 31 in Lunenburg Counties. He owned acreage commensurate with his slave holdings of about 40 to 45 acres per slave and owned a home and personal property in each county. In Nottoway, he lived near three thoroughbred race tracks and was kept busy, but by 1829 racing was slowly fading away from the Virginia countryside.

He had also developed a huge milling operation on Crooked Creek and had purchased over five hundred acres and dug over fifty acres of soil to build a dam to keep from flooding his neighbors. The mill was originally grist and flour. Now it was capable of powering the largest sawmilling operation in the county. There was also grist, cornmeal, fodder, flour, mash including grains for livestock, and a mill for extracting the syrup from sugar cane to make molasses and sugar. There were also several stills attached to the milling operation. He established a small foundry on the pond for metal work, cooperage, blacksmithing, and wheelwright operations. The entire property included 425 acres plus another 100 or so acres from the original plot purchased nearby. He added over 675 acres from the estate of Judge Frances Fitzgerald (purchased from his brother Judge John), which brought the total to over 1,200 acres plus the 500 acre milling operation.[26]

From the records, Edmund was not a particularly pious man, but he did send William, the elder, to Ebenezer Academy in Brunswick County. William graduated sometime around 1825 and returned home to work with his father.

Richard Irby was born fifth of six boys on September 28, 1825. At the age of fifteen, he was sent to Randolph Macon College to pursue his education. His guardian was his brother William. He reportedly rode from Nottoway to Boydton on horseback. He received his A.B. in 1844. Following graduation, Richard returned to his home and continued to apprentice with his older brother in the family businesses of operating a large plantation with vast land and slave holdings. On February 17, 1846, Richard's mother died. Shortly thereafter, the six sons divided the estate.

Following the death of his mother and having inherited Poplar Hill, Richard felt a need to share this windfall with a new bride. He sent word to his first cousin in Florida, William B., that he would like to marry his daughter, Francis Betty Freeman Irby (Fannie, b. 1830), and she soon arrived on a return train. They were married right away and moved into the plantation house.²⁷ In the 1850 Census, he is recorded as age 25, she as 18; the family included a daughter age 3; and a son age 1. They also owned several slaves, and the 1850 Slave Schedule shows a household black nanny, age 34, and black servant (butler), age 39.²⁸ At some point, Richard became involved in sponsorship and importation of immigrants into the United States. In the 1860 Census, the family is in District 3 of Nottoway County with land holdings worth over $30,000 and personal property worth over $43,000.²⁹ The census was taken July 24, 1860, and at that time the Irbys' children included Elizabeth, age 13 (at home), Freeman F., age 11, Ben., age 9, and Richard (Jr.), age 7 (all three in school), and Lewilling, son, age 5, and Mary C., age 1. Living with the family were Charles J. Seabrook, age 26, from Denmark, and Thomas Ryan, age 25, from Ireland, both working as painters. There were so many Ryans listed in subsequent census records, I was unable to track him.

When John Brown was captured, Irby helped organize a company of militia (which included six other RMC graduates, two students of RMC and an immigrant living in his home) in Nottoway County, and on April 22, 1861, the company of men was taken to Richmond in support of secession. An unusual member of the company of men was Charles J. Seabrook of Denmark. At the age of 27, he enlisted on April 22, 1861, into Company G, 18th Infantry, and was established a sergeant (which says a lot in this company). He was described as 5 feet, 8 inches tall, light complexion, and blue eyes. He was discharged on October 28, 1862.³⁰ In 1880, he was living in Talladega, Alabama, and in 1910, in Jefferson, Alabama.

Of the company, the colonel in command wrote, "The Nottoway men are of good education, high standing and strong health." But while in "Richmond, the mob scene of mobilization, this unit fared no better than any other. For three days the Nottoway recruits were quartered without rations in a warehouse. With the eventual issuance of food, the men were transferred to cattle stalls at the camp of instruction." Irby was established as a first lieutenant, Company G, 18th Virginia Infantry. In August 1861, the 18th Infantry began to move north to Centreville. In August 1861, "over a 1,000 man regiment generally had 300 able bodied men reporting for duty"—the rest were sick. By the end of October the 18th was beginning to prepare to serve out the winter season in Centreville. They "began to build log cabins with crude chimneys and crude furnishings interrupted occasionally by picket duty" or a skirmish nearby. "Centreville by November had become a huge 'Frontier-like settlement' of over 1,000 men of the 18th."³¹

On March 29, 1862, Irby was elected captain of Company G. On August 30 1862, during the Battle of 2nd Manassas, Irby was wounded in action with gunshots to his neck and breast. He was on detached duty from January until

March 1863, and in July 1863, he resigned his commission. He accepted a position with the Commissary General Department. He was paroled on April 19, 1865, at the Jones' House. But because he was working for the Confederacy, that was insufficient—he had to receive a presidential pardon. He filed for the pardon with the newly established Military District No. 1 (Virginia) in Richmond. It was granted on July 22, 1865 (as he was "worth over $20,000"), by the new temporary satrap, Governor F.H. Philpot, just in time for the Randolph Macon College Board of Trustees meeting on August 23.[32]

Following the war, Irby converted his mills to one major foundry operation and began producing stoves. After about two years he sold Poplar Hill to former first lieutenant Charles Betts Hardy, Confederate veteran of the 9th Cavalry. Irby and his family moved to Richmond to be in a better position to market and distribute his stoves. By 1870, he had almost completed the sale of his holdings in Nottoway County. The 1870 Census has him and family living in Henrico, Richmond, and his occupation is listed as husbandry.[33] But he and Francis were also settling their estate in Nottoway County. On December 22, 1873, they sold a couple hundred acres to Frances and Lucy White on Hungryhound Road, bounding the Little Nottoway River.[34] *The City of Richmond Directory* for the next 25 years proves to be an interesting resource. As early as 1877, Richard is listed as corresponding secretary and board of trustees, R-MC–Ashland; vice president, Richmond Stove Company, Ashland; vice president of Virginia Protective Life Insurance Company at 26 N. 9th St., Richmond (joined by his son Freeman in 1885); secretary and general agent, Virginia Bureau of Immigration, Freedmen and Abandoned Lands, 1214 E. Main Street, Ashland—"Searching to locate sold and relocated slaves before the war"; secretary-treasurer for the Virginia Mining and Manufacturing Company, 1214 E. Main Street, Ashland; and board of trustees, Merchants National Bank (Richmond and Petersburg). In 1885, he is also listed as secretary, Virginia Bible Society, 2nd Floor, 827 Main Street E., Richmond.[35]

The 1880 Census lists four more children, and then in the late 1890s the *Directory of Representative Business and Professional Men of Augusta and Stanton County, Virginia* states: "This embraces—First. Randolph-Macon College at Ashland for young men. Second. Randolph-Macon Academy at Bedford City. Third. Randolph-Macon Academy at Front Royal. Fourth. Randolph-Macon Women's College at Lynchburg. W.W. Smith, President, Lynchburg. Richard Irby, Sec., Ashland."[36]

In the 1900 Census, Irby is listed as owning his home at or on the Randolph-Macon College campus, and "Secr. RM Col." Lewilling is living there at age 43 and is working as a "Prof" or "Grom." Mary, the daughter, is keeping house, Sally (daughter age 27) with no notations and son, Moment

S., is a railroad clerk.[37] His four oldest sons (Freeman, Benjamin, Richard and Lewilling) appear to have graduated from RMC with their first cousins, William's sons. Richard died July 4, 1902, having served for forty-four years on the board of trustees. In 1898, he published the *History of Randolph-Macon College*. Now two of the unanswered questions are raised. How did Irby begin and maintain status as a spokesperson for RMC—or was it the way he wrote the history and reviewed the Methodist-college protocol of the era? Irby was a member of the board of trustees for almost 50 years with a number of accomplishments, including the book. He was a successful and well to do gentry planter, but there is no record of an honorary degree?

There is a Bennett Hall, Wills Hall, Corprew Blvd., and a town named Duncan which was formerly Duncan's Crossroads (maybe not related), a town, high school, and college named Olin, just to name a few shrines to the former faculty of RMC at Boydton, and many throughout the south to former students. Yet, in Boydton and Mecklenburg County, there are no accolades, no streets or buildings dedicated in honor of the college, only the decaying remains of a once majestic structure coveted by the almighty destination of nature as was taught in natural science at RMC in Boydton. Even College Avenue was renamed Jefferson Street.

CHAPTER 9

The War Years

The legislature had established a commissary and ordnance Company at RMC, along with the school of military tactics, in the spring of 1862. Essentially, an ordnance company was for the purpose of procuring or manufacturing medical chemicals, munitions, or salt. Therefore, a commissary was for the purpose of procuring supplies, food and clothing for the soldiers both on the battlefields and those passing by in need. Also, the commissary was charged with procuring food and supplies for the horses. Even before the military school and ordnance company were established, the January 21, 1861, issue of the *Tobacco Plant* had an ad that read: "Requesting citizens with spare guns, muskets, pistols (these do not have to be in repair), Bowie knives, flints, lead, molds for bullets, blankets, etc. to deliver them to either Dr. William A. Smith, President of Randolph Macon College or to L.E. Finch at the Roanoke Railroad office in Clarksville."[1]

In the archives of John W. Wootton (May 23, 1822–December 23, 1879) (presently in the possession of Virginia Dare Wright of Boydton), there are numerous receipts and documents for transactions during the war. For a farmer to be exempt from military service, a committee for the county board reviewed each case individually. The farmer had to be nearing the cut-off age for military service, of excellent character, own sufficient land, and have a proven record of successful farming. When granted a "farming exemption," the farmer was issued a license that allowed him to retain for his personal use a certain ration of product. The remainder would be "paid" to the Confederate government as part of the exemption or as part of the state Confederacy tax.[2]

Each year in December, an assessor would survey the farmers and complete the "Form of the Estimate and Assessment of agricultural products agreed upon by the assessor and the taxpayer." For the year of 1863, the form included "NOTE.—Each farmer and planter has the privilege of reserving fifty bushels of sweet potatoes, fifty bushels of Irish potatoes, one hundred bushels of corn, or fifty bushels of wheat, produced in the year 1863, and twenty bushels of peas or beans, but no more than twenty bushels of both, for his own use. In making the estimate and assessment, therefore, these quantities of the articles mentioned will be excluded therefrom."[3] In 1863, Wootton had an excess of 100 bushels of wheat and 70 bushels of corn. His tax was one-tenth of each. As can be easily seen, the surrounding farmers remaining would have been hard pressed to furnish the provisions needed by the college to sustain a continued operation. Being well into the war, seeking and receiving dispensation by the Confederacy would have been a difficult process.

There are a number of items not referenced, to include meat, tobacco, molasses and others. (These were used to pay the Confederacy state tax.) The tobacco crop was used to pay the war debt. Farmers were being heavily taxed by the Confederate States of America, state and county to maintain operations, and tobacco was the most readily accepted form of payment. In Mecklenburg County there were five tanneries and four of those were very large. Thomas Jones, mentioned earlier, owned one of the largest on Coleman's Creek at Boydton, and Goode on Allen's Creek near present day "old" landfill. Next was Richard Clausel Puryear's 80 acre tanning yard on Bluestone Creek at Spanish Grove near Christiansville with head tanner John D. Browne, and Brame's Tannery on the Roanoke River. But these tanneries were unable to keep up with production of the leather and hides needed by the Confederacy; and by the middle of 1864, they were producing very little. Operations of the Clarksville Ordnance were nearly stalled, and all four of the county commissaries were nearly empty.

To complicate this further, in the fall of 1864, following the capture of Petersburg and concerted efforts focused on Richmond, many of the Confederate troops were heading south to do battle with Sherman, who was laying down a swath of terror and destruction. As these Confederate troops passed through the county, they were seeking supplies of any and all kinds. Even while there they needed food, shelter, clothing and medical care. RMC could have been the haven they sought, as Dr. George Smith was still there. Likewise Drs. Jones and Jordan were in town with the drugstore, and several other doctors were nearby for aid. And let us not forget Professor Puryear, with his medical training, was still on campus. One documented instance is a dispatch to General A.R. Lawton, quartermaster general, at Macon, North Carolina. This would have been sent down river and returned by bateaux, as the railroad tracks had been removed in 1863, and melted down for the production of cannon. The dispatch reads:

14 March 1865
Gen A R Lawton at Macon
QM Gen from Cpt. J.H. Nichols
Detachment of Cavalry in Meck. Co.
for supplies, passing through
W/a QM Cpt. Stevens[4]

The cavalry was headed to North Carolina to join General Johnston's regiment. The commissaries were busy places, and the main building of Randolph Macon College was a perfect place for storage, processing and even triage medical care. This meant that a number of soldiers were working there, and many of those were on medical leave for wounds that took them off the battlefield but not out of the service. There would have been a constant movement of supplies. One receipt it shows, "13 Apr. 1864—John W. Wootton delivered Nov. 21 102 lbs of bacon & 500 bu of fodder to L.E. Finch for T.D. Dodson." Another reads, "13 Apr 1864—D.N. Carter 10 bu wheat 100 bu grain 5 hay to John M. Taylor, Agent by Thomas E. Reekes."

If there was a surplus of product from the ration, the farmer was allowed to sell same, otherwise there would be a county tax levied against the inventory. Further examples are found among the receipts:

- 12 December 1864 I hereby certify that I bought of John W. Wootton one barrel of corn and 1,000 lbs. of fodder at schedule prices, it being a part of his surplus at Ra-Ma College. William Carter by order of the Secretary of War.
- 12 December 1864 of J.W. Wootton 7 bu corn 481 lbs of fodder. J.N. Nichols, Cpt., County.
- 22 Nov 1864 of Samuel Farrar 8 bu corn and 600 lbs of fodder for a detachment of Philips Legion of Cavalry in route for the Army. Cpt. J.R. Sterns, AQM of Philips Legion.
- 6 Dec. 1864 Burton's Brigade, 1st Div. Cav. Corps of Va. Purch 1500 lbs of fodder + 40 bu of corn from John W. Wootton. Cpt. J.W. McCurry, AQM.
- 10 Feb 1865 Johnson's Division, Cpt. A. Kinney, AGS 330 lbs of bacon of John T. Wootton.[5]

Thus we have scant documentation of the commissary. As for munitions, salt for Mecklenburg County was being brought in from Saltville by the documentation of Wootton[6] and Dr. L.I. Rose archives (the latter originals are located at the Virginia Historical Society).[7] There is also a notation in Susan Bracey's book that Thomas R. Reekes (Jr.) was the salt procurement agent for Mecklenburg County. On one occasion, Reekes hired six of Judge Chambers' slaves to work from September to December 25, 1863, hauling salt to the county from Saltville, Virginia.[8]

Munitions were being produced by the Clarksville Munitions Factory and the wagon factories. I found no records of the Boydton wagon factory operating during the war. That leaves medical chemicals. That was a clear possibility. Professor Puryear had taught chemistry and conducted experiments for fifteen years when the war began. In the spring of 1863, the board of trustees granted permission to Professor Puryear and Professor Carr to establish a "classical school" at the hotel, making sure that none of the students would be allowed in the main buildings of the college, as they were being used for the commissary.[9] Since the hotel was just across the road from the chemistry professor's home and farm, this was a good arrangement. The war could have been the motivation for the young students to learn a lot of practical chemistry for their own survival and for the aide of their family members. They were bordered by the farms of Wootton, Reekes, Leigh, Carter, and Dodson. Also, the 1850 Census shows there were five boot and shoe makers in the neighborhood. Most were in their 30s and 40s, which would have exempted them from service due to age after 1861.

The biography of Puryear at the Virginia Baptist Historical Society states that "Puryear taught a 'Classical School' from 1863 to 1865." Further evidence is the biography of Francis H. McGuire. McGuire was born on June 4, 1850, in Mecklenburg County, Virginia, to the Rev. Francis McGuire and Mary Willing Harrison McGuire. He was taught at private schools and a classical school where he excelled. He entered Randolph Macon College in 1865; but with the move to Ashland, he took a year off to teach and save money for law school. He taught during the summers and graduated with an A.B. in 1870. He taught school for another year, and in the fall of 1871, he entered the University of Virginia School of Law. In 1874, he established a law practice in Richmond and became one of the founders of the Virginia State Bar Association. He was elected the first chairman. He married a Miss Notting and they had one daughter. He died on October 30, 1894.[10]

Confirmation was, of course, the board of trustees meeting in September 1864,[11] and that Irby wrote that in 1865, three A.M. degrees were awarded in June 1865. Also, receipts for the ordnance company of RMC are signed by F.D. Dodson, L.E. Finch, Thomas Reekes (Jr.), and John M. Taylor, sergeant. The Mecklenburg County Commissioners responsible to the Confederate government for tax and commissary collection were L.E. Finch, agent for RMC and Taylor's Ferry, R.M. Finch, agent for Clarksville ordnance and munitions, Thomas E. Reekes, agent for Taylor's Ferry, and A.S. Mason, agent for Taylor's Ferry and conscription of blacks to work on the fortifications in Norfolk, Petersburg, and Richmond.[12]

One additional factor we must consider is the locale of Mecklenburg County. There are four rivers with numerous spring fed streams and creeks. Until 1849, there were copper, silver, and gold mining operations which were abandoned for the California gold rush. Following reconstruction, mining was resumed in Southside by interested investors from New York and Pennsylvania in the 1890s. The low grounds along the waters were filled with wild herbs for medicinal use. Puryear should have been familiar with this information as he was a native, third generation, of one of the largest and wealthiest families in the county. Aside from the metals and herbs there were hundreds, if not thousands, of acres of orchards. One of the most common methods of storing fruits and berries for future use was to convert them into barrels of cider. Early medicine relied heavily upon caffeine, honey, liquor, cider, wine and tobacco which included hemp, marijuana and other herbal leaves to be blended and smoked or chewed.

Some of the common herbs which still exist in vast quantity are morning glory, garlic, ginseng, ginger, mint, nutmeg, ginkgo biloba, Jimson weed (loco weed), and some wild nuts that serve as a coffee substitute. Puryear's notes in 1851 to 1856 contain several chemical formulas for a variety of uses of potash, potassium, potassium bromide, potassium nitrate, and potassium carbonate. His specialty was fertilizer, but these chemicals have multiple purposes, and he had conducted experiments using them for over twelve years.[13]

He must have known that potassium is used in fertilizer, as is potash, but potassium nitrate is also used in fertilizer. Additionally, it is used as a preservative (of absolute necessity during the era), and it is used in gunpowder. Potassium bromide is used as a sedative, and potassium carbonate is used to make soap and glass.

Put into perspective, the contributions from Mecklenburg County to the commissaries could have been vast. There are indications of large quantities of molasses and honey being sold or used to pay taxes. This would have been used for cooking, candies and pastries, medicinally for a variety of gastrointestinal disorders and emotional problems, and some converted into mead for medicinal use as a sedative or analgesic. But the contributions from Boydton area for ordnance could also have been enormous with medical chemicals, hides, and even munitions. The metals found would have been taken to Clarksville ordnance for processing. From the perspective of a chemistry professor in Mecklenburg County, the war would have created a great challenge and opportunity for hands-on research and identification in the field. This could have included educating the locals still home and purchasing their harvests. It would certainly have included experiments in the laboratory for the benefit of the students and science, then supplying them to the Confederacy. (As is true of most history—how great it would be to have a journal documenting what happened.)

Documentation is also available that Ira I. Crenshaw (A.B. 1842), president of Buckingham Female Academy, was performing marriages in Mecklenburg County for Confederate soldiers and young and old couples in 1862, 1863, 1864 and 1865. It appears that he moved to Boydton in 1860. Dr. William A. Smith and the Rev. James Jamieson were also performing marriages, except (not in 1865 for the latter) they seemed to be marrying many of the local young ladies to men from other states. There are records for the class of 1861 A.M. graduates Wesley C. Vaden and William H. Judkins that they too were performing marriages in 1862 and 1863.[14]

Just prior to the college closing to students in March 1864, the last hurrah for the literary societies was an address delivered before them in March by Dr. James Armstrong Duncan (A.B. 1849, RMC), son of Professor David. Following the ceremony and celebration, the board of trustees voted to close the college on March 9, 1864. James appears as a sickly individual. In 1867, the *Tobacco Plant* had a story that Duncan had just returned to the pulpit following an extended stay in Philadelphia for recuperative purposes from his illness.[15] The board of trustees must have been aware of this when they considered him for president of RMC because he was the preacher of the Petersburg M.E. Church where Paul, Anthony Dibrell, and Cowles were members.

During Reconstruction, it was important for the board to distance the college from the Confederate politics. James Duncan was the son of an Irish immigrant and first generation Irish in the United States. His father had been a long term professor at RMC. Neither he nor his father served in the military. He was a preacher and writer. Thus, he was a good candidate to keep the college on a low profile with the Union occupation. James served as president from October, 1868, until he died of a prolonged debilitating disease on September 23, 1877.

In May 1864, the people in Mecklenburg County received word that General Kautz and General Wilson were pressing south toward them. The circuit court ordered that all county government records and papers be taken to a safe place.[16] Wilson was held up in Burkeville, but Kautz, with his regiment and two companies of Wilson's men, attacked the Stanton River Bridge on June 24 and 25, 1864. Having been defeated, they retreated through Charlotte County and crossed Mecklenburg County into Lunenburg County, looting and pillaging as they went.

The March 31, 1865, *Tobacco Plant* (last issue on microfilm for the year) carried a story of the evacuation of Richmond, a Battle at Sailors Creek in Farmville, and a story that Sheridan and his cavalry were coming to Southside and on to Danville.[17] This prompted the remaining militia into action to spread the word. Major General Philip H. Sheridan's goal, with his three divisions of cavalry, was to raid for supplies until in North Carolina, where he could join Sherman and attack General Johnston. On April 20, 1865, they arrived in Boydton and discovered the waters of the Roanoke River were high. Orders were given to construct a bridge near Abbeyville, and a detail was sent to begin work.

In the interim, Sheridan's men settled into preparations for their return home. After all, for them, the war was settled on April 9, when Lee surrendered. Now it is three weeks later, they are tired, still suffering, and headed away from their homes and families. The men organized a Union hospital in the main building of RMC with what would be called a "triage clinic" in today's language. Most of the downstairs rooms in the main building and the west building were used as stables for some of their horses. Upon completion of the bridge, the troops left Boydton for Abbeyville, about April 24, only to arrive at the bridge and learn that the war was over. Numerous soldiers, "bummers," deserters, and former slaves began a spree of looting and mayhem. An inventory from Dr. W.F. Wade's estate in St. Tammany discloses that some of Sheridan's men raided the home, which was in mourning, and stole $360.90 on April 25.[18] (These men were headed in the opposite direction of Abbeyville—must have been some of the numerous deserters that the Union had to contend with after April 9.)

Although Johnston had surrendered to Sherman at Durham Station on the 16th of April, when the surrender agreement reached Washington, D.C., following Lincoln's assassination, the sentiment was such among the legislative bodies of men that the terms were too liberal. Thus, General Grant was sent to Sherman's headquarters in Raleigh on April 24. He delivered the bad news on April 25 that the surrender was unacceptable. Once this was done, the following day, April 26, President Johnson signed a new surrender agreement for all remaining Confederate forces, based on the conditions that Lee had agreed to at Appomattox. Sheridan and his men returned to Boydton about April 27 on their way to Washington, D.C., and departed on April 28.

Sheridan left a detachment behind to secure the community. (Probably including his sick, injured, and some medical corps. I think it is safe to assume that those left behind were not happy. Even if he had asked for volunteers to stay, the war was over, and the men wanted to go home.) Resources indicate that Union soldiers filtered through town for several weeks attempting to locate and reunite with their units. With an army of many thousand—some on horseback and some in wagons, others in formation, and then others with wounds or sickness—the procession of soldiers stretched for many miles.

Adding to this, those who were looting and partaking of the bountiful spirits to excess; the procession lasted for several days.

Susan Cosby Rowlett published some years later:

> In the Spring of 1865, my brother, Charles, my senior by six or seven years, took me in his double buggy, driving his two grey horses, Hector and Tom, to visit my oldest brother, an Episcopal minister [the Rev. John C. Cosby] living in Boydton, Mecklenburg County, Virginia. Our home was in Halifax County, about forty miles away.
>
> We had not been at my brother's home many days before we heard many rumors of the coming of [General] Sheridan's cavalry, and of their many acts of brutality, etc. We were driving out in the country when a messenger arrived saying Sheridan was in town and making his headquarters at Randolph-Macon College, the Methodist theological seminary.
>
> Sheridan had 35,000 men. When we got home, we found everything in confusion. My two brothers immediately walked to town to get a guard to protect us and our home. I was a young girl and very much afraid of the Northern soldiers. While my brothers were away, a servant came in to say some soldiers—Germans—were demanding the smoke house key and threatened to break into the house if she did not give them the key. My brother's wife was sick in bed, but she said they should have the key. I tried to give the servant the key, but before I found it two men, seemingly drunk, were climbing up to the window and trying to break in. I looked out the window and saw my brothers returning and I waved my handkerchief.
>
> Immediately my brother Charles began running and soon reached us. He knocked the men down and threatened them with the guard, and all was quiet for a while, but the stragglers stole all our cakes and bread from the kitchen.
>
> Sheridan's officers were taking all the horses they could find. Our two horses were locked in the smoke house and my brother managed to keep them....
>
> In a day or two Sherman passed our house with 40,000 foot soldiers. I can never describe the terror which seized me during their stay. I never left my brother's side. I slept by him and followed him like a dog. A very tall general said he would be guard while they passed as he wanted some water. We had heard how they bullied our women, ruined their greenhouses, etc.
>
> This general had a bouquet of flowers on his coat. He took it off and handed it to me. I took it, then thought what my brothers, cousins and friends would think of me, and unconsciously dropped the flowers and put my foot on them. The general was furious and left us, but I have always been glad that I did prove I was not such an arrant coward after all.
>
> The next morning Sherman's army left Boydton for the army in Virginia, but for several days stragglers were passing in groups decked out in jewelry and other things they had stolen. My brother recognized some of the watches, breastpins, etc., but tho' he wished to take them from them, my brother Charles said, "No, I have Susie to take care of and you, your wife and we could get into more trouble interfering.[19]

General William Tecumseh Sherman's men arrived in Boydton on May 4, 1865. When most of them left on May 5, General Sheridan's unit was replaced by a detachment of Sherman's. The 14th and 20th Corps were under Sherman's command and passed through the county. There is documentation of these men raiding a home near present day Sudan (south of Clarksville),[20] of two raids being carried out in Christiansville (present day Chase City), and a raid in St. Tammany, plus other raids in Lunenburg County, all including theft of property, stores, livestock and property damage with home invasions and some deaths. That unit stayed for over a month; but with so many complaints of harassment by the local citizens, they were replaced in late June by the 126th Pennsylvania Infantry under the command of Captain Lulges, provost marshal.[21]

They stayed until the end of September. The troops took over the college buildings as headquarters and a depot for freedmen, their wives, and children. It seems the freedmen occupied the west building and at least one wing of the main building, as that was where the most damage was done.[22] The west building was eventually purchased in the 1870s by Colonel Thomas F. Goode and removed. Even after the soldiers left, the newly established Freedman's Bureau, freedmen and families continued to occupy the buildings long after September 1865. Where else were they going to go? They had left the plantations, and after all, the Union soldiers had invited them to live there. Possibly this could have been a factor in the board of trustees' rationale for closing the college. The buildings were ransacked and most window sills, doors, mantels, books, papers, and furniture were used as fuel for fires.

In any event, the board of trustees met in August of 1865 and vacated all faculty chairs with the exception of Professor President Smith. He was instructed to hire assistants to teach the new class of 1865–1866. Among the 58 students were 55 from Virginia and 26 under the age of sixteen. They must have received their instruction at Steward Hall, where many also resided with the supervision of a teaching assistant. The remainder must have lived with Dr. Smith, a teaching assistant in the Brown House and in the Puryear House. Dr. Smith resigned on July 12, 1866. In 1867, he, like several other graduates and faculty of RMC, chose to leave the tyranny of occupation in the South with its martial law, and move west. Under martial law, lawyers were not allowed to practice in the state, which prompted several to move. (Many of their stories are in the text with more found in Appendix B.) A couple of notable students from Mecklenburg County were Benjamin J. Hawthorne and Benjamin Lee Arnold, both graduates of the class of 1861 (see Appendix A).

The Methodist Episcopal, South, Conferences were at full throttle before the war in their expansion of colleges such as Central Missouri and West Tennessee. The effort to reestablish schools totaled over "200 colleges between

Faculty members of the old Corvallis College in 1882–83. From the left are E.E. Grimm, Ida B. Callahan, B.L. Arnold, president, B.J. Hawthorne, professor, Dr. Joseph Emory and W.W. Bristow (Division of Special Collections and Archives, Oregon State University, Corvallis, Oregon).

1822 and 1860,"[23] and after the war, the growth continued. Among the notable schools were Southwestern University of Texas with the first medical school in the state, Vanderbilt University also with a medical school in Tennessee, and Oregon Agricultural College (Oregon State University today). Other reasons for the migration were the severe depression following the military occupation, the appeal of "homesteading" in the western states, the uncertainty of reconstruction with former slaves serving in the legislatures and as government officials, and that which was not discussed—"shell shock." For some there was simply the need to leave the area that served as a stark reminder, in its presence, of the war and all that was lost.

One notable individual is the elusive Dr. Samuel David Sanders (listed as Saunders from South Carolina in 1842, and Sanders from Texas in 1859, in Irby, 1898). The records of Southwestern (established in 1875) and its root schools[24] lists 116 students named Sanders, but only one not attending Southwestern and that was John Sanders, 1859, Soele College. In any event, Samuel D. Sanders was born January 4, 1824, and raised into the ante-bellum plantation lifestyle in northeastern South Carolina. Although South Carolina was the third largest supporter of Randolph Macon's student and faculty population, this area of the state was not a particular "hot spot" for Methodists and students. Sanders was raised in Cheraw, Chesterfield County, "Pee Dee Country," South Carolina.

He entered Randolph Macon College at age sixteen in October 1836 sponsored by William Godfrey as his guardian. He graduated with an A.B. degree in June 1842 with fourth honors in his class. Some of his classmates and chums included William G. Connor, A.B., RMC, 1842, of South Carolina, and A.M. 1846 and D.D. 1869 in Tennessee; Professor (later Bishop) David Doggett, A.M., June 1842 (honorary), of Virginia, who became faculty at RMC that month; and Amos W. Jones, A.B. 1839, who served as principal of the Preparatory Department and received an A.M. in June 1842. There was also Henry E. Lockett, son of Colonel S.L. Lockett of Boydton (A.B. 1841); Thomas Lockett of Louisiana, son of Sam Lockett of Boydton (A.B. 1846); Warren DuPre of South Carolina (A.B. 1836 and A.M. 1840), who served as a tutor from 1838 to 1844; Holland N. McTyrire of Alabama, son of John McTyrire of Ritchie, Russell County, Alabama ((b. 1824; A.B. 1844), and who served as a tutor 1844 to 1845 and principal of the Preparatory Department; and Bishop William Wightman (D.D. 1846, RMC). Returning to South Carolina, Sanders completed the requirements for a medical certificate from Charleston Medical College.[25]

On January 26, 1848, he married Martha J. Pegues (b. 1826) from a prominent Methodist family in southeast South Carolina. She was acknowledged in notes of the South Carolina Historical Society in 1867 as being "well educated." Her younger brother, Rufus R. (b. 1830), was sponsored by his widowed mother, Jane, and graduated from RMC with an A.B. in 1852. Following the death of the Reverend Pegues, the family moved to the Cheraw area. The couple had three children: Mary J. (b. October 10, 1848), Harriett (b. around 1850), and Samuel G. (b. 1852). Harriett must have died young, as there is no mention of her in the 1867 records, and she was born after the 1850 census was taken in August that year. No 1860 census record is extant for the family, but in June 1859 Randolph Macon awarded Dr. Samuel D. Sanders (now of Texas) an honorary A.M. degree. And this is where the story of the elusive Dr. Sanders begins. Historically, an honorary A.M. was awarded by Randolph Macon to A.B. graduates who were teaching at the college level or who were being hired to teach there.

When the Civil War began, South Carolina was at the forefront. Dr. Sanders immediately responded to the call for troops to protect the state and enlisted in early 1861 into Company D, 21st South Carolina Infantry, but not as a physician. Instead he enlisted and was elected by the men of Company D to serve as a saber wielding, charging infantryman with the rank of second lieutenant.²⁶ This unit was under the command of fellow classmate Colonel Olin Dantzler (A.B. 1846). At first his unit was sent to the defense of Fort Sumter and Charleston, but when these were captured, most of the South Carolina troops moved to the defense of Virginia. In May 1864, he was promoted to first lieutenant, and at the Battle of Fort Fisher, North Carolina, when the commanding officer was killed, he was promoted to captain in December 1864. In December the fort on the island defending Wilmington and Cape Fear River was successfully defended but the Yankees returned with more troops on January 13, 1865; by January 15, they had captured the fort and island. Captain Sanders was captured, made a prisoner of war and eventually sent to Governor's Island for incarceration. He was finally released from confinement in June 1865 and sent home.²⁷

After entering the military, Sanders sent his daughter, Mary J. (age 12), to Columbia, South Carolina, where she attended Columbia Female College starting in September 1861 until graduating in June 1865. During her college years she and her father wrote to each other regularly until he was released from captivity. (Those letters are in the possession of the South Carolina Historical Society of Charleston.)

It appears that Dr. Sanders had difficulties in adjusting following the war. He abandoned his medical practice and the fields were left unattended. In September 1867 the family began their trip west to the mountains of South Carolina, where Samuel G. entered Wofford College (age 15 or 16). But instead of returning to the plantation, Samuel D. and Martha continued west until they arrived and settled, temporarily, in Jackson, Tennessee. Samuel met with his former classmate Amos W. Jones, who was now president of the Memphis Conference Female Institute. The 1869 college's catalog lists "Dr. S.D. Sanders, Professor of Ancient Languages and Mathematics" and "Mrs. S.D. Sanders, Assistant in Preparatory Department."²⁸

Neither name appears in subsequent catalogs but the Jackson archives librarian, Jack Wood, distinctly recalls seeing a photograph of Dr. Sanders in a local history book.²⁹ The reason for the recollection was that Dr. Sanders had a distinctive full, long beard, unlike any of the other professors in the picture, and he thought it somewhat odd for the time period (probably Jones' book about Southwestern). The couple may have moved on because during the war the Memphis Conference Female Institute had been occupied as a Union Hospital, Jones taught from his home, and the campus needed repairs when the Union soldiers left.

Amos W. Jones' wife, Carolyn M., was the first and only documented spouse to be buried in the Randolph Macon Cemetery (see Appendix D). She was 19 years and 10 months of age when she died on December 14, 1841.

Jones was born in Lewisburg, Franklin County, North Carolina, on December 28, 1815, the son of Amos and Mary Myrick Jones. He graduated with an A.B. from RMC in 1839, and that year was admitted on trial in the M.E. Conference of North Carolina. In 1841, he had full connection with the conference and took his A.M. degree from RMC in 1842.

In 1846, he transferred to the Memphis Conference in Tennessee and was appointed as a professor to the Memphis Conference Female Institute. In 1853, he purchased the institute and became its president. He served in that capacity until 1878, when it was taken over by his son, Amos Blanche Jones. While in Tennessee, he was married four more times. In 1880, his son left the institute, and he resumed the presidency until his death on September 13, 1892. At that time his wife, Mrs. A.W. Jones, took over as acting president and served until 1893, when Amos Blanche resumed the presidency. A. Blanche held the post until 1911.[30]

Dr. Sanders's obituary outlines his next movement to Smithville, Kentucky, in 1870, although I did not find him on the 1870 Census. Then from Kentucky he traveled to Huntsville, Texas, where he took charge of the Huntsville (Andrews) Female College in the fall of 1871. It isn't clear if his wife, Martha, was still alive, but in 1877, he abruptly departed Huntsville to join his son, Samuel G., in Georgetown, Texas.[31] (This suggests he may have been widowed at or before Huntsville.)

Samuel G. Sanders graduated from Wofford College in June 1871 (age 19) receiving highest honors in his class. He moved to Texas shortly thereafter, being offered a faculty position with Salado College, Salado, Texas (chartered February 8, 1860, following a camp meeting of the Methodist Episcopal Church, as a tuition-only based school). The school had a continuous pattern of growth until the early days of the depression; and in 1873, it began to suffer financially until its charter expired in February 1880, and no further students were graduated. The college closed in 1885. In 1874, Sanders was recruited for the newly established Southwestern University to serve as one of the main core of five faculty. His position was professor of modern languages. In short order he left to attend the University of Virginia for a year of postgraduate study. But it seems that while in Virginia he had more on his mind than studying; he married, and when he returned to teaching at Southwestern in 1879, he was now a family man. He and his wife, Mary, who was born in North Carolina in March 1852, had their first child almost as soon as they returned to Texas in late 1877.[32]

In 1881, Samuel G. was elected secretary of the faculty and held that position until June 1890. He and Mary had seven surviving children. They were Mary, born in 1878 (d. 1962) in Texas; Samuel D., born 1880, in Tennessee; Nannie, born 1883 (d. 1964) in Texas; Albert, born 1885 in Texas; Shipp, born 1888 in Texas; Martha P., born 1890 in Texas; and John Randolph, born 1892 in Texas. All of the children are recorded as attending Southwestern or the preparatory school, or both. As a matter of fact, John Randolph received his A.B. in 1912, Professor Shipp G. Sanders received his A.B. in 1908, Professor Albert G. Sanders received his A.B. in 1904, and Samuel D. Sanders received his A.M. in 1901. In 1906, Albert was working as a professor at Magdalena College, Texas, when he was nominated for and awarded the prestigious Rhodes Scholarship at Oxford, England, in 1907.[33]

Samuel G. had served as superintendent of Sunday schools for eleven years. "The congregation placed a stained glass window in the church behind and to the left of the pulpit when viewed by the congregation." Later, in a brochure entitled "The Book of Southwestern," Samuel G. is described: "No teacher in Southwestern ever made a deeper or more lasting impression for good."[34]

Professor Samuel G. Sanders died unexpectedly at the age of 42 on September 30, 1892, of typhoid fever. He left a wife with seven children, the oldest of whom was age 13 or 14 and the youngest a few weeks. Among other things, he was described by the president of the college as "the one man in the faculty in that day whose quiet influence directed the policy of the institution and placed it upon a solid foundation." The president went on to add that "his religion was the secret of his life and power. He carried it into his home and into the recitation room." A close friend and colleague of Sanders was Wesley Carroll Vaden, son of Wesley Childs Vaden of Virginia and graduate of RMC, with an A.M. 1861. W. Carroll's wife, Kate Lockett, was the daughter of M.B. Lockett, who was appointed to the Southwestern Board of Trustees in 1895. (Several Locketts attended and graduated from RMC in the 1840s, and one in 1862.) John Granbery, Jr., was also on faculty at Southwestern at the time, and his father, John Granbery, Sr. (RMC, A.B. 1848), was a bishop. Bishop Granbery left Vanderbilt, where he had been teaching in the 1880s; and in the early 1890s, he arrived in Texas to provide assistance to Southwestern.[35]

As for the development of Southwestern University, graduates of RMC, Boydton were everywhere. In 1859, the Rev. William G. Foote, son of Richard H. Foote of Warrenton, North Carolina (b. 1830; A.M. 1859, RMC), was professor of math and natural philosophy at Soule University, Chappell Hill, Texas (a root school of Southwestern).[36] He returned to his home state of Mississippi during the Civil War and served as a hospital steward. Dr. Craven (A.B. 1849, A.M. 1851, RMC, both honorary), former president of Trinity College, was selected as president of Soule in 1866,[37] but never showed up to accept the appointment, as Trinity did reopen after the war, and he resumed presidency of that institution. Even some rather dramatic stories can also be found from the Soule student body. In high school, I recall a teacher talking about Confederate soldiers being disenchanted with the United States after the Civil War, so they hired ships to take them to Brazil, where the antebellum lifestyle still existed. (By 1870, there were newspaper ads circulating in the United States and Great Britain offering excellent land sales opportunities in Brazil.[38]) It seems, as I recall from one professor in college, that about 5,000 former soldiers made the journey.

However, a nontraditional student arrived on the Soule campus in 1858. He was much older that the average adolescent student at age 23, and he was a veteran of the Nicaragua Campaign. His name was Francis McMullen McKenzie. After graduating he served in the Confederacy during the Civil War as a captain commanding a company of soldiers. Disgruntled at the loss, he and 154 other veterans left Texas and settled in Iguape, Brazil. He died there of tuberculosis in 1867 at about age 32. With so many families in Brazil, the M.E. Church began a concerted missionary effort.

Another nontraditional student was Thomas J. Jarvis (January 18, 1836–June 17, 1915) of North Carolina. Jarvis's family had a 300 acre farm but not much more, and Thomas spent most of his time working the farm. He occasionally attended a nearby common school whenever possible. At the age of nineteen, he decided to attend Randolph Macon College in Boydton, and in order to do that, he would teach during the summer. He graduated with honors, A.B. in 1860 and A.M. in 1861. Now he was a farmer and preacher.

Jarvis rose to the rank of captain during the Civil War, but in May of 1864, he was seriously wounded and lost most of the use of his right arm. Following the war, he was elected to the North Carolina House of Delegates, then the House of Representatives, speaker of the house, and in 1876, lieutenant governor of North Carolina. On February 5, 1879, he took over as governor when the presiding governor was elected U.S. senator. He was elected governor in 1880. President Cleveland appointed him as minister to Brazil in July 1885, a post he held until the fall of 1888, when he returned to his political life in North Carolina.[39]

Another North Carolina student was Samuel Lander of Lincolnton. Lander graduated from Randolph Macon College with an A.B. with highest honors in June 1852 and A.M. in 1855. He served as adjunct professor of modern languages at RMC from 1854 to 1855 and assistant professor from 1856 to 1857. He went on to become president of several colleges and founder and president of Lander University in South Carolina. His oldest son, John M. (b. December 127, 1858), graduated from college and taught for a period of time for his father. But he then chose to move toward missionary work as a

Methodist minister, and he traveled to Brazil. In 1889, he had accomplished all requisites to begin the Institute Metodista Granbery (Granbery College, Minas, Gerais, Brazil) with campus and faculty. In 1891, the Randolph-Macon College Board of Trustees sent J.W. Tarboux as a missionary to Brazil. Soon postgraduate work was offered at the institute, and in 1904, a dental school was established.[40]

Back to Samuel D. Sanders—"the elusive." Following Samuel G.'s return to Texas with his new bride and child soon to arrive, it appears that Dr. Samuel D. felt his time could better be occupied with his son and family instead of a failing college that was in the process of being closed. So he left the college in 1877 and moved to Georgetown to join his son. (The school closed in 1879, and the building was given to a program for black children.) The next record of Dr. Sanders is an 1881 photograph of Southwestern faculty. There on the

Dr. Samuel D. Sanders is among the Southwestern University Faculty, 1880–81. Seated, left to right: J.H. McLean, S.G. Sanders, and F.A. Mood. Standing: R.S. Hyer, S.D. Sanders, C.C. Cody, R.F. Young, and P.C. Bryce (Southwestern University Special Collections, Georgetown, Texas).

front row is Dr. Sanders with a beard, and he is seated with his son standing behind him. Otherwise there are no Southwestern nor Soule records or catalogues that list Dr. Sanders. Southwestern historian Dr. William Jones and archivist Kathryn Stallard suggest that he may have served as an adjunct, as needed.

In 1900, Dr. Sanders was living with the widow of his son, Mary, and her seven children, in a house on College Street. He was seventy-eight years old and listed as "father-in-law." It would certainly have made sense for Dr. Sanders to have moved in with the family immediately following the death of his son. (These were the days of no Social Security, retirements, benefits, etc.) The census records have a notation, not legible, that Mary is working, and possibly "at the college."[41]

"A knightly, chivalrous, Christian man, just, honorable and upright in all his dealings with men. He died as he lived in peace and without a complaint," was part of his obituary written in the *Georgetown Commerce* newspaper on January 30, 1903. It continued, "A brave Confederate soldier; noble Christian man, and a just and upright mason. He was interred at the Odd Fellows Cemetery. He died on Sunday morning, January 25, 1903, from heart failure. He was 81 years old.[42] Records of the I.O.O.F. Cemetery list not only his headstone (he also has a Confederate grave marker), but the markers for Nannie, Mary Shipp (daughter) and Samuel G. (except his date of death is listed incorrectly as 1929 instead of 1892).[43]

CHAPTER 10

A Procrustean Analysis

The first board of trustees meeting following the war must have been devastating to each and every member in a variety of ways. The college had closed officially in March 1864, and now it was August 1865. But in fifteen months (actually just three months of occupation by the Union soldiers), the college had gone from being a magnificent campus to mere grounds and buildings filled with soldiers, freedmen, and their families—all of whom had little respect for the property or the school. In my mind, to have arrived at the college and found the campus, rooms, and halls filled to capacity with filth, animals, crying babies, soldiers and the privies (when used) filled to the brim could only have made one's heart sink to the pit of his or her stomach. It would have pushed forth the tears of melancholy or the anger of a raging bull. Though this is pure conjecture on my part, as neither the board nor Irby even imply that the scourge was even obscene. Either my statement is unjustified, or they were politically astute and guarded as to the proper couching of a simple truth (much like present day written word).

A board meeting was scheduled for Petersburg on August 23, but a quorum did not attend. It was rescheduled to be held at the home of Richard Irby, secretary of the board, at Nottoway County on September 13, 1865. A quorum was in attendance, and the first matter of business was to appoint a committee of Dr. Smith plus four others to "estimate the damage to the college." The second item was to declare all professors' chairs vacated, as clearly in their present situation, they were not prepared to resume "business as usual."[1] (The preliminary report of Dr. Smith and the local trustees must have portrayed a bleak picture.) Dr. Smith was the only remaining professor, and he was authorized to hire assistants.

For some of the board, those who served in the military especially, this may have aroused a different set of responses, as most of the Confederate men in union prisons had not been paroled until late June and early July.

Some were still in the process of returning home in mid and late July (many dying en route or shortly after arrival home), while others remained in prison until as late as September. In addition, RMC was now the home of military rule for the county with union soldiers harassing local citizens into signing an "oath of allegiance to the United States government" (sometimes two or more[2]) and for food, handouts, souvenirs, and other valuables. There continued to be looting and general harassment toward the citizens—especially the elder "gentlemen" and the southern belles. These trustees, former Confederate soldiers, would only have been home about four months with the war still fresh in their senses. The reactions would also have been different for those who lost loved ones in the war, as many men died even as recent as April 1865 and later, and those were near Farmville, certainly part of RMC's territory (the latter at Nottoway).

With the vote of secession, there was no RMC company of men such as those at Hampden-Sydney or the University of Virginia. Most simply went home to serve and fight with family. Captain Richard Irby pulled together six alumni and, later, two students and wrote about his RMC Company G, 18th Infantry, which was actually listed as the Danville Regiment. But another unit, the 12th Infantry, had sixteen alumni and later a student. One of their officers was Captain Thomas Branch (Jr.), member of the board of trustees in 1876. But therein lies another problem—not the competition one would expect, but the remorse. Under Irby's command, Branch was shot twice in August 1862, was detailed in March 1863, and resigned in June 1863; Ferguson was wounded in action in June 1862 and a prisoner of war in July 1863; Hardy was wounded in June 1862; Muse suffered wounds twice; Scott (a cousin born in 1841) was wounded in June 1862 and killed in action in September 1862; and Crenshaw was killed in action in March 1865, less than six months before the board of trustees meeting. On the other hand, of the 12th Infantry, none were killed in action; two died of disease; two were wounded in action twice and two once; and three were captured and made prisoners. Also, Branch's brother, James, became the commanding lieutenant colonel. (This information comes from the Virginia regimental history books. See more on these men in Appendix B.)

Irby gives a few insights into his perceptions of the war in the text of his book, which was written sometime before 1898. Of the "War History," he writes, "Six Randolph-Macon men were enrolled in one company, and the casualties which befell these are here given from actual data."[3] Irby further adds, "The college premises were occupied after the close of the war for some time by the Federal forces. The main building was used as headquarters of the Freedman's Bureau, and the rooms filled with the 'wards of the nation'....

This closes the ante-bellum record."[4] It appears he made no visit to the school during the military occupation, and this was his war history—less than two pages. Then the next chapter begins, "College History After the War."[5]

> The period immediately succeeding the surrender of the Confederate army at Appomattox was one of the darkest and most discouraging that any civilized people was ever called to face. Virginia had been for four years the battle-ground over which great armies had marched and counter-marched and fought. Every home had felt the torture that "tried men's souls." Widows gathered their fatherless children around them to share the last crust of bread together, not knowing whether even that much could be found to-morrow. For miles along the highways over which the armies had marched, the bare chimneys only, marked the sites where comfortable houses had sheltered happy house-holds.

On the next page he continues:

> One of the saddest scenes this writer ever witnessed was at Nottoway courthouse. A few days after the surrender at Appomattox, he was summoned with other citizens of the county to attend a meeting called to confer with the military officers as to the best plans to be devised to prevent suffering among the people. Just as he entered the courthouse, where a number of people were assembled, he saw a venerable man of more than three-score years and ten standing before the officer, with tears streaming down his furrowed cheeks, and heard him say: "Every scrap of meat, every grain of corn, everything in the way of food I had, has been taken from me. I know not where. I shall get my meat or bread to-morrow." This man had been for many years one of the foremost men in the county, a senator in the General Assembly of Virginia, and for many years a trustee of Randolph Macon College.
>
> But poverty and penury were not all. The people were humiliated and despondent. Their state, "the mother of States and statesmen," had now the tyrant's heel upon her neck, and was styled 'District' (No. 1), a "conquered province"—her governor, first a refugee, then a prisoner. Military satraps filled the seats of judges and magistrates. The ignorant slave was often shown more deference than his former cultured master. Most of the flower of the manhood of the state had died by the sword or disease. The boys and girls of the next generation were growing up without the means of education, and helping to eak out a living for their widowed mothers.
>
> Such, in brief, was the condition of Virginia in the period succeeding the close of the war. What could the trustees of the college do under such circumstances as now surrounded them?

(What a surreal reverberation that must have caused to ripple through his mind while preparing his manuscript thirty years later.)

The senator he was referencing was most likely an older classmate of Richard's and a close family friend of the Irby's, Thomas H. Campbell (A.B. 1841, A.M. 1846, RMC). Campbell served for several years in the Virginia House of Delegates and from January 12, 1852, to 1859 as a state senator.[7] He did not serve in the Confederate military, and sometime around 1870, he became president of the Southside Railroad Organization and was one of the leaders in the removal of the college from Boydton. He remained active on the Randolph-Macon Board of Trustees after the move to Ashland.

Irby was born in 1825, and his older brother William was born in 1808. When their father died in 1829, Richard was only 4 years old. William became a member of RMC Board of Trustees, appointed in 1848. Richard's brother was his male role model and father figure, more so than just an older brother. He was also listed as Richard's guardian at registration in 1839 at RMC. During the Civil War, Richard had Company G, 18th Infantry (although most of his family joined either the 3rd or 9th Cavalry, including his young son-in-law John Lucas Irby), but William, wanting to be supportive of his younger brother, signed for his underage son, Julius Edmund Irby, 17, to enlist into Company G under the care of his uncle Richard on November 22, 1862. (Richard left the company in March 1863 and resigned from the military in June 1863 to work for the Confederate government.) Edmund stayed in Company G, and at Saylor's Creek on April 6, 1865, he was captured and made a prisoner of war. (Irby writes in his memoirs of the 18th Infantry that Edmund was wounded in action at Gettysburg, but the official regimental records do not confirm that.) He was sent to Point Lookout Prison, Maryland (suggesting he had been elected an officer), where he was confined until paroled on June 3, 1865.[8]

Another twist to this story involves William and his son. Part of Richard's pride in his brother was that William had attended Ebenezer Academy in Brunswick County and then Hampden-Sydney College, from which he graduated. Returning to the family farm, shortly after graduating from college and following his father's death, William began to invest his assets into land in the Pleasant Grove community of Lunenburg County. By 1860, the U.S. Census discloses that his wife, Sarah E. (Sarah Elizabeth Poindexter, age 39), and William "Little Billy" Irby (age 52) had seven children—six sons and one daughter. The four oldest children—Edmund (15), Fannie (12), Richard B. (10) and Wesley Childs (8) were in school. The family holdings in Pleasant Grove were listed as $26,000 in real estate and $62,000 in personal property.[9] One of William's best friends in nearby Blacks and Whites (Blackstone, Nottoway County) was Allen Crenshaw, father of RMC graduate Ira Irving Crenshaw (b. 1819; A.B. 1842). Together, these men built and began Crenshaw M.E., South, Church in Blacks and Whites.

At the end of the war, William had to report to the Lunenburg County Courthouse to swear an oath of allegiance to the United States government and receive his travel pass. On his return home from the courthouse, William was ambushed and held-up "near Little Nottoway River by Yankee stragglers.

They took his horse and treated him roughly, forcing him to walk home, a distance of five or six miles. The rough treatment and long walk resulted in his death on May 18, 1865."[10]

He did not have the opportunity to see many of his family members and son return home from the war. But then, Edmund was released from prison on June 3, 1865, and he arrived home on June 9, 1865, suffering from camp fever (which he had had for over a week before being released). He continued to suffer until the first week in July, when he died. Having lost her husband and oldest son within seven weeks, the war having ended only a month before that, William's widow had to sell many of her holdings to support her remaining five sons and daughter. To send her sons to Randolph Macon College, she liquidated some of her holdings. The sons started attending RMC in 1867 (Richard B. at age 17).[11]

Family lore states that eventually they settled in Ashland to save on costs, but each summer she and the children returned to Lunenburg County, Brown's Store District mailing address, in 1870. She had kept the family home to be used as a summer house. (It seems that several of the Nottoway County land holdings and large milling operations became the property of his brother, Richard, who converted the entire milling operation to a foundry for the production of stoves.) But the census records suggest that of William's sons, Richard B. had left RMC in 1870, and 20 year old Wesley C. appears to have graduated in 1870.[12] Sarah died on August 26, 1877.

It was at a similar meeting at Nottoway Courthouse that Richard Irby was brought before the Regional Military Tribunal (court) because he had an oath of allegiance," but since he had worked for the Confederacy that was insufficient. He was required to appear before a tribunal, to swear that he had released his slaves and file for a presidential pardon. Within two weeks, the acting Virginia governor, on behalf of the president, approved the pardon, based in part on Irby's substantial wealth.[13]

Irby's son-in-law, John Lucas Irby, enlisted into Company E, 3rd Cavalry (with a number of kinsmen) on April 1, 1864, and on May 9, 1864, his horse was shot during the skirmish at Mitchel's Shop. John was also wounded in action at Mitchel's Shop but soon returned to duty. He was at Appomattox and paroled on April 9, 1865.

It is most curious that Irby would state that he preserved the records and photographs of the men in his command (from March 1862 to March 1863), then furnish what appears to be misinformation about their military lives. Especially information about the period of service after March 1863, when he was detailed out of the regiment for three months, and this was followed by his resigning from the regiment. (Unless this was his personal and family memories that he had recorded, possibly in a journal. The Irby records were donated to the Virginia Historical Society in Richmond in 1930.[14])

The board of trustees met next on July 11 or 12, 1866, at which time there were nineteen members of the board of trustees present. Dr. Smith offered his letter of resignation as president following twenty years of service. His resignation was accepted and he began to make preparations to relocate his family to St. Louis, Missouri, to the Methodist Conference there in early 1867. Another resolution by Judge Chambers was offered to the board at this same meeting to protect and preserve the college's location in Boydton. The resolution passed by a vote of 12 to 6, but for many of the local board members, it was only a stall and not the end. The resolution included a provision that no board of trustees meeting could be held outside of Boydton. The last piece of business was a letter from Professor William B. Carr requesting reimbursement of the monies he had spent building a servants' house on the property in Boydton. The request was tabled for study of the property.[15]

Three A.M. degrees were approved, and the board voted to adjourn until August 18, 1866. One of the conditions for Dr. Smith's departure and relocation was that he wanted to be paid in full for the monies due him in back pay and the property he had sold the board in 1860, plus he wished to sell to the board the ten acres he had purchased that adjoined the president's house for a price of $90. He was owed a total of $7,342.21. In presenting his claim at the business meeting on August 16, 1866, he was adamant that either he was to be paid—in full, at once—or he was prepared to take the board to court that day. Professor Carr was informed, following this meeting, that his request for reimbursement was reasonable; but that the board had no funds available to reimburse his expenses.[16]

Even with coffers that were nearly depleted, he was paid in full. The board also voted to remove John G. Boyd as a member, as he had missed three meetings (he had moved to Baltimore). Arrangements were made to pick up students from the R&D and the R&G (Ridgeway) railroad stations for the college. Also the board voted to hire a servant to have the "college buildings and campus vacated [and] professors' houses brought into good order."[17]

Dr. Smith was still functioning as president pro tem awaiting the arrival of the new president on November 22, 1866. Corprew was still serving as treasurer and proctor. Smith was in charge of conducting the board of trustees meeting which was held in Norfolk in November, instead of Bishop John Early.

Smith had been in a state of declining health for a few years, so he waited until the spring of 1867 to move to St. Louis. Upon arrival, he was established as a minister in the St. Louis Centenary Methodist Church. Soon, the board of curators for the Normal School in Fayette, Missouri, offered Dr. Smith a seat on the board, and he accepted.

At its meeting in June 1868, the board of curators decided they needed a director of fundraising, and that individual should also be the new college president. After much discussion, expediency was of the essence, and the board invited Dr. Smith to accept the position. Due to his ill health, he declined. A recess was called, and three of the board members took him aside and offered all the assistance he could need if he would accept the position of president of the school. The meeting reconvened, and at the age of 66, Dr. Smith accepted.

In a state of melancholy concerning the aftermath of the war, following the board meeting of July 12, 1866, Colonel Townes wrote his grandson a letter on July 22, 1866.

> The loss of all my property or nearly all gives me now neither trouble or uneasiness having made up my mind philosophically to give in and think no more about it. Much trouble would surely destroy me and I therefore try to keep out of it. Had I been able to assist you I never would have consented to your return to Mississippi. But I felt then and now feel like a pauper and I am not sure that I shall not realize the feelings in all its horrors before I die (God knows). In addition to all my state, Confederate, and bank property of every kind and description I have lost, and shall lose, nearly the whole amount of my claims against individuals. Nearly every person is broke that owed me anything and all I have to depend on is what little produce I had on hand and I fear it will take all my rents to pay my taxes. I am only working three hands to try and make a little corn and do not believe that any person can make one cent by hiring negroes at one hundred and odd dollars to farm. I have rented out most of my land (all that I could) on shares. Our crops are very promising. We are now in the midst of a most distressing drought, not having any rain for four or five weeks. Our garden is completely burnt up. Have no vegetables at all except tomatoes and potatoes and if it doesn't rain shortly, there must be a famine in the land as the wheat crop was an entire failure. Your Uncle William is broke as well as the rest of the folks and has gone to work. I hope now he will quit horse trading as he has not credit. He is sued for more than he is worth. It is well for him that I retained the title to the land he lives on or his family would come to want without doubt. I am appointed a delegate to the Union Convention at Philadelphia which takes place on the 14th of August but do not think I can undergo the fatigue of the journey and shall not go unless nobody else can. In that event shall go help the country all I can. It will be a great and imposing meeting and if I was a young man would take great pleasure in attending.[18]

Of course, Uncle William was Captain Townes, Jr., and the land was Cuscowilla. It appears that Townes did attend Philadelphia, as he was not in attendance at the August 15 and 16 board meeting. At this meeting, the board established the new professors of the college, and Dr. Smith issued an advertisement to the *Tobacco Plant* for the October 19, 1866, issue:

Randolph Macon College, Virginia
FACULTY

REV, DR. J.C. BLACKWELL A.M., Professor in School of Chemistry and Natural Philosophy. He will also act as President until a Permanent appointment is made, which will be done at an early day.

O.H.P. CORPREW, A.M., Professor in School of Ancient Languages.

RICHARD W, JONES, A.M., Professor in School of Mathematics.

ERNEST LAGARD, A.B., Professor in School of Modern Languages.

Arrangements are made by which students who are unprepared for the regular classes may be instructed in the primary branches. The session will begin, last Thursday (27th) September and continue forty weeks, or ten lunar months.

TERMS. Payable half in advance, and the other half the first of February following, viz: For tuition and other College fees, according to the number of schools attended, about ... $99. All other expenses, including board (about $160), fuel, lights, &c, exclusive of pocket money and outfit, need not exceed $200.

Arrangements are made to transport students from Ridgeway Depot, on the Raleigh Railroad, whilst a conveyance leaves Roanoke Station, on the Richmond and Danville Railroad, on Mondays, Wednesdays and Fridays, and the Wolf Trap Depot, on the same road, on the same days, and Scottsburg, via Buffalo Springs, on alternate days—Tuesdays, Thursdays and Saturdays.

Address, for the present: Wm. A. Smith, Pres. pro tem. of Board Of Trustees[19]

The RMC board did not hire a new president; instead they selected the Reverend Blackwell as acting president and professor of moral philosophy. This left the chair of chemistry vacant. Some of the applicants considered and not hired by the board included Dr. F.J. (A.) Mettauer for chemistry and Alex Hogg for math—one a former graduate of RMC and the other, former faculty. The 1866 session was soon begun with the new faculty and 46 students, 39 from Virginia and still 16 under the age of 16. The board of trustees ordered that those under the age of 16 should be housed and taught separately from the older students.

Professor LaGarde's first teaching position was with RMC. Born in New Orleans in 1836, he was home schooled by his uncles, studied law and then medicine, but chose a career in journalism. In 1860, he was publisher and editor of *The Sentinel* newspaper in New Orleans. On February 11, 1861, he married Leonine Lafforgue, but soon thereafter, the war began. Instead of continuing the newspaper, he enlisted into Company C, 24th Louisiana Infantry Regiment, as a private. Following the Battle of Shiloh (Pittsburg Landing, April 5–6, 1862), his unit was disbanded. He came to Richmond as a volunteer to assist the Confederacy. He was directed to General Josiah Gorgas, commanding general of the Ordnance Department. He was established into Company A, 3rd Virginia Regiment of Local Defense for Richmond, for the duration of the war.

Following the war, he returned to New Orleans and went to work for a newspaper. Somehow he was recruited by the board of trustees for the chair of professor of modern languages, serving in that position from the fall term of 1866 to the summer of 1868. He then moved to Richmond and edited newspapers in Richmond and Petersburg for a short time, but then accepted another faculty position. In the fall of 1869 he became professor of English literature and modern language at Mount St. Mary's College in Emmitsburg, Maryland, where he stayed until retirement. He died there in 1914.[20]

Two southern states had not reorganized their governments under the conditions set forth by the Federal government by December 1865, and this infuriated President Andrew Johnson. After a political temper-tantrum, on "March 2, 1867, Congress passed an act that 'Whereas, no legal state governments exist ... in the rebel states ... said rebel states shall be divided into five military districts.' Over each a Federal general was appointed." This seemed to have no effect upon the college (except possibly the board of trustees, who wanted change). In August 1867, the student enrollment was 62, with all being from Virginia and North Carolina. For the third year in a row there continued to be 16 students under the age of 16. On September 23, 1867, the *Petersburg Index* published a story: "Rev. James Duncan returned to this city on Thurs. after an absence of several weeks of health. Pastor of Washington Street Methodist Episcopal Church we are glad to hear that he is somewhat improved."[21] This was D'Arcey Paul's church and he, with at least two other board members, were clearly aware of the Reverend Duncan's health issues.

In March 1867, following their meeting with President Thomas Carter Johnson, the Baltimore Conference furnished four new board of trustees members: the Rev. S.S. Rozel, the Rev. John Poisal, the Rev. S.S. Register and the Rev. John Landstreet. In June 1867, three members of the Virginia Conference received honorary D.D. degrees: the Rev. Nelson Head of Mecklenburg County, the Rev. John E. Edwards, and the Rev. W.W. Bennett. The board also discussed the number of empty buildings on the Boydton RMC farm, and it was agreed that Steward Hall, the preparatory department, and the hotel would become rental properties. It was also agreed to hire a janitor for the main building. On December 12, 1867, the board of trustees leased the preparatory building to Professor J.W. Jones for $2.50 per month to begin a preparatory school, and Steward Hall was leased to the Rev. M. Woodward for an undisclosed amount and purpose.[22] The following year, the board of trustees decided at their meeting on June 26, 1868, to waive the rent. In 1869, Steward Hall was again rented and became a photography studio which was advertising in the *Tobacco Plant* newspaper. On January 10, 1868, a paid advertisement appeared in the *Tobacco Plant*[23]:

> Randolph Macon College
> Anniversary celebration
> of the
> Franklin Literary Society
> January 17 at 7 ½ O'clock
> Eulogist:
> W.A. Browder, Ala.
> 1st orator, E.T. Jones, N.C.
> 2nd orator, F. Furr, Va.
> Marshals:
> W.J. Kilby, Va.
> J.A. Blackmon, Ala.

The keynote address was delivered by the Rev. Moses Drury Hoge, D.D., LL.D., and an extract is at the beginning of this book. Dr. Hoge was a most remarkable individual. He was born September 17, 1819, and raised near Hampden-Sydney College, which is where he attended college, earning an A.B. degree in 1839 as valedictorian. His father, Dr. Moses Hoge, was a professor there, following in the footsteps of his grandfather, Dr. Thomas P. Hoge (a medical doctor from Scotland), both professors reportedly having served as president of the college at varying times. From there, Moses entered Union Theological Seminary and became a licensed minister in 1844. In that year he became the reverend of the First Presbyterian Church of Richmond, and two years later he received his first charge, the Second Presbyterian Church of Richmond. He served in this church for over 50 years. He died on January 6, 1899.[24]

When the war began he enlisted as a private but was immediately established as a general and staff chaplain in Richmond. Following the Peninsula Campaign, in the fall of 1862, there was a great revival among the Confederate soldiers, and as many as 5,000 were being converted per day. With a great shortage of Bibles, Dr. Hoge commandeered a ship, ran a Lincoln blockade at Charleston, and again at Wilmington, and sailed for England to purchase Bibles from the British and Foreign Bible Society. He was met at port by his friend the Earl of Shartersbury, who had obtained a grant for 4,000 pounds to purchase Bibles and scriptures. With this grant, they purchased 15,000 Bibles, 50,000 testaments and 250,000 copies of the gospels and psalms bound together. Returning to Virginia, he distributed these to the chaplains and missionaries in the field, organized church building along the Rapidan River (37 churches were built the first year), and conducted revivals.

In April of 1865, when Richmond was being evacuated, "Into Dr. Hoge's church a hurried messenger came. The pastor read the note handed up to him, bowed his head in silent prayer and then said: 'Brethren, trying scenes are before us; General Lee has suffered reverses. But remember that God is with us in the storm as well as the calm. Go quietly to your homes, and whatever may be in store for us, let us not forget that we are Christian men and women. The blessing of the Father, Son and the Holy Ghost be with us all. Amen.'"[25]

It wasn't long before a messenger arrived from President Davis reporting that Richmond was being evacuated. President Davis believed that with the Reverend Hoge's reputation he would not be safe from the Union Army when Richmond was captured. The Reverend Hoge joined the Confederate cabinet in their removal from Richmond to the new capital, Danville, Virginia. Upon arrival in Danville, on April 4, 1865, the Reverend Hoge and Benjamin Judah, secretary of the Confederate States of America Treasury Department, were the house guests of John M. Johnston. His home was located on the southeast corner of Main and Banks Street in Danville, and it also housed the vault and Bank of Danville, where some of the CSA treasury would be stored. That Sunday, which was Palm Sunday, April 9, 1865, while in Appomattox, General Lee was surrendering the battlefield, the Reverend Hoge was preaching a service at the Presbyterian Church on Jefferson Street in Danville.

In the general and staff, a chaplain's pay was established at $80 per month with a ration allowance equivalent to that of a private—25 cents per day. Many chaplains were supplemented by their church or became missionaries of the church instead of enlisting. Even though a chaplain may have been with a unit throughout the war, he was not required to enlist into the Confederate military. Thus, there would have been no official record kept of their presence.

Not all matters relative to RMC were omitted in the newspaper, nor were they without humor. On January 31, 1868, it was published that "Venable Bishop Early is recovering from the effects of a congestive child with which he was attacked last week."[26] The paper soon changed owners, again, and there is no further reference to RMC.

The *Tobacco Plant* said in a February 20, 1870, editorial[27]:

> In June 1868, at the annual meeting of the board, the majority of the trustees then present determined to remove the college to Ashland, Hanover County, Virginia—the minority promptly filed a bill in the Circuit Court of Charlotte County, Judge Marshall presiding, setting forth the facts in the case, and asking for an injunction to prevent its removal. It was promptly granted. The majority had applied to General Stoneman, military governor of Virginia, and obtained an order to remove the apparatus, libraries and fixtures of the college to Ashland. When the majority attempted, through their counsel, to file an answer to this bill, they were ruled out of court for contempt (by Judge Marshall), having already ignored the civil tribunal by applying to the military authorities.

The committee that met with Stoneman was appointed by the board on June 25, 1868, and consisted of D'Arcey Paul, R.M. Smith and the Rev. Leroy M. Lee.[28]

The board appears to be picking and choosing committee members more wisely after 1866 and 1867. I found no reference to a military record for the three committee members. Paul, a Petersburg merchant; Lee a minister; and Smith, Esq., board of trustees in 1858 and appears later as a professor in Ashland (who died soon after relocating), were also not recipients of any degree from RMC. This committee was an excellent choice to approach the "satrap" Stoneman. Obviously, as recorded, it was previously discussed by this committee on July 8. So when the second committee arrived, they were immediately received and the petition immediately granted, but with the proviso of not undermining the court of jurisdiction.

Another committee was appointed to contact President Davis. At a meeting of the board called for on March 13, 1868, the agenda was "'to consider matters touching on the prosperity and permanence of the Institution,' a desperate stroke was planned." On motion, it was resolved that Dr. J.C. Blackwell, Judge E.R. Chambers, and J.J. Daley, Esq., be appointed a committee to correspond and if possible confer in person with Hon. Jefferson Davis and obtain full information as to the prospect of procuring him as president of the college."[29]

John S. James Daly, Esq., had entered Randolph Macon College in 1837 but only attended a couple of years. He was the son of Colonel Samuel Daly of Whittle's Mill area in north central Mecklenburg County and was born in 1820. He was licensed to practice law in the county in December 1840 and served for a number of years as the circuit court clerk. Also included on the committee were Capt. Richard Irby, secretary, Richmond Stove Company, and Thomas Branch, president, Merchants Bank.

President Davis was arrested by the Union Army and taken to Fortress Monroe, Virginia. To guarantee he would not escape, a surety bond was required. The surety bond was given and "under his name are those of his sureties, Horace Greeley's leading the signatures of Cornelius Vanderbilt, Gerritt Smith, Benjamin Wood and Augustus Schell, all of New York"[30] plus another twelve to fifteen.

"Davis had been approached informally earlier." This time "he stated that he had had offers that were better pecuniarily but none that suited his feelings as well."[31] There was a glimmer of hope and potential. But then the board determined their only options were to move or to stay with hope of a revival of the economy. If they moved, they would abandon over 400 acres of land and several substantial buildings and homes, along with other apparatus, to "a precarious market." The unclear thinking process of all or nothing, with no other options, leaves little room for discussion. (One option may have been to have sent board member and good friend of President Davis, Major Sutherlin, to discuss options with Davis.) But with their substantial holdings and starting anew with so little and surviving, there appear a vast number of options. Davis appears as just one of those small details that needed to be cleaned up before the final move was taken.

According to Irby, the next board of trustees meeting was June 24, 1868, with 30 members present. The Rev. J.E. Edwards made the motion to move to Ashland. It was adopted by a vote of nineteen to nine, but as Scanlon writes, this had more "the character of a coup d'état, one engineered by the laity of the board This is very different from the founding of the school, when the direction of affairs was in the hands of the clergy. By the time the full board met to ponder the future of the college, the decision was very nearly forced upon them."[32] To backtrack for a moment, according to Irby and Scanlon, Edwards made most of the motions during the meeting on that date—as though a prepared agenda. This included purchasing the buildings in Ashland from Irby, et al., a committee established to seek approval for the move from the legislature, the president of RMC to hire an agent to pack up and move—all in one fell swoop. But, coupling this with Scanlon, we find that "on May 5, 1868, the directors of the railroad heard through their president a letter from [Johnson] the president of Randolph Macon seeking inducements the company would give the college to move to Ashland. That town, on the railroad line, had come to the notice of the college's trustees in November, 1866, when the owners of a bankrupt hotel [complex of seventeen frame buildings] tried to sell it to the college."

It is clear that Johnson was using his railroad skills to the advantage of the college (notwithstanding the fact that Confederate Brigadier General Mahone was back in the state Senate following the war, and he was president of the railroad line that ran past Ashland). Also, it seems that the college was approached with the property for sale in Ashland about the same time Johnson arrived on campus before being whisked away to Baltimore (passing by Ashland or was a stop in Ashland already scheduled?) accompanied by John C. Blackwell in April 1867.

"The directors of the railroad decided that the college's presence would increase the population in Ashland, increase the property values of the town, and increase fares."[33] They offered the college: (1) to move the furniture, libraries, apparatus, professors and officers to Ashland free of charge; (2) that food from Bailey's Market in Richmond to the College would be done freight free; (3) they would deed the college a 19½ acre parcel of land (the old racetrack) free and clear; and (4) a variety package of discounted and free railroad fare passes for officers, families, trustees and professors was proposed. On May 13, 1868, Thomas Branch (Sr.), Richard Irby, and two investors purchased the hotel.

On May 20, 1868, President Johnson of RMC met with the Baltimore Conference in that city, seeking an $80,000 scholarship to fund the lost investments of the college due to the Civil War and to fund a chair, among other items. He gained their renewed permission to move the college campus to Ashland (although they were not part of the conference). A follow-up inducement negotiated through a ruse by Johnson netted on June 19, 1868, from the railroad, a draft for $1,500 to make necessary repairs to the hotel to begin operation of the college in Ashland on October 1, 1868.

The plan to remove the college was well orchestrated by Carter and a few select board of trustees members, executed and now almost complete.[34] According to Scanlon, a meeting was held on June 24, 1868, with 24 members present. There was much discussion as to whether it was a called meeting, because if so, it would violate the 1866 resolution passed in Boydton that no called meeting could take place outside of that town. Johnson presented a report, which was not kept with the minutes and subsequently lost, recommending relocation. One of the staunchest supporters of the move was the editor of the *Richmond Christian Advocate*, W.W. Bennett (a board of trustees member and later president of R-MC–Ashland), who wrote frequently of his opinion in an effort to persuade Richmonders, and I'm sure some board members, to join the campaign.[35]

Another meeting was scheduled for July 29, 1868, in Richmond. At this meeting, the committee to seek approval to relocate the college read into the record a letter to General Stoneman. They related that they are a new committee to follow up on what the previous committee had received from Stoneman on July 8 (this letter was not to be found in college nor conference records). Primarily, the Mecklenburg minority of the board of trustees filed suit in Prince Edward County court to prevent the move. The judge ruled in favor of the minority. The committee (apparently anticipating this) had already served notice to Stoneman of what was happening, apparently failing to mention the ruling by the Prince Edward County judge. Now they were officially asking his permission to move, and through his assistant adjutant, he wrote a reply the same day, "Authority is hereby given to the trustees of that college to remove that institution ... subject to the conditions set forth in a former letter from these headquarters, dated the 8th instant."

On July 30, RMC President Johnson submitted to the board his letter of resignation that starts, "The experiment upon which you are about to enter, with my aid and approbation, seems to me to demand that you should have the widest field for the choice of a man to fill the position that I now hold. The general troubled condition of the country, excluding many distinguished men from the arena of politics, in which the talent of Virginia and the South has heretofore been employed, and also the returning to this state many unemployed scholars and literary men, affords you a wide field of selection for this purpose.... I hereby resign."[36] Johnson had actually done what he was hired to do—shut down the college in Boydton, gain the support and backing of the Baltimore Conference and relocate the college with the aid of a railroad. The railroad company had worked in tandem with Johnson, but when, less than six months later, the new president, Duncan, ask for reduced fare passes for students, their response was quick and clear—"no" (the clout was absent). Johnson was gone, and the negotiations were done.

What took place had pitted "a small but vocal minority that bitterly opposed the move" against the majority-driven board of trustees, which insisted that the move from Southside Virginia was "imperatively demanded by educational interests of the church and the community at large" and quashed attempts to stop it. Boxes were packed, furniture moved and arrangements made with the railroad before any real obstacles could slow things down. "Left behind was a large bell, college papers and perhaps a trunk of what were presumed to be worthless bonds.... The lingering devastation of the Civil War had left the former campus at Boydton isolated, run down and largely deserted and an unlikely place for a lively academic community (nor a picturesque) for a last stand by local supporters."[37]

It really didn't matter what Boydton wanted, nor what they did, the college board was determined to move. There are no records of their having met with local officials, although the county government had signed contracts in March 1868 for a railroad to come through the county. A few wagons were loaded with as much as they could haul, and Randolph Macon left town. There is no record that they ever looked back.

CHAPTER 11

Boydton Has a Voice

Even as late as February 2, 1870, the "gentlemen" of Mecklenburg County were providing their emotional support toward Randolph Macon College. A story appeared in the *Tobacco Plant*, now under the new ownership of Langston Finch.[1] Finch was a graduate of the RMC Law Department in 1849 and had owned the Boydton Hotel. He was extremely active in Boydton and had been married in the RMC chapel. During the war, he was a commissioner of the local commissary and a staunch supporter of the college. He also served as a circuit Methodist Episcopal, South, minister for several of the Mecklenburg County churches for many years following the war. Between 1866 and 1870, there was no newspaper coverage of RMC except commercial advertising, as John Boyd sold out in 1865. Also, from May 1865 through most of 1866, newspaper publication was prohibited under military rule. This story appeared in the February 2, 1870 issue:

> Randolph Macon College—Rev. J.B. Kirkpatrick, the agent, has addressed an appeal to the citizens of Baltimore to come to the relief of Randolph Macon College, at Ashland, Hanover County, Va., a venerable institution of learning, which lost by the war seventy thousand dollars of its endowment fund. To recuperate that fund is felt necessary in order to secure the complete success and usefulness of the college, which has in the number in its students rapidly recovered from the prostration of the war, there being now on the roll not less than 100 young men. Encouraged by the general sympathy of Baltimore towards the South, and especially towards Virginia, an appeal is made to our citizens to contribute $80,000 to constitute the "Baltimore Professorship in Randolph Macon College," to be a perpetual monument to their generosity and appreciation of education.[2]

This commitment was reconfirmed at a Baltimore Conference meeting in May 1868. James M. Becker, Virginia Methodist Conference Historian, wrote in 2004 that "the Baltimore Conference of the Methodist Episcopal Church, South ... had no college. The move to Ashland was designed to elicit financial support and students from the southern Baltimore Conference. Ashland in 1868 was reasonably close to the center of the two conferences."[3]

Then in the issue of February 18, 1870, "a letter of importance to the community" is published in the editorial section.

> We have been requested to state that a meeting of the trustees of R.M. College, and the people of the county, will be held at our next county court to take some action with regard to the removal of that institution from our midst. Now that we are having civil law restored to us, let us endeavor to assert our rights, which have been so flagrantly violated, and to protect ourselves against the effort which is being made to convert our property into a pandemonium for insane negroes. This last act of the gentlemen who, by military law, have wrested from us our property, is the crowning act of all; it shows us to what lengths men will go when they have once departed from principle. We are pained when we think that gentlemen of their high position can persuade themselves, that "law or no law" they can trample the rights of a minority under foot.[4]

The salient points of the editorial of February 18 were published previously. There is one point that needs to be added. Following the above section, the next part of the text was:

> Litigation costs money, and without money the suit must stop. The minority of the trustees have no more personal interest in this suit than the rest of the citizens of Mecklenburg County; and it ought not to be expected of them to bear the entire burden to pay the expenses of this suit. They are not able even if they were disposed to do so. If the suit they have instituted proves successful (and I see no reason why it should not), will it not promote the interests of the entire county, and in fact a blessing to the community? The college in successful operation would enhance the value of land, furnish a good home market for produce, and bring annually into the county some twenty to thirty thousand dollars.[5]

Following this, the trustees of RMC and citizens held their meeting on February 21, 1870 (with three days' notice). The *Tobacco Plant* of February 23, 1870, gives these details about the meeting:

> On motion, E.A. Rawlins was called to the chair, and L.E. Finch appointed secretary. The chairman called on Judge E.R. Chambers to explain the object of the meeting, which was briefly done, in a quiet but clear manner. The following resolutions were then read by the secretary, and unanimously adopted by the meeting:
>
> "'Resolved,' That the minority of the Board of Trustees of Randolph Macon College, and the donors, and beneficiaries, by whose liberality the institution was built up and endowed, have rights and interests in it, which could not be divested by the arbitrary orders of a military commandant.
>
> "'Resolved,' That the closing of the college, and the removal of its library and apparatus, and other personal property to Ashland, after an injunction had been granted by a judge of the Circuit Court for the County of Charlotte, in which a suit had been instituted and which is still pending to litigate the rights of the

parties, was an act of lawless violence against the court, and disregard of the judicial authority of the state.

"'Resolved,' That the trustees of Randolph Macon College have no rights of property in the institution and no power or authority to sell, or convey it, and that the proposition to sell it to the state for an asylum for insane colored persons, is a continuance of the disregard of right and of law, in which its removal originated.

"'Resolved,' That the people of Mecklenburg, who paid of $10,000 as a bonus upon an agreement and stipulation that the college be located on its present site near Boydton, and who afterwards contributed at least $10,000 more to create an endowment fund, have claims and rights in the institution which it is their duty to vindicate and arrest.

"'Resolved,' That we have too much respect for the legislature to presume they will unite with the trustees in casting reproach and contempt on the judiciary of the state by wresting from it a judicial question of which it has taken cognizance, involving only legal rights, and which can only properly adjudicated in that forum.

"'Resolved,' That a committee of __ gentlemen be appointed, and they are hereby requested to prepare and present a memorial to the legislature, giving a statement of the facts and circumstances of the case, and respectfully requested that they do not, by purchasing the property, or by amending the charter, anticipate one arrest the action of the courts in the premises—but leave it for the judiciary to decide how far the civil rights of the people have survived the unregistered edicts of a military commandant."

On motion, the "blank" committee in the resolutions was filled by the chairman with five, viz: Messrs. E.R. Chambers, C.S. Hutcheson, T.F. Goode, William Townes, and Geo. B. Finch.

On motion, the chairman was added to the committee.

On motion, it was requested that a copy of the proceedings of this meeting be published in the county papers, and that the papers of Richmond and Petersburg be requested to copy the same.

E.R. Rawlins, Chairman[6]

On behalf of Randolph Macon College, William W. Bennett, editor, responded in the *Richmond Advocate* to the resolutions published on February 23 in the *Tobacco Plant*. The response was quick and a copy of the *Advocate* was sent to the editor, Finch. The following is the entire response to Bennett in the March 15, 1870, *Tobacco Plant*. It seems to warrant inclusion as to the position of the "silenced abandoned minority."

In an effort to quell some of the heated discussions taking place on the streets of the towns in the county, On Christmas day, 1869 an anonymous planter (reported to be Peyton R. Burwell from the Board of Trustees of the Christiansville Academy) sat down at his home somewhere in Mecklenburg County (he styled it "Piney wood") and wrote a letter to the editor of the *Tobacco Plant*, then being published in Boydton, having moved from Clarksville that year. It had been a hard year, there had been a severe drought, five months without any real rain. Many people had already left to seek homes in more favorable places.

The fine house that he would never build now was on the mind of "Overseer of the Road,"[7] as he signed himself:

> "Is it not a sad thing that so many of your friends neglected to build fine houses when they were able to do so? Some of us could have built a dozen such, but now have to be thankful for any that we can get. To what should we attribute this great neglect in our people? Was it for the want of industry? Or was it the effort of an example set us by our forefathers, our great and wise statesmen, for instance Randolph and Macon taught us by their example that wise men did not always build fine homes—they were men of large minds, large fortunes of land and negroes, yet they lived in very common houses. Our idea of a fortune was nothing less than two plantations and a hundred negroes, out of debt and a plenty of money. When that fortune was attained your correspondent intended to build a fine house to die in and be buried near, but just before the break of day the dark time came, and we have determined, having food and raiment, therewith to be content...."

Wednesday March 15, 1870 RANDOLPH MACON COLLEGE AGAIN[8]

* * *

The temper of the editor of the Richmond "Christian Advocate," ruffled by an editorial which appeared in this paper on the removal of R.M. College, was not tranquilized on reading the resolutions adopted by the people of Mecklenburg. Indignant as the editor is that a minority should dare to assert any rights in opposition to a preemptory order of the Virginia Conference, yet he felt that the resolutions placed him and those with whom he is acting on the defensive, and he attempts their justification. Let us review the defense and we will give the editor the full benefit of it.

The resolutions say that $10,000 was paid by the people of Mecklenburg on an agreement and stipulation that the College should be located near Boydton. This says the editor, "is vain imagination of the people near Boydton, the $10,000 was not offered as a bonus, but as a ground for the consideration of the committee, and to induce them to locate the college near Boydton." We know not what objection the editor has to the word bonus, and have no objection to his cashiering it; but he distinctly asserts that $10,000 was offered to induce the commissioners to locate the college near Boydton, the offer was accepted, the $10,000 was paid, and the college by the terms of the charter located near Boydton. This is all that the people of Mecklenburg claimed or asserted; and if this does not constitute a binding agreement for a valuable consideration, we would like for the editor to inform us what would be a binding agreement. "It was your anxiety," says the editor, "to get the college that induced the offer of $10,000, and not the anxiety of the commissioners to select the site." This sentence requires an expositor. Does the editor mean to say that a man's anxiety to purchase property after it has been bought and paid for and delivered will justify the purchaser in retaking it and appropriating it to his own use? It means this or it means nothing. Such are the paradoxes and absurdities to which those are liable who undertake to defend an unjust and hopelessly defenseless cause.

The resolutions state that the removal of the college, after an injunction had been awarded by Judge Marshall, was an act of lawless violence. The editor admits that the college being located by its charter near Boydton, it could not legally be removed without an amendment to the charter. The charter has not been amended, yet the college has been removed, its removal thus was clearly a violation of the law, and being done by the arbitrary order of a military satrap in violation of the law, it surely may be properly designated as an act of lawless violence. But the military power was not appealed to for permission to remove it.

The removal was by the trustees, acting in obedience to the instructions of the Methodist Conference; and the appeal to the military power was to protect them for violating the order of injunction awarded by Judge Marshall, and was an act of lawless violence.

Gen'l Stoneman, says the editor, was the "state, the legislature, and the power of the state, he might have altered the charter," &c. The judge who leads the minority and the judge who granted the injunction were his appointees. Now we do not know which is most reprehensible, the fawning adulation which thus magnifies and exalts the military power or the palpable violation of the truth of history in asserting that the judges were the appointees of the military authority.

The judges referred to were elected by the constituted authorities of the state, held their commissions and discharged their duties under the broad seal of the Commonwealth. Judge Marshall was elected by the people of his district in the year 1852, and has held the position as successor of Judge William Leigh for sixteen years. Judge Chambers was elected by the legislature of the state prior to the passage of the reconstruction, and before a military governor of civil affairs had been known in Virginia. Gen'l Stoneman had all faith and confidence in the ability and integrity of the judges of the state and held the military authority in subordination to them and when he granted his protection to a (?) majority for their violation of the law in removing the college, he stated to them it was a proper question for the court and its judgment would be carried out by him, and (re?ed) them to execute a bond in a large (pena?o) abide the results. The plea that the (m?ry) was the only power in the land being (?sified), all the defences founded upon it (?s) with it, and leaves the editor and those (with) whom he acts without defence.

The payment of $10,000 as a consideration for locating the college near Boydton is admitted, and the (?nce) of all necessity by appealing to the (military) power is proven by the history of the (S?) the people then are justified in calling it a violent and lawless set.

In misstating the tenure by which the judges held their offices we do not believe the editor designed willfully to misrepresent facts.

The gentlemen having boldly defied the law and the military power, which they invoked, having failed them, they now as a last refuge fly to the church as a sanctuary and claim the protection of its altars. "The College" says the editor "is in moral law and justice the property of the conference, the board of trustees were instructed by the conference to change it and they intend to obey its instruction." This lofty claim of ownership of the college by the conference, and the right to govern it, which divests the board of trustees of all, and converts them into mere menials or machines to register their edicts, is both novel and astonishing to the minority of the board, and never heard of by them until after the removal of the college, they saw it stated in the answer of the bill of the majority to the minority.

We will not borrow a favorite word of the editor, one used by him, when he is unable to deny a statement and unwilling to admit it, and call it a "gratuitous" claim—But we would ask with an honest wish to be enlightened, on what is the claim founded? Not on the charter, for the words Methodist Conference nor the word Methodist are not in it; and had they been there the charter would never have been granted. It would have been a palpable violation of Article iv. section 32, of the Constitution of the state, which declares "that the General Assembly shall not grant a charter of incorporation to any church or religious denomination."

Now is there any sect or denomination that claims ownership of a college in this state? William and Mary, it is true, is under the fostering care and patronage of the Episcopal Church, and it is wise and proper that it should be so, and a majority of the board of trustees being of that denomination, it is reasonable as vacancies in the body will be filled by one of the same denomination, and thus it will continue under the patronage of that church. In like manner Hampden Sydney College is under the patronage of the Presbyterian Church. But no Episcopal Convention or Presbyterian Synod has ever assumed to interfere with the trustees in the government of these colleges, much less to assume a right of property in them. It was intended by the charter that R.M. College should be under the care and patronage of the Methodist people, and that object, it was believed, was sufficiently secured by appointing in the charter a majority of gentlemen of that denomination trustees. But surely it was never contemplated that under the charter the Methodist Conference, as an ecclesiastical body, should have any more power or authority over it than any other religious denomination. And if the charter justified the high pretentions of the conference, it should be revoked and the corporation dissolved or the constitutional provisions before referred to become a dead letter.

The minority have studiously avoided the introduction of the Methodist Conference into the controversy; for the conference as a body they have the profoundest respect, and do not hold it responsible for any resolutions it may have adopted on the subject of the removal of the college. The resolutions were no doubt introduced by the trustees, who were members of that body, and the conference thinking they were the best judges of the best interest of the college and the Methodist people, adopted them without inquiry or investigation, totally ignorant that they were trespassing on the rights of others or violating the law of the land. The editor says that the removal of the college meets with the approval of the Methodist people around Boydton. This we pronounce a "gratuitous" assertion, and the vacant halls at Ashland proves it so. Where are the young men from the Piedmont regions of Virginia, from the Carolinas and Georgia, that used to crowd her halls near Boydton? They are at other schools or at home, because their fathers do not wish to have them buried in the swamps and slashes of Hanover, which they believed would be a noble result if they were sent to Ashland.

But the editor says, "he hopes there is good sense enough in the legislature not to remand R.M. College back to be buried without hope of resurrection in the old fields near Boydton. If the minority succeeds, its grave is dug; on its

grave stone will be written; died of a minority." Be it so. John Randolph and Nathaniel Macon can have no nobler inscription on their tombs than this;
DIED OF A MINORITY VAINLY CONTENDING FOR THE RIGHT, AGAINST THE WRONG AND INJUSTICE OF A LAWLESS MAJORITY.

But the editor says "the success of the minority will not defeat nor arrest the Ashland Randolph Macon College." Be it so. Give us our rights and we have no objection to the Methodist Conference building for itself a college at Ashland.

But we claim the charter, the name, and the franchises of R.M. College. Give us these, and we will not call in question what you may do elsewhere.

Paragraph 5 gives us some clues into the letter of July 8, 1868, from Stoneman, but this story appeared as an epitaph to the college in the *Tobacco Plant*. Finch began a new newspaper in 1870 the *Mecklenburg Herald*, based in Boydton.[9]

The Wednesday, June 29, 1870, issue contains an editorial: "College Peddling."[10]

> Suppose the legislature and the courts sanction the removal of Randolph Macon College to Ashland, and the people of Ashland and that vicinity shall take stock in the institution as located there, what would prevent a majority of the trustees, after getting the money from the people in and near Ashland for their purposes, from treating them as they have treated the Mecklenburg people, move the college to some other point, to suit the fancy or whims of the majority trustees, and so on; this principle, proposed to be established by these gentlemen, is an absurdity; yet, it is an outrage on common justice.
>
> Just think of it; most of the agents of the college have been Methodist ministers. Such men as Wm. D. Rowzie and H.B. Cowles would go to the people, and in the honesty and sincerity of their hearts sat to brother C and brother D we are trying to establish the college permanently at Boydton, and you are greatly interested in its being put on a permanent basis, it brings to your county annually some $30,000 or $40,000—your property will be greatly enhanced in value by it; your society will be improved; your children can be educated at your doors, where you can watch over them, and we think you should subscribe to it probably or five hundred dollars, they pay the money; and in a few years the majority trustees ignore the rights of these subscribers, refuse to submit the question to the arbitraments of the courts, apply to the military authority, override the law, and defy public sentiment. Such conduct can only be justified in our opinion on the unscriptural ground that these trustees are willing to do evil that good may come out of it.

The tide began to turn, and the editorials began to offer glimmers of hope and options beginning in July 1870. The county commissioners established a Randolph Macon Commission composed of Judge Edward Chambers, Colonel T.F. Goode and Lieutenant George Finch. In the *Mecklenburg Herald* issue of July 27, 1870, mentioned in the editorial column[11]: "We would be glad if the Committees on the Randolph Macon College and the Railroad Committee would make a report at an early day as convenient, so as to encourage us, or let us know the state these several enterprises. The Committee on Navigation of Allen's Creek from the mouth to Plank Road Bridge, are arranging to make an inspection of this stream at an early day. We have reasons to believe they will report favorably on this project; some half dozen good business men who know whereof they speak, pronounced this as a feasible scheme. We know of no enterprise that will pay better than this. If this arrangement was complete and a warehouse built at the long bridge, all the freight brought to Boydton and the surrounding country would be shipped to that point." However, with the beginning of a poorly structured, funded and operated public school system and remnants of the Freedman's Bureau floundering around the county, on August 10, 1870, the editorial took on a different tone[12]:

> Mecklenburg County today is as poorly supplied with the means and appliances for education as any county in the state. At the close of the war we had R.M. College near Boydton, an excellent institution, but which, some two years ago, under the unjust and unfortunate action of its trustees become peripatetic, and moved off to Ashland, where it has been gasping for breath ever since.—At this time we have not a school, either male or female, of sufficient éclat to command any respectable extent of patronage.—The great want of our community at this time is a first class female seminary.
>
> Make Boydton a centre, and describe a circle sixty miles in diametur, and in the whole area thus described we have not a single first class female school. But the question occurs, how shall we remedy this state of things? We know of no method more feasible than the formation of a joint stock company, with a capital of some six or seven thousand dollars.

A letter to the editor in the September 21, 1870, *Mecklenburg Herald* begins[13]:

> Dear Sir—A gentleman of this county, who I believe, is a member of the board of trustees of Randolph Macon College, suggested to me the other day the propriety of sending an application to the legislature to establish the state Agricultural College at this place. If I am correctly informed, the state has received three hundred thousand dollars for the establishment of such a college.
>
> Here are buildings which may be got at an almost nominal price, and we think this circumstance will go a great way in furthering our application. Action should be taken immediately to remove all obstacles, and to secure as much influence in our favor as possible, for other institutions in the state are making great efforts to obtain the endowment.
>
> (Little did they know that this offer was made much earlier to the college, June 26, 1867, with an average enrollment of 200 students, and RMC had already notified the state that its enrollment was too small, and it didn't qualify. This was a precursor program for R.O.T.C., offered to all but southern colleges by President Lincoln, in 1862, in an effort to bolster recruitment. Southern states were minimally included in 1867.)

One last attempt at "guilt" and "pleading" was attempted in the editorial of September 28, 1870, headlined "The Property of Randolph Macon College"[14]:

> We have learned with much pleasure that the Masonic Lodge of Boydton have passed a resolution recommending the purchase of this property by the Grand Lodge of the state for a college, to be under the control of the fraternity; and in furtherance of this object, have appointed a committee to wait upon our people and ascertain what they are willing to give by way of assurance that they desire such an institution in their midst.
>
> Now in this age we hope it requires no logic to prove that this enterprize, in which every man in Mecklenburg county, and more particularly every human being in our little village, is vitally interested—and were we to not be? In the advancement of our material interest alone, there would be a contest among us all to see who would come up to the scratch first, cheerfully, and who should have the honor of contributing the largest amount in the establishment on a firm footing of this most landable enterprize.
>
> We have had till within the last few years a flourishing college in our midst; had we ? wisely it would probably have been with us now. While it was here, it was certainly the chief attraction and ornament to this county and the most fruitful source of profit to Boydton and the surrounding country.
>
> For a period of thirty years the average annual amount of money thrown into circulation and spent among us in this immediate vicinity could not have been less than thirty thousand dollars. This income is gone from us forever, unless we avail ourselves of the advantage offered us by the existence of the buildings still untenanted, and give substantial evidence to the Masonic fraternity and to the world at large, by consecrating our means, our talents and our influence to the successful reconstruction of a college.
>
> Let this be done, and five years would not elapse before every acre of real estate within five miles of the institution would appreciate thirty-three and one-third per cent in its present value. It would attract emigration from abroad, and from other sections of our own country, and even our own state....
>
> Tell us not then, land-owner, that you have no money to subscribe to the reconstruction and rehabilitation of the college. If you have no money, your land is a most excellent substitute. It is the finest basis of credit in the world, because it is immovable and indestructible. If you can give your broad acres to build the Norfolk and Great Western Railroad, you can with more reason give your lands to the building up of a literary institution in our community. But we have enough to give to both enterprizes.

There was a story in December 1871 of Captain J.W. Jones (RMC alumnus), formerly of Brunswick Academy near Zion Church, Union Level, Virginia, holding recitals and orations for his students in the halls of RMC. (This was Southside University, which operated for about eighteen months.) "We hope the time will soon come, when these halls will again be resonant with the tread of many feet, and the hum of voices, attendant on a first class institution of learning, which shall be to Southside Virginia what old Randolph Macon was in days gone by."[15]

In the May 8, 1873, *Clipper* a brief notation was made of "Southside Liberality"[16]: "During the past week the Boydton subscriptions, in aid of the purchase of Randolph Macon College for Masonic purposes, have reached several thousand dollars."

Although there are a limited number of the original weekly issues of local newspapers on microfilm, there are no further references to RMC from 1874 to 1886 when the *Plant*, the *Herald*, the *Valley*, *Clipper*, and the other county newspapers were sold or went out of business. It would appear that in the midst of a depression, end of reconstruction, trying to rebuild family lives, and trying to build a place of worship, Boydton simply gave up or ran out of steam. Either way, the chapter closed.

The June 24, 1887, issue of the Clarksville *Banner of Truth* carried a state news story of Dr. Moses Hoge, chaplain of the First Regiment "Richmond Grays," who preached a sermon for their reunion in Richmond on Sunday, July 12, 1887. This story was followed by: "The commencement exercises of Randolph Macon College, Ashland were conducted on the 15 and 16 inst., Bishop A.W. Wilson delivering the oration before the two literary societies: Bishop Granbery and other church celebrities were present. Resolutions were adopted by the board of trustees, on the death of the Rev. W.W. Bennett late president of the college: There were nine graduates from the school for the term, and President W.W. Smith read a long list of names of students who had won distinctions in the lower classes."[17]

Appendix B, Roll of Honor, gives general description of many lives of RMC and the Boydton College community, their role in the military during the war, and for some, a thumbnail sketch following the war. The board had gotten wise very quickly about the sentiment between the North and South. The fact that the war was over did not take it away—in fact, it may have even deepened the resentment. Johnson, as a former Confederate colonel, was sent north in 1866 and 1867 to raise funds for the college. Of course, he was almost completely unsuccessful, but that was as expected. Another veteran was the Rev. J.E. Edwards (honorary A.M. 1858, RMC; board of trustees 1858; honorary D.D., 1867), a staunch advocate for the move from Boydton who made most of the motions on June 24 to move. He also served on several committees. At a later date, he purchased property and built a hotel in Ashland, which he subsequently donated to RMC. Edwards served in the 2nd Virginia Light Artillery Battalion (no rank found).

The second committee to approach Stoneman on July 29, 1868, was composed of D. Paul, R.M. Smith, Drs. L.M. Lee and (honorary D.D. 1867, RMC) J.E. Edwards, and N. Head (Dr. Nelson; honorary D.D. 1867, RMC). Edwards was the only veteran of the Virginia Conference group I could find who served in an artillery unit (most likely Utterback's Company). His son, William E. Edwards (A.B. 1862 and later a D.D., RMC), left Boydton upon graduation and went to Petersburg. He served as a chaplain at Drewey's Bluff. The committee returned the same day with a response from the 1st Military District, Stoneman.

Following the reading of this letter, President Johnson resigned his post; his resignation was accepted by a motion from the Rev. J.C. Granbery on July 30, 1868. Then another motion was made the same day by Dr. N. Head to move the college to Ashland to "be opened ... by October next." In this same motion, another resolve included, "This board has been actuated only by the solemn conviction that it was imperatively demanded by the educational interests of the church and the community at large, and the opposition which has been offered to this action by a minority of the trustees is deeply deplored by their colleagues of the board, who here now and hereby respectfully request that those members will withdraw their opposition, as injurious to the interests dear alike to all."[18]

According to Irby, at this meeting the board appointed a committee to take care of moving the college, which was composed of Irby, Paul, Branch, Head (who had been assigned as pastor of Providence Church, Forksville, in 1865 and was awarded an honorary D.D. by RMC in 1867) and the Rev. T.S. Campbell (an RMC trustee and the "old man" referred to by Irby in 1865). The committee to secure and elect a new college president was Bishop Early, Bishop Doggett, Dr. Head, Dr. L. Lee, Dr. J. Edwards, Dr. Rosser, the Reverend Cowles, the Reverend Granbery, and Richard Irby, treasurer.[19]

Sometime later, board's records reflect that Irby made a motion that "this board hold itself in readiness to make such arrangements as will secure to the county of Mecklenburg a high school at the present site of Randolph Macon College on terms such as may be desired, said school to be a preparatory school to the college."[20] (The college did begin two preparatory schools and a women's college, in the central part of the state, but no return to Boydton.) Then, as soon as the college opened in Ashland, the board of trustees recommended to the Commonwealth that the campus in Boydton be purchased by the state to become an asylum for Negroes. When all the dust settled the following advertisement was placed in *The Richmond Inquirer* (semiweekly edition) of June 7, 1872[21]:

> VALUABLE COLLEGE PROPERTY IN MECKLENBURG COUNTY, VIRGINIA FOR SALE AT PUBLIC AUCTION.—By virtue of a deed of trust, bearing date the 15th day of February, 1871, executed to the undersigned by Henry G. McGonegal, of the state of New York, and at the request of Randolph Macon College, the creditor secured thereby, I shall expose to sale as public auction, on the prem-

ises, at 12 o'clock, on FRIDAY, the 5th day of July, 1872, the valuable property known as the "RANDOLPH MACON COLLEGE PROPERTY," NEAR Boydton, in the county of Mecklenburg, Virginia. The main buildings, situated in a beautiful oak grove, are of elegant brick, four stories high, fire-proof, and contain a large and commodius chapel, three society halls, eight or ten lecture rooms, and a sufficient number of well-ventilated dormitories to accommodate from 175 to 200 students. The building of the Preparatory Department, near the main buildings, is also of brick, has two large recitation rooms, and will seat from 50 to 75 pupils. Those of the Boarding Department (two in number) are likewise of brick, and from their convenient arrangements are admirably suited to the purposes for which they were built. They have all the necessary outbuildings, with large gardens and lots attached. The mansion of the president and the different residences of the faculty (three in number) are handsome buildings, eligibly and conveniently located, and have all the desirable out-buildings, gardens, lots, &c., for the use and comfort of private families.

In addition to the property mentioned above, there are THREE HUNDRED AND SEVENTY ACRES OF LAND attached, the greater portion of which has been under cultivation, and is well adapted to the growth of all the products of this climate.

The above property will be sold together or in parcels to suit purchasers, as may be determined at the time and place of sale. Terms: A sufficient amount of cash to defray the expenses attending the execution of the trust and to pay two notes, one for $1,254, with interest from November 15, 1871, and the other for $1,272, with (interest) from February 15, 1872; and on a credit, as to $6,000, with interest from February 15, 1871, to February 15, 1874; and as to the balance, upon such terms as the grantor in said deed may decide; and upon his failure to do so, upon such terms as may be announced at the sale by the undersigned.

JOHN HOWARD, Trustee

J.S. Mason, Auction'r[22]
To Randolph Macon College, Boydton, Virginia—adieu.

Epilogue

The third stanza of Professor Puryear's first published poem in *The Saturday Post* in Philadelphia in 1848 ends with:

> Ere I shall fall to the arms of death,
> And to my God resign my feeble breath.
> Oh may my toils have won a brilliant name,
> And blessed my memory with a deathless fame.[1]

Appendix A
Salute to the Class of 1861

Based on information from the *Tobacco Plant* (as cited in Chapter 4), the following is a compilation of the students receiving diplomas and degrees, also those seniors having passed their second exam. Many of the junior class were included, as they were juniors in some subjects and seniors or graduates in others. There were some in the junior class (totaling eight) I didn't have enough information to track. I began the search by referring to the Virginia Confederate military service records published by Hewett in 1908[1] and then proceeded to research each of the students, since most all were from Virginia, in the Virginia regimental books.[2]

W.D. Adams, junior in Latin, enlisted into the 4th Infantry Battalion, Company B, Local Defense.

William A. Archer, son of Philmer W. Archer (former RMC student) of Mecklenburg County, received his diplomas in Spanish, ancient languages and chemistry, and natural philosophy. He was also a junior at the intermediate level in mathematics. He took an A.M. in June 1862. On August 20, 1862, he enlisted into the Company A, 3rd Cavalry, at Winchester, as a private. On April 30, 1863, he was in the battle at Fredericksburg, where he was captured and made a prisoner of war. In September he was paroled, exchanged and returned to his unit, and on September 10, 1863, he was detailed as the brigade courier. On July 29, 1864, he is listed as having transferred to an unnamed infantry company. No further record was found.

Benjamin Lee Arnold of Mecklenburg County (b. 1839) completed his A.M. degree in June 1861. He also received diplomas in German, moral philosophy, mineralogy and geology, and political economics and slavery. Following graduation, his autobiography relates he enlisted into Company G, 38th Virginia Infantry, with his friend and classmate Benjamin Hawthorne, but was soon disabled and released from the military (he is not listed in the regimental books). He then accepted a teaching post with several small southern colleges. In 1866 he married Addie Lea, daughter of the Rev. Solomon Lea of Leasburg (who was president of a nearby college). They had a son, Harry Lea (b. 1868), but Addie died shortly thereafter. His last position in the

South was professor of mathematics and natural science with West Tennessee College in Jackson, Tennessee. Arnold held this position for four years until being offered and accepting the presidency of the Corvallis College in Williamette Valley, Oregon, in September 1872.[3]

Arnold married a second time in 1878 to Minnie M. White, a graduate of Corvallis College, class of 1876. Her father was the Rev. T. B. White, pastor of the M.E. Church, South, in Albany, Oregon. White was a member of the college board of trustees and his family moved to Oregon from Louisiana. In 1878 they had a son, Ernest White Arnold. Ernest and Harry both graduated from Oregon Agricultural College and went for advanced studies to Johns Hopkins University. Neither married.

Harry entered Johns Hopkins in the fall of 1892 following his father's death. After five years he dropped out, just shy of his Ph.D. He accepted a teaching position in English in Kansas City. When the Spanish-American War began in 1898, he enlisted in the army as a private at age 30. He stayed in the military as an enlisted man. His final assignment was that of an ordnance sergeant, and upon completion of twenty years' service following World War I, he retired. He returned to Corvallis and rented a room where he resided for the next 30 years, until his death in 1948. With no surviving relatives, his estate was left to the city library and parks departments. There is a park named in his honor.

Harry's half-brother, Ernest, was also very smart and he too went to Johns Hopkins. He could read Latin and Greek. He earned advanced degrees from Johns Hopkins and University of California at Berkeley. He taught English at the University of Munich, Germany. He died at the age of 37 by accident (although many of his acquaintances suggest it was suicide) in 1915 in Stockton, California. President Benjamin Arnold died on January 30, 1892, in Eugene, Oregon, and is buried at Crystal Lake Cemetery.

P.H. Arnold was a junior in mathematics. He enlisted into Company A, 3rd Cavalry, on August 20, 1862, as a private at Winchester. On July 3, 1863, he was listed as missing in action at the Battle of Gettysburg. Later, he was presumed dead.

John G. Ayres of Buckingham County received his diplomas in chemistry and natural philosophy, ancient languages and mathematics. He was also a junior at the intermediate level in Latin. He enlisted on August 22, 1861, in Buckingham County into Company A, 57th Infantry, but was immediately transferred to the Quartermaster's Department and discharged from the 57th on September 21, 1861. No reason was listed.

Bennett W. Bagby of Powhatan received his diploma in French. He enlisted into Company D, 20th Infantry, at Richmond on May 28, 1861. He stated he was from Powhatan, was described as 5 feet, 9 inches tall, with dark complexion, hair and eyes. His stated occupation was teacher and his age was 23. His company arrived at Rich Mountain, Virginia, on July 6, 1861, most of the men were captured and all made prisoners of war. With no suitable jail or prison in Randolph County, they were paroled, stripped of their gear and rations and sent home on July 17, 1861. The company was discontinued, and in about the spring of 1863, Bagby enlisted into R.M. Anderson's Light Artillery Company near Richmond.

Robert W. Bailey of Amelia received his diplomas in chemistry and natural philosophy, ancient languages, mineralogy and geology, and mathematics. He enlisted as a private into Company H, 44th Infantry, on June 18, 1861, at Richmond and stated he was a student. He was home on furlough for being sick from November through December 1861. He was sick at Stanton and Amelia, from March 1862, for several months, through June 1862. Even so, he was elected a second lieutenant on May 1, 1862. He was wounded in action at Chancellorsville on May 3, 1863. He was listed as missing, wounded in Action at Gettysburg on July 2, 1863, and died of this wound. His remains were removed from Gettysburg after the war to Hollywood Cemetery in Richmond.

John R. Barr of Richmond received his diploma in French. He was also an intermediate junior in Latin and mathematics. He enlisted in Petersburg on August 16, 1861, into the 5th Cavalry for one year. He also served in Captain Allen's company, heavy artillery.

Thomas M. Beckman of Fauquier received his diploma in chemistry and natural philosophy. No record of any Confederate service was found.

Nathaniel P. Boyd of New Orleans, Louisiana, received his diploma in French and was an intermediate junior in Latin. He served in Company C, 2nd Mississippi Infantry.

Robert A. Boyd of Mecklenburg County received his diplomas in French, Ancient languages and mathematics. He enlisted into Company G, 38th Infantry, as a private on May 18, 1861, in Boydton. He was established as a sergeant. On July 16, 1862, he hired a suitable substitute and was discharged. He transferred to V.M.I. and graduated in 1863. He reenlisted into an engineering battalion under the command of General Lee and was at Appomattox for the surrender.

J. Thomas Brown of Richmond received his diploma in French. He enlisted into Parker's company of light artillery and was elected first lieutenant.

George E. Butler of Dallas County, Arkansas, received his diplomas in political science and slavery, Latin and mathematics. He was also an intermediate junior in Greek. He served in the 3rd Arkansas Infantry, Company I, and was established as chaplain (see Chapter 5).

William J. Carter, see Chapter 6.

Kenneth R. Cobb of Elizabeth City, N.C., received his diploma in chemistry and natural philosophy. He was also a senior in Greek and junior in Latin. He returned to Elizabeth City and enlisted into Company D, 43rd North Carolina Infantry.

A. Buford Coleman of Lunenburg received his diploma in Spanish. He was also a junior in Latin, Greek, mathematics and French. No Confederate record could be identified.

Samuel Francis Coleman of Cumberland was born September 4, 1842. He received diplomas in chemistry and natural philosophy; ancient languages; political economy and slavery; and French. He enlisted into Company G, 3rd Cavalry, as a private on July 12, 1861, at Yorktown. He was promoted to sergeant and detailed to Mitchell's Shop on May 9, 1864. He was captured and made a prisoner of war on May 17, 1864. On August 15, 1864, he was transferred to Point Lookout. On March 1, 1865, he was transferred to Elmira and paroled on March 2, 1865. He died on May 1, 1898.

Robert A. Compton of Mecklenburg County received diplomas in ancient languages and moral philosophy. He was a junior in mathematics. He possibly enlisted for a one year term into Company A, 49th Infantry, at Yorktown on June 16, 1861. He reenlisted into Company E of the 49th on April 30, 1862. On May 31, 1862, he was wounded in action in the arm at Seven Pines and hospitalized for most of June. His record is void until he was arrested on November 5, 1863, court-martialed on December 26, 1863, and ordered to forfeit six months in pay and was sent to jail for nine more months. He was released from confinement on August 15, 1864, and was at Appomattox for the surrender on April 9, 1865.

James R. Cowles of Petersburg received his diplomas in political economy and slavery and mathematics. (See Appendix B, 12th Virginia Infantry section.)

Watson S. Dibrell of Chesterfield received his diploma in French and was a junior in Latin and Greek.

Robert E. Dunn of Louisa received his diploma in Spanish and was a junior in Latin. He enlisted at Winchester as a private into Company D, 13th Infantry, on July 3, 1861. He was listed as a student. He was wounded in action in the hand on June 27, 1862, at Gaines Mill, and there is no further record of him.

William Emory Edwards of Lynchburg was born in Prince Edward County, Virginia, on June 10, 1842, the son of the Rev. John Ellis Edwards (RMC Board of Trustees 1857; D.D. 1867, RMC). William received a diploma in moral philosophy and was a junior in German. He received his A.B. in 1862. He served as a chaplain during much of the fighting at Drewry's Bluff in 1863 and 1864. Following the war, he became a clergyman for the ME, South, of the Virginia Conference. In 1885, he had a book published, *John Newson: A Tale of College Life*, Nashville, Tennessee.

His brother Landon Brame Edwards was a junior and senior at RMC, completing his schooling in 1863. Leaving school, he went to Lynchburg and joined J.W. Drewery's artillery company, where he served until 1865. Following the war, he went to New York University Medical School and received his M.D. in 1867. He returned to Lynchburg and was one of the principals in establishing the Virginia Medical Society. In April 1874, he began *Virginia Medical Monthly*, served on numerous boards and was a prolific writer.

E.H. Estes was a member of the junior class in mathematics. From eastern Mecklenburg County, he enlisted into Company K, 38th Infantry, at Cascade on June 2, 1861, as a private. He was furloughed and sent home on August 17, 1861. He soon returned to duty and was wounded in action at Seven Pines on May 31, 1862. He was sent to the hospital for treatment. He was promoted to third sergeant and assigned enrolling officer on August 31, 1862. Estes rejoined his unit and was elected second lieutenant on December 18, 1864. His military record lists him as having been a student of Randolph Macon.

William Hamilton Farrar enlisted as a student from RMC. He was a junior in Latin and French. He enlisted into Company F, 14th Infantry, at Boydton on July 21, 1862, as a private. Born in Mecklenburg County on October 13, 1842, he died in Baskerville on October 10, 1916. At Gettysburg, July 3, 1863, he was captured and made a prisoner of war. He was transferred to Chester Pennsylvania Hospital on July 31, 1863, and exchanged on March 4, 1864. He was wounded in action at Chester Station on May 10, 1864, and hospitalized on May 11, 1864, resulting in an amputation of his thumb. He was furloughed on May 23, 1864, and after returning to his company elected second lieutenant. He was paroled at Appomattox on April 9, 1865. Following the war, he returned to Mecklenburg County, where he was a successful farmer.

Virginius O. Gee, nephew of Jesse Gee, of Mecklenburg County, received his diplomas in chemistry and natural philosophy, French, ancient languages and mathematics. There is no record of any Confederate service. Following graduation, according to family history, he became headmaster of the Lombardy Grove Academy, where he served throughout the war and for many years thereafter.

Otis A. Glazebrook of Richmond was born October 13, 1845. He received his diploma in French. He was also a junior in German, Greek and Latin. Then, according to family history, he was sent by his family to V.M.I. for Confederate officer training. He fought under Lee and Jackson, and was a cadet at the Battle of New Market, where he was recognized for distinguished gallantry. He was at Appomattox for the surrender and returned to V.M.I., where he graduated with first honors. Following the death of his father, a strong Episcopalian, in September 1867, he entered the Episcopal Theological Seminary and received his A.M. in 1869. He was ordained a priest that year. After serving for six years in southern Virginia, he was sent to Baltimore in 1875 and then on to Christ Church, Macon, Georgia, in 1878.

Glazebrook married Virginia Calvert Key in 1866. In 1879, he was severely injured in a railroad accident and took a medical leave of absence to travel to Europe for medical care. Returning to the United States, he was elected chaplain to the University of Virginia in 1883. In 1885, he was appointed to St. John's Church in New Jersey. He was awarded the D.D. degree by the Diocese of New Jersey.[4]

William E. Goode of Charlotte County received his diploma in French. He enlisted into an artillery battery and was established as a corporal.

Clifton A. Hamner of Halifax County received his diplomas in political economy and slavery and in moral philosophy. He was also a junior in Greek and mathematics. He enlisted into Captain Paris's company, Stanton Hill Light Artillery.

Benjamin G. Harrison of Norfolk received his diploma in Spanish. He enlisted into Company K, 15th Cavalry, near Moseley's Church on March 27, 1862, with a stated age of 21. He was captured and made a prisoner of war at Suffolk on July 18, 1863. On August 4, 1863, he was paroled and exchanged at Fort Monroe, Virginia, and returned to his unit. There is no further record.

Benjamin J. Hawthorne from the Union Level area of Mecklenburg County was born in 1837 in Lunenburg County. His parents were John and Elizabeth A.M. Harper Hawthorne. He attended school as a young man in a one room log cabin, with Headmaster Barnes in charge. He basically attended a three month term in the winter when he could be spared from farm duties. Completing his education in June 1861 at Randolph Macon College, he received his diplomas in mineralogy and geology; Spanish; political economy and slavery; mathematics and ancient languages. He also received his A.M. degree. He enlisted into Company G, 38th Infantry, as a private and was appointed second lieutenant on December 11, 1861. He was promoted to first lieutenant on April 29, 1862. At Gettysburg, he suffered a gun shot wound to his left arm. From there, he was detailed to the Conscription Bureau. "While convalescing he organized a cavalry company and carried out military operations against Union guerrilla bands that were terrorizing the region." On November 15, 1863, for demonstrated bravery on the battlefield, he was promoted to captain. He was designated as the enrolling officer for the famous Brigadier General Armistead's brigade of Picket's division on December 26, 1864, but then, on, January 7, 1865, he was ordered to return to his command. He was paroled at Appomattox on April 9, 1865.[5]

Following the surrender, he walked the nearly 100 miles home and "the morning following his arrival he was in his neighbor's field with mule and plow tilling the cropland." He describes the time at home under military rule: "A day or so later I walked to town [Union Level]. A sentry stopped and told me to cut the Confederate buttons off my uniform. I told him I had no other clothes and no money to buy new buttons. He arrested me and took me to the Union officer in charge. I explained to him that my sole resources were 25 cents, which I was keeping for a rainy day. He wrote me a permit to wear my uniform with the brass buttons of the Confederacy on it. At almost every cross street I was challenged and told to cut off my brass buttons. Finally I carried my permit in my hand, and every time a soldier challenged me I would hand him my permit."[6]

According to General Order No. 4, April 29, 1865, it contained the "Button Order" which prohibited men from wearing any Confederate buttons. Punishment for violating this order all depended on the arresting officer and the legal system in place at the time: from a verbal reprimand to a monetary fine and even imprisonment. This general order also included the "Marriage Order" which prohibited marriages between two people that had not signed an oath of allegiance to the United States government. Until the oath was signed, no teacher could teach, no preacher could preach nor marry others, and no magistrate nor other elected or appointed official could serve in office. The general order was signed by General Halleck and sent to General Stanton, to be effective immediately; "Measures have been taken to prevent ... the propagation of legitimate rebels ... all under pains of imprisonment, etc."

Following his military service, Hawthorne was principal of an academy when he married Emma (b. 1848) around 1866. They began their long journey westward, first settling in Louisiana, where he was headmaster of a collegiate institute until 1870, when he was offered the position of president of West Tennessee College. He accepted and moved his family to Jackson, Tennessee, where he served as president until 1873. A former classmate, Benjamin Arnold, who had also been teaching at West Tennessee in 1870, had moved to Oregon and accepted a position with the Corvallis College of the M.E. Conference, South, in Oregon. In 1884 the college split into Corvallis as an M.E., South College and Oregon Agricultural College from the cadet portion. Arnold was being considered for the vacated position of president of Corvallis College. He recruited Hawthorne as his replacement, also to take over as the drill instructor for the cadets recruited under the newly established program funded through the Morrill Act.

Hawthorne accepted the offer and took the train to San Francisco and then the steamboat to Portland. From there he took a river boat to the village of Albany near the college and finally a stage to Corvallis. In the fall of 1873 he became the professor of languages at Corvallis College and the drill instructor for what was eventually to become ROTC (Reserve Officers' Training Corps) following World War I. The 1880 Census establishes that Hawthorne was professor of languages at an Oregon college. He, his wife and their three daughters were living in Benton, Oregon. In 1884 when Corvallis was divided, Hawthorne made application to the recently established (1876) Oregon State University and was accepted. He became the fifth member of the faculty. Over the next 25 years he taught over 30 different courses ranging from Greek, Latin, Ancient Hebrew, French and German to fertilizer, fruit, drainage and philosophy. He retired at age 69 in 1906.[7]

The eldest son was Wistar Hawthorne. When the Spanish-American War began, young men were scrambling to the recruitment offices in 1898. Wistar wasn't quite of age, but wanted to serve. When Professor Hawthorne learned of his desire, he stated: "Yes, Wistar is going. I know what it means, but I want him to go. When I was his age I thought it was right to fight with the South in the Civil War. I owe my boy to our country now.... As his fellow students laid Wistar away in the old Paco cemetery in Manila and stepped back while taps sounded the last call, we thought: 'The Hawthorne patriotism has paid in full.'" Another student serving with him was the center for the varsity football team, Arthur Gilleland, who was also killed.

The 1910 Census reveals Benjamin was age 72, living in Eugene, Oregon, and two of his daughters were still living with him. An ambitious man, Hawthorne retired from the University of Oregon in 1906 on a Carnegie pension after a total of 41 years of teaching. That year he began to read law and attend law school, completing all his studies in one year. He was licensed as an attorney in 1907. In 1913, he met with many former Confederate veterans on the Gettysburg Battlefield for their 50th reunion. He said, later, that there were so few survivors in attendance that each of them received special attention. Shortly after this, he was given the Southern Cross of Honor by the Daughters of the American Confederacy of Richmond, Virginia.

In 1920, he was widowed and living with one of his daughters. For his 85th birthday, he received a resolution written by the Oregon State Supreme Court justices wishing him "many more anniversaries [birthdays] with continued health and undiminished happiness." He is not on the 1930 Census, but family history is that he died that year at age 92. In fact he died on February 3, 1928, in Eugene, Oregon, at the age of 90. Several obituaries were written in the local newspapers, and they all referenced that he had, being of sound mind, written his own obituary earlier in the year, but no one published it that I could find.

William A. Hightower of Halifax County received his diploma in French. He was also a junior in mathematics. There is no record of Confederate service found.

Chandler V. Hill of Norfolk (b. 1840 in Portsmouth) received his diploma in French. He was also a junior in Greek and mathematics. He enlisted at Norfolk as a private into Company G, 6th Infantry, on April 19, 1861, for a one year term. His listed occupation was a student, and he was established as a sergeant. On October 27, 1862, he was reduced in rank to private and on April 1, 1864, promoted to corporal. On July 30, 1864, he was wounded in action at the Battle of the Crater and his arm was amputated. On April 9, 1865, he was paroled at Appomattox.

He returned to college after the war and in 1884 was a licensed practicing lawyer in Norfolk. He died in Norfolk on August 13, 1896, and is buried at Cedar Grove Cemetery, Portsmouth.

Robert N. Holstead of Richmond received his diplomas in ancient languages, Spanish and math. There was no record of any Confederate service found.

Caius Jacob Jones of Dinwiddie was born to Edgar and Elizabeth Archer Dunnivant Jones in 1842. He received his diplomas in mineralogy and geology; mathematics; political economy and slavery; Italian; and moral philosophy. He also received his A. M. degree. He served during the war as Jacob Jones and enlisted on June 23, 1861, in Smithfield, Virginia, as a private in Company I, 3rd Infantry. He was established as the company clerk and promoted to corporal on October 9, 1861, then sergeant in June 1862, and elected as a second lieutenant on January 1, 1863. On April 1, 1865, he was captured and made a prisoner of war and sent to Johnson's Island, Ohio.

He was paroled and released on June 18, 1865. He moved to Isle of Wright County, Virginia, after the war and died there on April 20, 1912.

James W. Jones of Brunswick County received his diplomas in mineralogy and geology; Spanish; political economy and slavery; moral philosophy; and chemistry and natural philosophy. He also received his A.M. degree. He enlisted into Company A, 5th Virginia Infantry, and was elected first lieutenant. Following the war, he moved to Mecklenburg County and began a school in Union Level. He advertised in the *Tobacco Plant* on December 15, 1869: "Principal Captain J.W. Jones, Zion Hill Academy, Union Level. Office Lombardy Grove. 20 students tops." A brief editorial said Captain Jones had a "well balanced and trained mind, refined and courteous manners, [and was] gentle and amiable yet firm and decided if needed."[8] When the Baptists (the Reverend McGonegal) purchased the RMC buildings in 1870 and established Southside University, Jones was hired as the head of the faculty, but the school closed a year later.

J.B. Jordan was a junior in math. No additional records could be identified.

William H. (Elliott) Judkins was born April 10, 1829, in Southampton County, son of Jarratt Wallace and Connie Whitehead Judkins. An older student at RMC on November 15, 1855, he married Mary Gray, and in December 1856, their first born was William Duncan Judkins. Mary died on August 3, 1858. William received his diplomas in mineralogy and geology; Spanish; political economy and slavery; Italian; moral philosophy; and mathematics. He also received his A.M. degree in 1861.

In 1880, he was working as a clerk in a dry goods store in Greensville County and was remarried to Alfretta C. Judkins. He was age 50, and she was age 26. He enlisted into Company H, 5th Cavalry, for one year in 1861–1862. In 1886, the Reverend Judkins had been awarded his D.D. by Randolph Macon Collage and is listed as a member of the board of trustees.

Phillip Lockett was born in Halifax County, but his family moved to Mecklenburg County in the mid 1850s. Phillip (b. 1842–c. 1904) enlisted as a 19 year old student from RMC into Company F, 14th Virginia Infantry. He was a junior in mathematics but also received a diploma in French in 1861. He was one of the four students involved in the scathing letter of April 3, 1861, to the Randolph Macon Board of Trustees (see Chapter 6). He was expelled because of this but appealed and received demerits instead.

Lockett enlisted as a private at Lombardy Grove on May 12, 1861. He was captured and made a prisoner of war at Gettysburg on July 3, 1863. He was sent to Fort Delaware and then transferred to Fort McHenry on July 7, 1863. On August 1, 1863, he was transferred to City Point and exchanged. Returning to his company, he was elected first lieutenant on April 6, 1864. At the Battle of Bermuda Hundred, he suffered gunshot wounds to the neck and shoulder on June 19, 1864. He was admitted to Richmond General Hospital on June 19, 1864, and sent home to Lombardy Grove on furlough on August 10, 1864. Returning to his company, he signed the clothing invoices on November 30, 1864, as the company commander. He was paroled at Appomattox on April 9, 1865.

He returned home to pursue his education and earned an A.M. at RMC. In 1869, he began a law practice with offices in Lombardy Grove and Boydton. He was elected and served as commonwealth's attorney for Mecklenburg County from July 1, 1875, to 1879. His younger sister, Myrta Lockett (Avary) (1857–1946), spent many hours during the war on her father's (Harwood Lockett, b. 1812) knee in the family tavern, known as Delony's Ordinary, in Lombardy Grove.

Myrta was mesmerized listening to stories of the war and its impact on Virginia. Following her schooling, she spent a number of years traveling. In 1884 she married Dr. James Corban Avary, a physician, and they moved to Atlanta, Georgia. In the 1890s they moved to New York. In 1903 her first book was published, *A Virginia Girl in the Civil War*, followed by *Dixie After the War 1861–1865* in 1906. In 1903 she separated from her husband and a few years later returned to Atlanta. She also edited and caused to be published the war diary of Mrs. James Chestnut, Jr. (Mary Boykin Chestnut) of South Carolina, *Diary from Dixie*. Probably her most successful book was *Diary of Alexander H. Stevens, Vice President of the Confederacy, During His Imprisonment in Fort Warren*, around 1910. According to Margaret Mitchell, author of *Gone With the Wind*, one of her progenitors and inspirations for writing the book was Myrta Lockett Avary. Myrta Avary died on February 14, 1946, in Atlanta. Much of her correspondence and other documents from 1868 to 1931 are with the Virginia Historical Society, Richmond.

Joseph E. Maxey of Powhatan County received his diplomas in ancient languages, and chemistry and natural philosophy. He was also a junior in math. He enlisted into Company K, 1st Artillery Battalion, as a private. He was transferred to the 2nd Artillery Battalion (L.F. Jones' company) and was promoted to corporal. In 1863, he was transferred to Captain William Kings' Saltville Light Artillery, which consisted of 19 men: a captain, four lieutenants including an artificer, and fourteen noncommissioned officers. This company experienced several attacks in the final year of the war, as the Union Army desperately wanted to capture the primary southern salt mines and destroy the railroad.

John B. Merritt of Brunswick County received his diploma in French. He enlisted into Company D, 3rd Light Artillery.

J.C. (Jessee Charles) Mundy (b. February 11, 1836 in Patrick County, Virginia) was a senior in Greek and Latin and intermediate junior in math. On October 11, 1860, he married Vicie Louisa Kinder. He enlisted into Company D, 19th Battalion of Heavy Artillery (Captain Joel Henry Campbell's company of heavy artillery), on March 24, 1862, at Amherst Courthouse and was established as a lieutenant. He was detached August 31, 1862, until October, when he returned to duty. He was promoted to captain on November 24, 1862. In February 1865, he was in Richmond on furlough. After the war his occupation was listed as farmer; he died in Tazewell County, Virginia, on July 3, 1919.

Walter Myrick of Greenville County received his diplomas in French and chemistry and natural philosophy. He was also a junior in math. He was born in 1841 to Benjamin and Ann Myrick and had eight brothers and sisters. He enlisted into Company B, 53rd Infantry, on July 15, 1861, at Jamestown, as a private. Shortly thereafter, he transferred to Company F and was promoted to sergeant on April 30, 1862. There is no further record.

Thomas Archer Perkins was a junior in Latin. He enlisted into Company I, 3rd Cavalry, on April 30, 1862, at Norfolk as a private. He was killed in action at Spotsylvania Court House on May 8, 1864.

H. (Hunter) B. Phillips was a junior in math. He was enlisted on June 13, 1861, at Leesburg by Captain Carter into Company B, 8th Infantry. At enlistment, he gave his occupation as student and his age as 22. He was described as 5 feet, 9½ inches tall, dark hair, eyes and complexion. From April through December 1862, he was listed as sick and from February 28 through October 5, 1863, he was assigned to the Quartermaster Department in Richmond. On October 5, 1863, he was given a disability discharge.

F.A. Princkard (Francis Asbury Pinckard; b. June 23, 1844, Northumberland County) was a junior in Latin, Greek, and math. He enlisted into Company F, 47th Infantry, as a private on June 1, 1861. His stated occupation was a student at RMC and he was established as a sergeant. On June 30, 1862, he was hospitalized and listed as a private. The record is silent until he was hospitalized again on December 31, 1864, where he is listed as a private. There is no further military record. Following the war, he returned home and in 1868 married Elizabeth Campbell. He died on November 23, 1903.

The Rev. George H. Ray, see Chapter 6.

James C. Reed of Bedford received his diplomas in ancient languages and French. He enlisted into J. D. Smith's company of light artillery and was promoted to sergeant.

Adolphus E. Richards was from Loudoun County, see Chapter 6.

William C. Richardson of Mecklenburg County received his diplomas in French, Spanish and ancient languages. No Confederate record could be verified.

E.A. (William) Shepherd was a junior in math at Randolph Macon College. He returned to his home in Danville and enlisted into Company E, 38th Virginia Infantry, on June 8, 1861, as a private. Later he was admitted to Richmond General Hospital with "Vulnes Seloperturn," and was transferred to Danville General Hospital on April 2, 1863. He was detailed to the Danville Arsenal on April 1, 1864, and then to the brigade Quartermaster Department on December 31, 1864, due to his medical conditions of burn of the leg and epilepsia. He would have served at the Battle of Stanton River Bridge on June 24–25, 1864. He was paroled at Appomattox on April 9, 1865.

Henry H. Sneed of Mecklenburg County received his diplomas in Spanish and political economy and slavery. He was also a junior in math. He enlisted into Company G, 38th Infantry, in Boydton as a corporal on May 18, 1861. In January 1862, he was promoted to fourth sergeant and assigned to the Commissary Department, Pickett's Division, on December 25, 1862. On May 1, 1863, he was promoted to third sergeant and returned to his company on December 31, 1864. He was paroled at Appomattox on April 9, 1865.

Robert Alexander Stainback of Brunswick County received his diploma in ancient languages. He was also a junior in math and German. He returned home and he, his father, Robert, and brother George enlisted on July 10, 1861, into Company E, 56th Infantry, as privates. Robert was soon captured and made a prisoner of war taken first to Fort Donaldson, then to a camp, and finally to Vicksburg for exchange. He was admitted to Charlottesville General Hospital. Upon release, he was elected first lieutenant. Following the company commander Captain Frasier's capture at Gettysburg on July 3, 1863, Stainback was promoted to captain on December 13, 1863. On January 24, 1864, he was listed as commanding officer.

During this time Robert's father (born in Brunswick County in 1804) had been admitted to a hospital but died of typhoid on April 25, 1862. Also, on September 29, 1864, his brother George was shot and killed in action.

Robert was captured again and made a prisoner of war on April 6, 1865, at Saylor's Creek. He was sent to Johnson's Island on April 17, 1865. He was paroled on June 20, 1865. He was described as 5 feet, 5 inches tall, florid complexion, dark hair and hazel eyes. He was born in 1843. He returned to Randolph Macon College, completed his studies in 1868, and married Belle West. Following graduation, they moved to Clarke County, Mississippi. In 1880, they were still there, with several children.

Oscar Malachi Styron of Princess Anne County received his diplomas in chemistry and natural philosophy, mineralogy and geology, moral philosophy, and political economy and slavery. He enlisted as a private on Canary Island, Virginia, into Company G, 6th Infantry, but was immediately furloughed to complete his studies at RMC. He was awarded his A.M. degree and then caught up with his unit on August 1, 1861. He was promoted to corporal on June 17, 1862, then to full sergeant on February 1, 1863. Shortly afterward he was wounded in action and hospitalized. He was given a medical discharge on March 27, 1863.

He was described as 6 feet tall, fair complexion, light hair and blue eyes. He was born on October 25, 1838, and died of his wounds on March 17, 1865.

Allen Talbott of Richmond received his diploma in French. He was also a junior in math. He enlisted into the 4th Battalion, Local Defense, and served as first lieutenant, G&S (General and Staff) adjutant.

Richard D. Thackston was a junior in math. He enlisted into Company D, 18th Infantry, on August 17, 1861. He was described as 5 feet, 6 inches tall, hazel eyes, dark hair and complexion. He transferred to Company F, but was sick and in the hospital on April 26, 1862. On July 3, 1863, he was captured at Gettysburg and made a prisoner of war. On February 8, 1865, he was paroled and exchanged at Fort Delaware. He returned home.

Wesley Childs Vaden of Chesterfield was born on August 23, 1841. His parents were Michael and Catherine Rowlett Vaden. He received his diplomas in chemistry and natural philosophy, German, French, mathematics and Spanish. He was also awarded his A. M. degree. Serving a one year term as chaplain for RMC, from 1861 to 1862, upon graduation, in June 1862, he accepted positions as pastor of Clarksville Methodist Church and professor of language with the Clarksville Female Collegiate Institute. He served in those positions through 1865. He married Sallie F. Sadler and they were both teaching at the Danville Female College in 1866. In 1867, Wesley was elected president of the college until replaced by Dr. John C. Blackwell in 1868. He then served as a minister in Farmville, Virginia. In 1880, they had six children and a sister-in-law living with them in Richmond, where he was working as a minister, and in 1890, they moved to Norfolk to serve a church there.

Dabney J. (Jordan) Waller (nickname "Baby"), Caroline County, was a junior in Latin and received a diploma in French. He was born on June 29, 1841, to Dabney and Caroline Waller. He enlisted on July 25, 1861, as a private into 2nd Battalion, Infantry, Local Defense, Waller's Battalion (this battalion had six Wallers listed with the colonel being Thomas Conway Waller (b. 1832) as a quartermaster). His stated occupation was a student at RMC. Waller's battalion became Company B, 9th Cavalry;

in March 1863 he was promoted to corporal and in November 1863 to sergeant. He was paroled at Ashland on April 29, 1865.

Following the war, he lived and married in Caroline County, and his son, Dabney J. Waller, Jr., was born in 1878. The family then moved to Madison County but subsequently returned to the family farm in Caroline County. He wrote a story for the library, which was published in Caroline County, "Waller's War: Reminisces—Wingfield." He died on April 12, 1925, and is buried at Walnut Hill.

Jordan P. Ware was born in 1839, in Caroline County. His parents were Albert G. and Judith T. Ware. He received his diplomas in mineralogy and geology; French; political economy and slavery; mathematics; and moral philosophy. He also was awarded his A.M. degree. He enlisted as a private, into Company K, 47th Infantry, on July 23, 1861. He was promoted to sergeant on November 1, 1861. On April 30, 1862, he was elected captain. On October 1, 1864, he was given a medical discharge, but died that same day at Petersburg.

John Wesley Watts of Amherst County, received his diplomas in chemistry and natural philosophy; moral philosophy; political economy and slavery; German; and mineralogy and geology. He was also awarded his A.M. degree. He was born April 22, 1840, to James Dillard and Lucy Ann Simms Watts. Watts was one of the four students expelled on April 3, 1861, for a scathing letter to the board of trustees, but on appeal was reinstated with demerits (see entry for Phillip Lockett, this appendix). He enlisted into Company F, 34th Infantry, at Halifax County, Virginia, on March 14, 1862. On January 4, 1864, he was detached to the Confederate Engineering Corps. He was wounded in action in the hand in July 1864. On April 8, 1865, he was hospitalized at Farmville General Hospital and paroled at that facility. He died on his farm in Halifax County in November 1898.

Thomas S. (Scott) West (b. January 25, 1842, in Appomattox County, moved to Bedford County in 1857) was a junior in French and Greek. He enlisted at Lynchburg into Company A, 2nd Cavalry, on May 22, 1861, as a private. He stated he had been attending Randolph Macon College and was a farmer, age 20. On September 10, 1862, he was promoted to fourth corporal, November 12, 1862, to third corporal and March 1, 1863, to second corporal. From April 30 to May 8, 1864, he was absent on horse detail. On November 29, 1864, he was elected second lieutenant and on February 27, 1865, was assigned as an aide to General Jubal Early. His horse was appraised on April 6, 1865, as being worth $3,300. He was paroled at Appomattox on April 9, 1865.

Following the war, he returned to Bedford County and his home—Bellevue, where he was listed as a farmer. In 1885, he was elected as county commissioner of revenue, a position he served for a number of years. He died on November 4, 1923, and is buried at Oakwood Cemetery, Bedford.

William Arthur Wheatley (b. January 4, 1843, in Memphis) was from Memphis, Tennessee. He received his diploma in political economy and slavery. He was also a junior in Latin and Greek and a senior in moral philosophy. He enlisted on June 20, 1861, at Capon Bridge into 1st Company E, 13th Infantry, as a private. He stated he was a student attending RMC. The company was disbanded and he joined General N.B. Forrest's cavalry in 1863. While on a 30 day furlough to his plantation in Carroll Parish, Louisiana, he obtained a suitable substitute for his cavalry assignment. Once he had found refuge for his slaves from Louisiana to Texas, he joined General Kirby Smith's Army. He was paroled at Shreveport, Louisiana.

Following the war, he returned to Memphis and married Elizabeth Bowen in 1867. He established a very successful real estate business in Memphis and later became a United States commissioner.

William Henry White was a freshman in 1861 but stayed at RMC until 1864. He was born April 16, 1847, in Norfolk to Colonel William White (Confederate 14th Infantry Regiment) and Henrietta Kemp Turner White. Following the closing in March 1864, William transferred to V.M.I. to train for the Confederacy as an officer. He was a cadet at the Battle of New Market. Completing his education at V.M.I., he entered the University of Virginia Law School.

He received his license to practice law the day after his 21st birthday, April 17, 1868, and he established his practice in Portsmouth, Virginia. In 1870, he was elected commonwealth's attorney for Norfolk. He married Lucy Carter Minor on November 4, 1869, and then Emma Gray on March 10, 1880. In 1900, he received a presidential appointment to the position of United States district attorney for Eastern Virginia.

William W. White of Southampton County was born in 1842 and received his diplomas in chemistry and natural philosophy, Spanish, political economy and slavery, moral philosophy and mineralogy and geology. He was also awarded an A.M. degree. In the 1880 Census, he is listed as age 38, single with two boarders in his home, a farmer and teacher. In 1910, he is listed as age 67 with his wife, Mary E., age 61.

William S. Williams of Rocheport, Missouri, received his diplomas in mineralogy and geology, ancient languages, chemistry and natural philosophy and mathematics. No further records could be identified.

William K. Woodson was a senior in Latin. He enlisted at Williamsburg into Company E, 15th Infantry, on June 14, 1861, as a private. At Sharpsburg, Maryland, he was wounded in action, captured, and made a prisoner of war on September 17, 1862. He was sent to Fort McHenry and paroled on September 23, 1862, sent to Fort Monroe, Virginia, and exchanged on October 17, 1862. He rejoined his company and was promoted to first sergeant on May 17, 1864. He was captured and made a prisoner of war again at Farmville on April 6, 1865, sent to Point Lookout, Maryland, and paroled on June 22, 1865.

Arthur Lee Wynne was born in 1843 to C.H. Wynne of Richmond, who was listed as a widower with Arthur and three sisters. Arthur received his diplomas in political economy and slavery, mathematics, chemistry and natural philosophy, Italian and moral philosophy. He was also awarded an A.M. degree. On September 23, 1862, he enlisted in defense of Richmond into 1st Virginia Howitzers Artillery Battery as a lieutenant. He was transferred on August 3, 1864, to Captain R.M. Anderson's light artillery company in Richmond and discharged on December 2, 1864.

Appendix B:
Roll of Honor

A painstaking effort was made to identify Confederate veterans associated with Randolph Macon through Confederate records, U.S. Park Service records, resource and archival records from Virginia, Alabama, Missouri, Georgia, South Carolina and North Carolina public libraries, Virginia regimental books, Google Search, ask.com, Footnote.com (Fold3.com) and Ancestor.com. I am pleased to report the following, with a proviso that I feel very confident that 95 percent are accurate, as listed, due to the correlations among the resources. There are a small number (10 at most) of early (pre–1846 graduates with an estimated age at graduation of 20 years) where no rank was given or the rank was private. For that group, they could be the Randolph Macon alumni or a possible son. Two or three at best are "possible" and so noted. One difficulty is that many chaplains and doctors didn't want the low Confederate pay and rations. There were many on the battlefields as missionaries and chaplains representing local churches and missionary groups that are not included because they didn't fill out the military forms. There are also a number of doctors in larger city hospitals who maintained their staff positions and medical school affiliations and only attended Confederate soldiers when they arrived. Occasionally they went to the field but they were paid by their primary employers—thus again no records are to be found. The only active militia records I found were several from North Carolina and South Carolina and a few from parts of Southside Virginia. (For the sake of brevity, Randolph Macon alumni with their stories written elsewhere in the text will not be repeated here. The Confederate record collection and Virginia regimental records were cited with Appendix A, thus not repeated.)

Confederate G&S

Within the Confederate States of America military structure were the command general and staff (G&S) officers who reported directly to a commanding general or the president himself. Of those officers, the following were alumni of Randolph Macon College.

Richard Boyd, M.D., was born February 9, 1835 (see Chapter 3).

James R. Branch (b. 1826; A.B. 1848; son of Thomas and brother of Thomas, see 12th Virginia Infantry section) stayed at RMC as a teaching assistant toward his A.M. degree, but there is no record he requested same. Returning to Petersburg, he enlisted into the 12th Virginia Infantry as a captain. He was transferred as captain of Company K, 16th Infantry, and then placed in charge as a captain of Pegram's light artillery. By June 1862, he was in charge of his own artillery company. The field report of Lieutenant General Theophilus H. Holmes, commanding the Department of North Carolina operations for June 30 through July 2, 1862, including Malvern Hill (Turkey Ridge), includes an appended statement about Captain Branch. "His conduct, as also that of the section of his battery (Branch's Artillery) with which he served, was excellent and worthy of praise." During the Seven Days' Battles, Colonel James Deschler, in his final field report before being killed on July 5, 1862, wrote, "Captain Branch of French's Battery has favorable notice of gallant conduct."[1] He was chief of artillery, Department of North Carolina. In 1862 he was promoted to major of the command general and staff and later promoted to lieutenant colonel of the general and staff heavy artillery defenses around Richmond.

William M. Cabell, son of widow Mary Cabell of New Glasgow, was born in 1825 in Amherst County, Virginia. He was described as 5 feet, 8 inches tall, black hair and brown eyes. He graduated with an A.B. in 1844 as a third honors man and went on to become a lawyer. On April 11, 1862, he formed a militia unit for the state which became the 2nd Company E, 41st Virginia Infantry, and he was discharged on June 18, 1862, by orders of the CSA War Department as being over the age of 35 and having prior militia experience. In 1897, he was practicing law, according to Irby.

John H. Claiborne, see 12th Virginia Infantry, this appendix.

David Clopton (A.B. 1840) was valedictorian of class of 1840 (see Chapter 5).

Oliver Hagen Percy Corprew, see Chapters 1, 2, and 5.

William S. Davis, see Chapter 2.

William G. DeGraffenreit was born in Charlotte Court House, Virginia, in 1823. He graduated from Randolph Macon College with an A.B. in 1846, attended the RMC Medical Department and graduated from a medical college. Dr. DeGraffenreit was appointed assistant surgeon to a Confederate hospital. Following the war, Dr. DeGraffenreit moved to Alabama. A story in the Tupelo *Mississippian* reported that on December 30, 1867, he and Methodist Episcopal, South, preacher Samuel Briggs made a house call on John R. Noah. During the visit "Briggs took up a stick of wood and struck DeGraffenreit in the head." The doctor fell into the fireplace, dead, whereupon John Noah got out of bed and Briggs proceeded to beat him to death with the stick. As Mrs. Noah was trying to escape, Briggs chased her down and beat her to death. No arrest had been made by January 2, 1868.[2]

William G. Foote was born in Warrenton, Fauquier County, Virginia, the son of Richard H. Foote. He completed his A.B. in 1848, probably attended the medical department and received his A.M. in 1852. He completed medical college and then relocated to Mississippi. When the war began, he was established as a steward in charge of a Confederate hospital in Mississippi.

Lucius J. Gartrell was born in 1821 and was a senior in 1844 but did not take a degree, according to Irby. He was the son of Joseph Gartrell of Washington, Wilkes County, Georgia. Following school, he returned to Georgia. When the war began, he enlisted into Georgia infantry's Collier Guard. This was established into the Confederate Army as the 7th Georgia Infantry Company. Gartrell was selected to serve out the war as a Georgia brigadier general of the G&S. Following the war, he established a law practice in Georgia.

Thomas F. Goode was born in Roanoke, Virginia, the son of Dr. Thomas Goode, and was educated by tutors until entering Episcopal High School in Alexandria, Virginia. Dr. Thomas Goode was famous for his having developed the Hot Springs, Bath County, Virginia, and he built the Homestead Resort around 1850 (today The Homestead). He came to Randolph Macon College and studied law with Judge Chambers, among other studies, receiving his A.M. in 1848. He was soon elected commonwealth's attorney for Mecklenburg County and was a delegate to the 1861 secession convention. In 1860 he organized Company C in what was to become the 3rd Virginia Cavalry, and he served as the captain. He was established into the Confederate G&S as a colonel. Due to his gallantry, bravery and skilled leadership, he was recommended to General Robert E. Lee by General J.E.B. Stuart in 1862 for promotion to brigadier general. Instead Goode chose to resign due to ill health and return to Mecklenburg County. He was elected commonwealth's attorney.

Following the war he established a law practice in Boydton, and in 1872 purchased some of the RMC property at auction and purchased Buffalo Lithia Springs resort in Mecklenburg County. His wife was Rosa C. Chambers, daughter of his professor, and they were married on November 22, 1860 (the week before he organized the Boydton militia). They had five children.[3]

John Cowper Granbery, son of Richard Granbery of Norfolk, Virginia (A.B. 1848; later a D.D.), graduated as first honors man, valedictorian. Following graduation, he became a minister in the M.E. Church, South. From 1854 to 1856, he served as chaplain for Randolph Macon College. Born in Norfolk, Virginia, on December 3, 1829, to Richard Allen and Ann Leslie Granbery, he married Jessie Massey in 1858, but she died in 1859. He went to the University of Virginia, where he served as college chaplain from 1859 to 1861. He was described as 5 feet, 9 inches tall. He remarried, to Ella Winston (1837–1906), on November 17, 1861, and they had eight children.

When the war began, he enlisted into the 11th Virginia Infantry on July 4, 1861, as a chaplain. He was captured at the Battle of Seven Pines on June 28, 1862, and made a prisoner of war. He had been shot in the head and left on the battlefield for dead. He was sent to Fort Warren prison in Boston Harbor, where he recovered from his wound. In 1863 he was exchanged and paroled. The remainder of the war he served as a Confederate command general & staff chaplain. Following the war, he was living in Richmond serving as an M.E. minister and had been appointed as a member of the RMC Board of Trustees in 1866. It was reported in the *Tobacco Plant* in 1870[4] that he was taking care of Dr. William A. Smith, who was quite ill. In 1875, he moved to Nashville, Tennessee, accepting a professorship with Vanderbilt University. He served in this position until elected bishop of the M.E., South, in 1882. He resigned in 1902 due to ill health. From 1889 to 1900, he was an infrequent lecturer on homiletics and pastoral theology with R-MC–Ashland.[5]

In June 1894, Bishop Granberry dedicated the new sanctuary for the Providence United Methodist Church in Forksville, Virginia, on the old Boydton to Petersburg Plank Road. It was the same church where the Rev. William H. Wheelwright had served as presiding elder in 1858. He was quoted in the church history as saying "for the earth bring forth fruit of herself; first the blade, then the ear, after that the full corn in the ear." He was elected president of the Randolph Macon College Board of Trustees. He died on April 1, 1907, and is buried in Hollywood Cemetery, Richmond.

John H. Guy, son of Samuel A., was born in 1834 at Long Creek, Louisa County, Virginia, and received his A.B. degree in 1851. Working as a lawyer, he enlisted on April 21, 1861, into Company B, 1st Virginia Infantry, as a private. He was established as a corporal but resigned on May 23, 1861. Later in 1861, he was captain of the Goochland Light Artillery, where he served through 1862. He was elected and served as a Confederate Virginia state senator from Goochland from 1863 through 1865. In Richmond, he was established by the Confederate Army on July 4, 1864, as lieutenant colonel in charge of the 2nd Battalion Virginia Reserves in Richmond. He was paroled on May 9, 1865. He established a law practice in Richmond following the war and died in Richmond on June 16, 1890.

Moses D. Hoge, see Chapter 10.

Charles E. Hooker, son of G. Hooker of Union Court House, South Carolina, was born in 1824. He was also a student (junior) in 1844 who did not take a degree. Irby writes that he was a South Carolina senator and later attorney general for the state. When the war began he was serving in the South Carolina militia. He was selected by the Confederate Army as G&S colonel in command of the South Carolina cavalry.

Lieutenant Colonel Thomas Carter Johnson, see Chapter 7.

Hezekiah Gilbert Leigh, Jr. was born in Mecklenburg County on a farm next to RMC on March 12, 1833. His father was on the original board of trustees, and his mother was Mary Jane Crump Leigh, daughter of Richard Crump from Northampton County, North Carolina. He received his A.B. at RMC in 1851, was a tutor from 1852 to 1853, and married Martha Alice Moody. They had four children. The two oldest were Nannie and Emmett. He taught for one year in a female academy in Aberdeen, Mississippi, then attended the University of Virginia Medical School for one year. He transferred to Medical College of New York, where he graduated with his M. D. He relocated his family to Petersburg and began a practice.

When the war began he enlisted into the 58th Virginia Infantry and was established as a surgeon. Almost a year later, he was selected as a G&S surgeon and transferred to a Confederate hospital in Raleigh, North Carolina. He served in that capacity until May 1865. He returned to Petersburg and resumed his medical practice. He died on October 17, 1898, and is buried in Blandford Cemetery.[6]

Woodson L. Ligon, whose guardian was D.S. Beacham of Cokesbury, Abbeville District, in South Carolina was born in 1819 and received his A.B. in 1840. When the war began he was established into the Confederate G&S, Commissary Department, and then transferred to the Engineering Department. No rank was given, but Irby writes he was a colonel (see Chapter 5).

Thomas J. Lockett was born in Boydton, Virginia, in 1825 and was the son of Sam Lockett. He graduated from RMC with an A.B. in 1846 and most likely the medical department. He completed medical college and moved to Louisiana. In 1861, Dr. Lockett enlisted into Company G, 14th Louisiana Infantry. He was immediately selected as a Confederate assistant surgeon and assigned to a Confederate hospital.

John Lyon, see 12th Virginia Infantry, this appendix.

Professor Robert T. Massie, see Chapter 7.

Peter A. Moses (A.B. 1858) enlisted into Company D, 34th Arkansas Infantry, and was established as the company chaplain. He was then recruited and established as a chaplain of the Confederate G&S.

Richard Samuel Fennell Peete was born in 1828 in Charlotte Court House, Virginia. He was sponsored at RMC by his guardian, L. Skidmore, also of Charlotte County. He received his A.B. in 1849, most likely attended the Medical Department and received his A.M. in 1852. He went on to the University of Virginia and completed his medical degree with high honors in 1853. He returned to Mecklenburg County, residing on land he had inherited, but following the war he relocated to Warren County, North Carolina, where he established a new medical practice. On February 22, 1864, one of his former patients died. In settling the estate, Alfred G. Boyd of Boydton, as administrator, authorized and made payment to Peete for a medical bill of $1,160. Peete enlisted into the military and was immediately established as a Confederate G&S surgeon. Following the war, he and his wife, Catherine Jane Nicholson Peete, had one son, Charles Henry Peete (b. November 24, 1878). Charles attended the Warrenton Military Academy and went to the University of Virginia. He graduated from medical school in 1903 with high honors and served during World War I and II as a surgeon. In Warrenton, he was a trustee, steward and Sunday school teacher for the Methodist Church for over 60 years.[7]

Professor William A. Shepard, see Chapter 7.

William Gabriel Starr (1840–1916; A.B. 1859) was entered into a trial as Methodist minister with the Alabama Conference in 1860. When the war began in 1861, he enlisted into the 47th Alabama Infantry, where he was established as a chaplain. The regiment immediately came to the defense of Virginia, and shortly after the Peninsular Campaign, he was established as a Confederate command general and staff chaplain until the end of the war. In 1865, he petitioned the Virginia Conference for a transfer, and it was granted. In 1899, he was selected as president of Randolph-Macon College–Ashland. He served in this capacity until 1902.

Allen Talbott, see Appendix A.

John W. Taylor (A.M. 1860) appears to have enlisted into the Confederate Army and been established as a chaplain in G&S. (There were 41 John. W.'s in the Virginia Confederate Armies, but only seven were Confederate, two quartermaster, one miscellaneous and four chaplains.)

Leroy M. Wilson was born in Norfolk, Virginia, in 1835. His widowed mother, Elizabeth J., saw to his education at RMC. He graduated with an A.B. in 1854 and settled in Boydton. He enlisted at Boydton on August 20, 1861, into Company A, 3rd Virginia Cavalry, as a private. He was detailed to the position of company clerk from September 1861 until March 1862. He was promoted to sergeant and detailed to the

Quartermaster Department but removed by the Confederacy and established as a captain, G&S, assistant quartermaster.

Confederate F&S

Also in the Confederate States of America command structure was the command field and staff (F&S) services. This was composed primarily of field officers for regiments or battalions but also included support services. These were the moving, fighting on the field soldiers.

Benjamin W. Arnold graduated from Randolph Macon College with an A.M. in 1860. He enlisted into Company E at Clarksville on May 12, 1961, along with his younger brother, Joseph D. He listed his age as 24 and his occupation as teacher. He was absent sick in March and April 1862, then admitted to Williamsburg Episcopal Hospital for 10 days beginning May 10, 1862. He was sick and at home from September 25 through November 1862, and then hospitalized at Williamsburg again May 7 through May 30, 1863. On September 10, 1863, he was appointed acting adjutant. On December 14, 1863, he was promoted to first lieutenant and established as the F&S company adjutant. He was wounded in action at Drewry's Bluff on May 16, 1864, admitted to Chimbarazo Hospital, and then sent to private quarters June 11–18. On April 6, 1865, he was captured and made a prisoner of war at Sailor's (Saylor's) Creek. He was sent to Old Capitol Prison in Washington, D.C., then, on April 17, transferred to Johnson's Island. He was released on June 17, 1865. He reported his home as being Boydton, Virginia, and was described as 5 feet, 8 inches tall, with dark hair and complexion.[8]

John Wilder Atkinson was born 1830 in Petersburg, Virginia. He was sponsored to attend RMC by Thomas Branch of Petersburg and received his A.B. degree in 1852. He enlisted April 23, 1861, as a private in Company A, 15th Virginia Infantry, at Richmond and was then established as captain of the company. On April 25, 1862, having completed his one year enlistment, he was dropped from the rolls. On June 6, 1862, he was appointed major, Confederate F&S, 19th Heavy Artillery Battalion, for the defense of Richmond. On December 18, 1862, he was appointed a lieutenant colonel in charge of the 10th Battalion of Virginia Heavy Artillery. On April 6, 1865, he was captured at Sailor's Creek and made a prisoner of war. He was first sent to Old Capitol Prison in Washington, D.C., and then transferred to Johnson's Island, Ohio. He was paroled on May 9, 1865, and allowed to return to Richmond. He was born in Lunenburg County, Virginia, on May 23, 1830, and was working as a tobacco merchant before the war. Following the war, he moved to Wilmington, North Carolina, and established a merchant business there until his death on October 26, 1910. He is buried at Oakdale Cemetery, Wilmington.

The Rev. John D. Blackwell, see Chapter 1.

Colonel Thomas T. Boswell, see Chapter 5.

The Rev. George E. Butler, see Appendix A and Chapter 5.

Brigadier General John R. Chambliss, see Chapter 4.

William H. Cheek (A.M. 1857) enlisted into Company E of the 9th North Carolina State Troops. This unit was brought into the Confederate Army as the 1st North Carolina Cavalry, and Cheek was established as F&S colonel in command.

Appendix B

Lieutenant Colonel Henry Eaton Coleman, Jr., see Chapter 5.

Olin M. Dantzler (A.B. 1846) was born in 1826, the son of Jacob Dantzler of Lewisville Depot, Orangeburg District, South Carolina (see Chapter 5).

James Ferguson Dowdell earned at Randolph Macon College an A.B. in 1840, A.M. in 1846, and LL.D. in 1867 (see Chapter 5).

David R. Duncan (A.B. 1855) joined his father in South Carolina, completing his A.M. degree there (see Chapter 2).

Tyree Finch, assistant quartermaster sergeant, see Chapter 3.

Brigadier General Samuel Garland, see Chapter 2.

Garland Brown Hanes (b. 1832), son of E.G. Hanes from Chambers Mill, Buckingham County, Virginia, received his A.M. in 1857. His brother, James C. (b.1834), was also an A.B. student at RMC and is discussed later. Garland enlisted on May 22, 1861, into Company F, 20th Virginia Infantry, as a lieutenant. He was elected captain. On April 15, 1862, he was established as major of the 57th Virginia Infantry. On May 7, 1862, he prepared a request to retire based on the fact that his entire command consisted of one captain, three lieutenants, five servants and fifty men. His resignation was accepted and he was dropped from the rolls that day.

Tazewell Lee Hargrove (April 6, 1830–December 16, 1889; A.B. 1848) was born at Catalpa Grove of Lynesville, Granville County, North Carolina, and was the son of J.W. Hargrove. Following RMC, he studied law and was licensed to practice in North Carolina. On May 15, 1861, he was elected to represent North Carolina as a delegate to the state convention for secession, representing Granville County.

Following secession, he organized and was established into Company A, 44th North Carolina Infantry, as a captain on March 28, 1862. He was promoted to major on June 10, 1862. On July 28, 1862, he was again promoted, this time to lieutenant colonel. In June 1863, as rear defense for the troop movement toward Gettysburg, he was defending the South Anna River Railroad Bridge at Hanover Junction. "Colonel Hargrove had only eighty or so men and it [was] reported that they held off an attack by 1,200 Union Army for four hours before all were killed or wounded and captured."[9] Colonel Hargrove was sent to several prisons before finally being transferred to Johnson's Island, Ohio. He was referred to as the "cussing Confederate colonel" and continued to speak out against the surrender until his death. He refused to take the oath of loyalty and died an unreconstructed Rebel. So angry the South surrendered, he preferred to remain in prison rather than take the oath. His aged parents went to Ohio and persuaded him to come home. On March 17, 1868, he married Mary Augusta Lamb (February 10, 1846–December 7, 1922), and they moved into their new home in Oxford, North Carolina. He established a law practice there, was elected to the state legislature in 1870, and then elected attorney general for North Carolina in 1873. He served in that capacity until 1877.[10]

Benjamin Z. (Zachery) Herndon was the son of William Herndon from Macon, Bibb County, Georgia. He was born in 1820 and graduated with his A.B. degree from RMC in 1842. When the war began he enlisted at Abbeville, South Carolina, into Company F, 5th South Carolina Reserves, Light Artillery. He transferred to Company A (Macbeth's Light Artillery) and was elected captain. He served in that capacity for a year from 1862 to 1863. On December 27, 1864, he was established as an F&S lieutenant colonel in the 1st Regiment, South Carolina State Troops, in command of the 3rd Regiment, Junior Reserves. He held this post until war's end.[11]

John W. Jones (A.B. 1859) enlisted on January 1, 1863, into the 25th Infantry and was established as F&S chaplain. On August 1, 1864, he resigned due to bad health.

Dr. William H. Jones was a surgeon, see Chapter 4.

John W. Leak was the son of Walter R. Leak of Rockingham County, Richmond, Virginia. He was sponsored by a North Carolina circuit, received his A.B. in 1838, and moved to North Carolina. His brother William C. was a student at RMC at the same time, but did not take a degree. John (b. c. 1818) was established into the F&S as a lieutenant colonel in command of the 23rd North Carolina Infantry.

Richard W. Leigh was born in 1831 to Hezekiah Leigh, presiding elder of RMC Circuit, benefactor, and neighbor to the campus in Boydton, Virginia. He graduated with an A.B. in 1849 and A.M. in 1853, and relocated to Mississippi. He enlisted in 1861 into Company A, 5th Battalion, Mississippi Infantry, as a lieutenant, but soon he was elected captain. He moved with his company to the defense of Virginia. In the report of Brigadier General Charles S. Winder, commanding First Brigade, Second Division, regarding the Battles of Gaines Mill and Malvern Hill, he writes, "I cannot speak too highly of the officers.... I must include the Irish Battalion, Captain Leigh."[12] Captain Leigh was then ordered to file his own report, as he was in command of a battalion and this he did. In 1863, he was established a major in the Confederate F&S with the 43rd Mississippi Infantry and later promoted to lieutenant colonel. According to Irby, he was killed at Murfreesboro, Tennessee.

Tennant Lomax from Alabama was born September 20, 1820, in Deadfall, Abbeville District, South Carolina. Both of his parents died when he was young, and his guardian, Matilda Lomax, insured that his education and that of his brother, Lucien, was provided through RMC. He graduated with an A.B. in 1840 and returned to Alabama, read law and established a law practice in Eufaula. In 1848 he raised a company of men, was elected their captain, and they were sent to Orizaba, Mexico, in 1848. Returning from the Mexican War, he married Sophie Shorter in 1849, but she died on March 18, 1850. He then moved to Columbus, Georgia, became the editor of the *Times and Sentinel* and received his A.M. from RMC in 1851. He was elected state printer of Georgia and served as president of the Democratic Convention. He returned to Alabama in 1857, married Caroline Billingslea Shorter, become a successful planter and was captain of a local militia unit, the Montgomery True Blues. They had two children, a daughter that died in infancy, and on April 29, 1858, a son, Tennent (Jr.). With the hanging of John Brown, Alabama Governor Moore appointed Lomax as F&S colonel and sent him to Pensacola to help the Florida Militia take possession of the forts and Navy yard. They returned to Montgomery within 30 days and the unit disbanded.[13]

Lomax enlisted in April 1861 into the 3rd Alabama Infantry and was elected lieutenant colonel. He was soon promoted to colonel by Colonel Withers and the unit moved for the defense of Virginia. At the Battle of Seven Pines on June 1, 1862, he was killed in action. On June 10, 1862, Major General Longstreet, commanding the Right Wing (3rd Brigade, 3rd Division), wrote in his report to General Lee that they had experienced torrential rains "with the woods filled with knee deep water and at times waist deep. The men pushed on through the undergrowth." Colonel Lomax had his horse shot from under him, likewise a second horse. "Colonel Lomax of the 3rd Alabama fell at the head of his command, gallantly leading them to victory." So exhausted following the battle, the men slept in their positions on the field that night. His body was recovered and sent to Montgomery for burial with full state honors, as he had been promoted to brigadier general the morning of the battle, effective June 1, 1862.[14]

Tennent, Jr., went on to college, became a successful lawyer and was elected solicitor of the district. In 1901, he was elected as a member of the Constitutional Convention.

George W. Magruder from North Carolina Circuit was the son of Dr. W.W. Magruder of Woodstock, Shenandoah County, Virginia. He was born in 1834 and graduated from RMC with his A.B. degree in 1854 and possibly attended the RMC medical department. He went on to medical school, relocated to North Carolina, and when the war began he was established with the 146th North Carolina Militia, F&S, as assistant surgeon. Later, he was promoted and established a Confederate G&S surgeon.

Adolphus W. Mangum, see North Carolina in this appendix, and see Chapter 3.

William T. Merritt, from Virginia, graduated with an A.B. in 1856 and A.M. in 1858. He enlisted for one year as captain and assistant surgeon for the 6th Virginia Infantry. He was assigned to an entrenched camp from November 13, 1861, through August 17, 1862. At that time he was established as an F&S assistant surgeon, acquired typhoid fever, and died August 21, 1862.

Lieutenant Colonel John Singleton Mosby, see Chapter 4.

Richard Holmes Powell was born November 2, 1821, at Monticello, Georgia, son of Norberne Berkeley and Elizabeth Holmes Powell (both from Amherst, Virginia). Norberne was a physician and had served several terms in both branches of the Georgia legislature. Richard graduated from RMC with an A.B. 1843, and he was also president of the Franklin Literary Society. He relocated to Alabama and became a successful planter with vast slave holdings. He married Mary Ann Polk in 1844, and they had seven children. He was awarded his A.M. from RMC in 1851. In 1856, he was elected mayor of Union Springs and re-elected several times. In 1860, he established the Bank of Union Springs.

He enlisted in April 1861 into the "Southern Rifles" and was elected captain. At muster, his company became part of the 3rd Alabama, under the command of Colonel Lomax, and Powell was promoted to major, F&S. He was wounded in action at Malvern Hill in 1862, and with the death of Lomax, he was promoted to lieutenant colonel. In 1864, he was wounded in action at Spotsylvania and was subsequently promoted to colonel.

Following the war, Powell returned to Alabama, and in 1868, was licensed to practice law. That year he was elected president of the Alabama Press Association and editor of the newspaper. A vigorously active humanitarian during Reconstruction, in 1882 he was elected to the state legislature. He was a Methodist lay leader and superintendent of Sunday schools, which were organized in his home. He wrote extensively for the *Union Springs Herald* and the *Southern Literary Messenger* under the pen name of "Cottager." He died in 1884 and is buried in Union Springs.[15]

The Rev. George H. Ray, see Chapter 4.

William McKendrick Robbins, see Chapter 3.

Edwin A. Thompson from North Carolina graduated with an A.B. from RMC in 1850. He enlisted in the 43rd North Carolina Infantry and was established as an F&S chaplain.

Major Phillip James Thurmond, see Chapter 4.

The Rev. Thomas A. Ware was born September 1, 1830, in Tuscumbia, Alabama, to Dabney and Elizabeth Ware. At age 18 he joined the Memphis M.E. Conference and served several churches until contracting malaria. He returned to Virginia and transferred to the Virginia Conference in the early 1850s. He was selected as chaplain for RMC from 1856 to 1857. In December 1863, he enlisted and was established as chaplain, 8th Virginia Infantry, and served until December 1864. Following the war, he married Jennie D. Pretlow on January 28, 1869, and continued to serve as a minister. He died on July 18, 1887, at Charlottesville, Virginia.[16]

The Rev. Major William Henry Wheelwright, see Chapter 5.

Lieutenant Colonel Wichtler, see Chapter 4.

Captains

James T. Alexander, see Chapter 2.

Robert P. Alexander, see Chapter 2.

Thomas S. Archer (A.B. 1841 and A.M. 1845) joined a South Carolina statewide militia and reserves unit in 1860. It became the 16th South Carolina Home Guard, in Spartanburg County. On July 1, 1863, it became the Greenville Home Guard, State Troops, with Archer elected the captain in command. Most of the war was quiet for the unit, but when President Jefferson Davis was retreating from Richmond via Danville and Greenville, the Union Army was in hot pursuit. Arriving near Greenville was Union General I.N. Palmer, who was met by the Home Guard. Underestimating the Home Guard, Palmer found himself in a situation more intense than his unit was capable of handling. He moved around Greenville and headed south to try and intercept the train at a later destination.[17]

Robert D. Baskerville, see Chapters 3 and 4.

John Edwin Blankenship, see Chapter 5.

George E. Booker, from Virginia (A.B. 1855 and A.M. 1857), enlisted into the 48th Virginia Infantry, and was appointed chaplain and captain on September 25, 1862. He was hospitalized for debilitas at Richmond from March 30, 1865, to April 2, 1865, and returned to duty. He was paroled on April 28, 1865.

Thomas W. Branch, see 12th Virginia Infantry, this appendix.

Charles Bruce, Jr., see Chapter 3.

Charles Bruce, Sr., see Chapter 3.

Harvey Chambers, see 1st Virginia Reserves, this appendix.

John R. Chambliss, Sr., see Chapter 2.

Archer D. Crenshaw, see 18th Virginia Infantry.

George B. Davis, see Chapter 3.

Benjamin C. Drew, A.B. 1850, was the son of Captain B.L. Drew of Bailey's Buoy, Surry County, Virginia. He enlisted into Company G, 13th Virginia Cavalry, on April 20, 1861. He was elected captain on August 22, 1862. He was sick and hospitalized in October 1862, November 22, 1862, and May 20, 1863. Following six more hospitalizations, he resigned due to ill health.

William W. Duncan, see Chapter 1.

Thomas Ashbury Gatch was born in 1832 and graduated with an A.B. in 1855. He became principal of the Home School in North Carolina that year and received his A.M. in 1857. He enlisted into Company H, 6th Virginia Infantry, on April 16, 1863, and was appointed first lieutenant. He was elected captain on July 30, 1863, and served in that capacity until paroled at Appomattox on April 9, 1865. He was described as 5 feet, 8 inches tall, florid complexion, light hair and blue eyes. Following the war, he moved to Baltimore, Maryland. He then relocated to Alabama. He is buried at Cedar Grove Cemetery, Norfolk, Virginia.

James C. Hanes (A.B. 1855) was the son of E.G. Hanes of Chambers Mill, Buckingham County, Virginia. His brother was Garland Brown Hanes (see Confederate F&S, this appendix). James (b.1834) enlisted on May 26, 1861, in Buckingham County into Company A, 57th Virginia Infantry, with his brother. He was appointed captain and put in charge of conscription duty. On April 1, 1865, he was captured at Five Forks and made a prisoner of war. He was sent to Point Lookout, Maryland, on April 5, 1865, took an oath, and was paroled and released on June 13, 1865. He was described as 5 feet, 9 1/2 inches tall, fair complexion, dark brown hair and light blue eyes. Following the war, he settled in Franklin County, Virginia.

John W. Hutcheson, see Chapter 5.

Richard Irby, see 18th Infantry and numerous references in the text.

Benjamin Franklin Jarratt, see Chapter 5.

Thomas J. Jarvis, see Chapter 3.

James W. Jones, see Class of 1861 Tribute.

Richard W. Jones, see 12th Virginia Infantry in this appendix and Chapter 5.

Thomas Jefferson Kroger (b. 1817) was the son of Major Joseph Koger from Indian Fields, Colleton District, South Carolina. He received his A.B. in 1838 and A.M. in 1851. Thomas enlisted into Company D, 41st Mississippi Infantry. When the unit was taken into the Confederacy, he was elected its captain.

Joel B. Leftwich (b. 1817) of Red Hill, Campbell County, Virginia, transferred from RMC in 1844 without taking a degree. In 1860, he was captain of a militia company in Castle Craig, Campbell County, at the age of 44. He was working as a lawyer. When the war began, his militia company became Company D, 42nd Infantry, and he was established as the captain on June 28, 1861. He was sick and on furlough from November 10, 1861, through December 5, 1861, and again from February 14, 1862, through April 1, 1862. He failed to be re-elected by his men and was dropped from the rolls on April 21, 1862. According to Irby, he went on to serve in the Virginia General Assembly.

Phillip Lockett, see Class of 1861 Tribute.

John B. McPhail, see Chapter 3.

Robert Alexander Stainback, see Class of 1861 Tribute.

Marcellus Stanley (A.B. 1841) enlisted into Carleton's company, "Troop City," of the Georgia Artillery and was elected captain. This company became Confederate 2nd Georgia Infantry, Stanley's Company, with Stanley still the captain in command.

John Dudley Thurmond, see Chapter 4.

John W. Thurmond, see Chapter 4.

William Dabney Thurmond, see Chapter 4.

William T. Thurmond, see Chapter 4.

William Townes, Jr., see Chapter 4.

Charles E. Williams (A.B. 1855) enlisted into Company I, 1st Battalion, Confederate Infantry. He was established as the regimental quartermaster (captain).

Oliver P. Williams (b. c. 1820) was the son of William Williams from Buckland Causey, Colleton District, South Carolina. He received his A.B. in 1841. He enlisted and served a 90 day contract at Camp Ida, Pocotaligo, South Carolina. He was elected captain of Company K, 11th Regimental Reserves, and served from November 19, 1862, to February 19, 1863.[18]

Henry W. Wingfield (A.B. 1853 and A.M. 1855) was born June 26, 1829, at the Marl Ridge estate in Richmond, Hanover County, Virginia, the son of Joseph B. Wingfield. He enlisted as a private on September 5, 1861, into Company H, 58th Virginia Infantry, but was selected as third lieutenant on October 15, 1861. On May 1, 1862, he was elected captain. He was wounded in the arm at Fredericksburg on May 4, 1863. Following this, he was absent by order on May 24, 1863, and five more times over the next twelve months, for three to five days each. At Winchester on September 19, 1864, he was captured and made a prisoner of war. He was sent to Fort Delaware, where he took an oath and was released on June 17, 1865. When he enlisted, he stated his occupation was as a teacher. He was described as 5 feet, 10 inches tall, light complexion, dark hair and blue eyes. He returned to Hanover County as a surveyor. He then became a professor with Randolph-Macon College–Ashland. He died on August 11, 1902, and is buried at Marl Ridge.

Luther Wright (A.B. 1858) became a teacher in Caroline County, Virginia. He enlisted into Company G, 47th Virginia Infantry, on August 2, 1861, as a lieutenant. On April 20, 1862, he was elected captain. On June 27, 1862, he was wounded in action at Gaines' Mill. He was wounded in action again on October 28, 1862, and while at Fredericksburg, again, on December 12, 1862. On April 25, 1863, he tendered his resignation, citing ill health in his family and only a small number of troops in his command (49 total with 10 of those on details). Colonel Mayo endorsed his resignation.

12th Virginia Infantry

One Civil War unit from Virginia stands out above the rest concerning Randolph Macon's successful and prominent graduates—the 12th Virginia Infantry from Petersburg. The historian for the unit, William D. Henderson, seemed so impressed with the unit that he did an extensive collection not only of their military histories, but civilian as well, before and after service. This unit includes 17 distinguished individuals from RMC.

James R. Branch, see Confederate G&S, this appendix.

Thomas W. Branch of Petersburg (b. 1831) was the son of the prominent Thomas Branch (the elder,1812–1888, RMC Board of Trustees 1846–1874). The Branch family established and operated a large wholesale grocery and commission merchant business in Petersburg on Old Street near D'Arcy Paul. Branch became a partner in the business upon completing his studies at RMC (BL&S 1859). On April 19, 1861, he enlisted as a corporal in Company A, 12th Infantry. On May 20, 1862, he was elected as a second lieutenant and detailed to Petersburg for conscription duty (drafting soldiers). On May 2, 1863, he was captured at Chancellorsville and made a prisoner of war. He was sent to Old Capitol Prison in Washington, D.C., and later exchanged. In January 1864, he was discharged from the 12th and enrolled as a captain of the Petersburg City Battalion Reserves. Following the war, the elder Thomas became president of Merchants National Bank (1867 in Petersburg and 1870 in Richmond) and served Randolph Macon College on a committee to approach Jefferson Davis, former CSA president, to become president of Randolph Macon.

Thomas W. (Jr.) took over the family business and was appointed to the RMC Board of Trustees (1876–1883). The Branch family established an endowment fund with the college. Partially funded by the family and in their honor, RMC built the Mary Branch Dormitory in 1905 and the Thomas Branch Dormitory in 1914.

John H. Claiborne was born March 10, 1829, in Brunswick County. His father was the Rev. John C. Claiborne from Brunswick County, who was one of the original members of the Randolph Macon College Board of Trustees. He received his A.B. in 1848, probably attended RMC medical department and received an A.M. degree in 1853 from RMC. After completing his A.B. degree and the medical department, he completed his M.D. with the University of Virginia in 1849. He went on to Jefferson Medical College, Philadelphia, for a residency and did his internship with the Philadelphia Hospital. In 1851, he relocated to Petersburg, where he began his practice. He served in the Virginia House of Delegates from 1855 to 1857 and the Virginia Senate from 1858 to 1862, from which he resigned. He enlisted into the Confederate government as a surgeon on February 17, 1862. From February 1862 until April 1865, he was in charge of the military hospital in Petersburg. Throughout his career, he published numerous articles, journals and books. He also received many awards, and was on the Virginia Board of Medical Examiners and a president of the Medical Society of Virginia. He was married twice, died on February 25, 1905, and is buried at the Blanford Cemetery in Petersburg.

Henry Brown Cowles, Jr., the son of a wealthy and prominent Methodist minister, the Rev. H. Brown Cowles of Petersburg completed his studies at RMC. Cowles was a reverend of the Virginia Methodist Conference and an agent for RMC. The family home was situated at the corner of Franklin and Jefferson Streets in old Petersburg. Henry enlisted on July 1, 1861, into the 12th Infantry. On May 20, 1863, he was hospitalized at Virginia Hospital in Petersburg for typhoid, but died.

James R. ("Tack") Cowles (b. 1842), Henry's brother, was a student at RMC. Completing his proficients in mathematics and political economy and slavery, he left Boydton and returned to Petersburg. There he enlisted, as a private, in Company E,

12th Infantry, on July 22, 1861. March through November 1862, he was on sick leave. On August 1, 1863, he was wounded in action during a skirmish at Brandy Station. He was hospitalized from August 1863 to September 1864. In September 1864, he was returned to light duty, serving out the war with Anderson's Quartermaster Corps. He was paroled at Appomattox on April 9, 1865. Following the war, he moved to Goldwaithe, Texas, where he became a judge.

William Hoomes Davis, son of Williams T. Davis, president of Petersburg Female College, and a student at RMC, enlisted into Company E, 12th Infantry, in June 1862 as a corporal. On April 1, 1863, he was promoted to sergeant. On May 7, 1863, he contracted a fever and died at Chancellorsville.

His older brother, Richard Beale Davis, also attended RMC and earned an A.B. 1862. He was a businessman in Petersburg. He also enlisted in Company E, 12th Infantry, early into the war. At the Battle of Seven Pines in June 1862, he was wounded by a shell fragment to the face. He was wounded a second time at the Battle of the Crater, in Petersburg on July 14, 1864, with a gunshot to the right arm. He was paroled at Appomattox on April 9, 1865. Returning home, he attended the University of Virginia School of Law from 1866 to 1870 and established a law practice in Petersburg in January 1871. He married Annie Warwick Hall on April 20, 1875, and they had seven children, of whom five lived to adulthood. He was elected to the Virginia House of Delegates the same year.

He was selected as a member of the RMC Board of Trustees in 1876 and served several years. He was also on the board of trustees for the Virginia Normal School Board of the State, and served a term as president. He was elected city attorney for Petersburg in 1880 and served in this position until 1902, when he was elected to the Virginia Legislature again. He was appointed assistant attorney general for the State of Virginia in 1912, and served in that position until his death in 1914.

William S. Davis, valedictorian of the class of 1859 at RMC, was originally from Warren, North Carolina. After graduation, he moved to Petersburg. On May 14, 1862, he enlisted as a private in Company F, 12th Infantry, and on June 6, 1862, he was promoted to sergeant. When promoted, he was assigned to assist Lt. Branch with conscription duty in Petersburg. He was paroled at Appomattox on April 9, 1865. He died in Petersburg, of a stroke, in 1914.

Leroy S. Edwards of Petersburg (b. 1839) left RMC (A.B. 1858 and A.M.1866) and enlisted April 19, 1861, as a private in Company E, 12th Infantry. On June 1, 1863, he became a sergeant. On May 8, 1864, he was captured at Spotsylvania Court House and made a prisoner of war. He was transferred to Belle Plain Field Prison, then transferred to the union prison at Elmira, New York, on August 12, 1864. He was paroled on February 25, 1865, and transferred to Aikens Landing for exchange. He died in 1900.

Richard W. Jones received his A.B. from RMC in 1857 and his A.M. degree in 1860, with majors in math, physics and chemistry. He enlisted on February 22, 1962, from Greensville County into Company I, 12th Infantry, and was elected captain on May 1, 1862. He was regimental commander from August 30 to September 14, 1862, but not promoted to major until July 30, 1864. He was in command of the regiment at Appomattox in April 1865 and paroled on April 9. Following the Civil War, he became professor of math for Randolph Macon College from 1866 to 1868, when the college closed in Boydton. His father, Richard, was reported as being the largest landowner in Greensville County and had served in the Virginia House of Delegates. Richard W.'s second cousin was Senator John Y. Mason (see Chapter 5).

Anthony M. Keiley was born on September 12, 1833, in Patterson, New Jersey, into an Irish immigrant family of John D. Keiley and Margaret Keiley (b. August 5, 1809, in Dummanaway. Ireland; died April 26, 1887, in Richmond, Virginia). The family moved to Petersburg, Virginia, around 1835. He stated to the Confederate Army that he graduated with his A.B. degree from RMC in 1854 and moved to Petersburg. There he published *The South Side Democrat*. He continued his studies and was admitted to the Virginia State Bar in 1859. He was the oldest of seven children. His youngest brother became a Catholic priest (as the family was staunch Catholic) and his older brother was knighted by the pope. One sister was a teacher and the middle brother became a politician in Brooklyn, New York.

He opposed secession, but on April 19, 1861, enlisted into Company E, 12th Infantry, as a sergeant. On October 13, 1861, he was promoted to second lieutenant and assigned as a judge advocate on courts-martial duty. On May 1, 1862, he was promoted to first lieutenant. He was wounded in action at Malvern Hill on July 1, 1862, severely in the foot and was hospitalized from July to December 1862. At Gettysburg, his foot gave out and he did not participate in the charge. On December 1, 1863, he resigned. He became editor of the *Petersburg Express* during 1864 and 1865, but he also enlisted into Archer's Battalion, Virginia State Reserves. He was captured and made a prisoner of war on June 9, 1864, at Petersburg, and taken to Point Lookout, Maryland. He was transferred to Elmira, New York. Due to an outbreak of scurvey, 1400 prisoners were deemed unfit and sent to Baltimore for exchange on October 1, 1864. Finally, Anthony and a group of prisoners were sent to Hilton Head, South Carolina, and released in November 1864. He returned as editor of the *Petersburg News* in 1865 but was imprisoned at Castle Thunder, Richmond, by Federal troops, for writing anti-northern editorials. He was released on June 4, 1865.

Anthony was founder of *Petersburg Indexes* along with Major E. Branch, and he wrote a book on his experiences as a prisoner of war, *In Vinculis*, published in 1866. He was raised Roman Catholic, and on November 1, 1865, he married a Jewish woman, Rebecca Davis from Richmond. He served in the Virginia House of Delegates from 1863 to 1871. He and his wife moved to Richmond in 1870 with their two children; he was elected and served as nayor of Richmond during Reconstruction from 1871 to 1876. In 1874, he had a pamphlet published: "History of the Catholic Church in Richmond." He was city attorney from 1881 to 1885. On April 2, 1885, he was nominated, by the president of the United States, as envoy extraordinary and minister plenipotentiary to Italy. Unfortunately, he had given a speech in Richmond in 1871 blasting the Pope. He and the Italian foreign minister recommended he be withdrawn as a nominee. He was then nominated on April 29, 1885, by President Grover Cleveland as minister to Austria-Hungary, but since his wife was a Jew, the foreign minister from there recommended his name be withdrawn. It was not, but he did resign, and was sent to Cairo, Egypt, as a justice to the International Court. He was transferred to Alexander, Egypt, on June 22, 1886, and appointed chief justice of the International Court.[19] He resigned and moved to London, living there from 1900 to 1905. While visiting Paris, he was struck and killed on the Place de la Concorde, January 27, 1905, by a runaway horse.

John Lyon (b. August 22, 1827) graduated with an A.B. from RMC, class of 1844, and earned his A.M. in 1847. He then graduated from the University of Virginia with an LL.B. (bachelor of laws) and established a successful law practice in Petersburg. In 1860, he married Margaret Springs (b. 1836) of Charlotte, North Carolina, and when the Civil War began they had one daughter, Mary A. Also living in the home was Margaret's father or much older brother, Lewy Springs (b. 1815). Lyon's home and office were on "Lawyer's Row," West Bank Street. Before Virginia officially seceded, Lyon enlisted into Company B, 12th Infantry, on April 19, 1861, as a captain. On December 16, 1861, he was detailed as judge advocate for courts-martial duty. On April 23, 1862, he was detailed as an inspector and muster officer of General Mahone's Brigade. He resigned on August 1, 1862, to accept an appointment to the offices of the Confederate Judge Advocate's office, War Department, in Richmond. He held this position until the end of the war. Finally receiving his pardon from President Johnson, he returned to his law practice in Petersburg. In 1875, he and his family moved to Richmond, where he continued a law practice until 1889. That year he accepted a position in Washington, D.C., as an attorney for the Land Patent Office of the Department of Interior. He died in Washington, D.C., on November 3, 1897, and was buried at Blanford Cemetery in Petersburg.

John Henry Maclin was born in Brunswick County, Virginia, in 1839 and attended RMC. He enlisted on August 19, 1861, as a private in the Brunswick Guards, Archer's Battalion of Volunteers. On December 28, 1861, he was transferred to Company E of the 12th Infantry as a private. On April 28, 1862, he was given a medical discharge as unfit for military service, but he enlisted again in 1863 into a cavalry company. Again he was discharged. Following the war, he moved to Petersburg and became a senior partner in John H. Maclin and Son Tobacco Company. This was one of the largest in Virginia. He died April 1, 1923, and is buried at Blanford Cemetery in Petersburg.

Alex Mallory (A.B. 1858) of Greensville County, Virginia, enlisted into Company I of the 12th Virginia Infantry on February 22, 1862, and was established as a sergeant. Having furnished a suitable substitute in the person of W.G. Talley (age 45 and not subject to conscription), Mallory was discharged on October 7, 1862.

Joseph Richard Mason (b. April 3, 1831) of Brunswick County, Virginia, received his A.B. degree from RMC in 1851. On July 3, 1855, he married Charlotte Ashby of Culpeper and they had 10 children. Following the war, he returned to his life as a planter in Brunswick County and became a lay leader in the Methodist Church. In 1860, he was working as a merchant for the Petersburg Wholesale Commission. He enlisted into the 12th Infantry, but was soon captured on September 14, 1862, at Crampton's Gap and made a prisoner of war. He was sent to Fort Delaware Prison and then exchanged at Aiken's Landing on October 6, 1862. Returning to the 12th Infantry, he was promoted to corporal in July 1864. He was paroled from Appomattox on April 9, 1865. He was reported to be an accomplished violinist. He died April 4, 1918, and was buried at Warfield, Brunswick County.

John S. Moore was born in 1829 in South Hill, Mecklenburg County, Virginia. He was residing in Brunswick County, Virginia, when sent to Randolph Macon College by his widowed mother, Elizabeth Moore, of South Hill. He graduated with an A.B. in 1848. On January 10, 1858, he married Sarah from Gaston, North Carolina. His listed occupation was farmer, and on February 22, 1862, he enlisted into 2nd Company I, 12th Infantry, as a private. He enlisted in Greensville County, Virginia, and in November 1863 was furloughed due to a bowel problem. He was detailed to the ordnance company (apparently in Danville, Virginia) from February through September 1864 as a blacksmith. In June 1864, he was treated at the Confederate hospital in Danville for a wound in action (must have been received at the Staunton River Bridge Battle) to his finger. He was paroled at Appomattox on April 9, 1865. He died May 31, 1890.

14th Virginia Infantry[20]

The 14th Virginia Infantry of Boydton was named the "Chambliss Grays" in honor of Colonel John R. Chambliss, Jr., who retired from the Boydton Cavalry on June 14, 1860. There were 11 men from Randolph Macon in the unit. The 14th Virginia Infantry was composed of 10 companies of men with two companies from Mecklenburg County. Company E was from Clarksville and Company F from Lombardy Grove. Of the men in the ten companies in 1861, by war's end, only 23 had survived.

Varney O. Andrews was a nineteen year old student at Randolph Macon College when the war began. He enlisted into Company F at Lombardy Grove on May 12, 1861, and was established as a fourth corporal. He was sick in September and October 1862, but at Gettysburg on July 3, 1863 he was captured, made a prisoner of war and sent to Fort McHenry Prison. On July 7, 1863, he was transferred to Fort Delaware and then to Point Lookout on October 26, 1863, where he remained until exchanged on February 13, 1865. That is also the same date he was hospitalized at Chimborazo Hospital in Richmond, and there is no further record of him.

Benjamin L. Arnold graduated from RMC with an A.B. in 1862. He enlisted as a private into Company F at Lombardy Grove following graduation, but then transferred into Captain Branch Jones Epes' company of heavy artillery at Fort Drewry on November 18, 1862. He transferred back in March 1864, and was then absent sick from May through October 1864. On February 1, 1865, he was admitted to Chimborazo Hospital for spermatorrhea. Following his release on March 27, 1865, he was again admitted on May 18, 1865, for chronic diarrhea, although he had been paroled on April 29, 1865.

Benjamin W. Arnold, see Confederate F&S, this appendix.

Joseph D. Arnold graduated RMC with an A.B. in 1860 and enlisted into Company E in Clarksville on May 12, 1861. His stated age was 22 and his listed occupation was that of teacher. He was absent sick during March and April 1862. On July 1, 1862, he was wounded in action at the Battle of Malvern Hill. He was wounded in the right arm severely enough that it had to be amputated on July 2, 1862, at Chimborazo Hospital. He was retired by a medical board on April 23, 1864, but still listed in the Invalid Corps on December 16, 1864.

Hugh D. Bracey, see Chapter 1

William H. Bracey, see Chapter 1.

William S. Davis graduated from Randolph Macon with an A.B. in 1859 and enlisted into Company E, 14th Infantry, as a private on April 30, 1862. He was absent on leave to North Carolina and discharged on July 27, 1862. See Chapter 1.

Anthony Dibrell graduated from Randolph Macon (A.B. 1858 and A.M. 1860) and was from a family of men who fought in the Revolutionary War and the War of

1812. He enlisted into the 1st Company, Company D, Richmond Howitzers. He transferred into Company E, 14th Infantry, as a private. He was later assigned to R.M. Anderson's light artillery unit as a corporal.

Lieutenant Joseph C. Hutcheson, see Chapter 5.

John L. Johnson graduated from Randolph Macon with an A.B. in 1859 and enlisted in Company F, 14th Virginia Infantry, on July 17, 1861, at Jamestown Island, as a private. He was back in Mecklenburg County during March and April in 1862 for being sick and at home convalescing, but stayed two extra months and was listed as AWOL (absent without leave). This seemed to cause him no harm, because on May 14, 1863, he was promoted to second lieutenant. He was killed in action at Gettysburg on July 3, 1863.

William H. Jones, see Chapter 3.

Robert T. Massie, see Chapter 5.

Charles Wesley Ogburn, see Chapter 4.

1st Virginia Reserves

The 1st Virginia Reserves was referred to as the "old men and young boys" regiment. Companies A and C were primarily composed of men from Mecklenburg County, but the 1st Reserves covered over 10 counties with seven identifiable connections to RMC.

William A. Brame graduated from RMC with an A.B. in 1850 and A.M. in 1856. He enlisted on April 22, 1864, in Company A, 1st Virginia Reserves, and was established as a sergeant, to defend the Stanton River Bridge. From December 4 to December 28, 1864, he was furloughed to Farmville General Hospital, and then was home for 60 days with rubella. Originally from North Carolina, following his A.B. degree, he relocated to Mecklenburg County. Following the war, he was a resident of the Oakley community and is buried at Ephesus Methodist Church on Trottinridge Road.

Harvey H. Chambers (b. 1845), son of Professor Edward Chambers, attended Randolph Macon, completed law school and established a law practice in Boydton. He enlisted on January 6, 1864, in Company E, 1st Reserves, and was elected its captain on April 20, 1864. He was sent home on furlough October 24, 1864, and listed as AWOL on December 28, 1864. He was transferred by General Kemper to regular service, to Camp Lee, Virginia, where he served out the remaining months of the war. Once paroled, he returned to Boydton and established a law practice. In 1867, when his father did not run again for justice of the peace, they ran the practice together. On June 3, 1870, he and Charles Alexander (much his elder) met at Boydton for a duel. Being the son of a prominent justice, following the duel, he immediately left Mecklenburg County, not knowing the outcome of the shooting. Alexander had been shot twice but survived and went on to become a justice in the county. Harvey relocated to Olcolona, Mississippi, and his father died very soon thereafter. In 1915 he retired, and made application for and received a Civil War pension.

W.H. Christian was another honors man from the class of 1851 (A.B.; b. 1828) from New Kent County, Virginia, but listed his residence as the RMC Circuit in Boydton in 1849. His oration at graduation was "Christianity, a Nation's Palladium." He enlisted into Company C, 1st Reserves, on March 1, 1864, where he remained until April 1865. He remained close to RMC until the move to Ashland in 1868. At that time he also moved to Ashland and became more involved in the college.

William D. Garner enlisted as a private from Boydton in Company H, 1st Reserves, on April 22, 1864. Following the Battle of Stanton River Bridge he was assigned to guard the bridge until December 31, 1864. At that time, he was detailed as a county guard, primarily in Boydton, until the end of the war.

John Y. Graves (b. 1820) married Mary (b. 1822) around 1839. They had two children: Frances (b. 1840) and Elizabeth Scott Graves (b. 1842). He enlisted as a private in Company A, 1st Reserves, on April 22, 1864, in Boydton. He was assigned as a conscript guard to Boydton for the duration of the war.

R.H. Williams was the son of William Williams of McFarlands, Lunenburg County, Virginia. He was born in 1830 and graduated from RMC with honors in the class of 1851 and with his A.B. degree. Stating he was from Nottoway County, Virginia, he enlisted into Company D, 1st Reserves, on August 18, 1864, as a private, at the Staunton River Bridge. He remained a guard there until April 1865.

18th Virginia Infantry

Richard Irby helped organize the 18th Virginia Infantry on April 22, 1861, following the convention's vote to secede. He listed his occupation as farmer and was first selected to serve as first lieutenant and later captain. He died July 4, 1902, and is buried at Blackstone, Virginia (see Chapter 5).

The Rev. John D. Blackwell, see Chapter 1.

Archer Dibreld Crenshaw (b. 1838) was from Nottoway County, Virginia, and was a graduate of Randolph Macon College with his A.B. degree in 1858. He listed his occupation as teacher when he enlisted into Company G, 18th Infantry, on May 25, 1861, as a private. He was promoted to sergeant on April 23, 1862, and hospitalized at Chimborazo Hospital, in Richmond, in June 1862. The report states "he was taken away by his mother without permission." No charges were filed. He returned to duty in July 1862 and was elected captain on December 14, 1863. During Lee's retreat from Richmond, near the Battle of Saylor's Creek (Farmville, Virginia), Archer was shot and killed in action March 31, 1865, on White Oak Road.

The Rev. Richard Ferguson (b. October 22, 1838) was a graduate of Randolph Macon (A.B. 1858), and on April 22, 1861, he enlisted into Company G, 18th Infantry. He listed his occupation as farmer. He was selected as a first lieutenant on November 21, 1861. He was furloughed as sick from December 1861 until February 1862. When he returned to his unit, they were being reorganized and he was demoted back to private in April 1862. On June 30, 1862, he was appointed to adjutant of the regiment (first lieutenant) but was wounded in action that day at Frazier's Farm. He recovered quickly and was with his regiment at the Battle of Gettysburg. A story circulated about him referring to him as "Preacher" Ferguson. "Ferguson, reluctant to take orders with which he disagreed, was deliberately very slow in moving his cannon when retreat had been ordered. After most of the soldiers, and probably all the officers, had passed, Ferguson loaded his cannon quickly and fired. His shot received no reply.

The cannon ball is said to have been the last one fired at that Battle of Gettysburg."[21] He may have fired the last shot but was captured on July 3, 1863, and made a prisoner of war. On February 24, 1865, he was exchanged at Johnson's Island Prison. He died on June 1, 1930.

Samuel Hardy was the son of Elisha Hardy of Blackface, Nottoway County, Virginia, born in 1825. He graduated in the class of 1846 with his A. B. degree from Randolph Macon College. He stated his occupation as teacher when he enlisted into Company G, 18th Infantry, on April 22, 1861. He was established as first sergeant and was promoted to second lieutenant on November 29, 1861. He was wounded in action in the left arm at Gaines Mill on June 27, 1862. His wound was severe enough that his arm had to be amputated. He resigned his commission on October 8, 1862. He died in 1881.

Richard Irby, Randolph Macon class of 1844, helped begin Company D, 18th Virginia Infantry, which was referred to as the Nottoway Grays. The 18th had seven men with Randolph Macon histories.

Edward H. Muse was a student at Randolph Macon when the war began. He finished his school year and returned home to enlist into Company G, 18th Infantry, on June 30, 1861, as a private. On April 20, 1862, he was established as a sergeant. He was wounded in action, in the neck and shoulder, at the Battle of Frazier's Farm on June 30, 1862. He returned to duty and was wounded in action again at the Battle of Gettysburg on July 3, 1863. Recovering from his wounds, he was detailed to the Danville Ordnance Company in the fall of 1864, following the Battle of Stanton River Bridge. Subsequently he was hospitalized in April 1865 at Farmville Hospital and paroled from there. Following the war, he moved to Quincy, Florida.

Benjamin Irby Scott (b. 1841) also listed his occupation as teacher when he enlisted into Company G, 18th Infantry, on May 29, 1861, at the age of 19. A graduate of Randolph Macon College (A.B. 1858, A.M. 1860), he enlisted and served as a private. He was bruised by a musket ball at Gaines Mill on June 27, 1862, but returned to duty. He was killed in action on September 14, 1862, at the Battle of South Mountain.

38th Virginia Infantry[22]

The 38th Virginia Infantry was composed of 10 companies of men. Two of those companies were from Mecklenburg County. Company G was from Boydton and Company I, from Clarksville. It was reported that they were extraordinary at Seven Pines, Malvern Hill, Gettysburg and Five Forks. Yet they had charges of "confusion, demoralization and stampeding before the enemy"[23] in four other battles.

Jesse P. Bagby, A.B. 1854 and A.M. 1857 from the North Carolina Conference, enlisted on May 10, 1861. He gave his occupation as schoolmaster and birthplace as Mecklenburg County. He enlisted in Powhatan County, Virginia, in Company G, 38th Infantry, as a private at age 38. He was described as 5 feet, 9 inches tall, dark complexion with black eyes and hair. On October 2, 1861, he was given a medical discharge for bronchitis.

Thomas H. Boyd, see Chapter 2.

John Wesley Bugg (1835–1903) had worked for Dr. Smith for many years. Later in life he laughed and told that he attended Randolph Macon, daily, longer than anyone and never took a degree. His younger brothers enlisted in the Confederate Army and he stayed behind with Dr. Smith through the transition. In late 1861, he married a young woman from North Carolina. Then, on March 13, 1862, he enlisted as a private in Company G, 38th Virginia Infantry, in Boydton. (Shortly after his younger brother enlisted in 1861, William Henry Bugg [1837 –1861] died of disease.) His other brother, James Richard Bugg (b. 1839), had been promoted to sergeant. To protect his older brother, Sergeant James Bugg had him detailed as an ordnance wagon guard in June 1862. John Wesley wrote home of how he would watch the battles taking place through a "spy scope."[24] He was captured and made a prisoner of war at Saylor's Creek (Farmville) on April 6, 1865. He was sent to Newport News, where he took an oath and was paroled on July 1, 1865. He was described as 5 feet, 10 inches tall, fair complexion, light hair and blue eyes. He returned to Boydton just in time to assist Dr. Smith with his move to Missouri. Subsequently, Bugg went on to be a respected auctioneer and businessman. He married and they had eight children. For over fifteen years he served as magistrate and coroner for the Chase City District during Reconstruction.

William J. Carter, see Chapter 4.

Green A. (M.) Jackson, from Virginia, received his A.B. degree 1858. The only military record in the Confederate Army is that he was discharged from Company A, 38th Infantry, on February 25, 1865, as a private, from Kentuk, Virginia.

James W. Jackson was the son of Waddy J. Jackson of Union Level, Mecklenburg County, Virginia. He graduated with his A.B. degree in 1849 and A.M. 1852, and recorded his occupation as teacher. He enlisted into Company B, 38th Virginia Infantry, on June 4, 1861, and was established as a second lieutenant. From February 15 through March 1862, he was detailed to recruiting service. He was not re-elected and was dropped from the rolls on May 1, 1862. (See 22nd Battalion, Virginia Infantry, in this appendix for his brother, Robert A . Jackson.)

Local Defense Militia

Edward S. Brown was the son of Daniel Brown from Cartersville, Cumberland County, Virginia. He graduated with his A.B. degree in 1843 & his A.M. in 1854. He enlisted and served as a sergeant, first in Company D, then E, 122nd Militia. He was a lawyer and became a Virginia state legislator.

The Rev. W.H. Christian of Diamond Grove, Brunswick County, Virginia, was born in 1833. His guardian was John E. Christian of Brunswick County. Christian received his A.B. degree from RMC in 1851. When the war began, he enlisted and served in Company I, 149th Militia. He is also listed as 1st Virginia Reserves and in the 49th Virginia Infantry.

John F. Dance graduated from RMC with an A.B. in 1850 and A.M. in 1855. He served in the 1st Battalion, Virginia Cavalry, Local Defense.

Henry B. Eldridge was born in 1822. He was the son of Bowling Eldridge of Brooklyn, Halifax County, Virginia. He graduated from RMC with his A.B. degree in 1843. He enlisted and served in Company A, 2nd Battalion, Local Defense.

Richard B. Holstead of Virginia graduated with an A.B. in 1858 and A.M. in 1861. He served in Company F, 3rd Infantry, Local Defense.

Thomas M. Isbell, A.B. 1836, served in Company E, 3rd Virginia Reserves.

John S. Jackson was the son of Thomas Jackson from Blackface, Nottoway County, Virginia. He was also the brother of James F. Jackson, who enlisted in the 38th Infantry. He received his A.B. degree in 1853. When the war began he enlisted and served in McNeil's Company, 2nd Virginia Cavalry, State Line Defense.

Thomas L. Jackson was a third son of Thomas and the brother of John and James. He received his AB degree from RMC in 1856. He is listed as being born in Petersburg, Virginia, on November 11, 1840. He enlisted at Amelia Court House into Company A, 1st Virginia Cavalry, State Line Defense, on May 9, 1861. It was quite an active unit, and he was promoted to corporal and reassigned to Company G, assigned to recruiting, on February 14, 1862. He re-enlisted on April 26, 1862, and was named first sergeant. On April 11, 1865, he was promoted to first lieutenant. He was paroled on April 21, 1865. His listed occupation was that of farmer, and following the war, he moved to Maryland in 1870. In 1895, he moved to Arkansas.

The Rev. George B. Jones was from Boydton and the guardian of his brother, Benjamin (b. 1822), who was also a student at RMC, but did not take a degree. He received his A.B. in 1841 and A.M. in 1844. He was described by Irby as first honors man and a fine scholar. He enlisted into Company D of the 4th Infantry Battalion, Local Defense, Petersburg. In July 1864, when Union General Kauntz attacked Petersburg, Jones was killed in action (see Chapter 4).

Professor Godfrey Staubley, see Chapter 4.

Benjamin H. Thackston (A.B. 1858, RMC) enlisted in Henley's Local Defense in September 1864 to provide guard for the City of Richmond. This became the 3rd Virginia Local Defense, and after the evacuation of Richmond, the regiment moved to assist the Confederate troops at Sailor's Creek.

Artillery

One of the more popular artillery units was Captain Robert M. Anderson's. The company was organized in Richmond on November 9, 1859, as the 1st Richmond Howitzers, by Captain Edward S. McCarthy. It became Company H, 1st Virginia Artillery, in 1861. When Captain McCarthy died on June 4, 1864, it became R. M. Anderson's Independent Artillery Company, as a part of Cabell's Battalion of Artillery.

Another artillery unit that attracted a lot of attention was Pegram's company of light artillery. This company was established in Petersburg by Captain James Branch (see Confederate G&S, this appendix) as part of Company C, 12th Infantry. When Branch was promoted to major in May 1863, the company became an independent light artillery company led by Captain Richard G. Pegram.

Two other popular artillery units favored by the graduates were Captain G. Ailken Brown's company of horse artillery, which was organized on August 9, 1862, and was at one time part of Stuart's horse artillery. The other was Captain Branch Jones Epes' company of Virginia heavy artillery. This unit was organized in Dinwiddie County on September 2, 1861. It moved to Richmond for the defense of that city and was reorganized in 1862, with Captain Epes being elected. They were assigned to Major Francis W. Smith's battalion.

George W. Armistead of Virginia (A.B. 1857, A.M. 1860) was born October 4, 1835, in Hampton, Virginia. He was the son of Robert A. and Martha Savage Armistead. He was licensed to practice law in 1859, having completed his law training at RMC, and was principal of Ashland Female Seminary from 1860 to 1861. On July 18, 1861, he enlisted at Richmond into Hankins' light artillery company. This became 4th Company, Richmond Howitzers, and he was elected first lieutenant. This company was disbanded in late 1862. On July 21, 1863, he enlisted into the Surry Light Artillery as a private, but was established as a sergeant. On November 14, 1863, he was appointed as acting master, Provisional Navy. He taught midshipmen physics on the training ship CSS *Patrick Henry*. During the evacuation of Richmond, he was selected as a member of President Davis's escort south out of Richmond. He was paroled in Charlotte, North Carolina.[25]

Following the war, he returned and practiced law in Richmond until 1876. That year he moved to Tennessee. He first became editor of the *Bulletin* in Bolivar, Tennessee, and later editor of *The Issue*, a Nashville temperance newspaper. He died in Hopkinsville, Kentucky, on March 20, 1915. He was buried in Mt. Olivet Cemetery, Nashville.

B.L. Arnold (A.B. 1862) served in Epes' company, heavy artillery (possibly Thomas R. Epes, A.B. 1842, RMC). He also served in the 14th Infantry (see that section, this appendix).

William H. Bass was from Virginia (A.B. 1841 and A.M. 1844). His son William K. served as principal of the Preparatory Department in Ridgeway, North Carolina, in 1859 to earn his A.M., but took no degree from RMC. When the war began, he enlisted into Company K, 1st Artillery (see North Carolina section, this appendix).

John E. Christian was the son of William H. and brother of William H. (graduate of RMC) from Diamond Grove, Brunswick County, Virginia. He was born in 1832 and graduated with his A.M. degree from RMC in 1858. He enlisted and served in Kirkpatrick's company of light artillery.

The Rev. John E. Edwards of Virginia (A.M. 1853, honorary, and D.D 1863) served in the Virginia 2nd Light Artillery. Following the war, he served on the board of trustees for RMC for a number of years.

Landon Brame Edwards of Virginia (A.B. 1863, RMC) enlisted into Drewery's company, Virginia artillery, in Chesterfield County.

Aurelius T. Gill of Virginia received his A.B. at RMC in 1859. He enlisted into the Virginia Light Artillery, 38th Battalion, near Richmond.

Thomas J. Jarvis (A.B. 1860 and A.M. 1867) was a second lieutenant in J.W. Drewery's artillery company (see Chapter 3).

James E. Sebrell (b. 1833) was the son of William J. Sebrell of Farmers Grove, Southampton County, Virginia. He completed his A.B. degree in 1853 his A.M. in 1856. He moved to Sussex County as a teacher at the Newville Academy. After two years, he began a Sebrell School in Sebrell, Virginia. With the call to war, he enlisted into Company A, 18th Battalion Artillery, for the defense of Richmond and was established as the sergeant major. He served in that capacity until April 9, 1865. From 1865 to 1892, he was a merchant in Sebrell. In 1873, he was elected treasurer of the county and served until 1886. In 1892, he was elected commissioner of accounts for Southampton County and held that post until 1904. In 1904, he was selected cashier of the People's Bank of Cortland, and was still in that position in 1915.

Alex Sydnor, see Chapter 2.

3rd Virginia Cavalry[26]

The cavalry were the horse soldiers of the war. The Boydton militia cavalry became Company A, 3rd Virginia Cavalry, under the command of Captain Thomas F. Goode. Although many of the alumni enlisted into a local cavalry unit in their hometown, 15 enlisted into the 3rd Virginia.

The 3rd Virginia Cavalry consisted of eleven companies of men and the largest was Company A from Mecklenburg County. It fought in all fourteen major Virginia and Pennsylvania battles and was engaged in numerous skirmishes from 1861 to 1865. It was on the front line of defense and offense during the early days of Richmond campaigns and in Petersburg.

John Davidson Blackwell, see Chapter 1.

Lieutenant George B. Finch, see Chapter 3.

Thomas E.(R.) Fitzgerald was the son of B.W. Fitzgerald from Nottoway Court House, Nottoway County, Virginia. He graduated from RMC with his A.B. degree in 1850. When the war began he enlisted into Company E, 3rd Virginia Cavalry, at Nottoway Court House on May 27, 1861, as a private. Almost immediately, he was promoted to corporal. He was paroled on April 21, 1865, at Burkeville. He died in 1893.

John Valentine Hutcheson, see Chapter 5.

Thomas L. Jones, see Chapter 2.

Robert Moore of Virginia (A.B. 1858) enlisted into Company A, 3rd Virginia Cavalry, at Fredericksburg on November 25, 1862. He was established as a corporal. He was wounded in action at Gettysburg on July 3, 1863, and again at Buckland Mills on October 19, 1863. In July 1864, he was detailed to enrollment duty until Appomattox on April 9, 1865.

James Northington (b. 1833) was a student at RMC in 1850, but does not appear to have taken a degree. He enlisted into Company A, 3rd Virginia Cavalry, for one year. He was established as a sergeant. Upon completion of his service, he returned to Mecklenburg County. In 1864, he began a school in the Providence M.E., South, Church in Forksville, Virginia.

Albert Theodore Powell was born on February 18, 1842, at Norburn Hill in Nottoway County. He attended RMC 1858 to 1860, and transferred to Emory and Henry. He attended there from September 1860 until December 1861 without taking a degree. He went to Dinwiddie and enlisted as a private into Company I, 3rd Cavalry, on February 27, 1862. On November 3, 1862, he was wounded in action at the skirmish at Upperville. His record is incomplete, but his biography from 1915 relates that he was wounded in action twice and captured and made a prisoner on three occasions.[27] His military record shows that he was discharged on December 17, 1863, and then hospitalized for scabies at a Confederate hospital in April 1865, from which he was paroled.

Following the war, he worked as a teacher in Mecklenburg County and studied law. He married Louisa Jones Thweatt (b. 1843) while in Mecklenburg County. In 1871, he was licensed to practice law, and in 1873 elected commonwealth's attorney for Dinwiddie County.

Professor Bennett Puryear, see Chapter 5.

John L. Puryear, see Chapter 3.

Sergeant Reuban Puryear, see Chapter 3.

George Ray, see Chapter 4 and Class of 1861.

Lieutenant William F. Small, see Chapter 4.

John M. Tucker , see Chapter 2.

Benjamin R. Williamson, see Chapter 2.

Leroy M. Wilson, see Confederate G&S, this appendix.

Cavalry

David R. Doggett, see Chapter 4.

Armstreat E. Fowlkes was the son of John, born in 1831 at Nottoway Court House, Nottoway County, Virginia. He completed his A.B. degree in 1851 and an A.M. in 1854, both from RMC. When the war began, from Nottoway County, he enlisted into Company G, 9th Virginia Cavalry. He was established as a second lieutenant at Boonsboro. On September 15, 1862, ten privates in his company were captured and made prisoners of war. Six privates were killed in action and so was Fowlkes.

Robert S. Isbell was born March 24, 1836, in Lynchburg, Virginia, to Robert (a miller) and Angelina Isbell. In 1850, there were eight siblings including George the elder, with William and David being younger. He enlisted into Company B, 2nd Cavalry, on May, 13, 1861, and was established as a corporal. On January 1, 1862, he was promoted to sergeant and this was followed by a promotion to first sergeant on December 15, 1862.[28] On May 8, 1863, he was elected to second lieutenant and served out the war at that rank. Following his military service, in 1880, he is listed as living at home with his parents and his occupation is given as a miner.

Lieutenant William A. Jamieson, see Chapter 4.

Robert M. Mallory was born in 1829, the son of Colonel J.B. Mallory of Stony Point, Brunswick County, Virginia. He received his A.M. degree from RMC in 1855. When the war began, he enlisted as a private into Company I, 6th Cavalry, on May 4, 1861. He was transferred to the 13th Virginia Infantry as a quartermaster sergeant. His only record is that he was discharged on March 20, 1865, but not swearing the oath of allegiance to the United States, he had to apply for a pardon (which was three pages long and on file with the National Archives, with the appended pardon from President Johnson). It was granted.

John (James) D. Proctor was the son of Christopher, from City Point, Prince George County, Virginia. He was born in 1832 and graduated from RMC with his A.B. degree in 1853 an A.M. in 1856. When the war began, he enlisted at Greenville City in the 13th Virginia Cavalry. The only record of his service indicates he was paroled in Richmond on May 20, 1865.

Walter (William) H. Shay was the son of Henry Shay of Lancaster Court House, Virginia. Born in 1830, he completed and received his BL&S degree in 1854. When the war began, he enlisted into Company D, 9th Cavalry, on June 16, 1861, along with J.W. Brent. From July to October 1861, Shay was listed as sick with consumption and unfit for duty. Brent died of consumption on August 12, 1861. On November 1, 1861, Shay received a certificate of disability discharge. Not giving up, on February 15, 1863, he re-enlisted into the same company and was on their final roll on October 24, 1864. Following the war, Shay married the widow of Brent in 1876.

44th Virginia Cavalry Battalion

This unit was Thurmond's Partisan Rangers,[29] detailed in Chapter 4.

Lieutenant Elias Thurmond, see Chapter 4.

Lieutenant Richard Claiborne Thurmond, see Chapter 4.

Lieutenant Robert Given Thurmond, see Chapter 4.

1st Battalion, Virginia Infantry

James B. Dugger, Jr., was the son of James B. Dugger of Boydton. He graduated from Randolph Macon College with an A.B. in 1855. Early into the war, he enlisted into the 1st Battalion, Virginia Infantry, "the Irish Battalion."

9th Virginia Infantry

Claudius G. Phillips of Virginia (A.B. 1858) enlisted on May 18, 1861, at Chuckatuck in Nasemond County, Virginia. He enlisted into Company F, but was detailed as a nurse and clerk to a Richmond hospital until April 1864, when he was discharged.

16th Virginia Infantry

James H. Peay of Virginia, A.M. 1860, was conscripted into Company F, 16th Infantry, on April 11, 1862, at Huger Barracks near Norfolk. He was hospitalized on June 9, 1862, in General Hospital 21 with typhoid. He returned to duty on July 23, 1862. On April 30, 1863, he was captured and made a prisoner of war at a bridge crossing the Rapidan River. On May 1, 1863, he was sent to Old Capital Prison in Washington, D.C. He was paroled and released on May 10, 1863. He returned to Company F. On August 29, 1864, he was killed in action at Burgess Mill.

17th Virginia Infantry

James Sangster was the son of Edward, from Fairfax County in northern Virginia. He was born in 1831 and graduated with his A.B. from RMC in 1853. It seems probable that he was the same James that enlisted into Company A, 17th Infantry, on June 19, 1861, as a private. At Camp Pickens, he was promoted to corporal on June

25, 1862. On June 30, 1862, he was captured and made a prisoner of war at the Battle of Frazier's Farm. He was sent to Fort Columbus, New York, and transferred to Warren, Massachusetts. On July 31, 1862, he was exchanged. At Manassas he was wounded in action on August 30, 1862, and on September 8, 1862, he died from his wound.

20th Virginia Infantry

P. Fletcher Ford (A.M. 1860) enlisted into Company F on August 29, 1861, in Buckingham County. He was established as fourth corporal, but on July 30, 1862, he was elected second lieutenant. He was killed in action at Gettysburg on July 3, 1863.

Edwin S. Hardy (A.B. 1859) enlisted into Company C on May 20, 1861, at St. John's Church in Lunenburg County. He was established as a sergeant, but was discharged on August 24, 1861, due to a hepatic disorder. He was listed as a twenty-one year old school teacher.

22nd Battalion, Virginia Infantry

Robert A. Jackson was the son of Waddy J. Jackson of Union Level, Mecklenburg County, Virginia. He completed his A.B. degree from RMC in 1852. He is also the brother of James Jackson (see 38th Infantry, this appendix). Robert enlisted into Company D of the 22nd Battalion, at Lombardy Grove, on January 20, 1862. He was appointed second lieutenant and described as having a dark complexion. He was killed in action at the Battle of Seven Pines on June 28, 1862.

Pittman R. Venable of Virginia received his A.B. in 1858. He enlisted in Company E in Drakes Branch on January 22, 1862, as a private for a term of 12 months. He re-enlisted as a second corporal on August 23, 1862. He was hospitalized from July 22 through August 6, 1862. He was killed in action at Chancellorsville on May 3, 1863.

41st Battalion, Virginia Infantry

Benjamin F. Jarrett, see Chapter 4.

44th Virginia Infantry

Lieutenant William T. Bailey (A.B. 1856), see Chapter 3.

Thomas C. Elder graduated from RMC with an A.B. in 1854 and A.M. in 1857. He enlisted as a private in the 44th Virginia Infantry Regiment for six months early in the war.

49th Virginia Infantry

William H. Christian graduated from RMC with an A.B. in 1851. He enlisted into the 49th Infantry (see 1st Virginia Reserves and Local Defense Militia, this appendix).

52nd Virginia Infantry

Jacob M. Palmer (A.B. 1851) was born December 30, 1829, the son of Horace Palmer (Sr.) and brother of Horace Palmer, Jr. (graduate of RMC), from Macon Depot, Warren County, North Carolina. Following graduation, he married Elizabeth Frances Rodwell (b. December 3, 1830) on August 9, 1853. When the war began, he enlisted into Company C, 52nd Infantry. During the war, his wife died and he returned home to take care of their child. He married for a second time on February 28, 1865, to Sophie George Finley and they had five children. In 1870, he became divine master of the Grange of the Patrons of Husbandry, in Six Pound, Warren County, North Carolina. He died January 18, 1877.

54th Virginia Infantry

Peter A. Moses was born in 1830 at Charlotte Court House, Charlotte County, Virginia, the son of S.F. Moses. He graduated from RMC with his A.B. degree in 1855. When the war began, he enlisted in Company C at Christiansville on March 4, 1862. He was captured and made a prisoner of war at Lenoir Station, Tennessee, on June 19, 1863. He was exchanged at Montgomery White Sulpher Springs Hospital on September 3, 1863. He was transferred to Company K, and again captured and made a prisoner of war, this time at Marietta, Georgia, on July 3, 1864. He was sent to Camp Douglas, Illinois, then transferred to Point Lookout, Maryland, on March 23, 1865. He was paroled on June 21, 1865. He was a long time resident of Montgomery County and active member of United Confederate Veterans. With old age, he moved into the Camp Lee Old Soldiers Home, where he died on March 23, 1907, at age 73. He is buried in Salem Cemetery.

56th Virginia Infantry

Thomas T. Boswell, see Chapter 3.
Lieutenant Frank W. Nelson, see Chapter 3.

58th Virginia Infantry

The Rev. Peter F. August was born in 1821 at Fredericksburg, Virginia. Having entered the M.E. South, Virginia, Conference, he was selected as RMC chaplain for the year 1852–1853. When the war began, August enlisted in 1861 into the 58th and was an F&S regimental chaplain for the duration of the war. Following the war, he continued the ministry until his death on September 30, 1887.

North Carolina[30]

William H. Bass (A.B. 1841, A.M. 1847) was elected lieutenant colonel of the 34th Regiment, 9th Brigade, Halifax County, North Carolina Militia, F&S, November 6, 1861. In early 1862, he moved out of the county, returned to Virginia and enlisted into an artillery unit (see Artillery, this appendix).

Braxton Craven, see Chapter 2.

William Abraham Darden (May 15, 1836– June 2, 1890) was born in Greene County to William Augustus and Harriett Speight Darden. He was educated in neighborhood schools and came to Randolph Macon with plans to complete a program in law. His poor eyesight forced him out at the end of his junior year in 1860. In April 1861, he enlisted into Company A, 3rd North Carolina Infantry ("Greene County Rifles," Captain R. H. Drysdale's command), where he was elected second lieutenant. He was elected to the 1861–1862 North Carolina Secession Convention.

Again attempting to enter the Confederate service, he helped organize Company F, 61st Infantry Regiment, where he was elected second lieutenant and later captain. He was captured and made a prisoner of war defending Fort Harrison, Virginia, on September 30, 1864. He was sent to Fort Delaware and paroled from there in June 1865. He married the first time on August 13, 1857, to Sarah Speight Moore; they had three children and she died on August 25, 1863. He married a second time to Catherine Speight Adams on January 26, 1869, and they had seven surviving children. In 1884, he was elected to serve in the North Carolina House of Representatives, and in 1888 was elected as the first business agent of the North Carolina's Farmers State Alliance. He died several years later and is buried at his home, Speight's Bridge in Gates County.[31]

William H. Denton (A.B. 1841) enlisted on April 10, 1862, into the 101st Regiment, 25th Brigade, "Lower Fork" Burke County, North Carolina Militia, and was elected a first lieutenant.

William C. Doub (A.B. 1844, A.M. 1847) enlisted on March 10, 1863, into the 71st Regiment, 17th Brigade, Pfafftown District of Forsyth County, North Carolina, and was elected second lieutenant. Doub had been working as professor of languages at Greensboro Female College and later became a professor with Trinity College. He died not long after the war, around 1870.

John W. Ellis, see Chapter 3.

John P. Fuller of North Carolina (A.B. 1856, RMC) enlisted into the 33rd North Carolina Infantry Regiment.

Charles H. Hall was the son of J.H. Hall of Fayetteville, North Carolina. He was born in 1831 and graduated from RMC with his A.B. degree in 1855. When the war began, he enlisted into Company I, 20th North Carolina Infantry.

J. W. Heartsfield (B.Eng. and Sc. 1859) enlisted into Company I, 1st North Carolina Infantry, where he was selected as first sergeant.

William H. Jones (A.M. 1860) served as a major in the 48th North Carolina Infantry Militia Regiment.

Samuel Lander, see Chapter 2.

Addison Lea (A.M. 1851) enlisted into Company A, 50th North Carolina Infantry, where he was established as a sergeant (see Chapter 2).

John F. Long (A.B. 1858) enlisted into Company G, 61st North Carolina Infantry. He was established on March 31, 1862, in the 79th Regiment, 19th Brigade, of the Iredell County, North Carolina, militia as surgeon.

Adolphus W. Mangum was the son of E.G. Mangum of Deal Creek, North Carolina. He was born in 1834 and completed his A.B. degree at RMC in 1857. Early in the war he enlisted in Company B, 6th North Carolina Infantry, where he was established a sergeant (see Chapter 3).

A.C. Massenburg was born in 1834, the son of N.B. Massenburg of Louisburg, North Carolina. He graduated from RMC with his A.B. degree in 1854. He enlisted into Company K, 32nd North Carolina Infantry, and was established as a sergeant.

Henry D. Milam was born in 1842, the son of Nathan Milam of Macon Depot, Warren County, North Carolina. He completed his degree requirements and graduated with an A.B. in 1853. He enlisted into Company B, 34th North Carolina Infantry, Mallett's battalion.

Frank X. Miller, B.Eng.&Sc. 1859, enlisted into the 10th North Carolina State Troops, which at organization entered into the Confederacy as Company B, 1st North Carolina Artillery. He was established as a sergeant.

Lewis Miller was born in 1827, the son of Daniel Miller from Kinston, Lenoir County, North Carolina. He graduated from RMC with an A.B. degree in 1849 and his A.M. degree in 1853. Miller enlisted into Company K, 16th North Carolina Infantry. He later transferred to the 21st North Carolina Infantry, and then to the 61st N.C. Infantry. No rank was given.

Edwin G. Moore (A.B. 1857 and A.M. 1860) enlisted into Company A, 24th North Carolina Infantry.

Thomas J. Overby (A.B. 1859) enlisted into Company I, 23rd North Carolina Infantry. Following the war, he received his A.M. in 1866 from Randolph Macon College.

Horace Palmer, Jr., see Chapter 2.

Benjamin F. Simmons (A.M. 1854) enlisted into Company K, 63rd North Carolina State Troops. At organization this became the 5th North Carolina Cavalry, and he was elected second lieutenant. He transferred to Company B, 8th North Carolina Infantry, and was elected first lieutenant. He died of disease shortly thereafter.

William S. Smith, the elder, principal of RMC Preparatory Department, enlisted in the North Carolina Militia, of the Soda Hill District, 98th Regiment, Watauga County, 24th Brigade of Volunteers, on February 15, 1862. He was elected captain of the unit.

John B. Williams (A.B. 1857) enlisted on August 21, 1861, into Captain Hughes' volunteers, 29th Regiment, 7th Brigade, Greene County, North Carolina Militia, and was elected a lieutenant.

Georgia[32]

Edward A. Adams was born in Clarksville, Mecklenburg County, Virginia, as the son of William Adams. He graduated from RMC with his A.B. degree in 1850 and an A.M. in 1853. After graduation, he relocated to Georgia. When the war began, he enlisted and served as a corporal in Company I, 46th Georgia Infantry.

Joseph (Josiah) F. Askew was the son of the Rev. Josiah L. Askew of Mt. Yeassah, Habersham County, Georgia. He was born in 1816 and graduated from RMC with an A.B. degree in 1839 and A.M. in 1842. He enlisted into Company E, 1st Georgia Infantry Regiment.

Burwell K. Harrison was born in 1818, as the son of William Harrison, of Macon, Georgia. He graduated with an A.B. degree from RMC in 1840. When the war began, although 43 years old, he enlisted into the 14th Georgia Battalion of cavalry, where he was established as the first sergeant (see Chapter 3).

Henry Mettauer was in the Medical Department at RMC (see Chapter 1).

Mississippi[33]

George W. Blain (A.B. 1837, A.M. 1841) served in Company D, 5th Mississippi Infantry.

William W. Hereford was the son of William Hereford of Martinsville, Henry County, Virginia. Following his graduation from RMC with his A.B. degree in 1841, he relocated to Mississippi. When the war began, he enlisted into the 1st Battalion, Mississippi Cavalry, Cole's company (Miller's, later), and was established as a sergeant.

Texas

Alexander F. Hogg was the son of Lewis Hogg, Jr., of Yorktown, York County, Virginia. He was born in 1831 and was one of the first students to receive the new BL&S degree at Randolph Macon College in 1854, followed by an A.M. degree 1859. He applied for a teaching position with RMC in 1866, but was not considered. Following graduation, he relocated to Texas and when the war began, he enlisted into Company F, 20th Texas Cavalry. After the war, he returned home to Virginia (see Chapter 4).

John W. Hutcheson, see Chapter 5.

Henry E. Lockett was the son of Colonel S.L. Lockett of Boydton. He was born in 1818. He graduated from RMC with his A.B. degree in 1838 and A.M. 1841. After graduation he relocated to Texas. When the war began he enlisted, at age 44, along with his son Henry (Jr.) in Company C, 20th Texas Infantry. He was elected first lieutenant and his son second lieutenant.

Felix F. (H.G.) Taylor was the son of Judge John W. Taylor of Vicksburg, Mississippi. He was born in 1822, and graduated with his A.B. degree from RMC in 1843. He relocated to Texas, and when the war began, he enlisted into Company D, 12th Texas Infantry.

Alabama[34]

Willie M. Person was born in 1822, the son of P. Person of Franklinton, Franklin County, North Carolina. He graduated from RMC with an A.B. degree in 1844 and his A.M. in 1848. Following graduation, he relocated to Alabama, and when the war began, he enlisted into Company E, 28th Alabama Infantry.

William F. Samford, see Chapter 3.

Dallas Smith was born in 1827, the son of James H. Smith of Tuskegee, Macon County, Alabama. He graduated from RMC with his A.B. degree in 1848. When the war began, he enlisted into the Eufaula, Alabama, Light Artillery.

John C. Wills, see Chapter 2.

South Carolina[35]

Many of the graduates of RMC from South Carolina served and were established into the F&S, the G&S or were elected captains.

Thomas S. Arthur was born in 1820. His guardian for his attendance at RMC was F.G. Thomas, M.D., of Cokesbury, Abbeville District, South Carolina. He graduated from RMC with an A.B. in 1841 and A.M. degree in 1845. When the war began, he enlisted into Company K, 16th South Carolina Infantry.

David R. Duncan, see Chapter 1.

William H. Lawton was born in 1821 and was the son of Joseph M. Lawton, of Robertsville, Beaufort District, South Carolina. He graduated from RMC with an A.B. in 1843, and was South Carolina minister when the war began. He enlisted into Company H, 1st Regiment, of the Charleston Guard.

Rufus R. Peques of South Carolina (A.B. 1852, RMC) enlisted very early for the defense of Charleston in the 2nd Regiment, South Carolina Infantry. He enlisted for a six month period at Fort Sumter (see Chapter five).

Arkansas

Christopher Thrower (A.B. 1859) enlisted into Company E, 1st (Cloquett's) Arkansas Infantry.

Tennessee

Leonidas O. Rives (A.B. 1854, A.M. 1857) enlisted into Company A, 4th Tennessee Infantry, and was established as a sergeant.

Louisiana

Ernest LaGarde, see Chapter 6.

Charles Stuart, see Chapter 1.

Appendix C: Faculty and Graduates of Randolph Macon College, Boydton, Virginia

According to Irby, Randolph Macon College awarded 403 degrees to 294 students from 1832 to 1859. To receive the degree of A.B., students had to complete requisite courses in language, math, natural science and ethics, and have a recommendation from faculty. The student had to file a request to receive his degree. To receive an A.M. during this time frame an A.B. student could pursue three years of professional study (work—with no real guidelines) and claim an A.M. In 1835 through 1865 degrees conferred included fifteen doctorate of divinity (which had to be recommended by the faculty), 145 A.M. degrees and 256 A.B. degrees. From other sources I have added 24 additional names, bringing the total to 427 degrees, 315 graduates, 15 D.D. degrees, 152 A.M. degrees, plus most of the class of 1861 is not listed (see Appendix A). The following is an alphabetical listing of those students, the degree received and year in which received. An asterisk denotes Civil War service that could be identified (166), X denotes known dead (four) by 1861, and † denotes a later member of the board of trustees. An X with KIA (killed in action) or DOD (died of disease) indicates those who died in the war and the year. An ‡ indicates verification of no Civil War military service. The state they are from is indicated, when known. I am certain the military service and dead numbers are seriously understated. Information in parentheses is not found in the records of Irby or Scanlon.

Adams, Edward A.(W.)	A.B. 1850, A.M. 1853	VA*
Adams, Richard E.G.	A.B. 1837, A.M. 1840	VA†
Archer, William A.	A.M. 1862	VA*†
Armistead, George W.	A.B. 1857, A.M. 1860	VA*
Arnold, B.L.	A.M. 1862	VA*

Faculty and Graduates of Randolph Macon College 277

Arnold, Benjamin J.	A.M. 1861	VA (WVA)‡
Arnold, Benjamin W.	A.M. 1860	VA*
Arnold, Joseph D.	A.B. 1860	VA*
Arthur, Thomas S.	A.B. 1841, A.M. 1845	SC*
Askew, Josiah F.	A.B. 1839, A.M. 1842	GA*
(Atkinson, John	A.B. 1852	VA)*
Bagby, Adam C.	A.B. 1859	VA
Bagby, Jesse P.	A.B. 1854, A.M. 1857	VA, NC*
Bailey, William T.	A.B. 1856, A.M. 1859	VA* KIA
Baird, Charles W.	A.B. 1836, A.M. 1841	VA
Bass, William H.	A.B. 1841, A.M. 1844	VA*
Batte, William H.	A.B. 1839, A.M. 1842	VA
Beale, R.H.	A.B. 1847	TN
Beard, Clough S.	A.B. 1837	SC
Benaugh, George W.	A.B. 1843	VA X
Bennett, the Rev. W.W.	D.D. (1867)	VA‡†
Blackwell, John C.	A.B. 1835, A.M. 1840, D.D. 1860	VA‡†
Blackwell, John D.	A.B. 1848, A.M. 1862	VA*
Blackwell, John D.	A.B. 1859, (A.M. 1866)	VA*
Blackwell, William F.	A.B. 1845	VA
Blain, George W.	A.B. 1837, A.M. 1841	VA*
Blake, Thomas W.	A.B. 1843	NC
Blanch, Ezekiel A.	A.B. 1838, A.M. 1841	VA‡
Booker, George E.	A.B. 1855, A.M. 1858	VA*
Boswell, Thomas T.	A.B. 1845	VA*
Boyd, John G.	A.B. 1845, A.M. 1848	VA†
Boyd, John G.S.	A.B. 1854	VA
Boyd, Richard	A.B. 1854	VA*
Bracey, Hugh D.	A.B. 1851 (MED)	VA*
Brame, John T.	A.B. 1838, A.M. 1841	NC*
Brame, William A.	A.B. 1850, A.M. 1856	NC, VA*
Branch, James R.	A.B. 1848	VA*
Branch, Thomas W.	BL&S 1859	VA*
Brandon, Victor M.	A.B. 18	VA
Brown, Edward S.	A.B. 1843, A.M. 1854	VA*
Burnley, George W.	A.B. 1839, A.M. 1842	VA
Butler, J. (George) E.	A.B. 1862	AR*
Cabell, Lewis W.	A.B. 1837	VA
Cabell, William M.	A.B. 1844	VA*
Campbell, Thomas H.	A.B. 1841, A.M. 1846	VA‡†
Carter, William J.	A.B. 1861	VA*
Carter, William N.	A.B. 1855	VA*
Chamberlain, John L.	A.B. 1859	NC*
Cheek, William H.	A.B. 1854, A.M. 1857	NC*
Christian, John E.	A.B. 1855, A.M. 1859	VA*
Christian, William H.	A.B. 1851 (D.D. 1869)	VA*†
Claiborne, John H.	A.B. 1848, A.M. 1853	VA*
Clark, Archibald	A.B. 1844, A.M. 1847	VA

Clegg, Baxter	A.B. 1838	NC*
Clemons, Junious L.	A.B. 1837, A.M. 1840	NC
Clopton, David	A.B. 1840, A.M. 1851	GA, AL*
Compton, R. (Robert) A.	A.M. 1862	VA*
Conner, Francis A.	A.B. 1838, A.M. 1844	SC
Conner, William G.	A.B. 1842, A.M. 1846, D.D. 1869	SC, TN, TX*
Conner, William G.	A.M. 1857	TN
Corprew, Oliver H.P.	A.B 1846, A.M. 1849	VA*†
Cowles, Henry B., Jr.	A.B. 1859	VA* DOD 1863
Cowles, William I.	A.B. 1857, A.M. 1860	VA
Craven, Baxter	A.B. (Hon.) 1849, A.M. (Hon.) 1851	NC*
Crenshaw, Anthony D.	A.B. 1858	VA* KIA 1865
(Crenshaw, Archer D.	A.B. 1861	VA* KIA 1865)
(Crenshaw, Ira I.	A.B. 1842	VA)‡
Crenshaw, William N.	A.B. 1851, A.M. 1854	VA*
Croft, Isaac C.	A.B. 1837, A.M. 1842	SC
(Crute, Charles B.	? Med.	VA)
(Crute, J.W.	A.M. Law	VA)‡
Dance, John F.	A.B. 1850, A.M. 1855	VA*
Dantzler, Olin M.	A.B. 1846	SC* KIA 1864
Davis, John	A.B. 1846	VA
(Davis, Richard Beale	A.B. 1862	TN)*
Davis, Wilbur F.	A.B. 1857, A.M. 1860	NC, VA
Davis, William H.	A.B. 1859	VA* DOD 1863
Davis, William S.	A.B. 1859	NC*
Davis, Williams T.	A.M. 1848 (Hon.)	VA‡
Deems, the Rev. Charles F.	D.D. 1853	NC‡
DeGraffenreidt, Wm. G.	A.B. 1846	VA*
Denton, William H.	A.B. 1841	SC*
Dibrell, Anthony	A.B. 1860	VA* KIA 1865
Disoway, Gabriel P.	A.M. 1838 (Hon.)	NY
Doggett, the Rev. D.S.	A.M. 1842 (Hon.), D.D. 1847	VA†
Doggett, Rowland	A.B. 1852, A.M. 1855	VA
Doub, William C.	A.B. 1844, A.M. 1847	NC*
Dowdell, Hon. James F.	A.B. 1840, A.M. 1846, LL.D. (1867)	GA*
Dowdell, James F.	A.M. 1851	AL
Drake, Henry F.	A.B. 1851	NC
Drew, Benjamin C. (E.)	A.B. 1850	VA*
Dugger, James B.	A.B. 1855	VA*
Duncan, David	A.M. 1838 (Hon.)	VA‡†
Duncan, David R.	A.B. 1855	SC*
Duncan, James A.	A.B. 1849, A.M. 1852, (D.D.)	VA‡
DuPre, Warren	A.B. 1838, A.M. 1840	SC‡
Edwards, the Rev. John E.	A.M. 1853 (Hon.), D.D. (1867)	VA†*
(Edwards, Landon Brame	A.B. 1863	VA)*
Edwards, Leroy S.	A.B. 1859 (A.M. 1866)	VA*
Edwards, William E.	A.B. 1862, (D.D.)	VA*
Elder, Thomas C.	A.B. 1854, A.M. 1857	VA*

Faculty and Graduates of Randolph Macon College 279

Eldridge, Henry B.	A.B. 1843	VA*
Epes, Thomas R.	A.B. 1842	VA*
Eppes, George F.	A.B. 1838	SC
Fanning, James F.	A.B. 1844	GA
Ferguson, Richard	A.B. 1858	VA*
Finch, George B.	A.M. 1860	VA*
(Finch, Langston E.	Law 1849	VA)‡
Fitts, James M.	A.B. 1838, A.M. 1841	NC‡
Fitzgerald, Thomas F.	A.B. 1850	VA*
Foote, William G.	A.B. 1849, A.M. 1852	MS*
Ford, P. Fletcher	A.M.1860	VA* KIA 1863
Forster, Frank X. (Francis)	A.B. 1846, A.M. 1849	SC
Fowlkes, Armstreat E.	A.B. 1851, A.M. 1854	VA* KIA 1862
Friend, George W.	A.B. 1848	VA
Fuller, John P.	A.B. 1856	NC*
Garnett, Thomas H.	A.B. 1839	VA
Gatch, Thomas A.	A.B. 1855, A.M. 1858	VA*
Gee, Jesse	A.B. 1837	VA*
Gill, Aurelius T.	A.B. 1859	VA*
Gillespie, John L.	A.B. 1844, A.M. 1860	VA
Gilliam, Robert C.	A.B. 1841	SC
Goode, Robert S.	A.B. 1836	VA
(Goode, Thomas F.	A.M. Law 1848	VA)*
Gordon, Thomas B.	A.B. 1841, A.M. 1844	GA, VA
Granbery, John C.	A.B. 1848, D.D. 1869	VA*†
(Gregory, Flavious J.	A.B. 1846 Med.	VA)*
Guy, John H.	A.B. 1851	VA*
Haley, Argyle	A.M. 1859	VA
Hall, Charles H.	A.B. 1853	NC*
Hamlin, George W.	A.B. 1854	VA
Hanes, Garland B.	A.B. 1854, A.M. 1857	VA*
Hanes, James C.	A.B. 1855, A.M. 1858	VA*
Hardy, Edward T.	A.B. 1846, A.M. 1849	VA X
Hardy, Edwin S.	A.B. 1859	VA*
Hardy, James W.	A.B. 1837, A.M. 1840	GA X
Hardy, Samuel	A.B. 1846	VA*
Hargrove, Tazwell	A.B. 1848	NC*
Harrison, Burwell K.	A.B. 1840	GA X
(Hawthorne, Benjamin J.	A.M. 1861	VA)*
Head, the Rev. Nelson	D.D. (1867)	VA‡
Heartsfield, John W.	BL&S 1859	NC*
Hereford, William W.	A.B. 1841	MS*
Herndon, Benjamin Z.	A.B. 1842	SC*
Hill, Christopher D.	A.B. 1838	NC
Hill, William P.	A.B. 1860	VA
(Hite, Benjamin H.	A.B. 1856, Med. 1857	VA)*
Hogg, Alex	BL&S 1854, A.M. 1859	VA, TX*
Holstead, Richard B.	A.B. 1858, A.M. 1861	VA*

Horseley, William A.	A.B. 1837	VA
Howard, George	A.B. 1846, A.M. 1853	VA
Howard, John	A.B. 1844, A.M. 1847	VA
Humphreys, John T.	A.B. 1859	VA
(Hutcheson, Joseph C.	A.M. 1861	VA)*
Ingram, Robert M.	A.B. 1837	VA
Irby, Richard	A.B. 1844	VA*†
Irby, Walter M.	BL&S 1857	VA
Isbell, Robert S.	A.B. 1858, A.M. 1862	VA*
Isbell, Thomas M.	A.B. 1836	VA*
Jackson, Green A.	A.B. 1856, A.M. 1859	VA*
Jackson, James W.	A.B. 1849, A.M. 1852	VA*
Jackson, John S.	A.B. 1853	VA*
Jackson, Robert A.	A.B. 1852	VA* KIA 1862
Jackson, Thomas (the Rev.)	D.D. 1838	England
Jackson, Thomas L.	A.B. 1856	VA*
(Jamieson, William A.	A.B. 1860, LAW 1861	VA)*
Jarvis, Thomas J.	A.B. 1860, (A.M. 1867)	NC*
Jenkins, Benjamin	A.M. 1848 (Hon.) Missionary	China
Jerman, Thomas P.	A.B. 1846	SC‡†
Johnson, John L.	A.B. 1859	VA* KIA 1863
Johnson, Thomas C.	A.B. 1842. A.M. 1847	VA, MO†*
Jones, Amos W.	A.B. 1839, A.M. 1842	NC‡
(Jones, Caius Jacob	A.M. 1861	VA)
Jones, George B.	A.B. 1841, A.M. 1844	VA* KIA 1864
Jones, Henry F.	A.M. 1844	NC
(Jones, James W.	A.M. 1861	VA)*
Jones, John W.	A.B. 1859	VA*
Jones, Richard W.	A.B. 1857, A.M. 1860	VA*
Jones, Thomas H. (the Rev.)	A.B. 1841, A.M. 1844	VA
Jones, Turner M.	A.B. 1845, A.M. 1848	NC‡
Jones, William M.	A.M. 1860	VA*
(Judkins, William H.	A.M. 1861	VA)‡
(Keiley, Anthony M.	A.B. 1854	NJ)*
Kirkpatrick, J.	BL&S 1854	
Koger, Thomas J.	A.B. 1838, A.M. 1851	SC*
Lander, Samuel	A.B. 1852, A.M. 1855	NC*
Lawton, William H.	A.B. 1843	SC*
Lea, Addison	A.B. 1836, A.M. 1851	NC, MS*
Leak, John W.	A.B. 1838	NC*
Leigh, Hezekiah G.	D.D. 1853	NC† X
Leigh, Hezekiah G. (Jr.)	A.B. 1851, A.M. 1854	VA* DOD 1864
Leigh, Joseph	A.B. 1857	VA
Leigh, Richard W.	A.B. 1849, A.M. 1853	VA* KIA 1864
Ligon, Woodson L.	A.B. 1840	SC*
Lockett, Benjamin F.	A.B. 1846	VA
Lockett, Henry E.	A.B. 1838, A.M. 1841	VA*
Lockett, Thomas J.	A.B. 1846	VA*

Lomax, Lucien H.	A.B. 1842, A.M. 1849	SC‡
Lomax, Tennent	A.B. 1840, A.M. 1851	SC, AL* KIA 1862
Long, John F.	A.B. 1851	NC*
Lyon, John	A.B. 1844, A.M. 1847	VA*
Magruder, George W.	A.B. 1854	NC*
Mallory, Alex	A.B. 1858	VA*
Mallory, Robert M.	A.B. 1852, A.M. 1855	VA
Mangum, Adolphus W.	A.B. 1854, A.M. 1857	NC, VA*
Mann, Alfred T. (the Rev.)	A.B. 1836, D.D. 1854,	GA Conf. GA*
Martin, the Rev. John S.	D.D. (1867)	MD
Marvin, Bishop Enoch M.	D.D. (1867)	TN
(Mason, Joseph Richard	A.B. 1851	VA)*
Massenburg, A.C.	A.B. 1854	NC*
Massie, Thomas E.	A.B. 1843, A.M. 1855	VA
Massie, Waller	A.B. 1843	VA
(McGuire, Francis H.	A.B. 1870	VA‡)
McTyeire, Holland N.	A.B. 1844	AL‡
Merritt, Embry	A.B. 1853	VA
Merritt, William T.	A.B. 1856, A.M.1859	VA* DOD 1862
Milam, Henry D.	A.B. 1853	NC*†
Miller, F.X.	BL&S 1859	NC*
Miller, Lewis	A.B. 1849, A.M. 1853	NC*
Montgomery, Henry T.	A.B. 1837	VA
Moody, John	A.B. 1847	VA
Moore, Edwin G.	A.B. 1857, A.M.1860	NC*
Moore, John S.	A.B. 1848	VA*
Moore, Robert	A.B. 1858	VA*
Moore, Samuel	A.B. 1854, A.M. 1857	VA
Moore, Smith W.	D.D. (1867)	TN
Moran, the Rev. Robert S.	D.D. (1868)	NC
Morris, Richard G.	A.B. 1848	VA
Moses, Peter A.	A.B. 1855, A.M. 1858	ARK*
Mullen, Francis N.	A.B. 1837, A.M. 1840	NC
Myers, Edward H.	A.B. 1838, A.M. 1841	FL‡
Newton, Robert (the Rev.)	D.D. 1843	England
Ogburn, Benjamin W.	A.B. 1852, A.M. 1855	VA
Ogburn, John F.	A.B. 1852, A.M. 1855	VA
O'Hanlon, James	A.B. 1851	NC
Orgain, John A.	A.B. 1838	VA‡
Overby, Thomas J.	A.B. 1859 (A.M. 1866)	NC*
Palmer, Horace (Jr.)	A.B. 1852	VA*
Palmer, Jacob M.	A.B. 1851	VA*
Palmer, Reuben	A.B. 1851	VA
Parham, Edwin E.	A.B. 1850	VA
Parham, Richard S.	A.B. 1844	VA X
Paul, Samuel B.	A.M. 1855 (Hon.)	VA
Peay, James H.	A.M. 1860	VA* KIA 1864
Peete, R.S.F.	A.B. 1849, A.M. 1852	VA, NC*

Penny, William W.	A.B. 1857	MO
Peques, Rufus R.	A.B. 1852	SC*
Person, Willie M.	A.B. 1844, A.M. 1848	NC* X
Phillips, Claudius G.	A.B. 1858	VA*
Pierce, Alexander B.	A.B. 1848	NC*
Pierce, George F. (the Rev.)	A.M. 1838, (Hon.) (Bishop, LL.D. 1867)	GA, AL‡
Pierce, James L.	A.B. 1840, A.M. 1851, DD 1869	GA
Pierce, Lovick	D.D. 1843	GA‡†
Poisal, the Rev. John	D.D. (1867)	MD†
Powell, Richard H.	A.B. 1843, A.M. 1851	AL*
Proctor, James D.	A.B. 1853, A.M. 1856	VA*
Puryear, Bennett	A.B. 1847, A.M. 1850	VA‡
Reese, Dr. Joseph T.	A.B. 1842, A.M. 1845	GA*
Register, the Rev. Samuel G.	(D.D. 1867)	MD†
Reid, N. F. (the Rev.)	A.M. 1850 (Hon.)	NC†
Rives, James (John) F.	A.B. 1843, A.M. 1846	MS*
Rives, L.O.	A.B. 1854, A.M. 1857	TN*
Robbins, Wm. McK.	A.B. 1851, A.M. 1854	NC*
Rogers, Thomas H.	A.B. 1844, A.M. 1847 Med.	VA X
Roszel, the Rev. S.S.	(D.D. 1867)	MD†
Russell, Thomas B.	A.B. 1838	SC
Samford, William F.	A.B. 1837, A.M 1846, LL.D. (AL)	GA, AL*
Sangster, James	A.B. 1853	VA* KIA 1864
Sargent, T. B. (the Rev.)	D.D. 1854 (Baltimore Conf.)	MD
Saunders, Samuel D. (Dr.)	A.B. 1842, A.M. 1859 (Hon.)	SC, TX*
Scott, Benjamin I.	A.M. 1860	VA* KIA 1862
Scott, Samuel B.	A.B. 1841	VA
Sebrell, James E.	A.B. 1853, A.M. 1856	VA*
Sehon, Edward W.	D.D. 1846	KY
Shay, W.H.	BL&S 1854	VA*
Shelton, John W.	A.B. 1845	NC
Shepard, William A.	A.B. 1857, A.M. 1860	MA, VA*
Shipp, A.M. (Prof.)	D.D. 1859 (Wofford Col.)	SC‡
Simmons, Benjamin F.	A.B. 1844, A.M. 1851	NC* DOD
Sledd, Robert W.	A.B. 1855, A.M. 1858	VA
Smith, Dallas	A.B. 1848	AL*
Smith, Hampden S.	A.B. 1843	NC
Smith, James F.	A.B. 1839, A.M. 1843	SC
Smith, Oliver G.	A.B. 1855	NC
Smith, William A.	D.D. 1843	VA‡†
Stamford, William F.	A.B. 1837	GA‡
Stanley, Marcellus	A.B. 1841	GA*
Starr, William G.	A.B. 1859, A.M. 1862	VA*
Stewart (Stuart), Charles	A.B. 1845, A.M. 1848	VA*† DOD 1863
Stewart, Theophilus	A.B. 1837, A.M. 1841	GA
(Styron, Oscar Malachi	A.M. 1861	VA)*
Sutton, Joseph	A.B. 1842	VA
Taylor, Felix H.G.	A.B. 1843	MS*

Taylor, John W.   A.M. 1860   VA*
Thackston, Benjamin H.   A.B. 1858   VA*
Thackston, Thomas C.   A.B. 1854, A.M. 1857   VA
Thomas, James R.   A.B. 1838, A.M. 1841   GA
Thompson, Edwin A.   A.B. 1850   NC*
Thrower, Christopher   A.B. 1859   AR*
Thurmond, Richard W.   A.B. 1853   VA*
Tillet, John   A.B. 1840   NC
Vaden, Wesley Childs   A.M. 1861   VA‡
Venable, Pittman R.   A.B. 1858   VA* KIA 1863
Waddill, Nathaniel R.   A.B. 1843   VA
Wadsworth, Edward   A.M. 1851   AL
Wadsworth, Edward S. (the Rev.)   A.B. 1841, A.M. 1844, D.D. 1847   NC, AL†
Walker, John C.   A.B. 1843, A.M. 1846   VA
Ware, Jordon P.   A.M. 1861   VA* DOD 1864
Washington, James R.   A.B. 1838, A.M. 1842   NC, GA
Wightman, James W.   A.B. 1838, A.M. 1842   SC
Wightman, W.M. (the Rev.)   D.D. 1846   SC†
Williams, Charles E.   A.B. 1848   VA*
Williams, Henry H.   A.B. 1852   VA
Williams, John   A.B. 1852, A.M. 1859   NC
Williams, John B.   A.B. 1857   NC*
Williams, Oliver P.   A.B. 1841   SC*
Williams, Richard H.   A.B. 1851, A.M. 1853   VA*
Williams, William S.   A.M. 1862   MO
Williamson, James J.   A.B. 1837   VA
Wills, John C. (Prof.)   A.M. 1859 (Hon.)   VA*
Wilson, Leroy M.   A.B. 1854   VA†*
Winans, William   D.D. 1843   MS
Winfield, John O.   A.B. 1836   VA
Winfield, Robert H.   A.B. 1850, A.M. 1853   VA
Wingfield, Henry W.   A.B. 1851, A.M. 1855   VA*
Wright, James T.   A.B. 1845   VA
Wright, Luther   A.B. 1859   VA*
Wyatt, Richard O.   A.B. 1858, A.M. 1861   VA
Wyche, George E.   A.B. 1842, A.M. 1845   NC
Young, Thaddeus L.H.   A.B. 1854, A.M. 1857   VA

Faculty and Tutors

Presidents

Blackwell, John C., Acting President, September to December 1866
Duncan, James A., President, October 1, 1868, to 1877
Garland, Landon C., Acting President, 1836 to September 1838; President, September 1838 to November 1846
Johnson, Thomas C., President, December 1866 to July 1868

Olin, Stephen, President, March 1834 to November 1836
Parks, the Rev. Martin P., Acting President, September 1832 to March 1834
Smith, William A., President, December 1846 to July 1866

Professors

Blackwell, John C., Moral Philosophy 1866; Chemistry 1867 to July 1868; Mathematics, September 1861 to June 1864 (several stories throughout)

Blanch, Ezekial A., Mathematics and Astronomy, November 1846 to June 1850 (see Chapter 2)

Blankenship, J.E. (Major), Mathematics, September 1861 to April 1864; Military Tactics, January 1862 to September 1862 (see Chapter 7)

Carr, William A., Ancient Languages, 1856 to June 1864 (1865) (see Chapter 7)

Chambers, Edward R., Law, 1842 to 1863, 1866 to 1867 (several stories throughout)

Corprew, Oliver H.P., Natural Philosophy, 1852 to 1854; Ancient Languages, 1854 to 1857 and September 1866 to July 1868 (several stories throughout)

Deems, the Rev. Charles F., Chemistry, January 1848 to January 1849 (see Chapter 3)

Doggett, the Rev. David S., Moral Philosophy, June 1842 to November 1846 (see Chapter 2)

Duncan, David S., Ancient Languages, 1836 to 1852; Natural Philosophy 1852 to 1854 (see Chapter 2)

Garland, Landon C., Chemistry, 1832 to June 1836

Hardy, James W., Assistant Professor, Chemistry, June 1837 to 1840; Professor, Chemistry, June 1840 to June 1847 (see Chapter 2)

Johnson, Thomas C., Moral Philosophy, 1867 to June 1868 (see Chapter 7)

Jones, Richard W., Mathematics, September 1866 to July 1868 (see Appendix B, 12th Virginia Infantry, and Chapter 5)

LaGarde, Ernest, Modern Languages, September 1866 to July 1868

Lander, Samuel, Assistant Professor, September 1854 to June 1855; Professor, September 1856 to June 1857 (see Chapter 3)

Lupton, Nathaniel T., Natural Sciences, September 1857 to June 1858

Massie, Robert T., Mathematics and Astronomy, June 1859 to July 1861 (see Chapter 7)

Mettauer, Dr. Francis Joseph, Medicine and Medical Treatment, March 1847 to December 1862 (see Chapter 2)

Mettauer, Dr. Henry Archer, Therapeutics, Midwifery and Medical Jurisprudence, around 1851 to 1855 (see Chapter 2)

Mettauer, Dr. John Peter, Medicine and Surgery, March 1847 to December 1862 (See Chapter 2)

Moore, John S., Natural Philosophy, September 1854 to January 1856

Olin, Stephen, Moral Philosophy, March 1834 to December 1836 (see Chapter 1)

Parks, the Rev. Martin T., Mathematics and Astronomy, 1834 to June 1836 (see Chapter 1)

Pierce, the Rev. George F. of GA, Ancient Languages, June 1835 to June 1837

Puryear, Bennett, Chemistry, September 1858 to March 1864 (1864–1865) (several stories throughout)

Shepard, William A., Assistant Professor, September 1860 to June 1861 (see Chapter 7)

Sims, the Rev. Edward D., Moral Philosophy, 1832 and 1833; Ancient Languages, 1833 to 1836; English Literature and Language, September 1838 to May 1842 (see Chapter 1)

Smith, William A., Moral Philosophy, November 1846 to July 1866 (see Chapter 3)
Stuart, Charles B., Chemistry, September 1849 to June 1857 (see Chapter 2)
Tolefree (Tolfree), Robert C., M.D. of New York, Natural Science, September 1836 to June 1837
Turner, Lewis, Mathematics and Astronomy, September 1861 to January 1862 (see Chapter 8)
Wheelwright, the Rev. Major William H., Military Tactics, September 1862 to March 1864
Wightman, the Rev. William May, Moral Philosophy, March 1837 to June 1837 (see Chapter 4)
Wills, John C., Mathematics and Astronomy, September 1850 to June 1859 (see Chapter 4)

Chaplains of RMC

Andrews, the Rev. G.W., 1853 to June 11, 1854 (died)
Archer, Peter W., 1849–1850
August, the Rev. Peter F., 1852–1853
Blackwell, John D., 1850–1852
Brown, the Rev. Alexander Gustavus, 1857–1858
Granberry, John Cowper, 1854–1856
Jamieson, the Rev. James, 1832–1833 and 1866–1867 (part-time 1864–1865)
Lewis, James M., 1867–1868
Manning, Jacob, 1844–1845
Pearson, the Rev. Charles C., 1859–1860
Ray, the Rev. George Henry, 1860–1861
Vaiden, the Rev. Wesley C., 1861–1864
Ware, the Rev. Thomas A., 1856–1857

Principals of Boydton Preparatory (closed 1859)

Bass, William K., 1854 to 1855 (Ridgeway Preparatory in 1859)
Blackwell, John C., 1837 to 1839 (see Chapter 1)
Crawley, Charles W., 1856 to 1857
Daub, William, 1844 to 1845
Davis, William S., 1845 to 1848 (see Chapter 2)
Davis, Williams T., 1848 to 1852 (see Chapter 6)
Foote, William G., 1852 to 1853
Foster, Fisher A., September 1835 to June 1836
Garland, Hugh A., January to March, 1832 (see Chapter 1)
Gatch, Thomas A., 1857 to 1858
Isbell, Robert S., 1858 to 1859
Jones, A.B., 1836 to 1837
Kennedy, James S. (of Emory and Henry), 1853 to 1854
Lea, Lorenzo, March 1832 to 1835 (see Chapter 1)
Lea, Solomon, 1839 to 1841 (see Chapter 1)
Stuart, John W., 1855 to 1856 (see Chapter 2)

Tutors

Blanch, Ezekiel, 1838–1840, 1842–1843 and 1845–1846, tutor of French
Corprew, Oliver H. P., 1846 to 1849
Crenshaw, Ira I., 1842 to 1845
Dean, the Rev. J.A., 1850 to 1851
DuPre, Warren, 1838 to 1844
Enslin, Theodore, 1840–1841, French (in 1842 listed as dead)
Harris, William L., Languages, 1839 to 1840
Lander, Samuel, 1852 to 1854
Leigh, H.G., Jr., 1851 to 1854
McTyeire, Holland N., 1844 to 1845
Rogers, Thomas H., 1844 to 1847
Shepard, William A., 1854 to 1860 (Laboratory Assistant)
Young, Thaddius H. L., 1854 to 1857

Appendix D: Randolph Macon Cemetery

In Munsey Moore's *Mecklenburg County Cemeteries* (Vol. 2, 1996), for Randolph Macon, he lists an article that was published in the *Richmond Times Dispatch*. Although undated, it appears to have been written by historian W.H. Hill, which would date the story to the later 1950s. The published list of the graves in the cemetery and their inscriptions follows:

Andrews, G.W. "Born in Glouchester Co., 24 Oct 1808 who joined the Virginia Conf. of the Meth Ch in 1841 and who died 11 June 1854. He died in faith."

Arnold, Wm. M. of Campbell County, who died 19 September 1855, age 21. "Erected by the Franklin Literary Society."

Cowles, Alice Francis, who departed this life 17 December 1841, age 3 years and 5 months.

Dollinger, Frederick George, born 27 January 1822, Württemberg, Europe, died 29 July 1860. (He was a merchant who had a grocery and confectionery in the neighborhood, which was frequented by students and faculty alike.)

Douthitt, Alpha, died 16 November 1833 in his 17th year (died during second session of Randolph Macon).

Garland, Spotswood, infant son of Professor Landon C. Garland, who became president of RMC and subsequently first chancellor of Vanderbilt University.

Jones, Carolyn M. "In memory of who departed this life in full triumph of faith 14 Dec 1841. Aged 19 yrs 10 mos of conjugal affection by A. W. Jones to whom she addressed these parting words—'My dear husband I shall meet you in Heaven.'"

Speed, the Rev. R.A. "Victory over death and the grave." Erected by the class of 1853–54.

Yancey, Eliza, died 1852 (keeper of one of the student boardinghouses near the college).

This accounts for nine graves in the cemetery, but it is obvious that some of the text in the story is not to be found on the tombstone and was added by the writer. In February 2011, John and Betty Caknipe visited the cemetery. About 200 yards behind (north) Steward Hall is a swamp between the hall and grave sites. Around the back side of Steward Hall is dense undergrowth and a creek between the dead end road and grave sites (about 250 yards south), which prevents access by vehicle. Finally locating the cemetery atop a hill, we found it appears haphazard in the layout. It covers an area of about 75 square yards, and we could easily detect 13 scattered, sunken grave sites without a marker, or only a stone as a marker. We also located a double sunken site, with flat stones marking two distinct graves. There were six graves with granite rectangular foot stones that were not engraved and had no head stone; four graves were located with headstones that were unreadable (skilled cleaning may help to restore them), and eight graves were at least partially readable. At least 33 graves are readily distinguishable.

Aside from the lack of maintenance since the 1950s or before, the area has been timbered (at least once), which encourages undergrowth. Several trees in and close to the cemetery that were not harvested, have died and fallen down across grave sites and headstones. A couple of locations were so thickly covered we were unable to determine whether any graves were under the timber. Most all the cemetery is covered with periwinkle. One grave site, that of Cowles, was placed (most likely) with an oak tree planted near the head of her grave. The tree appears to have died several years ago and has broken in half (about a three foot center, at least a 100 year old oak) and the top half with limbs covers a lot of the cemetery's northern half.

To revisit the individuals listed earlier:

Andrews—The gravestone has Rev. G.W. Andrews and is near the southeast side. I found no record of his graduating from RMC. He is not listed as being in Boydton in the 1850 Census. The records, timeframe and headstone would suggest that he was the college chaplain for the academic year 1853–1854, and he was an M.E. reverend at RMC with a headstone outlining same.

Arnold—Stone is in good shape and reads, "By the members of the F & L Society. To the memory of Wm. M. Arnold of Campbell Co., Virginia, who died Sept. 10, 1855, Age 21 years." The grave is located in the southeast side of the cemetery. (There were a number of Arnolds from this family who attended RMC.)

Cowles—The top of the grave stone is in a root of the tree but when the tree fell, it drove the bottom half of the marker into the ground. On the top of the stone is the word "Sacred." The grave is in the center of the cemetery. This was most likely the daughter of the Rev. Henry B. Cowles, RMC agent and member of the board of trustees, selected in 1842, whose home was next to the college.

Dollinger—The stone has been broken off by a tree, with the bottom half driven into the ground. The stone is readable and in good shape (both halves). It is located to the west of center. Dollinger came to Boydton sometime before 1850 and was listed in the 1850 Census as a jewelry maker from Germany. He had a jewelry store in the Exchange Hotel of Boydton but with few citizens, and at least two other jewelers in town, Dollinger appears to have become an accomplished businessman by providing what the community wanted—food (possibly, with a little jewelry counter in a back corner).

Douthitt—Grave marker not found. For him to have been a second season (year) student he would have been in the first enrolled classes.

Garland—The stone is southeast of the center and simply lists: "Spotswood Garland July 19, 1845 July 28, 1846."

Jones—This stone has also been broken in half with the bottom half driven into the ground. The name is partially readable: ?aroline M. Jones. The top of the stone is marked "In Memory of." It is located central west side. (Amos W. Jones of North Carolina graduated in June 1839 with an A.B. degree. Following his wife's death, he earned an A.M. in June 1842.)

Speed—The former postmaster, was not found. He was 24 years old and appointed the postmaster in 1851 while a senior finishing his education at RMC. He appears to not have taken a degree, was listed as Reverend and still in the Boydton area in 1853–54 when he died. He must have been in the A.M. program.

Yancey—The grave marker is in an expansive rock walled (over 3 feet high) area, large enough for four graves, and hers is in the southwest corner of the enclosure. A tree has fallen across the rock walls. The stone needs to be cleaned, as there is a lot of writing on it that is not readable. Her date of death is readable as 15 October 1854. Her grave is on the central west side near the old road. Her story is well documented in this text, as are the deaths of her husband and father (which may be two of the unmarked graves).

One additional marker was found, that of a small child. It was located in the central east side and bore the inscription: "Our Little ROSE Age 13 mos J. & K. W???? [Wills, I believe] 1851." When Professor John C. Wills and family arrived at the college in 1850, they are listed in the Census records as John, age 30, wife Catherine (could be Katherine), age 25, Willie, a son age 2, and Rosaline (Rose), born September 1850. Thus, she would have died in the fall of 1851, at age 13 months. In the 1860 Census, John Wills and family, now residing in Alabama, includes a four year old daughter, Rosine M.D. Wills.

Very near this small stone is another rock wall enclosure for what appears to be a child. The wall is about 3 feet high by 3 feet wide by about 4 1/2 feet long. There was no marker found inside. This could be the grave site for one of Bishop Doggett's children. He had one child whose clothes caught fire, and the child died sometime between 1842 and 1846, during which time Bishop Doggett was a professor at RMC. The history is that sometime, earlier or later, he had another son who died under the same tragic circumstances.

At the north central part of the cemetery is wrought iron fencing remains that appear to have some graves enclosed (about a 10 foot by 10 foot area). With the brush, these were not identified. At the northeast corner was another section marked with an ornamental wire fencing which has fallen down, and with undergrowth, covers another section of graves. By the type of fencing I would date it to post 1850 (maybe even much later), and the wrought iron could have been earlier.

From the text, the double marked graves would appear to be for Samuel (1844) and Francis Bugg (soon after June 1865). The family history indicates they were buried with a simple unmarked stone. Near these two, in the southwest part of the cemetery, is one sunken grave site which could be that of Betsey Hatsel (1850s, Francis's mother). To the southeast of the double graves are four unmarked sites.

From this information, we know the cemetery was designated before the chapel was built in 1837. The oldest gravesite dates to 1833. The cemetery is atop a hill situated between two streams (one, now a swamp). A road was graded from the front of the chapel to the cemetery that ran between Steward Hall and the Samuel Bugg home, on Steward Hall property. This would have, most likely, been done upon completion of the chapel, perhaps in 1838.

With three faculty children, one child of a future member of the board of trustees, two students, one former graduate and postmaster (possible graduate student), one boarding house steward, one wife of a student, two seamstresses, a carpenter, a merchant and a minister, one could summarize that the cemetery was for the Randolph Macon family. At least 20 graves (possibly even double that number under the downed trees) are still unidentified. After all, this was the only Methodist sanctuary and cemetery in the community. It most likely also included the graves of any of the servants and slaves.

Chapter Notes

Prologue

1. John G. Boyd, *Tobacco Plant*, January 17, 1868. This newspaper series was begun in 1853 by Boyd, a graduate of RMC. The format remained consistent through his ownership through 1865. The first page of the paper featured local ads and national and international news. Page 2 had local news and stories with a few ads. Page 3 had statewide advertising, and Page 4 had more national advertising.

Chapter 1

1. Virginia Haskins Bugg, "Rehobeth M.E. Church, Boydton Charges, Mecklenburg County, Virginia," Brunswick-Mecklenburg Sesquicentennial Number, *Richmond Christian Advocate*, Vol. 89, No. 24 (June 21, 1934), p. 19.

2. Board of Trustees, "Catalogue of the Students, and Charter and Laws of Randolph Macon College, with the Names of the Trustees and Faculty, and the Course of Studies" (Richmond, printed by P.D. Bernard, opposite Exchange Bank, 1848).

3. Richard Irby, *The History of Randolph-Macon College* (Richmond, VA: Whittet and Shepardson), p. 18. Randolph Macon College did not use the hyphen when it was located at Boydton. The college adopted the use of a hyphen when it moved to Ashland.

4. James M. Becker, "Randolph-Macon College and Boydton," *Heritage*, bulletin of the Virginia Conference Historical Society of the United Methodist Church, Vol. 30, No. 1 (Spring 2004), p. 16.

5. Becker, p. 16.
6. Becker, p. 16.
7. Becker, p. 17.
8. Stephen E. Bradley, Jr., "Edward Droomgoole's Canaan," *Heritage*, bulletin of the Virginia Conference Historical Society of the United Methodist Church, Vol. 30, No. 1 (Spring 2004), p. 3.

9. John Abernathy Smith, "Ebenezer Academy: A Methodist School for Virginia," *Heritage*, bulletin of the Virginia Conference Historical Society of the United Methodist Church, Vol. 30, No. 1 (Spring 2004), p. 6.

10. Rev. H.H. Smith, "Ebenezer Academy," Brunswick-Mecklenburg Sesquicentennial Number, *Richmond Christian Advocate*, Vol. 89, No. 24 (June 21, 1934), p. 8. There was also a story about the academy in the Brunswick heritage book.

11. Smith, p. 8.

12. Southside Virginia Genealogical Society, *Brunswick County*, Vol. 1, 2001, Heritage Book Series, commemorating history in Piedmont Virginia and North Carolina counties (Waynesville, NC: Wadsworth, 2001).

13. Maud M. Turpin, "For God So Loved and Irishman," Brunswick Mecklenburg Sesquicentennial Number, *Richmond Christian Advocate*, Vol. 89, No. 24 (June 21, 1934), p. 5; and Ancestor.com.

14. Southside Virginia Genealogical Society, *Brunswick County*, Vol. 1, 2001, pp. 13, 386, 387.

15. William S. Powell, ed., *Dictionary of North Carolina Biography* (six volumes) (Chapel Hill, NC: University of North Car-

olina Press, 1979), Vol. 2, E.T. Malone, Jr., pp. 105, 106.

16. Ibid., Vol. 3, pp. 185–187, Clyde Wilson Hutcheson, p. 3; and Warren County Heritage Book Committee, *Warren County, North Carolina*, Vol. 1, 2002, p. 1.

17. According to Scanlon (p. 31) and Irby (p. 29), this had been a controversial issue from the start and the General Assembly wanted to insure that this was a college, not another school of theology.

18. Board of Trustees, 1848, p. 8. During this time frame, "seminary" was more generic in use. The term "college campus" was not used in Boydton. According to Scanlon, "campus" became popular after the Civil War.

19. The Virginia General Assembly established Mecklenburg County and Charlotte County from the vast Lunenburg County. The new courthouse for the county was located at what was called Mecklenburg Courthouse. It was south of the center of the county by one mile to accommodate those living below the river. Mecklenburg Courthouse was chartered as a town in 1812 and became Boydton, named for the founder, Alexander Boyd.

20. Susan L. Bracey, *Life by the Roanoke* (Richmond, VA: Whittet and Shepardson, 1977), Mecklenburg County Bicentennial Commission, p. 297. Cedar Crest was reportedly occupied by Sheridan's men for three days in April 1865, when they were en route to North Carolina. The home is currently a private residence.

21. Mecklenburg County Circuit Court Record Book 5, 19 August 1850.

22. Hezekiah G. Leigh, Archives.org, www.archives.org/stream/history.

23. Bracey, p. 332.

24. Mecklenburg County Circuit Court Record Book 6, September 19, 1855 notes. This area is generally referred to as the Piedmont region. (If Greenville County were added to the territory it would also be the colonial thoroughbred and quarter horse Mecca of the United States. Many of the board of trustees for Randolph Macon College garnered much of their sizable estates from the race tracks. Alexander McKay-Smith, *The Colonial Quarter Horse* (Richmond, VA, 1983), index.

25. Irby, p. 31.

26. T.A. Gayle, "Zion M. E. Church, South," Brunswick-Mecklenburg Sesquicentennial Number, *Richmond Christian Advocate*, Vol. 89, No. 24 (June 21, 1934), p. 31.

27. A.M. Rowland, ed., "Brunswick-Mecklenburg Sesquicentennial Number," *Richmond Christian Advocate*, Vol. 89, No. 24 (June 21, 1934), pp. 33, 35.

28. Southside Virginia Genealogical Society, *Mecklenburg County*, Vol. 1, 2006, Heritage Book Series.

29. James Scanlon, *Randolph-Macon College: A Southern Heritage 1830 to 1967* (Charlottesville: University of Virginia Press), 1983, pp. 77, 78.

30. Jackie Reeves Wood, University of Memphis Libraries, Lambuth Campus, Jackson, TN, Records of "Lorenzo Lea Chronology" and *Journal of the North Mississippi Conference of the Methodist Episcopal Church*, 1876, Lea Obituary. In other documents, per e-mail of March 15, at the archives of North Carolina State, their parents are listed as Captain Gabriel Lea of Revolutionary War fame and Sarah McNeil.

31. Ibid., records and e-mails (February 29, 2012, March 9 and 15, 2012) of data about Amos W. Jones. Memphis Conference Female Institute 1869 Catalogue and *Journal of the North Mississippi Conference of the Methodist Episcopal Church*, 1876.

32. Ibid., files.

33. Bracey, p. 344.

34. Gerald Gilliam, "Mecklenburg Vignettes," 1994, Charlotte County, Virginia, pp. 78– 80.

35. Moore, Munsey A., *History of The Boyd Tavern (Boydton Hotel)*, (The Boyd Family Foundation, self-published, 1990), p. 9.

36. Gilliam, 1994, pp. 79, 80.

37. Moore, 1990, p. 10.

38. Ibid., 1990.

39. *Tobacco Plant*, April 20, 1860, p. 2.

40. John Caknipe, *Around Clarksville: Images of America* (Mt. Pleasant, SC: Arcadia, 2009).

41. Bracey, pp. 133–134.

42. *Tobacco Plant*, March 6, 1861, p. 2.

43. For many of the graduates I added a notation of their year of birth, where they were from, and their parent or guardian. This information, throughout this text, for matriculates before 1853 came from the matriculation records of Randolph Macon College. Richard Slatten, "Matriculation Book:

Randolph Macon College, Part 1," transcribed and copied for *The Virginia Genealogy Society, Magazine of Virginia Genealogy*: August 1984, Vol. 3, 1837 to 1839, pp. 7–17. Part II, December 1984, Vol. 4, 1839 to 1847, pp. 32–40. Part III, February 1985, Vol. 1, 1847 to 1851, pp. 20–29.

44. Irby, p. 31; and Anne S. Rose, *The Faculty of Randolph-Macon College during the 1800s* (Ashland, VA: Randolph Macon College, 2009), p. 22.

45. Scanlon, p. 54.

46. Anne Rose, p. 21.

47. I toured the home with the permission of the current owner, V. Novell Evans. Upon entry, there is a grand hallway 10 feet wide for the length of the home. At the end of the hallway is a reverse-flight stairway leading to the second floor. The first floor is a basic two by two, or two rooms on each side of the hallway, approximately 14 feet by 16 feet each. Two rooms downstairs and the stairwell contained closets. Upstairs was a bedroom, about 12 feet by 20 feet, with a study area to the side in the attic area. Downstairs, the ceilings were 14½ feet high. The kitchen was a separate unit and attached to the right rear of the home. (It is gone.) Underneath the left side of the home was the servants' quarters. This was one room, about 20 feet by 20 feet, with a fireplace and window. The ceiling was finished, as were the walls, with stucco, and the floor was brick. The window has several wooden dowels across the opening, appearing as though they are bars, but they were used to keep the animals out.

48. Scanlon, p. 56, and Anne Rose, p. 21.

49. *South Carolina Biography Dictionary*, Vol. 2 (St. Claire Shores, MI: Somerset, 2000), p. 126.

50. Nelson Harris, *Virginia Tech* (Mt. Pleasant, SC: Arcadia, 2004), p. 6.

51. Walter James Edgar, ed., *South Carolina Encyclopedia* (Charleston, SC: University of South Carolina Press, 2006), and *South Carolina Biography Dictionary*, Vol. 2, p. 2.

52. Edgar, *Encyclopedia*.

53. Irby, p. 80.

54. Rhonda Shelton, September 2010 interview, Association for the Preservation of Virginia.

55. Mike Wright, *What They Didn't Tell You About the Civil War* (Novato, CA: Presidio Press), 1996, p. 8.

56. Tim Pyatt, *Duke Illustrated: A Timeline of Duke University History, 1838 –2011* (Durham, NC: Duke University Archives, 2011), April 1865 to January 1866.

57. Ibid.

58. Samuel Lander, Jr., "Private Journal of Samuel Lander, Jr.," Randolph Macon College, 1850–51, p. 37.

59. Board of Trustees, "Catalogue of the Students, and Charter and Laws of Randolph Macon College, With the Names of the Trustees and Faculty, and the Course of Studies" (Richmond, printed by P.D. Bernard, opposite Exchange Bank, 1848).

60. Scanlon, p. 97.

61. Powell, Vol. 3, "Lindley S. Butler," p. 37.

62. University of Oregon, Special Collections and Archives, copies of RMC documents from file of Benjamin J. Hawthorne plus copies of documents from other professors at RMC Boydton and documents by R-MC–Ashland President Duncan.

63. Mecklenburg County Will Book 15, p. 238.

64. U.S. Census records, 1850.

65. Irby, p. 82; Tyler, Vol. 3, p. 214; and Hutcheson, p. 2.

66. Anne Rose, p. 28.

67. Douglas Summers Brown, *Chase City and Its Environs, 1765–1975*, (Richmond, VA: Whittet and Shepardson), 1975, pp. 43–45.

68. Brown, 1975, pp. 49, 50.

Chapter 2

1. Circuit Court Record Book 7, 1865 to 1869.

2. *Regimental Books of Virginia Troops Serving During the Civil War*, sponsored, authoritative, controlled issue series (1,000 signed and numbered copies published by M.E. Howard, Lynchburg, Virginia 1983 to date); Thomas F. Nanzig, *3rd Virginia Cavalry*, 1989. All of the Civil War information, for the individuals throughout this book, is a composite of regimental books, fold-3.com, Ancestry.com, ask.com, state biography books, and if available, heritage books and genealogy books.

3. In all probability, of those listed in the "Roll of Honor" and "Class of 1861" sections of this text, if the individual returned

home from college and began the practice of law, he was most likely trained at RMC.

4. Scanlon, p. 109; and Deed Book 33, p. 452, June 13, 1850.

5. Emancipation documents for the family were recorded in Mecklenburg County Circuit Court Book 5, pp. 245 and 246, including their registration as free blacks in the county. It appears that the Evans descendants remained in the college farm area; several of the current day homes next to the college are owned by members of the Evans family. The presidents' home and Randolph Macon Cemetery have been owned, for several generations, by the Evans family.

6. *Petersburg Index*, 1866, p. 1.
7. Anne Rose, p. 9.
8. Scanlon, p. 85.
9. Ibid., p. 85.
10. Ibid., p. 84.
11. Scanlon, p. 89.
12. Anne Rose, pp. 10, 11.
13. *Tobacco Plant*, December 8, 1869, p. 2.
14. Anne Rose, p. 14.
15. Ibid., p. 21.
16. Tyler, Vol. 3, p. 53.
17. David Moltke-Hansen and Sallie Doscher, eds., *Manuscript Guide*, Charleston: South Carolina Historical Society, 1979), 28–356/425. Relevant contents synopsis: "Account Book, David Duncan of Norfolk [VA] Academy, 1822 to 1828"; "David Duncan Letters, 1842 to 1851, and Family Photos"; and "Letters of Elizabeth Duncan Lomax written from Abbeville, South Carolina, 1840 to 1865." Also, Wallace, p. 53.
18. Anne Rose, p. 11.
19. Dr. Phillip Stone, Wofford College Archives, telephone conversations, 2011.
20. Tyler, Vol. 3, pp. 168, 169.
21. Moltke-Hansen and Doscher.
22. David Duncan Wallace, *History of Wofford College 1854–1949*, (Nashville, TN: Vanderbilt Press, 1951), reprinted for Wofford College (Spartanburg, SC: Reprint Company, 2003), p. 54.
23. Stone; Ibid.
24. Moltke-Hansen and Doscher.
25. Lander, p. 37, 38.
26. U.S. Census records, 1850, 22nd Regiment, Mecklenburg County.
27. Oklahoma Historical Society, "Chronicles of Oklahoma," 2001, Vol. 15, 2, June 1937, resolution online.
28. *Tobacco Plant*, three issues in 1859 and 1861.
29. Ibid.
30. Heritage Book Series, Warren County Heritage Book Committee, *Warren County, North Carolina*, Vol. 1, 2002, p. 5, 6; and Powell, Vol. 2, p. 184.
31. *Tobacco Plant*, March 15, 1870, p. 2.
32. *Tobacco Plant*, May 14, 1870, p. 2.
33. H.C. Gregory, "Brunswick-Mecklenburg Sesquicentennial Number," *Richmond Christian Advocate*, Vol. 89, No. 24 (June 21, 1934), p. 17.
34. Ibid.
35. James Sheppard and Louise Sheppard, *The Heritage of Jamieson Memorial Methodist Church, 1830 to 2001* (Clarksville, VA: self-published by the church, 2001), p. 40.
36. Heritage Book Series, Warren County Heritage Book Committee, Vol. 1; and Powell, Vol. 2, p. 217.
37. Anne Rose, p. 19.
38. Herbert Clarence Bradshaw, *History of Prince Edward County, Virginia* (Richmond, VA: Dietz Press, 1955), pp. 161, 352–356.
39. Per a discussion with a McGraw-Page archivist, when I met with her there in May 2012.
40. Anne Rose, p. 19.
41. Bradshaw, pp. 352–356.
42. Carstairs Bracey, p. 39; Parish, p. 91; Heritage Book Series, *Mecklenburg County*, p. 283.
43. Carstairs Bracey, *The Bracey Family of Virginia* (self-published, 1952), p. 39; Timothy A. Parrish and Edward Crews, *14th Virginia Infantry* (1995), p. 90; Heritage Book Series, *Mecklenburg County*, p. 284.
44. Lyon Gardiner Tyler III, ed., *Encyclopedia of Virginia Biography* (New York: Lewis Historical Publishing, 1915), Vol. 5, pp. 704, 705.
45. Rowland, p. 19, a letter he received from H.T. Hutcheson outlining the history of Easters Church.
46. U.S. Census, 1950, 98th Regiment, Boydton.
47. Why two in one year is unknown, except one was for the 98th Regiment and one for the 22nd Regiment; both began with and included the RMC neighborhood.

48. U.S. Census records, 98th Regimental District, Boydton, 1860.
49. Bracey, p. 131.
50. File of William Baskervill, Sr., loose documents and letters, Duke University Archives.
51. Irby, p. 82.
52. Heritage Book Series, *Warren County*, p. 108.
53. U.S. Census records of the neighborhood, starting with the college, in the 22nd Regiment, Boydton, 1860.
54. Scanlon, p. 43.
55. Virginia Woody Wright, unpublished archived records of John W. Wootton and family from 1850 through 1890.
56. Ibid.
57. I read the lone, final checkbook of RMC Boydton (1861 to 1863) while visiting the archives, at the Randolph-Macon College campus in Ashland, VA, in May 2012.
58. Ibid.
59. Wright—part of the archives is a copy of the deed with notations as to the distribution to heirs. The deeds were also recorded in the Mecklenburg County Deed Books.
60. Mecklenburg Circuit, *Church Book for the Mecklenburg Circuit Commencing 1833 at Randolph Macon College*, p. 134 (through about 1860), copy in possession of Rubinette Neimann, Harrisburg, VA. In 2010, she sent me three e-mails with data from the book, relative to the Wootton (Wootten and Wooten) family. (Original donated by her to McGraw-Page Library Archives.)

Chapter 3

1. Scanlon, p. 90.
2. Ibid.
3. Ron A. Bugg, CWO-3, Retired, U.S. Army, several interviews, and unpublished family archives of the John Bugg family, a work in process, 2010.
4. Ibid.
5. Eliz Pettus Puryear, "Letter to the Editor—Reminiscense," *Chase City Progress*, November 1888 (reprinted on June 8, 1900, p. 1). The writer was Elizabeth Pettus Puryear, at the time a young, teenager living north of the college, in nearby (9 miles) Christiansville. She was the oldest daughter of Richard Clausel Puryear.
6. Lander, Jr., pp. 29, 33, and others.
7. Mecklenburg County Deed Book 36: 558, December 15, 1862.
8. U.S. Census, 22nd Regiment, Boydton, 1860.
9. Ibid.
10. Board of Trustees, "Catalogue of the Students, and Charter and Laws of Randolph Macon College, With the Names of the Trustees and Faculty, and the Course of Studies" (Richmond, printed by P.D. Bernard, opposite Exchange Bank, 1848).
11. Samuel T. Pierce, Jr., *Zeb's Black Baby* (Henderson, NC: Harper Prints, 1955).
12. Irby, p. 89.
13. Powell, Vol. 2, Margaret H. Hites, pp. 95, 96.
14. William Johnston, North Carolina Methodist Historian, e-mail to the author, August 2012 ("Caswell Circuit," "Granville Circuit," "Oxford Station" ministers).
15. Pyatt, p. 1859.
16. Duke University Archives, visit and records review, September 2012, index file.
17. John Caknipe, "Christiansville Academy," series, *The News Progress*, June 2011.
18. Douglas Brown, p. 85.
19. William B. Jones, *To Survive and Excel: The Story of Southwestern University, 1840–2000* (Georgetown, TX: Southwestern University, 2006), p. 117.
20. Rowland, p. 13.
21. Scanlon, pp. 82, 83.
22. Ibid., p. 69.
23. James Sheppard, "Land by the Rivers—Garlands I," *Mecklenburg Sun*, April 16, 2008.
24. Ibid., "Land by the Rivers—Garlands II," April 23, 2008.
25. Irby, p. 122.
26. Editorial, *Tobacco Plant*, August 9, 1861, p. 2.
27. Parrish and Crews, *Regimental Books of Virginia Troops Serving During the Civil War*, p. 89.
28. Scanlon, p. 62.
29. Lander, p. 39.
30. Ibid. (a second journal from 1855–56, among other documents, is included on the blog, website).
31. Powell, Vol. 3, p. 10.
32. The Lander history comes from William L. Sherrill, *A Brief History of the Lander Family* (Greensboro, NC: Advocate Press), 1918, http://openlibrary.org/books;

and Dr. DeWitt B. Stone, Jr., e-mail to the author, February 12, 2012, special assistant to the president, Lander University (and grandson of Samuel Lander, Jr.).
33. Weymouth Jordan, *North Carolina Troops* (Raleigh, NC: Department of Archives and History, 1998), p. 147.
34. Ibid.
35. Stone e-mail, February 12, 2012.
36. Southern Historical Collection, University of North Carolina, Chapel Hill, which includes numerous letters home that he wrote from the College. Some references online via Google.
37. Ibid., online, Google biography.
38. Ibid.; and Powell, Vol. 3, Brenda Marks Eagles, p. 207.
39. *Tobacco Plant*, August 2, 1861, p. 2.
40. Powell, Vol. 3, p. 316.
41. Powell, Vol. 2, p. 318.
42. Scanlon, p. 105.
43. *Tobacco Plant*, 1859, p. 2.
44. Powell, Vol. 2, p. 208.
45. Telephone conversation with Lyle Lankford, campus historian, Vanderbilt University, Nashville, Tennessee, March 2011.
46. Powell, Vol. 2.
47. Pyatt, *Timeline*, April 1865 to January 1866.
48. Powell, Vol. 3, Homer M. Keener, pp. 49, 50.
49. Irby, p. 69.
50. Irby, p. 69; and Scanlon, p. 69.
51. *Tobacco Plant*, January 19, 1865, p. 2.
52. Irby, p. 134.
53. *Tobacco Plant*, January 2, 1868, p. 2.
54. Irby, p. 136.
55. Anne Rose, p. 7.
56. James Sheppard and Louise Sheppard, *The Heritage of Jamieson Memorial Methodist Church 1830 to 2001* (Clarksville, VA: self-published by the church, 2001), appendix.
57. Heritage Book Series, *Warren County, North Carolina*, Vol. 1, 2002.
58. Ibid., p. 615.

Chapter 4

1. Irby.
2. *Tobacco Plant*, June 10, 1859, p. 2.
3. *Tobacco Plant*, June 17, 1859, p. 2.
4. *Tobacco Plant*, June 24, 1859, p. 2.
5. *Tobacco Plant*, Special Edition, September 23, 1859, four pages.
6. *Tobacco Plant*, October 14, 1859, p. 2.
7. Ibid., October 7, p. 2.
8. Ibid., October 21, 1859, p. 2.
9. Irby, p. 49.
10. Boyd, September 1859.
11. Frank C. Tucker, *Central Methodist College: One Hundred and Ten Years* (Fayette, MO: Central Methodist University, 1969); Wikipedia; and Ancestor.com. Following John Wills' death in 1878, the family moved to Fort Wayne, Indiana. In 1885, John C. Wills (Jr.), age 17, moved from Fort Wayne, Indiana, to Detroit, Michigan, to become a tool maker. He became acquainted with and was accepted as an apprentice by Henry Ford working from his garage. Wills was one of the designers of the Model T car. In 1904, when Ford Motor Company was formed, he was appointed as chief designer and metallurgist. In 1919 he received a $1.5 million severance package from Henry Ford. With his investments, he had acquired over $4 million before he received his buyout.
12. *Tobacco Plant*, September 30, 1859, p. 2.
13. Ron A. Bugg, John Bugg archives, a copy of the invitation.
14. Southwestern University: Root Institutions, student directory with photos, http://www.swedu/lib/.
15. Wright, archives.
16. Boyd, November 25, 1859, p. 2.
17. Ron Bugg; Ibid.
18. The letters were briefly reviewed by this author during my visit to the archives in May 2012.
19. Boyd, August 23, 1861, p. 2.
20. U.S. Census records, 1880, 98th Regiment, Lombardy Grove.
21. North Carolina regimental book; and Thomas F. Nanzig, *3rd Virginia Cavalry*, 1989, p. 110.
22. Ancestor.com; and fold3.com.
23. Ibid., Amnesty papers, heading, on fold3.com.
24. Irby, p. 144.
25. Scanlon, p. 68.
26. Time Life Editors, Civil War book series, *Confederate Ordeal: The Southern Home Front* (Alexandria, VA: Time Publishing, 1984), p. 68.

Chapter 5

1. William E. Bugg, "Journal of William Emanuel Bugg" (Southside Regional Library, Boydton, Virginia, unpublished journal, 1890).
2. *56th Infantry*, regimental book.
3. Powell, Vol. 3, pp. 96, 97.
4. Ibid.; James W. Wall, p. 97.
5. Circuit Court Record Book 5.
6. Munsey Moore, "Columns From Stone," *The News Progress*, Chase City, Virginia, Monday, October 3, 1983; Powell, Vol. 4, George V. Taylor, pp. 368, 369.
7. Birmingham-Southern University Archives.
8. Thomas McAdory Owen, ed., *History of Alabama and Dictionary of Alabama Biography*, Four Volumes (Chicago, IL: S.J. Clarke, 1921), reprinted (Spartanburg, SC: Reprint Company, 1978), Vol. 3, pp. 352–355.
9. Owen, Vol. 4, p. 1492.
10. Board of Trustees, "Catalogue of the Students, and Charter and Laws of Randolph Macon College, With the Names of the Trustees and Faculty, and the Course of Studies" (Richmond, printed by P.D. Bernard, opposite Exchange Bank, 1848).
11. Rowland, pp. 33, 35, 37.
12. Becker, p. 17.
13. Irby, p. 85.
14. Irby, p. 82; Ancestor.com; and email from Virginia Minnich, biography of Harrison, source referenced "Historic Oakland Tour Harrison Clan Fall," James Lawrence Harrison III.
15. Ibid., p. 83; Ibid.
16. Owen, Vol. 3.
17. Ibid.
18. Ibid.
19. Ibid.; fold3.com; Ancestor.com; and Google search.
20. Owen, Vol. 3, p. 502.
21. Powell, Vol. 3, pp. 225, 226.
22. Ibid.
23. Owen, Vol. 1, and Anne Rose, p. 21.
24. Walter James Edgar, ed., *South Carolina Encyclopedia*, 2006.
25. The National Historical Society, Inc., *War of the Rebellion: Historical Records of the Union and Confederate Armies*, Series I, Vol. 2, Part I, "The Peninsular Campaign" (Washington, D.C.: U.S. Government Printing Office, 1884, reprint), pp. 922, 923.
26. Powell, Vol. 2, Noble J. Tolbert, p. 152.
27. Powell, Vol. 3, William S. West, p. 86.
28. Boyd, July 1, 1859, p. 2.
29. Ibid.
30. Ibid.
31. Jack K.T. Smith, "Historic Tulip, Arkansas," dissertation (University of Arkansas, 1989), p. 11.
32. Eliza P. Hackley and Ethel C. Simpson, eds., *Tulip Evermore: Letters of Emma Butler 1857–1887* (Fayetteville: University of Arkansas Press, 1985), p. 23.
33. Ibid., p. 24.
34. Ibid., p. 25.
35. Ibid., p. 216.
36. Wright archives.
37. Puryear journal at Virginia Baptist archives.
38. Ibid.
39. Nanzig, p. 107.
40. Rowland, p. 48.
41. Bracey, p. 267.
42. Powell, Vol. 2.
43. Ruffner, Kevin C., *Regimental Series, 44th Virginia Infantry*.
44. Boyd, June 21, 1861, p. 2.
45. William A. Young, Jr., and Patricia A. Young, *56th Virginia Infantry, Regimental Series*, 1990.
46. Ibid.; brief notations of sales ads in the 1868 *Tobacco Plant*; a note on a *Confederate Veteran Magazine* from 1936; and 1930 Census records.
47. Jeffrey C. Weaver and Patti O. Weaver, *1st Virginia Reserves, Regimental Series*, 2002, p. 242.
48. Ron A. Bugg, "Military Death Records for the Clarksville Memorial" (unpublished monograph, Clarksville, Virginia, 2004.)
49. Heritage Book Series, Granville County Heritage Book Committee, *Granville County, North Carolina*, 2002, pp. 334, 335, 336.
50. Richard Logan Coleman, *Colonel Henry Eaton Coleman: 1838–1894*, self-published in Halifax County, 1897, p. 2.
51. Heritage, *Warren County*; Ibid.
52. Coleman, pp. 4, 5; Jordan, p. 144.
53. *Battle of Stanton River Bridge, Regimental Series*, pp. 61, 62.
54. Coleman, p. 8.
55. Hutcheson, p. 9.
56. George L. Sherwood, Jr., and Jeffrey C. Weaver, *20th Virginia Infantry, Regimental Series*, 1991.

57. Ibid.
58. Herbert F. Hutcheson, 11 page draft, historical incidents and anecdotes about Randolph Macon College, Boydton, prepared in 1937 for the *South Hill Enterprise*, from Hutcheson and friends in the county court and government. In the scrapbooks of his deceased former secretary, Mary McKinney, in the possession of Glen and Lisa Gillispie, Chase City, Virginia.
59. John Caknipe, "Richard Clausel Puryear," *The News Progress*, "Unsung Heroes" series, 2009 and 2010.
60. Tyler, Vol. 5, pp. 1094, 1095.
61. Nanzig, p. 107.
62. Bracey, p. 267.
63. Parish, p. 94.
64. Mecklenburg County Circuit Court Record Book 6.

Chapter 6

1. Hutcheson, p. 9.
2. Ibid.
3. G. Howard Gregory, *38th Virginia Infantry, Regimental Series*.
4. Ancestor.com.
5. Mecklenburg County Deed Book 137; James Sheppard and Louise Sheppard, appendix.
6. Heritage Book Series, Southside Virginia Genealogical Society, *Mecklenburg County, Virginia*, 2006, 565.
7. 1880 U.S. Census records, Union Level District.
8. Bracey, p. 345.
9. Hutcheson, p. 8.
10. Boyd, December 7, 1860, p. 2.
11. Anne Rose, p. 24.
12. 1860 U.S. Census records, Harrisonburg, VA.
13. Nanzig, p. 129.
14. 1880 U.S. Census, Richmond.
15. Tyler III, Vol. 3, p. 277.
16. Myrta Lockett Avery, *A Virginia Girl in the Civil War 1861–1865* (New York: D. Appleton, 1903; reprinted, Laverge, TN: Kissinger Legacy Reprints), p. 53.
17. Ibid., p. 378.
18. Tyler, Ibid.
19. 1870 U.S. Census record, Danville.
20. *Midland Express*, Negro newspaper published in Boydton, 1893; three issues on microfilm, February 13, 1893, p. 2.
21. Referenced by Boyd in several editorials in the *Tobacco Plant*.
22. Scanlon, p. 81.
23. Irby, p. 42.
24. Lander, Jr., p. 35, 45.
25. *41st Infantry Battalion, Regimental Series*.
26. Wallace, p. 50.
27. Powell, Vol. 4, Louise L. Queen, p. 334.
28. *35th Virginia Infantry, Regimental Series*.
29. Hugh C. Keen and Horace Mewburn, *43rd Virginia Cavalry Battalion, Mosby's Regiment*, 1993.
30. Jeffrey C. Weaver, *Thurmond's Partisan Rangers and Swain's Battalion of Virginia Cavalry*, 2001.
31. Ibid.
32. Ibid.
33. Time Life Books of the Civil War series.
34. Irby, p. 153.
35. Ibid.
36. Alfred Boyd, administrator receipts from 1846 thru 1863. A copy in the possession of Larry Smith, of Boydton, purchased at a yard sale, with a copy of some of the receipts given to this author.
37. Wright archives.
38. Boyd, receipts.
39. Wright archives.
40. Boyd, *Tobacco Plant*, May 16, 1861, p. 2.
41. U.S. Census records for 1860, 1870 and 1920.
42. Boyd, *Tobacco Plant*, June 28, 1861, p. 2.
43. Advertisements, *Petersburg Index*, Petersburg, Virginia, January 30, 1865, p. 3.
44. Sheppard, appendix.
45. James M. Francisco, ed., *Tobacco Plant*, Clarksville, Virginia, selected issues on microfilm, January 24, 1867, p. 3.
46. U.S. Census record, Richmond, 1880.
47. Jones, W., p. 117, http://southwestern.edu/library/documents/ToSurviveAnd Excel.pdf.
48. Bracey, p. 279.
49. Bracey, p. 279.
50. Ibid.
51. Rowland, p. 19.

Chapter 7

1. Nanzig, p. 124, and Parish, p. 133.
2. Tom Bennett, "The Civil War and

O.S.U.," *The Oregon Stater*, Oregon State University Alumni Association publication, Vol. 78, No. 3, June 1994, from the Division of Special Collections and University Archives, University of Oregon Libraries, p. 10.

3. Myrta Lockett Avary, *Dixie After the War* (New York: Doubleday, Page, 1906), p. 125.
4. Avary, p. 126, 127.
5. Google search.
6. Irby, p. 146, Trustees Minutes, February 1862, p. 531.
7. Ibid.
8. Baptist archives, loose documents.
9. William Townes, Jr., *Roanoke Valley*, August 2, 1878, p. 2.
10. Tyler, Vol. 1; and Baptist archives.
11. Parrish and Crews, *14th Virginia Infantry*.
12. Townes, December 30, 1871, p. 2.
13. William E. Henderson, *12th Virginia Infantry Regiment*, 1984.
14. Scanlon, p. 153.
15. Anne Rose, p. 7.
16. Trustees minutes, December 1862, p. 550, and September 14, 1864.
17. Board of Trustees minutes book, July 186.7
18. U.S. Census, 1900, Washington, D.C.
19. Google search.
20. *11th Virginia Infantry, Regimental Series*; Google search; and Ancestor.com, Civil War records.
21. U.S. Census record, 1900, Oklahoma; and Ancestor.com.
22. Ibid., 1910.
23. Wright archives.
24. Lillian (Elizabeth) Wootton Thompson Samuelson, *Ancestors of John T. Wootton of Mecklenburg County, Virginia* (genealogy monograph published in Guilderland, New York, 2005).
25. Wright archives.
26. Ibid.
27. Ibid., photocopy of a letter to the editor of the *Clarksville Times*, with the date and signature cut off.
28. Tyler, Vol. 5, p. 588.
29. Ibid.; and Parrish and Crews, regimental records.
30. Townes, social column, *Roanoke Valley*, August 20, 1878, p. 2.
31. Susan A. Riggs, *21st Virginia Infantry*, 1991 *Regimental Series*.

32. Nanzig, *Regimental Series*.
33. Ron Bugg, "Clarksville Memorial," death records.
34. Mecklenburg County Deed Book 37-298.
35. Ron Bugg, J. Bugg archives. John Wesley's grandson, Roland Pickett Bugg, followed in the family traditions. "Pickett," as he is called in 2012, was born in 1916 in Mecklenburg County. His father was the owner of Buggs Island in the Roanoke River southeast of Boydton, among other farms. At age 25, on February 3, 1941, he was drafted into the Chase City, Virginia, unit of the Army National Guard, Company E, 29th Division, 116th Regiment—the same unit his three younger brothers served in. At 6:30 a.m. on June 6, 1944, he was a platoon sergeant and led his men in an assault during the invasion on Omaha Beach. During World War II, he received two Purple Hearts and was wounded on several occasions, but declined the medals.

Following World War II, he was called to the ministry in 1953. He served as Methodist chaplain in a number of municipal positions in Hampton, Virginia, and as a visiting pastor for numerous Methodist churches in Virginia. During the making of the movie *Saving Private Ryan*, he served as a consultant. Finally retiring to his home in Virginia Beach area at age 93, he decided it was time to come home. So he purchased a small farm in Mecklenburg County and returned "home" in 2010. ("For one Veteran, no idea what he would get into," *Mecklenburg Sun*, pp. 1, 4, November 7, 2012.)

36. Board of Curators, *Central College Catalogue*, 1859, University Archives, Central Methodist University, Fayette, Missouri.
37. Becker, p. 27.
38. Francisco, January 24, 1867, and May 10, 1867, plus others. The same ad. It didn't change with the season.
39. Virginia Baptist archives loose documents.
40. Irby, p. 151.
41. Francisco, May 10, 1867, p. 2.

Chapter 8

1. Virginia Baptist archives loose documents.
2. Ibid.

3. Ibid.

4. Ibid. His son Bennett Puryear (Jr.) was born on January 9, 1884, at Richmond and was primarily home schooled by his father. He joined his brother, Charles, at Texas A&M in 1901 and graduated in 1905. Completing his bachelor's degree, he enlisted into the United States Marine Corps on September 21, 1905, as a second lieutenant. Having served in Cuba, World War I, Washington, D.C., Haiti, and the Philippine Islands, in 1940, he was assigned as executive officer, Quartermaster Department, United States Marine Corps Headquarters, and promoted to major general. He retired following World War II and lived in Arlington, Virginia, until his death on February 11, 1982.

5. Tyler, Vol. 3, p. 287, and Anne Rose, p. 17.

6. U.S. Census, June 14, 1880, Halifax County, Virginia; and Ancestor.com.

7. Wallace, pp. 51, 52.

8. Owen, pp. 1140, 1141.

9. Tucker, p. 46.

10. Ibid.

11. Ibid., p. 47.

12. Ibid., p. 48.

13. Ibid., p. 49.

14. Ibid., pp. 51, 52.

15. Ibid., p. 52

16. Robert Rackley, research assistant, Central Methodist University, several e-mails and telephone conversations in 2011 and 2012.

17. Scanlon, p. 119; Trustees minutes, Book II, June 1867, p. 248.

18. Ann Rose, p. 15.

19. Michael A. Cavanaugh, *6th Virginia Infantry, Regimental Series*, 1988.

20. 1880 U.S. Census record, Fayette, MO.

21. Verne Dyson, ed., County of Fayette, *Picturesque Fayette and Its People*: A Review of Fayette, Howard County, Missouri (Fayette, MO: The Advertiser, L.B. White Publishing, 1905), p. 48.

22. 1900 U.S. Census record, Fayette, MO.

23. Mary Virginia Irby, notes and unpublished manuscripts in the files in the Burkeville Public Library, in Nottoway County, 2009, notes of the Irby reunion held in 1985 with over 400 in attendance. Notes were donated to the library for vertical files.

24. Ibid.

25. Ibid.; and Will Book VI: 198.

26. Ibid., and Nottoway County Deed Books.

27. Ibid.

28. U.S. Census record, 1850 Nottoway County, and Slave Schedule Census, Nottoway County.

29. U.S. Census record, Nottoway County, 1860.

30. James L. Robertson, *18th Virginia Infantry*, 2nd ed., regimental series

31. Ibid.

32. Fold3.com, Civil War pardons.

33. U.S. Census, 1870, Henrico County.

34. Nottoway County Deed Books.

35. City of Richmond Directories 1877–1890, online.

36. *Dictionary of Representative Business and Professional Men of Augusta and Stanton County, Virginia*, 1890 edition, online.

37. U.S. Census record, 1900, Ashland, Virginia.

Chapter 9

1. Boyd, January 21, 1861, p. 2.

2. Wright archives.

3. Ibid.

4. Ibid.

5. Ibid.

6. Ibid.

7. Latinus Irving Rose, "Journal and Business Records, 1859 through 1869"; a copy is in the possession of Steven and Gray Rose, Lacrosse, Virginia (originals on file with the Virginia Historical Society, Richmond, Virginia).

8. Bracey, p. 291.

9. Virginia Baptist archives.

10. Tyler, Vol. 3, p. 340.

11. Board of Trustees minutes; local board members met with Puryear at the college in September 1867.

12. Wright archives.

13. Virginia Baptist archives.

14. Mecklenburg County Marriage Records.

15. Francisco, May 10, 1867, p. 2.

16. Mecklenburg County Circuit Court Record Book 8.

17. Boyd, *Tobacco Plant*, March 31, 1865, p. 2.

18. Alfred Boyd, documents.

19. Susan Cosby Rowlett, "Reminiscence of the Civil War," *Southside Virginia Highlights*, Roanoke River Branch, Association

for the Preservation of Virginia Antiquities, Fall 1993, pp. 4, 5.
20. John Taylor Lewis, Jr., ed., *Ole Marster's Cedar Grove*, 2nd Edition (Castleton, NY: Hamilton, 2006), pp. 24, 25.
21. Ron Bugg, John Bugg archives.
22. Scanlon, p. 117. South Carolina troops online, fold3.com: "2nd Regiment, South Carolina Infantry" and "21st South Carolina Infantry."
23. Becker, p. 21.
24. Southwestern University: Root Institutions, student directory with photos, http://www.swedu/lib/.
25. Irby, pp. 90, 143.
26. Ibid.; Fold3.com.
27. Ibid.
28. Jackie Reeves Wood, University of Memphis Libraries, Lambuth Campus, Jackson, TN, brief records and e-mails, February 29, 2012, and March 9 and 15, 2012.
29. Jackie Wood, telephone conversation, February 28, 2012.
30. Wood, biography and few notes about Jones.
31. "Obituary of Dr. Samuel D. Sanders," *Georgetown Commerce*, Georgetown, Williamson County, Texas, Friday, January 30, 1903. www.arlingtonlibrary.org/files/journal.
32. William B. Jones, pp. 129, 130; http://southwestern.edu/library/documents/ToSurviveAndExcel.pdf.
33. www.rhodeshouse.ox.ac.uk/section/rhodes-scholars-complete-list.
34. Jones, p. 174.
35. Jones, p. 175.
36. Southwestern University: Root Institutions.
37. Jones, p. 172.
38. Betty Antones de Olivaria Brasilia, "North American Immigration to Brazil: Tombstone Records of the 'Campo' Cemetery," *The Virginia Magazine*, book review section, Vol. 87, No. 4, pp. 495, 496; and Mike Wright, pp. 281-283.
39. Powell, Vol. 3, pp. 273, 274, June Dunn Parker.
40. William L. Sherrill, *A Brief History of the Lander Family* (Greensboro, NC: Advocate Press, 1918), http://openlibrary.org/books; Stone e-mail.
41. U.S. Census record, Georgetown, Texas, 1900.
42. Obituary, Ibid.
43. http://www.three-legged-willie.org/cemetery/ioofgeorgetown.

Chapter 10

1. Irby, pp. 166, 167.
2. Bugg archives and Wright archives.
3. Irby, pp. 159, 160.
4. Ibid.
5. Irby, pp. 164, 165.
6. Irby, pp. 165, 166.
7. "Nottoway County Senators 1835-1860," taken from *The General Assembly of Virginia July 30, 1619-January 11, 1978: A Bicentennial Register of Members*.
8. James L. Robertson, *18th Virginia Infantry, Regimental Series*.
9. U.S. Census record, Nottoway County, 1860; and Mary Virginia Irby, notes and unpublished manuscripts in files at the Burkeville Public Library, Nottoway County, 2009. Notes of the Irby reunion held in 1985, with over 400 in attendance, donated to the library.
10. Mary Irby files.
11. Ibid.
12. U.S. Census records, Ashland and Lunenburg County, 1870.
13. Fold3.com, Civil War records, pardons.
14. Mary Irby files.
15. Richard Irby, p. 168; and board of trustee records for the meeting.
16. RMC board of trustee records for that date.
17. Ibid.
18. Lewis, Jr., pp. 25-27.
19. Thomas Thackston, *Tobacco Plant*, October 19, 1866, p. 3.
20. Rose, p. 16.
21. *Petersburg Index*, social column, September 23, 1867.
22. Scanlon, p. 117.
23. Langston Easley Finch, ed., *Tobacco Plant*, January 10, 1868, p. 2.
24. Tyler, Vol. 3, p. 214.
25. Avery, pp. 9, 56, 57.
26. Finch, January 31, 1868, p. 2.
27. Ibid., February 20, 1868.
28. Irby, p. 174.
29. Scanlon, p. 123.
30. Avery, p. 226.
31. Scanlon, p. 123.
32. Ibid., p. 125.

33. Ibid., p. 126.
34. Ibid., p. 128.
35. Ibid., p. 129, 130.
36. Ibid., p. 132, 133.
37. Jack Trammell and James E. Scanlon, "Celebrating 175 Years: 1830–2005," *R-MC* alumni magazine, Part III, Spring 2005, p. 3.

Chapter 11

1. Finch, February 2, 1870, p. 2.
2. Ibid.
3. Becker, p. 28.
4. Finch, February 18, 1870, p. 2.
5. Ibid.
6. Finch, February 23, 1870, p. 2.
7. Finch, December 25, 1869, p. 2.
8. Finch editorial, March 15, 1870, p. 2.
9. Finch editorials, "The Property of Randolph Macon College," *The Mecklenburg Herald*, Clarksville, Virginia, June 29, 1870, p. 2.
10. Ibid.
11. Finch, *Herald*, July 27, 1870, p. 2.
12. Finch, August 10, 1870, p. 2.
13. Finch, September 21, 1870, p. 2.
14. Finch, September 28, 1870, p. 2.
15. Finch, December, 1871, p. 2.
16. A.J. Wootton and N.J. Wootton, *The Clipper*, Chase City, VA, May 8, 1873, p. 1.
17. Thomas Thackston, *Banner of Truth* (one issue only), Clarksville, VA, June 24, 1887, p. 2.
18. Irby, p. 178; and Trammell, Spring 2005.
19. Irby, p. 179.
20. Ibid.
21. *Richmond Inquirer*, July 7, 1872, p. 2.
22. Gerald Gilliam, "1872 Sale of Randolph-Macon College in Boydton," *Southsider*, Vol. 17, No. 1, January 1999.

Epilogue

1. This is the last stanza of the poem Puryear published in *The Saturday Post* in 1848. He copied it into his journal, which is part of the collection at Virginia Baptist Historical Society archives at the University of Richmond, Fred Anderson, curator.

Appendix A

1. Janet B. Hewett, ed., *Virginia Confederate Soldiers: 1861 to 1865. Name Roster*, Vol. 1, A–K, and Vol. 2, L–Z, arranged by Joyce Lawrence (Washington, D.C.: Broadfoot), 1908.
2. *Regimental Books of Virginia Troops Serving During the Civil War*, sponsored, authoritative, controlled issue series (1,000 signed and numbered copies) published by M.E. Howard, Lynchburg, Virginia, 1983 to date.
3. Tom Bennett, "The Civil War and O.S.U.," *The Oregon Stater*, Oregon State University Alumni Association publication, Vol. 78, No. 3, June 1994, from the Division of Special Collections and University Archives, University of Oregon Libraries.
4. http://www.VMI.edu, archives online.
5. University of Oregon, Special Collections and Archives, copies of RMC documents from file of Benjamin J. Hawthorne, copies of documents from other professors at RMC Boydton, and documents by R-MC–Ashland President Duncan. This is in addition to the regimental book, and to the lengthy story by Tom Bennett.
6. John C. Burtner, "College to Aid in Agricultural Centennial, University of Oregon," copy of *The Sunday Oregonian*, Portland, Oregon, September 2, 1928, a front page story which includes an 1882–1883 photograph of the faculty, including two RMC–Boydton graduates.
7. James Sheppard and Louise Sheppard, *The Heritage of Jamieson Memorial Methodist Church 1830 to 2001* (Clarksville, VA: self-published by the church, 2001); and stories and advertisements in the *Tobacco Plant* newspaper.
8. www.fold3.com (formerly "footnote.com"), Civil War records collection.

Appendix B

1. National Historical Society, War of the Rebellion: Historical Records of the Union and Confederate Armies, Series I, Vol. 2, Part I and II, "The Peninsular Campaign," Serial Nos. 12 and 13, U.S. Government Printing Office, 1884 (reprint).
2. "Strange Story," Tupelo Mississippian newspaper, reprinted in the Public Ledger

of Petersburg, Virginia, September 21, 1867.
3. Tyler, Vol. 3.
4. Finch, Tobacco Plant, January 13, 1870, p. 2.
5. Anne Rose, pp. 13, 14.
6. Ibid., p. 17.
7. Warren County Heritage Book Committee, Warren County, North Carolina, Vol. 1, 2002.
8. Parrish and Crews, p. 84.
9. Granville County Heritage Book Committee, Granville County, North Carolina, 2002.
10. Clark, Vol. 1, Granville County, section 236; and Pierce, Jr., Zeb's Black Baby.
11. Robert S. Seigler, South Carolina Military Organization Demographics: The War Between the States (Charleston Historic Press, 2008), p. 42.
12. National Historical Society, Vol. 2, p. 570.
13. Owen, Vol. 4, p. 1063.
14. National Historical Society, Vol. 1, p. 941.
15. Owen, Vol. 4, p. 1383.
16. Anne Rose, p. 28.
17. "South Carolina C.S.A.: Statewide Units, Militia and Reserves," library manuscript, North Myrtle Beach, SC, public library.
18. Ibid.
19. Ancestor.com, census records, Civil War amnesty records, family genealogy records, war pension records (master's thesis, James M. Bailey, George Washington University, about Anthony Keiley, online), http://www.ancestor.com.
20. Parrish and Crews, pp. 83–156.
21. Bracey, p. 292.
22. Gregory, pp. 77–132.
23. National Historical Society, Vol. 2, p. 541.
24. Ron Bugg, archives.
25. Weaver, 4th Company, Richmond Howitzers, p. 160.
26. Nanzig, pp. 94–136.
27. Tyler, Vol. 5, p. 615.
28. Trask, 16th Infantry, p. 233.
29. Jeffrey C. Weaver, Thurmond's Partisan Rangers and Swain's Battalion of Virginia Cavalry.
30. Louis H. Manarin, North Carolina Troops 1861 to 1865, Vol. 1, began a series of Civil War soldiers' service records, first volume published in1963, with subsequent volumes about every three years hence. The latest is Vol. 18.
31. Powell, Vol. 2, p. 15; H.G. Jones.
32. Fold3.com (formerly "footnote.com"), Civil War records collection; Ancestor.com census records, Civil War, amnesty records, family genealogy, http://www.ancestor.com .
33. Ibid.
34. Owen, 1921.
35. Robert S. Seigler, South Carolina Military Organization Demographics: The War Between the States (SC: Charleston Historic Press, 2008); "South Carolina C.S.A.: Statewide Units, Militia and Reserves," library manuscript, North Myrtle Beach, SC, public library; South Carolina troops online, fold3.com, "2nd Regiment, South Carolina Infantry," and "21st South Carolina Infantry."

Bibliography

Books

Avery, Myrta Lockett. *A Virginia Girl in the Civil War 1861–1865*. New York: D. Appleton, 1903. Reprinted, Laverge, TN: Kissinger Legacy Reprints.

_____. *Dixie After the War*. New York: Doubleday, Page, 1906.

Beale, Brigadier General R.L.T. *9th Virginia Cavalry*. Richmond, VA: R.F. Johnson, 1899.

Board of Curators. *Central College Catalogue, 1859*. Fayette, MO: University Archives, Central Methodist University.

Board of Trustees. *Catalogue of the Students, and Charter and Laws of Randolph Macon College, with the names of the Trustees and Faculty, and the Course of Studies*. Richmond, VA, printed by P.D. Bernard, opposite Exchange Bank, 1848.

Boddie, John Bennett. *Southside Virginia Families*, Vol. 1. Redwood, CA: 1955. Reprinted with Vol. 2, 1956.

_____. *Southside Virginia Families*, Vol. 2. Baltimore, MD: Genealogical Publishing Company, 1956.

Bracey, Carstairs. *The Bracey Family of Virginia*. Self-published, 1952.

Bracey, Susan L. *Life by the Roanoke*. Richmond, VA: Whittet and Shepardson, 1977, Mecklenburg County Bicentennial Commission, pp. 250–290.

Bradshaw, Herbert Clarence. *History of Prince Edward County, Virginia*. Richmond, VA: Dietz Press, 1955.

Brown, Douglas Summers. *Chase City and Its Environs: 1765–1975*. Richmond, VA: Whittet and Shepardson, 1975.

Burwell, Letitia M. *A Girl's Life in the South Before the War*. New York: Frederick A. Stoker, 1895. In cooperation with New York Public Libraries, Research Library.

Cage, Anthony J. *Southside Virginia in the Civil War*. Lynchburg, VA: H.E. Howard, 1999.

Caknipe, John, Jr. *Around Clarksville: Images of America*. Mt. Pleasant, SC: Arcadia, 2009.

Clark, Eva Turner. *Frances Epes: His Ancestors and Descendants*. New York: Richard D. Smithey, 1942.

Clark, Walter. *Dictionary of North Carolina Biographies*, Vol. 1. Chapel Hill, NC: University of North Carolina Press, 2001.

Coleman, Richard Logan. *Colonel Henry Eaton Coleman: 1838–1894*. Halifax County, VA: self-published, 1897.

Dyson, Verne, ed., and County of Fayette. *Picturesque Fayette and Its People: A Review of Fayette, Howard County, Missouri*. Fayette, MO: The Advertiser, L.B. White Publishing Co., 1905.

Craig, Edna Crenshaw. *Its Waters Returning*, . Danville, VA: U.R.E. Press, printed by the Delmar Company, Charlotte, NC, 1989.

Cummings, A.B. *Landmarks of Nottoway County*. Richmond, VA: W.M. Brown, 1970.

Edgar, Walter James, ed. *South Carolina Encyclopedia*. Charleston: University of South Carolina Press, 2006.

Guernsey, Alfred, and Harry Alden, eds. *Harper's Pictorial History of the Civil War*. New York: Fairfax Press, 1867; reprint undated.

Hackley, Eliza P. and Ethel C. Simpson, eds. *Tulip Evermore: Letters of Emma Butler 1857-1887*. Fayetteville: University of Arkansas Press, 1985.

Harris, Nelson. *Virginia Tech*. Mt. Pleasant, SC: Arcadia, 2004.

Heritage Book Series. Commemorating history in Piedmont Virginia and North Carolina counties; proposed by the area historical-genealogical societies. Waynesville, NC: Wadsworth, under the name of County Heritage. Southside Virginia Genealogical Society, *Mecklenburg County, Virginia*, 2006, and *Brunswick County*, Vol. 1, 2001. Cora St. John and Jacqueline Gray, et al., eds., *Charlotte County, Virginia*, Vol. 1, 2007, and Vol. 2, 2011. South Boston–Halifax County Museum of History and Fine Art, *Halifax County, Virginia*, 2007. Southside Virginia Genealogical Society, *Lunenburg County, Virginia*, 2008. Mildred C. Guss, et al., eds., *Nottoway County, Virginia*, 2005. Granville County Heritage Book Committee, *Granville County, North Carolina*, 2002. Jan E. Reese, Mark Pace, Judy E. Stainback, et al., eds., *Vance County, North Carolina*, 2004. Warren County Heritage Book Committee, *Warren County, North Carolina*, Vol. 1, 2002.

Hewett, Janet B., ed. *Virginia Confederate Soldiers: 1861 to 1865*. Name Roster, Vol. 1, A–K, and Vol. 2, L–Z, arranged by Joyce Lawrence. Washington, D.C.: Broadfoot, 1908.

Hill, William B. *Land Along the Roanoke: An Album of Mecklenburg County, Virginia*. Richmond, VA: Whittet and Shepardson, 1957.

Hutcheson, Nat. *"What Do You Know About the Horses?* Boydton, VA: self-published, 1959.

Irby, Richard. *The History of Randolph Macon College*. Richmond, VA: Whittet and Shepardson, 1898.

Jordan, Weymouth. *North Carolina Troops*. Raleigh, NC: Department of Archives and History, 1975.

King, Myrtle C. *A Civil War Diary, 1856 to 1890, of Anna Long Thomas Fuller*. Granville Public Library, Oxford, North Carolina.

Lefler, Hugh T. *History of North Carolina Families and Personal History*. Four volumes. New York: Lewis H. Blanch, 1956.

Lewis, John Taylor, Jr., ed. *Ole Marster's Cedar Grove*. 2nd edition. Castleton, NY: Hamilton, 2006.

Manarin, Louis H. *North Carolina Troops: 1861 to 1865*. Vol. 1 began a series of Civil War soldiers' service records, published in 1963, with subsequent volumes about every three years hence. The latest was Vol. 18 in 2011.

Mathis, The Rev. Harry R. *Along the Border*. Oxford, NC: Cable Press, 1964.

McKay-Smith, Alexander. *The Colonial Quarter Horse*. Richmond, VA, 1983.

Mitchell, Vivian P. *Pioneer Methodist Preachers: Charter Members of the North Carolina Conference, February 1837*.

Moltke-Hansen, David, and Sallie Doscher, eds. *Manuscript Guide*. Charleston: South Carolina Historical Society, 1979. "Account Book: David Duncan of Norfolk, VA Academy 1822 to 1828," "David Duncan Letters 1842–1851 and Family Photos," and "Letters of Elizabeth Duncan Lomax written from Abbeville, South Carolina, 1840 to 1851."

Moore, Munsey Adams. *Cemetery and Tombstone Records of Mecklenburg County*. Vol. 1. Chase City, VA: self-published, 1982.

Moore, Munsey A. *History of The Boyd Tavern, Boydton Hotel*. The Boyd Family Foundation, self-published, 1990.

Moore, Munsey Adams, and Margaret Moore. *Cemetery and Tombstone Records of Mecklenburg County*, Vol. 2. Chase City, VA: self-published, 1987.

National Historical Society. *War of the Rebellion: Official Records of the Union and Confederate Armies*, Series I, Vol. 2, Part 1, "The Peninsular Campaign." Washington, D.C.: U.S. Government Printing Office, 1884, reprint. Part II, Serial Numbers 12 and 13, U.S. Government Printing Office, 1884, reprint.

Neale, Janet Gayle, ed. *Brunswick County,*

Virginia: 1720–1975. Brunswick County Bicentennial Committee. Richmond, VA: Whittet and Shepardson, 1975.

Owen, Thomas McAdory, ed. *History of Alabama and Dictionary of Alabama Biography.* Four volumes. Chicago, IL: S.J. Clarke, 1921; reprinted, Spartanburg, S.C.: Reprint Company, 1978.

Pierce, Samuel T., Jr. *Zeb's Black Baby.* Henderson, NC: Harper Prints, 1955.

Powell, William S., ed. *Dictionary of North Carolina Biography.* Six volumes. Raleigh: University of North Carolina Press, 1979.

Puryear, Jay, ed. *The Puryears of America.* Idaho: self-published, 2002.

Pyatt, Tim. *Duke Illustrated: A Timeline of Duke University History, 1838–2011.* Durham, NC: Duke University Archives, 2011.

Randolph-Macon College. *The John P. Branch Historical Papers of Randolph-Macon College, Department of History and Government,* New Series, Vol. 3, December 1954, diary of Edward Dromgoole Sims and private journal of Samuel Lander, Jr.

Regimental Books of Virginia Troops Serving During the Civil War. Sponsored, authoritative, controlled issue series, 1,000 signed and numbered copies. Lynchburg, VA: H.E. Howard, 1983 to date: Jeffrey C. Weaver, *Virginia Home Guard,* Mecklenburg County, 1994; Jeffrey C. and Pattie O. Weaver, *1st Virginia Reserves,* 2002; Jeffrey Weaver, *Miscellaneous Heavy Artillery,* 1994; *First Company, Richmond Howitzers (Disbanded), Brunswick Rebel, Johnston Southside, United, James City, Lunenburg Rebel, Pamunkey Heavy Artillery and Young's Harbor Guard,* 1996; G.L. Sherwood and Jeffrey L. Weaver, *59th Virginia Infantry,* 1994; C. Howard Gregory, *5th Battalion Virginia Infantry Appomattox, Virginia,* 1999; *8th Virginia Infantry,* 1988; *53rd Virginia Infantry,* 1999; Michael A. Cavanaugh, *6th Virginia Infantry,* 1988; *4th Virginia Infantry Battalion;* John E. Divine, *8th Virginia Infantry,* 1983; *11th Virginia Infantry;* William E. Henderson, *12th Virginia Infantry Regiment,* 1984; Timothy A. Parrish and Edward Crews, *14th Virginia Infantry,* 1995; Benjamin H. Trask, *16th Virginia Infantry,* 1986; James L. Robertson, *18th Virginia Infantry,* 2nd edition, 1984; George L. Sherwood, Jr., and Jeffrey C. Weaver, *20th Virginia Infantry Regiment;* Susan A. Riggs, *21st Virginia Infantry,* 1991; Thomas M. Rankin, *22nd Virginia Battalion,* 1999; Terry D. Lowry, *22nd Virginia Infantry Regiment,* 1988; Alex L. Wiatt, *26th Virginia Infantry,*1984; Johnny L. Scott, *34th Virginia Infantry Regiment,* 1999; Hugh C. Keen and Horace Mewburn, *43rd Virginia Cavalry Battalion, Mosby's Regiment,* 1993; Thomas F. Nanzig, *3rd Virginia Cavalry,* 1989; Robert Driver, *5th Virginia Cavalry,* 1997; *58th Virginia Infantry,* 1990; Michael P. Musick, *6th Virginia Cavalry,* 1990; Kevin C. Ruffner, *44th Virginia Infantry,* 1994; Richard B.Kleese, *49th Virginia Infantry, 1st Battalion, Virginia Cavalry, Local Defense;* William A. Young, Jr., and Patricia A. Young, *56th Virginia Infantry,* 1990; "2nd Virginia Artillery Regiment," Joseph Wootton records; Lawrence McFail, Jr., *Danville in the Civil War,* 2004; Lee Wallace, *Richmond Howitzers;* Robert H. Moores, *Miscellaneous Disbanded Light Artillery;* Jeffrey C. Weaver, *Thurmond's Partisan Rangers and Swain's Battalion of Virginia Cavalry;* Capt. Greg E. Eanes, *Wilson-Kautz Raid and the Battle of Stanton River Bridge,* 1999.

Reynolds, Emily B., and Joan R. Faunt. *South Carolina Biography.* Columbia, South Carolina, Archives, 1964.

Robinson, Quay Hawks. *The Hendrick/Palmer Families.* Lawrenceville, VA: Brunswick, 1994.

Rose, Anne S. *The Faculty of Randolph-Macon College During the 1800s.* Ashland, VA: Randolph-Macon College, 2009.

Rowland-Jones, Toby. *Civil War Generals: Virginia.* Williamsburg, VA: Bicast, 2000.

Scanlon, Professor James Edward. *Randolph Macon College: A Southern History, 1825–1967.* Charlottesville: University of Virginia Press, 1983.

Scott, John. *His Partisan Life With Colonel John S. Mosby*. New York: Harper and Brothers, 1867.
Seigler, Robert S. *South Carolina Military Organization Demographics: The War Between the States*. Charleston Historic Press, 2008.
Sheppard, James, and Louise Sheppard. *The Heritage of Jamieson Memorial Methodist Church, 1830 to 2001*. Clarksville, VA: self-published by the church, 2001.
South Carolina Biography Dictionary, Vol. 2, . St. Clare Shores, MI: Somerset, 2000.
St. John, Jeffrey, and Kathryn St. John. *Landmarks 1765-1990: A Brief History of Mecklenburg County, Virginia*. Boydton, VA: Mecklenburg County Board of Supervisors, 1990.
Stewart, John. *Confederate Spies at Large: Lives of the Lincoln Conspiracy—Tom Harbin and Charles Russell*, Jefferson, NC: McFarland, 2009.
Time Life Editors. Civil War, book series, *Confederate Ordeal: The Southern Home Front*. Series. Alexandria, VA: Time Publishing Company, 1984. *Spies, Scouts and Raiders: Irregular Operations*, 1988.
Tucker, Frank C. *Central Methodist College: One Hundred and Ten Years*. Fayette, MO: Central Methodist University, 1969.
Tyler, Lyon Gardiner III, ed. *Encyclopedia of Virginia Biography*. Five volumes. New York: Lewis Historical Publishing Company, 1915. Vol. 2, Vol. 3, Vol. 5.
Virginia Historical Society, ed. *Encyclopedia of Virginia Biography*. Fairfax County, VA, January 5, 1905.
Wallace, David Duncan. *History of Wofford College 1854-1949*. Nashville, TN: Vanderbilt Press, 1951. Reprinted for Wofford College by the Reprint Company, Spartanburg, SC, 2003.
Wright, Mike. *What They Didn't Teach you about the Civil War*. Novato, CA: Presidio Press, 1996.

Periodicals

Advertisement. "Danville Museum of Fine Arts and History." *Mecklenburg Sun*, Clarksville, VA, September 2012.
Advertisements. *The Daily Express*, Petersburg, VA, September 5, 1865, Southern Female College, and November 8, 1865 (freedmen), also sale ad for Lombardy Grove and parade.
Advertisements. *Midland Express*, Boydton, VA, 1893 to 1895 (three issues used, on microfilm).
Advertisements. *Petersburg Index*, Petersburg, VA, January 19, 1865 sales ads, Flat Creek and Clarksville, VA.
Advertisements. *Petersburg Index*, September 23, 1867.
Anderson, Sterling P., Jr. "St. James' Episcopal Church (Boydton)," *Southside Virginia Highlights*, Roanoke River Branch, Association for the Preservation of Virginia Antiquities (Fall 1993).
"Battlefield Bible," battlefield editorial, *Petersburg Index*, Aug. 2, 1861.
Becker, James M. "Randolph-Macon College and Boydton." *Heritage*, bulletin of the Virginia Conference Historical Society of the United Methodist Church, Vol. 30, No. 1 (Spring 2004), pp. 15–29.
Bennett, Tom. "The Civil War and O.S.U." *The Oregon Stater*, Oregon State University Alumni Association publication, Vol. 78, No. 3, June 1994, from the Division of Special Collections and University Archives, University of Oregon Libraries.
Boyd, John G. *Tobacco Plant*, Clarksville, VA, selected issues on microfilm, 1853 through 1865. The ones used are: (closed from April 65 to January 1866), July 28, 1861; March 31, 1865; July 21, 1861; August 9, 1861; September 23, 1859; October 25, 1859; June 17, 1859; June 10, 1859; Septmeber 24, 1858; August 23, 1861; September 30, 1859; December 17, 1860; July 1, 1859; October 14, 1859; April 22, 1860; December 15, 1859; March 23, 1867; November 25, 1859; December 10, 1859; December 2, 1859; December 19, 1859; December 10, 1859; December 30, 1859; December 7, 1860; April 22, 1860; May 15, 1861.
Bradley, Stephen E., Jr. "Edward Droomgoole's Canaan," *Virginia United Methodist Heritage*, bulletin of the Virginia Conference Historical Society of

the United Methodist Church, Vol. 30, No. 1 (Spring 2004), pp. 1–5.

Brasilia, Betty Antones de Olivaria. "North American Immigration to Brazil: Tombstone Records of the 'Campo' Cemetery," *The Virginia Magazine*, book review section, Vol. 87, No. 4, pp. 495, 496.

Brubaker, John H. III. "The Last Capital: Danville, Virginia, and the Final Days of the Confederacy," Danville Museum of Fine Arts, 1979.

Bugg, Virginia Haskins. "Rehoboth M.E. Church, Boydton Charges, Mecklenburg Coun-ty, Virginia," Brunswick-Mecklenburg Sesquicentennial Number, *Richmond Christian Advocate*, Vol. 89, No. 24 (June 21, 1934), p. 19.

Burtner, John C. "College to Aid in Agricultural Centennial, University of Oregon," *The Sunday Oregonian*, Portland, September 2, 1928, front page story which includes an 1882–1883 photograph of the faculty, including two RMC Boydton graduates.

Caknipe, John, Jr. "Richard Clausel Puryear (son of John)," *The News Progress*, Chase City, VA, March 16, 2011.

_____. "Richard Clausel Pryear (son of Samuel)," *The News Progress*, Chase City, VA, May 27, 2009.

_____. "Unsung Heroes: Rev. Leonidas Lydwell Nash," *The News Progress*, Chase City, VA, August 3, 2011.

The Confederate, newspaper of Raleigh, North Carolina, October 30, 1864, on microfilm (only issue) at Boydton Regional Library.

Editorial, *Richmond Whig*, November 7, 1865, referencing Danville troops.

Finch, Langston Easley, ed. Editorials: "The Property of Randolph Macon College," *The Mecklenburg Herald*, Clarksville, Virginia, June 29, 1870; July 27, 1870; July 30, 1870; August 10, 1870; September 21, 1870; December 1872.

Finch, Langston Easley, ed. *The Tobacco Plant*, September 25, 1869; February 20, 1870; February 18, 1870; February 26, 1870; December 8, 1869; June 22, 1870; March 22, 1869; February 2, 1870; March 15, 1870; May 8, 1873; January 17, 1875.

Francisco, James M., ed. *Tobacco Plant*, Clarksville, Virginia, selected issues on microfilm, 1858 through 1875. The ones used are: October 19, 1866; January 24, 1867; May 10, 1867.

Gayle, T.A. "Zion M.E. Church, South," Brunswick-Mecklenburg Sesquicentennial Number, *Richmond Christian Advocate*, Vol. 89, No. 24 (Richmond, Virginia, June 21, 1934), p. 31.

Gilliam, Gerald. "1872 Sale of Randolph Macon College in Boydton," *Southsider*, Vol. 17, No. 1 (January 1999).

_____. 1994 issue with a story on pages 78–80 titled "Mecklenburg Vignettes."

Haycox, Ernest. "Dr. B.J. Hawthorne, Pioneer Educator," *Portland Oregonian*, January 20, 1922, plus several other newspaper clippings undated from the Archives of the University of Oregon, Eugene, Oregon.

Kyte, Susan. "For one veteran, no idea what he would get into," *Mecklenburg Sun*, Clarksville, Virginia, November 7, 2012 (Roland Pickett Bugg).

Lander, Samuel, Jr. "Private Journal of Samuel Lander, Jr., Randolph Macon College, 1850–51." *John P. Branch Historical Papers of Randolph-Macon College*, Vol. 3 (a second journal from 1855–56 among other documents, are included on the blog, website).

Lea obituary, *Journal of the North Mississippi Conference of the Methodist Episcopal Church*, 1876, provided by Jackie Wood, University of Memphis Libraries, Lambuth Campus, Jackson, TN, as part of an e-mail.

"Life and Letters of Stephen Olin II," reproduced in the *Spartanburg Herald*, Spartanburg, South Carolina, September 5, 1926.

Midland Express, negro newspaper published in Boydton, 1893, three issues on microfilm.

Moore, Mrs. Joe E. Undated letter to the editor (c. 1960) in the *Clarksville Times*, referencing her great grandmother, Martha Bedford Jeffress, during the Civil War.

Moore, Munsey A. "Columns From Stone," *The News Progress*, Chase City, Virginia, Monday, October 3, 1983.

"Obituary Memories—Hugh Garland, in memory of, 1839." *Petersburg Index*, November 9, 1865.
Owen, William L., ed. "For Congress," *The Mecklenburg Herald*, Clarksville, Virginia, September 28, 1870.
Petersburg Index, September 23, 1867, social column, p. 2.
Pettus, Eliza Puryear. "Letter to the Editor—Reminiscense," *Chase City Progress*, November 1888 (reprinted on June 8, 1900).
Richmond Inquirer, July 7, 1872, p. 2.
Roberts, F.B. *The Chase City Progress*, Chase City, Virginia, 1905.
Rowland, J.M., ed. Brunswick-Mecklenburg Sesquicentennial Number, *Richmond Christian Advocate*, Vol. 89, No. 24, June 21, 1934, reprinted by the Old Brunswick Circuit Foundation, 2009. "Bishop John Early in Southside Virginia," pp. 45–46. "Boydton in 1867," Leroy M. Wilson, G.B. Finch, p. 48. "Edward Dromgoole," p. 49. "For God So Loved an Irishman," Maud M. Turpin, pp. 5–6. "History of Canaan Church, Mecklenburg Circuit," pp. 31, 32. "History of Kingswood Church, Mecklenburg Circuit," pp. 33–34.
Rowlett, Susan Cosby. "Reminiscence of the Civil War," *Southside Virginia Highlights*, Roanoke River Branch, Association for the Preservation of Virginia Antiquities, Fall 1993.
Sheppard, James. "Land by the Rivers: A Railroad Came to Clarksville I" (Story 377), *Mecklenburg Sun*, Clarksville, Virginia, Fall 2012. "Land by the Rivers: Garlands I," *Mecklenburg Sun*, April 16, 2008. "Land by the Rivers: Garlands II," *Mecklenburg Sun*, April 23, 2008.
Smith, The Rev. H.H. "Ebenezer Academy," Brunswick-Mecklenburg Sesquicentennial Number, *Richmond Christian Advocate*, Vol. 89, No. 24 (June 21, 1934), p. 8.
Smith, John Abernathy. "Ebenezer Academy: A Methodist School for Virginia," *Heritage*, Bulletin of the Virginia Conference Historical Society of the United Methodist Church, Vol. 30, No. 1 (Spring 2004), pp. 6–14.

Social news, *Roanoke Valley*, August 20, 1878 (visit to Boyd from Texas).
"Strange Story," *Tupelo Mississippian*, reprinted in the *Public Ledger* of Petersburg, Virginia, September 21, 1867.
Thackston, Thomas. *Banner of Truth* (one issue only, newspaper), Clarksville, Virginia, June 24, 1887.
Tobacco Plant, Clarksville, Virginia, March 10, 1867; January 10, 1868; January 16, 1868; January 31, 1868; March 10, 1868; October 27, 1868; December 20, 1868; June 25, 1867; January 24, 1867.
Townes, William, Jr. *Roanoke Valley*, Boydton, Virginia, December 30, 1871, and August 20, 1878.
Townes, William, Jr. *Tobacco Plant and Quid Nunc*, published one recorded issue in Clarksville, Virginia, 1869.
Trammell, Jack, and James E. Scanlon. "Celebrating 175 Years: 1830–2005," four part special to the *R-MC* alumni magazine, Part I, Fall 2004; Part II, Winter 2004; Part III, Spring 2005; and Part IV, Fall 2005.
Trout, W. E. III, ed. "Bateaux and River Boats of the James," *The Tiller*, Spring 1995, quarterly newsletter, Virginia Canals and Navigation Society.
Watson, Walter A. *Notes on Southside Virginia*, from the Virginia State Library, records furnished by Irby family, March 1930.
Wootton, A.J., and N.J. Wootton. *The Clipper*. Chase City, Virginia, May 8, 1873, p. 1.

Archives and Collections

Birmingham-Southern College Archives, Library of Special Collections and BSC Library Archives, www.bsc.edu/library/.
Boyd, Alfred. Administrator receipts from 1846 through 1863. A copy in the possession of Larry Smith of Boydton purchased at a yard sale, with a copy made for this author, brought to the Southside Regional Library for review.
Census Records of the United States government: 1840, 1850, 1860, 1870, 1880, 1900, 1910, 1920 and 1930.

Bibliography

Duke University Archives, the David M. Rubenstein Rare Book and Manuscript Library files of William Baskervill, William H. Phillips, J.F.W. Boyd and Company, Boydton Hotel, note of R.P. Alexander and Alfred Boyd papers.

Flannigan, Mrs. Nate. Scrapbook, 1899, unpublished, collection of newspaper and magazine illustrations of famous (to her) people. (Sketch of the Rev. W.C. Starr, D.D., from an old newspaper on final page in poor condition, copied and sketched by the late Arlene McKinney Wootton in 2011.)

Gilliam, Gerald. "Boyd Family Records, notebook labeled 'Rainey Letters,'" Southside Regional Letters, Boydton, Virginia (advertisement of sale of Sydnor estate).

Hutcheson, Herbert F. Eleven page draft, historical incidents and anecdotes about Randolph Macon College, Boydton, prepared in 1937 for the *South Hill Enterprise*, from Hutcheson and friends in the county court and government. In the scrapbooks of his deceased former secretary, Mary McKinney, in the possession of Glen and Lisa Gillispie, Chase City, Virginia, pp. 1–11.

Irby, Mary Virginia. Notes and unpublished manuscripts from files in the Burkeville Public Library in Nottoway County, 2009, including notes of the Irby reunion held in 1985 with over 400 in attendance.

Mabry, W. Alexander. *The Diary of Edward Dromgoole Sims: June 17–August 2, 1834*. Ashland, VA: Randolph-Macon College, 1954.

McGraw-Page Library Archives. Checkbook, Randolph Macon College—Boydton, 1862 and 1863, Randolph-Macon College, Ashland, VA.

McGraw-Page Library Archives. Minutes from the Randolph Macon College Board of Trustees meetings in 1863, and the August 1864, special called meeting in Boydton.

Mecklenburg Circuit. *Church Book for the Mecklenburg Circuit Commencing 1833 at Randolph Macon College* (through about 1860), copy in possession of Rubinette Neimann, Harrisburg, Virginia, 2010 (original donated by her to McGraw-Page Library Archives).

Mecklenburg County Circuit Court Books, Vols. 5, 6 and 9.

Mecklenburg County Deed Books 32–325, 32–350, 33–466, 367–425, and several others enumerated in text "Men Licensed to Practice Medicine."

Mecklenburg County Marriage, Death and Birth Records: 1800 to 1860 (most also on microfilm reels at the Southside Library in Boydton)

Mecklenburg County Register of men licensed to preach, 1800 to 1860.

Mecklenburg County Tithe Record, partial, Fall 1765.

Mecklenburg County Will Books: 15–258 and others enumerated in the text.

Minutes of the Concord Baptist Association Annual Conferences, 1869 to 1890. Selected volumes referencing Bennett Puryear, South Hill, Virginia.

Nottoway County Deed Books: 6–300, plus 14 others pre–1813 and 11 after.

"Nottoway County Senators: 1835–1860," from *The General Assembly of Virginia July 30, 1619–January 11, 1978: A Bicentennial Register of Members*.

Nottoway County Will Books: VI-198, VI-296, VI-525.

Rose, Dr. Latinus Irving. Journal and business records, 1859 through 1869; a copy is in the possession of Steven and Gray Rose, Lacrosse, Virginia (originals on file with the Virginia Historical Society, Richmond, Virginia).

"Senators Representing Nottoway County from 1835 to 1860," from *The General Assembly of Virginia July 30, 1619–January 11, 1978: A Bicentennial Register of Members*. Richmond, VA, 1978.

Slatten, Richard. "Matriculation Book: Randolph Macon College, Part 1," transcribed and copied for *The Virginia Genealogy Society, Magazine of Virginia Genealogy*, August 1984, Vol. 3, 1837 to 1839, pp. 7–17.

_____. Part II, December 1984, Vol. 4, 1839 to 1847, pp. 32–40.

_____. Part III, February 1985, Vol. 1, 1847 to 1851, pp. 20–29.

"South Carolina C.S.A.: Statewide Units, Militia and Reserves," library manuscript, North Myrtle Beach, S.C., public library.

"South Carolina: Smiling Faces. Beautiful Places," historical districts map by Department of Tourism, 2010.

Southwestern University, Smith Library Center, Special Collections, Georgetown, Texas (several resources).

"Story of Ashbury" (Leigh L., Perquimans Co., NC, November 23, 1795), University of North Carolina Archives, Chapel Hill, North Carolina; online references.

University of Memphis Libraries, Lambuth Campus, Jackson, TN, records of "Lorenzo Lea Chronology."

_____. brief records and emails (February 29, 2012; March 9 and 15, 2012) of data about Amos W. Jones, Saunders, and the Memphis Conference Female Institute 1869 Catalogue.

University of North Carolina, Chapel Hill, Archives, papers of Charles Puryear.

University of Oregon, Special Collections and Archives, copies of RMC documents from file of Benjamin J. Hawthorne plus copies of documents from other professors at RMC Boydton and documents by R-MC Ashland President Duncan.

Virginia Baptist Conference Historical Society, Professor Bennett Puryear Collection, Archives, University of Richmond, Richmond, VA (site visit and records review, Summer, 2010).

Virginia Methodist Conference, Glen Allen, VA (several resources).

William R. Perkins Library, "Portraits in the Gothic Reading Room," Duke University, c. 2005.

William R. Perkins Library, "Uncommon Leaders: The Presidents of Duke University." Duke University Archives, Durham, NC, 2004).

Wofford College Archives, telephone conversations, 2011.

Wright, Virginia Woody, unpublished archived records of John W. Wootton and family from 1850 through 1890.

Brochures and Monographs

Bugg, Ron A. "Military Death Records for the Clarksville Memorial," unpublished monograph, Clarksville, Virginia, 2004.

Bugg, William E. "Journal of William Emanuel Bugg," unpublished journal, Southside Regional Library, Boydton, Virginia, 1890.

Clark County Historical Association, brochure, "The Civil War in Clark County, Arkansas," c. 2005.

Heritage Convocation Bulletin, "Old Randolph Macon College Historic Highway Marker," dedication pamphlet, October 29, 1994.

Hollister, Gayle. "Kin and Kin to Kin," self-published manuscript, now online, Virginia, c. 1973.

Jones, Joe B., Scott Hudlow, and Charles M. Downing. Report, *A Phase II Cultural Resource Investigation of Archaeological Sites 44MC482, 44MC484, and 44MC 485, and the Randolph-Macon College Historic District, Proposed Route 58 Widening Project, Route 15 to Boydton, Mecklenburg County, Virginia. Project: 6058–058-E25, PE101, C501*, William and Mary Center for Archaeological Research, Williamsburg, Virginia.

Smith, Jack K.T. "Historic Tulip, Arkansas," dissertation. Fayetteville: University of Arkansas, 1989.

Interviews and Correspondence

Bugg, Ron A., CWO-3, Retired, U.S. Army. Several interviews with and unpublished family archives of John W. Bugg, a work in process, 2010.

Danville Museum of Fine Arts and History, formerly Major William T. Sutherlin Home (last Capitol of the Confederacy). Field trip, photographs and tour, April 2013.

Johnston, William. North Carolina Methodist Historian, e-mail to the author, August 2012, "Caswell Circuit," "Granville Circuit," "Oxford Station" ministers.

Language professor's house, Joe and Martha Ware, Boydton—photo taken by author.

Lankford, Lyle. Telephone conversation with author; campus historian, Vanderbilt University, Nashville, Tennessee, March 2011.

Minnich, Virginia Puryear Newton, e-mail, July 21, 2011, to author, re: ancestry.com Burwell Kendrick Harrison research story.

Rackley, Robert, research assistant, Central Methodist University. Several emails and telephone conversations in 2011 and 2012.

Shelton, Dr. William, and Rhonda Shelton. Interviews by author in 2010, 2012 and 2013, of the inactive Southside Virginia Historical Society and occupant-owners of Steward Hall, Randolph Macon College in Boydton, Virginia, since the 1960s.

_____. Copy of letter they received, dated July 14, 1996, from "Carolyn of Richmond," (rest of name and address deleted in the copy) outlining her research about Hezekiah Leigh and family.

Stallard, Kathryn. E-mails to the author, February 2012; director of Special Collections and Archives, A. Frank Smith, Jr., Library Center, Southwestern University, Georgetown, Texas.

Stone, DeWitt B. Jr. E-mail to the author, February 12, 2012; special assistant to the president, Lander University (and grandson to Samuel Lander, Jr.).

Internet Resources

Ancestor.com. Census records, Civil War amnesty records, family genealogy records, war pension records. http://www.ancestor.com.

Bailey, James H. Master's thesis, George Washington University. "Anthony M. Keiley and "The Keiley Incident." *Virginia Magazine of History and Biography*, Vol. 67, no. 1 (Jan. 1959), pp. 65–81. http://www.jstor.org/stable/4246511.

City of Richmond Directories: 1877–1890. http://search.ancestry.com/search/db.aspx?dbid=4419.

A Directory of Representative Business and Professional Men of Augusta and Stanton County, Virginia, 1890 edition. Rohrer & Diamond, 1899. FHL Collection 6015631–6015632. Digital version at Ancestry.com.

Fishbach, Michael R. Records of Disposition, internet archive, ourmedia.org, professor of history at R-MC Ashland, Irby, eBook, Open Library, edited December 17, 2011.

Heritage Quest, census searches through Southside Regional Library, Boydton, Virginia, www.heritagequestonline.com/. http://www.archive.org/stream/historyofrandolph.

Jones, William B. "To Survive and Excel: The Story of Southwestern University, 1840–2000." Georgetown, TX: Southwestern University, 2006. http://southwestern.edu/library/documents/ToSurviveAndExcel.pdf.

Moore, W.H. *Historical Oration on the Life and Labors of Rev. Hezekiah G. Leigh D.D.* https://archive.org/details/historicaloratio01moorInternet Archive.

New Bern Craven County Public Library, Will Abstracts. http://newbern.cpclib.org/research/wills/willsbl.htm.

"Obituary of Dr. Samuel D. Sanders," *Georgetown Commerce*, Georgetown, Williamson County, Texas, Friday, January 30, 1903. http:// www.arlingtonlibrary.org/files/journal1903pdf.

Oklahoma Historical Society, *Chronicles of Oklahoma*, 2001, Vol. 15, No. 2, June 1937. Digital.library.okstate.edu/chronicles/vol5/vol5,228.html.

The Rhodes Trust, Rhodes Scholars: Complete List, 1903–2013. www.rhodeshouse.ox.ac.uk/section/rhodes-scholars-complete-list.

Samuel Lander Documentary Project, www.Samuel-lander-movie.blogspot.com.

Sherrill, William L. *A Brief History of Rev. Samuel Lander, Senior, and His Wife Eliza Ann (Miller) Lander: Their Two Sons William Lander and Samuel*

Lander, and Their Grandson Samuel A. Weber. Greensboro, NC: Advocate Press, 1918. https://archive.org/details/briefhistoryofre00sher.

Sketch received from the Old Brunswick Circuit Foundation, quarterly meeting, held at Ebenezer Academy in September 2012. Sketch of Ebenezer Academy donated to the foundation by artist V. S. Manson, dated August 30, 2001. http://www.oldbrunswick.org/sites.html.

South Carolina troops, 2nd Regiment, South Carolina Infantry, and 21st South Carolina Infantry. http:// www.fold3.com/civilwar/sc.troops.

Southwestern University: Root Institutions, Student Directory with Photos, http://www.swedu/lib/.

"Three-legged Willie." http://www.three-legged-willie.org/cemetery/ioofgeorgetown.

Virginia Military Institute. "Garland," "Glazebrook," "Boyd," and others. http://www.VMI.edu, archives:

Index

Adams, Catherine Speight 272
Adams, Edward A. 273, 276
Adams, Richard E.G. 276
Adams, W.D. 148, 231
Adams, William 273
Adkins, A.K. 90
Ainger, Sophia 35
Alabama 3, 28, 31, 39, 44, 51, 95, 103, 106–110, 117, 141, 169, 181, 183, 196, 244, 245, 248, 250–254, 274, 275
Alexander, James T. 94–96, 98, 253
Alexander, Mark, Jr. 98
Alexander, Mark, III 98, 99
Alexander, Nathaniel 7, 8, 12, 13, 98
Alexander, Dr. R.P. 98, 99
Alexander, Robert P. 96–98, 124, 253
Alexander, Sally P. 99
Alexander family 8, 43
Allemong, Ella Virginia 174
American Bible Society 82
Anderson, Edwin A. 253, 283
Anderson, Fred 3, 302
Anderson, John Thompson 76
Anderson, Mary Jane 106
Anderson, Phillip 76
Anderson, T.F. 166
Anderson's Light Artillery 232, 237, 243, 261, 265
Andrew College 33, 84
Andrews, Rev. G.W. 285, 287, 288
Andrews, Varney C. 260, 261
Andrews Female College 198
Archer, Allin 71
Archer, Peter W. 275
Archer, Philmer 71, 136, 231

Archer, Thomas S. 253
Archer, W.A. 149
Archer, William A. 151, 152, 159, 231, 276
Archer's Battalion 258, 259
Armistead, George W. 266, 276
Armistead, Martha Savage 266
Armistead, Robert A. 266
Armistead's Brigade 131
Arnold, B.L. 159, 194
Arnold, Benjamin 36, 148, 159
Arnold, Benjamin J. 149–153, 277
Arnold, Benjamin L. 231, 232, 236, 260, 276
Arnold, Benjamin Lee 195, 266
Arnold, Benjamin W. 249, 277
Arnold, Ernest White 232
Arnold, Harry Lea 231
Arnold, Hartwell 54
Arnold, Joseph D. 249, 260, 277
Arnold, Keziah 148
Arnold, Minnie M. White 232
Arnold, P.H. 149, 232
Arnold, Phoebe 148
Arnold, Solomon 148
Arnold, William M. 287, 288
Arnold, Addie Lea 231
Arthur, Dr. F.G. 275
Arthur, Thomas S. 275, 277
Asbury, Bishop Francis 9, 11, 20
Asbury, New Jersey 82
Asbury Mission 31
Askew, Rev. Joseph (Josiah) L. 273, 277

Atkins, S.G. 121
Atkins, William T. 129, 147
Atkinson, John Wilder 249, 277
August, Rev. Peter F. 271, 285
Avory, Dr. James Corban 239
Avory, Myrta Lockett 138, 238
Ayres, John G. 151, 152, 232

Bagby, Adam C. 88, 277
Bagby, Bennett W. 150, 232
Bagby, Capt. 99
Bagby, Jesse P. 263, 277
Bagby, John 54
Bailey, Robert A. 151
Bailey, Robert W. 149, 152, 232
Bailey, William T. 118, 120, 260, 277
Bailey's Buoy 254
Bailey's Market 215
Bain, George W. 56
Baird, Charles W. 27
Baird, Rev. Mr. 114
bank (building in Fayette) 180
Bank of Courtland 267
Bank of Mecklenburg 118, 119
Bank of Thurmond 143
Bank of Union Springs 252
Baptist, Richard L. 45, 128
Baptiste, Richard H. 25, 66
Baptiste, Richard H., Jr. 25
Baptiste, Samuel G. 25
Barr, James R. 149, 150, 233
Baskervill, Charles 16, 25
Baskervill, John W. 25
Baskervill, Dr. Robert 56, 253
Baskervill, William R. 25

315

Index

Baskervill, William, Sr. 55
Baskerville, George D. 61
Baskerville, George, Jr. 61
Baskerville, Capt. Robert Dortch 124, 134
Baskerville, North Carolina 74, 234
Bass, Rev. Rowland G. 76, 105
Bass, William H. 206, 271, 277, 285
Batte, William H. 277
Battle, William S. 146
Beale, Elizabeth Tayloe Corbin 154
Beale, R.H. 277
Beale, Walter, III 2
Beard, Clough S. 277
Becker, James 8, 168, 218, 291
Beckman, Thomas M. 149, 233
Benaugh, George W. 277
Bennett, Rev. William W. 211, 216, 220, 227, 277
Bigger, Capt. David 39, 74
Blackmon, J.A. 212
Blackwell, Rev. Dr. John Chapman 34, 35, 51, 54, 155, 168, 210, 214, 215, 241, 277, 283–285
Blackwell, Rev. John Davenport 36, 54, 128, 163, 249, 262, 277, 285
Blackwell, John Davidson 35, 36, 88, 267, 277
Blackwell, William F. 277
Blackwell, William T. 13
Blain, George W. 274, 279
Blake, Thomas W. 277
Blanche, Elizabeth 102
Blanche, Emily Fitts 73
Blanche, Ezekiel 43, 71, 73, 95, 102, 277, 284, 286
Blanche, Mary Alexander 43
Blanche, William E. 128
Blandon, Capt. Green 24
Blankenship, Rev. Capt. Prof. James Edwin 159, 162, 163, 253, 284
Blankenship, Margaret "Maggie" 253
Booker, Capt. Rev. George E. 253, 277
Border Grange Bank 138
Bostick, Mary Ann Aliza 28
Boswell, Martha Nelson 122
Boswell, Col. Thomas T. 120–122, 249, 271, 277
Bourland, H.A. 172, 176
Bowles, H.C. 105
Bowles, Dr. Samuel 175

Boyd, Alexander 21, 22, 38
Boyd, Alexander, Jr. 16, 62, 69, 292
Boyd, Alfred G. 128, 146, 147, 248
Boyd, Frances W. 7, 25, 126
Boyd, Isabella 25
Boyd, J. 56
Boyd, John 112, 139, 218
Boyd, John E. 146, 147
Boyd, John G. 77, 208, 277, 291
Boyd, Lucy Goode Finch 128
Boyd, Martha Emmett 128
Boyd, Nathaniel P. 150, 233
Boyd, Dr. Richard 78, 95, 128, 146, 245, 277
Boyd, Robert A. 150–153, 233
Boyd, Sally 77
Boyd, Tabitha Walker 128
Boyd, Thomas H. 99, 263
Boyd, William Henry 123
Boyd and Goode 106
Boyd Hotel 7, 21, 38, 292, 305
Boyd Street 75
Boyd Tavern 22, 24, 62, 69
Boydton Academy 15, 35, 38, 61
Boydton cavalry 96, 127, 147
Boydton cemetery 89
Boydton Circuit 56
Boydton Courthouse 16, 23, 41
Boydton Dirt Road 14, 67
Boydton drug store 97
Boydton Hotel 22, 62, 69, 119, 126, 127, 146, 176, 218, 292
Boydton Institute 58
Boydton masonic lodge 226
Boydton Methodist Church 56, 118
Boydton militia 100, 125, 130, 246, 267
Boydton Plank Toll Road 62, 69, 114, 127, 162, 247
Boydton Preparatory Department 100, 161, 285
Boydton Presbyterian cemetery 41, 129, 132, 291
Boydton Presbyterian Church 38, 56, 132, 134, 135
Boydton Savings Bank 26, 45, 61, 128
Boydton wagon factory 189
Bracey, Betty A. Simmon 60
Bracey, Carstairs 304
Bracey, Dr. Hugh David 60, 260, 277

Bracey, Mary Cornelia Dupuis-Yongue 60
Bracey, Olivia 60
Bracey, Pascal 59
Bracey, Susan 134, 188, 292, 304
Bracey, William Hicks 59, 260
Bradley, Dr. Stephen 9, 291
Brame, David 7
Brame, Elizabeth 66
Brame, John 14
Brame, Dr. John Baker 75
Brame, John T. 14, 74, 75, 277
Brame, Karen Happuch 66
Brame, Robert Harper 75
Brame, Samuel 66
Brame, Sarah P. 14, 74
Brame, Thomas R. 76
Brame, William A. 261, 277
Brame Tanning Yard 98, 187
Branch, Maj. E. 258
Branch, E.A. 90
Branch, James 204, 245
Branch, Capt. James 265
Branch, Maj. James 268, 277
Branch, Capt. Thomas, Jr. 204, 245, 256, 257, 277
Branch, Thomas W. 214, 216, 228, 245, 249, 253, 256
Branch's Artillery 256
Brandon, Victor M. 277
Brazil 79, 120, 200, 201
Briggs, Samuel 245
British and Foreign Bible Society 212
Brooks, James 66
Brooks, Wanda 2
Browder, W.A. 212
Brown, A.S. 84
Brown, Rev. Alexander Gustavos 84, 285
Brown, Daniel 20, 264
Brown, Edward S. 19, 264, 277
Brown, Fanny A. Cooksey 84, 285
Brown, Capt. G. Aitken 265
Brown, J.T. 149
Brown, J. Thompson 150, 233
Brown, James L. 19
Brown, John 25, 32, 47, 96, 183, 254
Brown, John D. 187
Brown, Nancy 84
Brown "house" 19, 44
Brown "Store District" 207
Bruce, Hon. Col. Charles 125, 253
Bruce, Capt. Charles, Jr. 125, 126, 253

Index

Bruce, James 14, 18, 130
Bruce, John 125
Brunswick Academy 10, 74, 226
Brunswick Circuit 10, 11, 309, 313
Brunswick County 9–12, 39, 43, 44, 101, 102, 106, 182, 206, 238–240, 256, 259, 264, 268
Brunswick Grays 10
Brunswick Guards 101, 259
Buckingham County 15, 18, 36, 44, 58, 88, 151, 152, 168, 230, 232, 234, 270
Buckingham Female Institute 9, 11, 14, 35, 44, 113, 191
Buffalo Junction 69, 133
Buffalo Springs Resort 20, 26, 27, 62, 75, 97, 102, 210, 246
Bugg, Francis (Hatsell) 37, 68, 69, 146, 289
Bugg, James 55
Bugg, James Richard 264
Bugg, John 68, 167
Bugg, John W(esley) 55, 96, 167, 168, 263, 264
Bugg, Mary Francis 68, 69, 146, 163
Bugg, Roland Pickett 299
Bugg, Ron A. 3, 295-297
Bugg, Samuel 32, 69, 289
Bugg, Sarah Leona Ingram 163
Bugg, Virginia Haskins 7, 146, 291
Bugg, William Emanuel 297
Bugg, William Henry 264
Bugg family 76
Bullock, Ann Harriett 123
"bummers" 164, 192
Burnley, George W. 277
Burwell, Letitia 304
Burwell, Mary Cole 38
Burwell, Peyton R. 74, 220
Burwell Armistead 15
Butler, Alexander 115
Butler, Charles 115
Butler, Emma 115
Butler, Rev. George Emory 115, 116, 149, 150, 152, 159, 233, 249, 277
Butler, Henry A. 115
Butler, Mary Wyche Reeves 115
Butler, R.E. 66

Cabell, Lewis W. 245
Cabell, Mary 245

Cabell, William M. 245, 277
California 29, 105, 115, 117, 190, 232
Calvary Church 18
Campbell, Archibald A. 43
Campbell, Elizabeth 240
Campbell, Joel Henry 239
Campbell, Rev. T.S. 228
Campbell, Thomas H. 205, 279
Canaan 9–11, 291
Capers, Bishop Rev. William 31, 156
Carlisle, Prof. James Henry 50, 141, 142
Carney, I. 56
Carr, Georgia 162
Carr, Panthea 162
Carr, William, Jr. 162
Carr, Prof. Capt. William B. 88–90, 94, 97, 155, 159, 161, 162, 189, 208, 284
Carr, Dr. William P. 162
Carrington, Dr. Cabell 125
Carrington, Mildred 166
Carter, David Norfleet 66, 96, 146, 147, 164, 188
Carter, Elizabeth A. 65
Carter, Maj. George Waigle 96
Carter, J.D. 148, 149
Carter, J.T. 46, 264, 275
Carter, John 158
Carter, John T. 17, 66
Carter, Karen Happuch Brame 66
Carter, Margaret E. 57
Carter, Pattie B. 168
Carter, Rev. William 66, 130, 134
Carter, William J. 130, 131, 149–153, 233
Carter, William N. 66, 163, 277
Catholic 10, 34, 48, 153, 258
Cawthorne, Mary Ellen White 85
certificate of disability 60, 61, 73, 109, 118, 241, 242, 259, 260, 263
Chalmers, W.M. 148, 149
Chamberlain, John L. 89, 277
Chambers, Edward R. 41–43, 54, 61, 71, 77, 78, 96, 97, 128, 175, 208, 214, 220, 222, 224, 241, 261, 284
Chambers, Harvey H. 42, 253, 261
Chambers, Lucy Goode Tucker 41

Chambers, Mary F. 107
Chambers, Rosa C. 246
Chambers, Virginia Betts 41
Chambers County, Alabama 103, 169
Chambers Mill 250, 254
Chambliss, John, Jr. 99
Chambliss, Col. John R. 95, 96, 99, 249, 253, 260
Chambliss "Grays" 123, 129, 260
Chase City, Virginia 56, 75, 117, 119, 168, 194, 264, 298, 299
Chase City Clipper 165
Chase City hospital 75
Chase City Progress 70
Cheek, Charles C. 49
Cheek, William H. 249, 277
Chestnut, Mary Boykin 239
Childs, John W. 76
Christian, John E. 264, 266, 277
Christian, Rev. W.H. 264
Christian, William H. 261, 266, 270, 277
Christiansville 25, 31, 39, 55, 71, 75, 117, 127, 128, 144, 167, 168, 181, 194, 271, 295
circuit rider 11, 17, 73, 74, 85
Claiborne, Rev. John C. 256
Claiborne, John H. 277
Claiborne, Dr. John T. 133, 245, 256, 277
Clark, Archibald 278
Clay, Virginia 107
Clegg, B. 56
Clegg, Rev. Baxter 78, 102
Clegg, David 78
Clements, J.S. 56
Clemons, Junious L. 278
Clopton, Dr. Alford 106
Clopton, David 103, 106, 107, 245, 278
Clopton, Martha E. Ligon 107
Clopton, Mary F. Chambers 107
Clopton, Sarah Kendrick 106
Clopton, Virginia Clay 107
Cobb, K.R. 149
Cobb, Kenneth Arthur 152, 174, 233
Cobb, R.R. 149
Cogbill, Benjamin D. 126, 155, 156
Cogbill, Benjamin E. 156
Cogbill, Bettie W. 156
Cogbill, Harriett H. Boyd 126
Cogbill, Harriett R. 156
Cogbill, Laura B. 156

Index

Cogbill, Lucy Boyd 126
Cogbill, Mary T. 156
Cogbill, Virginia 156
Coleman, A. Buford 149, 157, 233
Coleman, Gene 2
Coleman, Col. Henry Eaton, Jr. 73, 122–125, 131, 250
Coleman, Samuel Francis 150–152, 233
Coleman, William 66
Coleman Creek 98, 187
Coleman's Ferry 122
College Avenue 16, 185
college "hotel" 17, 20, 43, 51, 71, 162, 189
Collier, Dabney 74
Collier County, Georgia 246
Colquitt's Brigade, 6th Georgia 60
Compton B.A. 149, 151, 152
Compton, R.A. 159
Compton, Robert A. 233, 278
Concord Baptist Association 174, 310
Conner, Francis A. 278
Conner, Sarah Tillman 79
Conner, William G. 110, 134, 196, 278
Connor, William G. 278
Conrad, Bear 136
Conrad, Elizabeth 136
Conrad, Janetta 136
Conrad, Susan 136
Conrad, Thomas 30, 98
Conrad, Virginia 136
Conrad, William 136
conscription 59, 121, 140, 146, 164, 254–259
Conscription Act 59
Conscription Bureau 189
Cooksey, Fannie A. 84, 285
Corinth Female Academy 21
Corprew, Adeline 180
Corprew, Adeline (Ada) T. Rogers 25
Corprew, Francis 51
Corprew, Mary 47
Corprew, Oliver Hagen Percy 25, 48, 51, 53, 62, 71, 96, 97, 113, 14, 178–180, 208, 210, 245, 278, 284, 286
Corprew, Thomas 26
Corprew, Thomas Jefferson 180
Corprew Boulevard 181
Cosby, Dabney 37
Cosby, Dabney, Jr. 37
Courthouse Branch 75
Covington, R.C. 53

Cowan, Rev. Mr. 16
Cowles, Alice Frances 287, 288
Cowles, Rev. Henry B. 43, 86, 191, 224, 228, 256
Cowles, Henry H., Jr. 89, 113, 256, 278, 289
Cowles, James R. 150, 152, 234, 256, 257
Cowles, William I. 278
Craddock, Elizabeth 175
Craddock, Dr. J.M. 175
Craven, Braxton 32, 33, 74, 83, 84, 199, 272, 278
Crawford, "Frank" 47, 83
Crawley, Charles W. 285
Creek Indians 31, 107
Crenshaw, A. Debreld 89, 204, 253, 278
Crenshaw, Allen 44, 206
Crenshaw, Anthony D. 262, 278
Crenshaw, Archer D. 202, 253, 278
Crenshaw, Ira Irving 44, 181, 191, 206, 275, 278, 286
Crenshaw, Mary Cabiness 44
Crenshaw, William N. 278
Croft, Isaac C. 278
Crowder, Dr. Harold 3
Crowder children 102
Crute, Dr. Charles B. 58, 278
Crute, Judge J.M. (W) 58, 278

Daley, J.J. 128, 214
Daly, John S. James, Esq. 214
Daly, Col. Samuel 214
Dance, John Fletcher 51, 264, 278
Dance, Rev. Matthew M. 51
Dance, Matthew S. 51, 76
Dance, William G. 51
Daniel, Ann Harriett Bullock 123
Daniel, Nathaniel Chesley 123
Daniel, Sallie 123
Dantzler, Jacob M. 110, 250
Dantzler, Col. Olin M. 110, 197, 250, 278
Danville Arsenal 122, 240
Danville Bank 138, 213
Danville CSA Capital 233
Danville CSA Hospital 122, 240
Danville District, Arkansas 163
Danville Female College 35, 36, 49, 102, 132–136, 138, 154, 161, 241

Danville male academy 136
Danville, Museum of Fine Arts and History 138, 139, 311
Danville Ordnance Company 137, 194, 263
Danville Regiment 204
Darden, William Abraham 272
Darden, William Augustus 272
Darden, Harriett Speight 272
Davenport College 80
Davidson, A.F. 96
Davis, A.J. 148, 149
Davis, Elizabeth 54
Davis, Elizabeth Ann Jones 54
Davis, Elizabeth Taylor Corban Beale 154
Davis, Capt. George B. 121, 154
Davis, President Jefferson 41, 44, 112, 137, 138, 213, 216, 266
Davis, John 278
Davis, Joshua 54
Davis, M.H. 58
Davis, Martha Evans (Mattie) 161
Davis, Rebecca 258
Davis, Richard Beale 257, 278
Davis, Sallie Virginia Dante 123
Davis, Stephanie 3
Davis, Susan Swepson 123
Davis, Wilber T. 278
Davis, William Hoomes 151, 257, 275
Davis, William S. 54, 89, 113, 122, 252, 260, 278
Davis, William S. (son of Joshua) 54, 245, 284
Davis, Williams T. 35, 138, 159, 161, 214, 215, 253, 256, 278, 284, 287
Davis, Abrams and Lyons 146
Daws, Howell Wilkerson 66
Daws, Sallie A. 66
Day, Mary 108
Dean, Rev. James A. 102, 286
Deems, Annie Disoway 83
Deems, Prof. Rev. Dr. Charles F. 30, 74, 81–83, 90, 278, 284
Deems, Edward M. 83
Deems, Rev. Francis M. 83
Deems, Theodore Disoway 83
De Graffenreidt, John 102, 173
De Graffenreidt, Thomas 102

Index

De Graffenreidt, William 102, 245, 278
demerits 93, 140, 230, 242
Denton, William H. 272, 278
Dibble, Samuel 141
Dibrell, Anthony 191, 260, 278
Dibrell, W.S. 149
Dibrell, Watson S. 150, 234
Dickinson College 82, 174
diplomas 87, 92, 100, 131, 136, 142, 153, 154, 169, 177, 231–243
Dirtson, Anna White 31
Disoway, Annie 83
Disoway, Gabriel 82, 278
Dodson, Edward 74
Dodson, F.B. 189
Dodson, T.D. 188
Doggett, David 140, 142, 268
Doggett, Bishop Rev. Prof. David Seth 45, 46, 90, 136, 146, 228, 278, 284, 289
Doggett, John 46
Doggett, Martha Ann Gwathney 46
Doggett, Mary Smith 46
Doggett, Rowland 278
Dollinger, Frederick George 287, 288
Doub, John 73
Doub, Peter 73, 74
Doub, William C. 74, 272, 278
Douthitt, Alpha 287, 288
Dowdell, James F. 278
Dowdell, Hon. Col. James Ferguson 103, 108, 109, 169, 250, 278
Dowdell, James Render 109
Dowdell, Miss Farley 108
Dowdell, Sarah H. Render Lewis 108
Dowdell, Susan Lewis 103
Dowdell, "Warwick" 103
Dowdell, "Zeno" 103
Drake, Henry F. 278
Draper, Antonia Coetannas de Parva Pereia Gardner 39
Draper, Dr. John 39, 40, 58, 127
Draper Boarding School 31
Draperville 39
Dred Scott decision 76, 77, 84
Drew, Capt. Ben C. 254, 278
Drew, Edward 9, 10, 11, 39, 61, 304
Drew, Edward, Jr. 11
Drew, Edward Dromgoole Sims see Sims
Drew, George Coke 11

Drew, Rebecca Mary Walton 11
Drew, Thomas 12
Drew University 75
Dromgoole's chapel 11
Drysdale, Capt. R.H. 272
Duffy, Kate E. 178
Dugger, James A. 66
Dugger, James B. 269
Dugger, James B., Jr. 144, 163, 269, 278
Dugger, Richard A. 144
Dugger and Gary (tailors) 144, 145, 163
Duke 4, 74, 80, 83, 293, 310
Duke, Sallie 72
Duncan, Alice Amanda Needler Piedmont 48, 54
Duncan, David R. (Elder) 45
Duncan, David R. (Younger) 48
Duncan, Prof. Rev. Dr. David S. 45, 48–50, 54, 69, 90, 141, 142, 191, 233, 284
Duncan, DeArcey Paul "Old Pad" 48
Duncan, Pres. Rev. Dr. James Armstrong 48, 49, 54, 191, 211, 211, 217, 278, 283, 302
Duncan, Mary Eliza 50
Duncan, Robinson 49
Duncan, Thomas C. 48
Duncan, Van 54
Duncan, Bishop Rev. William Wallace 48, 149, 254
Duncan, South Carolina (formerly Duncan's Crossroads) 48, 185
Dunn R.E. 149, 151
Dunn, Robert 234
DuPre, Warren 24, 86, 87, 113, 114, 141, 175, 196, 278, 286

Eagle Point Mills 65
Early, Elizabeth B. 18
Early, Bishop John 12, 17–19, 42, 43, 176, 208, 213, 228, 309
Early, Gen. Jubal 18, 242
Early, L.L. Hunter 18
Early, Thomas H. 18
Early, William Ashby 18
Easter, John 11, 61
Easters Church 61
Eaton, Charles 123
Eaton, Lt. Col. Charles, Jr. 123
Eaton, James 123
Eaton, Gen. Thomas 123
Eaton, Col. William 123

Eaton, William, Jr. 123
Ebenezer Academy 9–11, 74, 106, 182, 206, 292, 313
Edmonds, Capt. 122
Edmondson, Sheriff Charles F. 125
Edwards, John E. 214, 215, 227, 228, 266, 278
Edwards, Rev. John Ellis 234
Edwards, Landon Brame 234, 266, 278
Edwards, Leroy S. 88, 257, 278
Edwards, Rev. Dr. William Emory 144, 149, 152, 154, 228, 234, 278
Elder, Thomas C. 270, 278
Eldridge, Henry B. 264, 274
Eldridge Bowling 264
Emory, Dr. Joseph 195
Emory and Henry 34, 76, 102, 179, 267, 285
Emory College 34, 50, 103, 110, 178
endowment 50, 86, 88, 91, 92, 113, 141, 176, 177, 218, 220, 225, 256
Enslin, Theodore 286
Epes, Capt. Branch Jones 265
Epes, Thomas R. 265, 279
Eppes, George F. 279
Estes, E.H. 149, 234
Evans, Edward John (slave) 54
Evans, Edward, Jr. (slave) 43
Evans, Elizabeth (Slave) 42
Evans, John (slave) 43, 44, 54, 294
Evans, Lucy (slave) 43
Evans, V. Norvel Hansard 29, 293
Exchange Bank 66, 164
Exchange Hotel 26, 44, 144, 288

Fanning, James F. 279
Farinholt, Capt. Benjamin F. 122
Farmville, Virginia 37, 58, 59, 75, 77, 154, 191, 204, 241
Farmville Female College 21, 35
Farmville General Hospital 242, 261, 262, 263
Farrar, Hettie 117
Farrar, Martha W. 74
Farrar, Samuel G. 74, 125, 126, 129, 188, 250, 278
Farrar, W.H. 149
Farrar, William Hamilton 234

Index

Ferguson, Rev. Richard "Preacher" 204, 262, 263, 279
Few, Dr. William Preston 80
Field, Dr. Alexander 16
Fields, John 26
Fields United Methodist Church 67, 165
15th Virginia 249
5th Virginia Cavalry 135, 238
56th Virginia Infantry 10, 120, 271, 297
53rd North Carolina Regiment 83
Finch, Rev. Adam 74, 127
Finch, Adam T., Jr. 75
Finch, Adam Tyree 75
Finch, Edwin T. 118
Finch, Elizabeth D. Morton 75
Finch, George B. 100, 108, 118, 128, 220, 224, 267, 279
Finch, John F. 74
Finch, Langston Easley 42, 56, 119, 127, 128, 186–188, 218–220, 224, 279
Finch, Lucy 74, 127
Finch, Lucy Goode 128
Finch, Martha W. Farrar 74
Finch, R.M. 188
Finch, Richard Henry 119
Finch, Tabitha Walker Boyd 128
Finch, Tyree 128, 250
Finch, William Carrington 75
1st Georgia Infantry 273
First National of Bank Sheffield 107
1st North Carolina Artillery 273
1st North Carolina Infantry 80
1st Virginia Artillery 205, 245
1st Virginia Cavalry 265
1st Virginia Infantry 247
1st Virginia Reserves 121, 122, 253, 261, 264, 270
Fitts, Ann Elizabeth 73
Fitts, Emily 23
Fitts, Rev. Henry 72
Fitts, James M. 73, 279
Fitts, Mary Parham 72
Fitts, Sallie Duke 72
Fitzgerald, B.W. 267
Fitzgerald, Judge Francis 182
Fitzgerald, Thomas F. 267, 279
Fitzgerald, W.R. 138
Flourney, Lt. Col. 122
Foote, Richard H. 199, 246

Foote, Rev. William G. 199, 245, 279, 285
Ford, P. Fletcher 270, 279
Forster, Prof. Frank (Francis) X. 177–179, 279
Forster, Julianna 29
Fort Fisher, North Carolina 61, 197
14th Virginia Infantry 54, 59, 60, 98, 126, 129, 134, 167, 234, 238, 243, 260, 261, 266
4th Alabama Regiment 109
41st Virginia Infantry 94, 245
44th Virginia Infantry 120, 269, 270
46th Georgia Infantry 273
43rd Battalion Virginia Cavalry (Mosby's Rangers) 142
Fowlkes, Armstreat E. 268, 279
Fowlkes, John 268
Franklin College 28
Franklin County, North Carolina 44, 123, 198, 252, 274
Franklin County, Virginia 136, 254
Franklin Literary Society 5, 19, 87, 114, 140, 212, 287
Friend, George W. 279
Fuller, John P. 272, 279, 281
Fuller, Kimberly 2
Fuller, Mrs. Willie 177
Furr, F. 212

Gannaway, Pres. Pro Tempore William T. 33
Garland 13, 15, 47, 250, 287, 288
Garland, Hugh 15, 27, 35, 38, 42, 76, 77, 285
Garland, Landon 31, 37, 38, 42–47, 83, 90, 283, 284, 287
Garner, William D. 262
Garnett, William Edward 174
Gartrell, Gen. Joseph 246
Gartrell, Lucius W. 246
Gatch, Capt. Thomas Asbury 254, 279, 285
Gee, Benjamin 101
Gee, Frances W. Harper 101
Gee, Jesse 18, 19, 279
Gee, Jesse Q. 19, 101
Gee, Martha Euphemia Clementine Rose 101
Gee, Mary Susan Smith 18, 119
Gee, Virginious O(liver) 19, 101, 150–152, 235
General Assembly, North Carolina 111, 162, 205, 223, 254, 292
General Assembly, Virginia 7, 8, 12, 30, 89
Geoghegan, Virginia Puryear Mason 122
Georgetown, Texas 3, 76, 96, 155, 198, 201
Georgetown Academy 38
Georgetown College 174
Georgetown Commerce 202
Georgetown Institute 30
Gholson, James H. 24
Gholsonville 11
Gill, Aurelius T. 89, 229, 266
Gill, Flourney 139
Gill, Susan 31
Gilleland, Arthur 237
Gillespie, George 64
Gillespie, John L. 279
Gillespie, Mary 141
Gillespie cemetery 141
Gilliam, Gerald 3
Gilliam, Robert C. 274
Gilliam Street 74
Gillispie, Alex 64
Gillispie, Glen 4
Gillispie, Lisa 3, 4
Glazebrook, Dr. Otis A. 149, 150, 235
Glazebrook, Virginia Calvert Key 235
Godfrey, Joseph 136
Godfrey, William 196
Goode, M.A. 146
Goode, Martha 106
Goode, Osborne 13
Goode, Robert S. 274
Goode, Sarah 13
Goode, Thomas 16, 48, 106, 246
Goode, Col. Thomas 128, 220
Goode, Thomas F. 96, 97, 98, 128, 194, 224, 246, 267, 279
Goode, Walter 61, 99
Goode, Ward 106
Goode, William E. 150, 235
Goode, William O. 7, 12, 13, 99
Gordon, H.D. 22
Gordon, Thomas B. 279
Gorgas, Gen. Josiah 210
Granberry, Ann Leslie 246
Granberry, Ella Winston 246
Granberry, Jesse Massie 246
Granberry, Bishop John Cowper 67, 79, 165, 177, 199, 201, 227–229, 246, 247, 265, 285, 299

Index 321

Granberry, John Cowper, Jr. 199
Granberry, Richard Allen 246
Granville County, North Carolina 13, 72, 89, 122, 123, 250, 295
Graves, Elizabeth Scott 262
Graves, Francis 262
Graves, John Y. 262
Graves, Mary 262
Gray, Emma 243
Gray, J.T. 149
Gray, Mary 238
Greeley, Horace 214
Greensboro, Alabama 114, 155, 174
Greensboro Female College 35, 45, 73, 74, 79, 98, 112, 132, 141, 272
Greensboro Preparatory 82
Gregory, Dr. Flavious Joseph 60, 61, 279
Gregory, H.C. 56
Gregory, Joseph 60
Gregory, Joseph C. 60
Gregory, Mary Elizabeth Lee 60
Gregory, William 23
Gregory, Zachariah 60
Guy, Capt. John H. 279
Guy, Samuel A. 247
Gwathney, Martha Ann 46

Haley, Argyle 279
Halifax, William of 175
Halifax County, North Carolina 271
Halifax County, Virginia 20, 122, 124, 175, 181, 182, 193, 235, 237, 238, 242, 264
Halifax Volunteers 126
Hall, Annie Warwick 257
Hall, Charles H. 257, 272, 279
Hall, J.H. 257, 272
Hamblets 64
Hamilton and Graham 146
Hamlin, George W. 279
Hamner, Clifton A. 149, 150, 153, 235
Hampden-Sydney College 16, 38, 40, 57–59, 75, 127, 204, 206, 212, 223
Hanes, E.G. 250
Hanes, Capt. Garland Brown 250, 279
Hanes, Capt. James C. 254, 279
Hardy, Lt. Charles Betts 184
Hardy, Edward S. 58, 279
Hardy, Edward T. 279

Hardy, Edwin J. 270
Hardy, I. 56
Hardy, Prof James W. 46, 51, 204, 279, 284
Hardy, Prof. Joseph W. 90
Hardy, Melissa 263
Hardy, Samuel 263, 279
Hargrove, J.W. 250
Hargrove, Mary Augusta Lamb 250
Hargrove, Col. Tazewell Lee 250, 279
Harpers Ferry 32, 109
Harris, William L. 65, 286
Harris County, Georgia 108
Harrison, Benjamin G. 238
Harrison, "Col." "Squire" Burwell Kendrick 106–108, 151, 274, 279
Harrison, Elizabeth Woodson Robertson 106
Harrison, William 106, 274
Harrison County, Texas 43
H(e)artsfield, John W. 89, 279
Hatsel, Betsey 69, 289
Hatsel, Frances 69
Hawthorne, Benjamin 16, 150–153, 194, 195, 231, 235–237, 279, 293
Hawthorne, Wistar 236
Head, Rev. Dr. Nelson 167, 211, 227, 228, 279
Helper, Hardie 102
Helper, Hinton 102
Hereford, William W. 274, 279
Herndon, Benjamin Z. 250, 279
Herndon, William 250
High Point Female Normal College 79
Hightower, W.A. 149, 150
Hill, Mrs. A. 279
Hill, Allen Christopher 174
Hill, C.W. 149, 150
Hill, Chandler W.(V.) 237
Hill, Christopher D. 279
Hill, Russell 68
Hill, W.H. 257
Hill, William P. 279
Hinton Hall Academy 34
History of Randolph-Macon College (Irby) 1, 185
Hite, Benjamin H. 279
Hoge, Dr. Moses 227
Hoge, Moses D. 5, 247
Hoge, Moses Drury 212
Hoge, Rev. 213
Hoge, Dr. Thomas P. 212

Hogg, Alexander 78, 210, 274, 279
Hogg, Lewis, Jr. 274
Holstead, Richard B. 264, 279
Holstead, Robert N. 151, 152, 237
Holt, Amelia Phillips 55
Holt, David 55
Holt, Elizabeth McGehee 55
Holt, Jacob 24, 37, 55, 56, 119, 123
Holt, Thomas 55, 56, 119
Holt, W.N. 149
Holt, William K. 56, 119
Home, William H. 71
The Homestead 106
Horseley, William A. 280
hospitals 18, 37, 59–61, 75, 78, 111, 121, 122, 124, 131, 142, 161, 192, 197, 199, 234, 238, 240, 242, 245–249, 253, 256, 260–263, 267, 271
House of Commons, North Carolina 12
House of Delegates: North Carolina 200; Virginia 7, 13, 16, 24, 61, 98, 99, 138, 140, 165, 205, 256, 257, 258
House of Representatives: Alabama 106; Confederate 79; North Carolina 71, 112, 119, 200, 272; United States 12, 38, 76, 107, 110, 112
Howard, Gen. 171
Howard, George 280
Howard, John 229, 280
Howard, John W. 94
Howard, Rebecca W. 51
Howard, William A. 23, 37, 44, 51
Howard, William Travis 57
Howard College 174
Howard County, Missouri 180
Howard Female College 177
Howell, Harrison 147
Hughes, Capt. 273
Hughes, D.T. 66
Hughes, R. 149
Hughes, William 52
"Humbug Hotel" 55
Humphreys, John T. 88, 113, 280
Hunter, Hon. Charles E.(G.) 247
Hutcheson, Col. Hon. Judge Charles Sterling 42, 61, 129, 165, 220
Hutcheson, Harriett Elizabeth Palmer Millby 167

322 Index

Hutcheson, Herbert F. 310
Hutcheson, John T. 61
Hutcheson, John W. 129, 274
Hutcheson, Hon. Capt. John William 169, 254
Hutcheson, Joseph 61
Hutcheson, Joseph C. 61, 129, 150–153, 261, 280
Hutcheson, Joseph Cabell 166
Hutcheson, Joseph V. 129, 267
Hutcheson, Joseph Valentine 165
Hutcheson "scholarship" 165

Indian Fields 254
Indian Territory Oklahoma 53
Inge, David 69
Ingram, Robert M. 280
Ingram, Sarah Leona 163
Irby, Ben 183
Irby, Benjamin 185
Irby, Edmund 181, 206
Irby, Edward 206
Irby, Elizabeth 183
Irby, "Fannie" 182
Irby, Francis Betty Freeman 182
Irby, Francis Briggs Lucas 181
Irby, Freeman F. 183, 185
Irby, Janice 206
Irby, John Lucas 206, 207
Irby, Julius Edmund 206
Irby, Lewelling 183–185
Irby, Mary C. 183, 184
Irby, Mary Virginia 300, 301, 310
Irby, Moment S. 184
Irby, Richard 171, 181, 182, 189, 195, 203, 207, 215, 225, 254, 262, 280, 291
Irby, Capt. Richard 204, 214
Irby, Richard, Jr. 183, 185
Irby, Richard B. 206
Irby, Sarah E. 206
Irby, Sarah Elizabeth Poindexter 206
Irby, Walter M. 280
Irby, Wesley Childs 206
Irby, William 181, 206
Irby, William B. 181, 182
Irby, William "Little Billy" 206
Irby, William of Sussex 181
Isbell, Angelina 268
Isbell, E.S. 94
Isbell, Robert 268
Isbell, Robert S. 159, 268, 280, 285
Isbell, Thomas M. 265, 289

Isle of Wight County, Virginia 178, 238

Jackson, Green A. 264, 280
Jackson, James 265
Jackson, James W. 280
Jackson, James T. 265
Jackson, John S. 265, 280
Jackson, Robert A. 264, 270, 280
Jackson, Thomas 265
Jackson, Rev. Dr. Thomas 280
Jackson, Thomas L. 265, 280
Jackson, Waddy J. 264, 270
James, George W. 65
Jamestown, Virginia 234, 261
Jamieson, Andrew 132
Jamieson, Rev. James 56, 130, 132–136, 154, 191, 285
Jamieson, William A. 36, 130, 133, 280
Jamieson, Lt. William A. 268
Jamieson Memorial M.E. Church 18, 50
Jarrett, Benjamin Franklin 140, 254
Jarvis, Rev. Bannister Hardy 119
Jarvis, Elizabeth Daley 119
Jarvis, Mary Woodson 119, 120
Jarvis, Capt. Gov. Thomas Jordan 119, 120, 200, 234, 266, 280
Jarvis Hall (East Carolina University) 200
Jefferson, Samuel 53
Jefferson, Alabama 183
Jefferson City, Missouri 177
Jefferson Street 38, 185, 213, 256
Jeffress, James Hamet 164
Jeffress, Joseph H. 96
Jeffress, Martha Bedford 164
Jeffress, Nancy Bedford Mosely 164
Jeffress, Richard D. 96
Jeffries, Dr. Howell L. 16
Jenkins, Benjamin 280
Jerman, Cornelia Klipstein 85
Jerman, Edward 85
Jerman, Lucy Beverly Sydnor 85
Jerman, R.H. 85
Jerman, Dr. Thomas Palmer 85, 280
Johns Hopkins University 106, 108, 232

Johnson, Pres. Andrew 99, 158, 170
Johnson, John 126
Johnson, John L. 88, 261, 280
Johnson, Martha R. Scott 168
Johnson, S.P. 128
Johnson, Col. Pres. Rev. Thomas Carter 114, 168–170, 211, 215–217, 227, 228, 247, 283, 284
Johnson's Division 188
Johnson's Island, Ohio (prison) 49, 103, 121, 237, 241, 249, 250, 263
Johnston, John M. 213
Johnston, Gen. Joseph E. 33, 188, 192
Jones, A.B. 255
Jones, Mrs. A.W. 198
Jones, Alexander 26
Jones, Rev. Amos 94, 198
Jones, Amos Blanche 198
Jones, Amos W. 21, 44, 196, 197, 280, 287, 289
Jones, Col. Benhring 143
Jones, Caius J. 150–153, 237, 280
Jones, Carolyn M. 197, 287, 289
Jones, E.T. 212
Jones, Edgar 237
Jones, Elizabeth 54
Jones, Elizabeth Archer Dunnivant 251
Jones, George B. 154, 265, 280
Jones, Glenna 18
Jones, Harriett G. 46
Jones, Henry F. 49, 280
Jones, Capt. Prof. J.W. 211, 226, 238
Jones, Jacob 237
Jones, James W. 150–153, 238, 254, 280
Jones, John W. 16, 88, 251, 280
Jones, L.F. 239
Jones, Mary Myrick 198
Jones, Richard W. 178, 179, 210, 254, 257, 280, 284
Jones, Samuel Goode 106
Jones, Sarah Pauline 143
Jones, Thomas Goode 106
Jones, Rev. Thomas H. 280
Jones, Thomas L. 96, 97, 187, 267
Jones, Dr. Tingnal 16
Jones, Turner M. 44, 280
Jones, Dr. William B. 76, 155, 192, 202
Jones, William H. 272

Jones, Dr. William H. 96, 97, 129, 184, 259, 267
Jones, William M. 280
Jones, William N. 125
Jones House 184
Jordan J.B. 238
Jordan, John Parker, Esq. 87, 113
Jordan, Dr. Miles W. 97, 187
Jordan, Samuel P. 97
Jordan, W.F. 149
Judkins, Alfretta C. 238
Judkins, Connie Whitehead 238
Judkins, Jarrett Wallace 238
Judkins, Mary Gray 238
Judkins, William Duncan 238
Judkins, William Elliott 280
Judkins, Rev. William H. 150–153, 191, 278
Justice 8, 22, 42, 61, 64, 107, 109, 134, 156, 165, 237, 258, 261

Kearney, John 60
Keiley, Anthony M. 258, 280
Keiley, John D. 258
Keiley, Margaret 258
Keiley, Rebecca Davis 258
Kennedy, James S. 285
Kilby, W.J. 212
Kingswood United M.E. Church 18, 105
Kinney, Capt. A. 164, 188
Kirkpatrick, Rev. J. 75, 78, 280
Kirkpatrick, Rev. T.D. 218
Kirkpatrick's Company (light artillery) 266
Knight, James 139
Knights of the Golden Circle 85
Kroger, Maj. Joseph 254
Kroger, Thomas Jefferson 254, 280

Lagard, Prof. Ernest 210, 275, 284
Lagard, Leonine Lafforgue 210
LaGrange College 39, 46, 51, 102, 103
Lander, Elizabeth (Eliza) Ann Miller 78
Lander, John M. (McPherson) 70, 200
Lander, Laura Ann McPherson 79
Lander, Martha (Mattie) McPherson 79

Lander, Samuel, Jr. 33, 51, 70, 78, 79, 140, 200, 272, 280, 284, 286, 295, 296, 312, 313
Lander, Dr. Samuel, Jr. 50
Lander, Lt. Samuel, Jr. 80
Lander, Rev. Samuel, Sr. 78, 79
Lander, William Tertius 79
Lander "Chapel" 79
Lander College 78–80
Lander University 200
Landstreet, Rev. John 211
Lanier, L.T. 106
Lanier, Mary Jane Anderson 106, 108
Lanier, Robert Sampson 106, 108
Lanier, Sidney Clopton 106–108
law school (RMC) 41–43, 137, 164; professors 41, 58, 77, 97, 218
Lawton, Gen. A.R. 187, 188
lawyers 13, 15, 20, 31, 38, 41, 47, 49, 53, 73, 76, 78, 79, 98, 103–109, 112, 118–120, 128, 133, 136, 158, 166–169, 189, 210, 214, 237, 243–246, 250–253, 257, 259, 261, 264, 266, 268, 272, 278–280, 284, 294
Lea, A. 56
Lea, Addie 231
Lea, Addison 35, 272, 280
Lea, Elizabeth 54
Lea, Georgia Hunt 20
Lea, Harry 231
Lea, Lorenzo, Jr. 21
Lea, Lorenzo Dow 20, 21, 33, 76, 285
Lea, Mary Ann Medley 20
Lea, Miss A. 21
Lea, Sarah McNeil 20
Lea, Solomon 35, 45, 54, 112, 231, 285, 292
Lea, William 20
Lea, William F. 20
Leak, John W. 251, 280
Leak, Walter R. 251
Leak, William C. 251
Lectures on Domestic Slavery 84
Lee, Jesse 11
Lee, Dr. L.M. 227, 228
Lee, Rev. Leroy M. 44, 214
Lee, "Light Horse" Harry 60
Lee, Mary Elizabeth 60
Lee, Gen. Robert E. 106, 125, 157, 192, 213, 233, 235, 246, 251, 262

Leesburg Academy 20
Leftwich, Capt. Joel B. 254
Leigh, Ernest 247
Leigh, H.G. 56, 89
Leigh, H.G., Jr. 286
Leigh, H. Gilbert 52
Leigh, Hezekiah 12, 14, 43, 54, 61, 62, 77, 189, 280
Leigh, Hezekiah, Jr. 14, 62, 247, 280, 281
Leigh, Joseph 280
Leigh, Julia Ann Crump 52
Leigh, Martha Alice Moody 247
Leigh, Mary Jane Crump 247
Leigh, Nannie 247
Leigh, Richard M. 61
Leigh, Capt. Richard W. 251, 280
Leigh, W. 56
Leigh, William 52
Leigh, Judge William 222
Leigh, Rev. William 52
Letcher, Bertonia 35
Letcher, Gov. John B. 35, 36, 87, 144, 155
Letcher, John D. 36
Lewis, Rev. James M. 285
Lewis, John W. 15
The Life of John Randolph of Roanoke 77
Ligon, Governor 101
Ligon, Martha E. 101
Ligon, Robert T. 187
Ligon, Woodson L. 105, 247, 280
Lincolnton Female College 80
Lockett, Benjamin F. 280
Lockett, Harwood 138, 239
Lockett, Henry E. 196, 274, 280
Lockett, Henry E., Jr. 274
Lockett, Kate 155, 199
Lockett, M.B. 155, 199
Lockett, Myrta 138, 238
Lockett, P. 149–151
Lockett, Phillip 138, 140, 154, 238
Lockett, Col. S.L. 196, 274
Lockett, Sam 196, 248
Lockett, Samuel L. 16
Lockett, Thomas 196
Lockett, Thomas J. 248, 280
Lofty Oaks Academy 165, 166
Logan, Richard 124
Lomax, Caroline Billingslea Sharter 251, 281
Lomax, Lucien 50, 252, 281
Lomax, Matilda 251
Lomax, Tennent 50, 251

Lomax, Tennent, Jr. 251, 252
Lombardy Grove 18, 26, 62, 98, 120, 123, 127, 134, 238, 239, 260, 270
Lombardy Grove Academy 101, 235
Lombardy Grove Baptist Church 55
Long, Judge Benjamin Franklin 110
Long, John F. 272, 281
Long, Rev. John S. 170
Long Creek, Virginia 247
Loving, Rev. Robert G. 20
Lupton, Ella Virginia Allemong 174
Lupton, Prof. N.P. 51
Lupton, Nathaniel T. 70, 174, 284
Lynch, Julia Matilda (Hanna) 29
Lyon, John 99, 248, 258, 259, 281

Maclin, Alexander 26
Maclin, Elizabeth 14
Maclin, James 14, 20
Maclin, John Henry 259
Maclin, Nathaniel 14
Macon, Nathaniel 8, 12, 224
Macon, Georgia (Bibb County) 59, 106, 108, 235, 250, 274
Macon, North Carolina 187, 188
Macon County, Alabama 275
Macon County, Georgia 103
Macon Depot 73, 271, 271
Magruder, George W. 252, 281
Magruder, Gen. G.W. 75
Magruder, Dr. W.W. 252
Mahone, Maj. Gen. 97, 140, 180, 215, 259
Mallory, Alex 259, 281
Mallory, Col. J.B. 268
Mallory, Robert M. 268, 281
Mallory, Secretary 131
Malvern Hill, Battle of 48, 73, 126, 245, 251–253, 260, 263
Mangelsdorf, Paul C. 171
Mangum, Adolphus Williamson 80, 81, 252, 272, 281
Mangum, Ellison Goodloe 80, 81, 272
Mangum, Elizabeth Harris 80

Mangum, Laura Jane Overman 84
Mangum, William Preston 81
Mangum, Wylie P. 81
Mann, Rev. Alfred T. 281
Manning, Rev. Jacob 66, 85, 285
Mansfield Female College 52
Manson, V.S. 10
Marion, Maj. Gen. Francis 31
Martin, Rev. John S. 281
Martin, Martha 95
Marvin, Bishop Enoch M. 281
Mary Branch Dormitories 256
mason 37, 66, 146
Mason, A. S. 189
Mason, Charlotte Ashby 259
Mason, Senator John Y. 258
Mason, Joseph Richard 259, 281
Mason, Robert F. 122
Mason, S.G. 54
Mason, Virginia Puryear 122
Masonic Lodge 202, 226, 227
Massenburg, A.C. 273
Massenburg, T.N. 273
Massie, Lucy Waller 13
Massie, Robert T. 71, 90, 94, 114, 160, 248, 261, 284
Massie, Sarah Maria 13
Massie, Dr. Thomas 13
Massie, Thomas E. 281
Massie, Waller 281
Maxey, Joseph E. 149, 151, 152, 239
May, James 74
Mayo, Col. 255
Mayo, Mrs. Henry Wise 174
McAdam, James 54
McAden, James 66, 76
McCarthy, Capt. Edward S. 265
McCurry, Capt. J.W. 188
McGonegal, Dr. Henry 56, 228, 238
McGowan, Rev. J.E. 118
McGuire, Rev. Francis 189
McGuire, Francis Harrison 189, 281
McGuire, Mary Willis 189
McKendree, Bishop 47
McKenzie, Capt. Francis McMullen 200
McKinsey, J.A. 149
McPhail, Col. John B. 121, 255
McPhail, Paul 121
McTyeire, Amelia Townsend 178

McTyeire, Bishop Rev. Dr. Holland Nimens 47, 83, 87, 176, 178, 286
Mecklenburg, North Carolina 53
Mecklenburg Circuit 11, 37, 49, 66, 105, 295
Mecklenburg Circuit Court 92, 292, 294
Mecklenburg County cemeteries 287, 305
Mecklenburg County Clerk 133
Mecklenburg County commissioners 189
Mecklenburg County jail 24, 55
Mecklenburg Courthouse 21, 43, 55, 292
Mecklenburg Female College 163
Mecklenburg "Guards" 120
Mecklenburg Herald 224, 225
Mecklenburg "Rifles" 131
Mecklenburg "Spartans" 120
Mecklenburg Sun 295, 298
medical schools/departments: Charleston 196; Hampden-Sydney 59; Jefferson (Philadelphia) 57, 60, 248, 256; New York University 14, 234, 247; Oregon Agricultural College 195, Paris 29; Pennsylvania 40, 57; Randolph Macon 25, 42, 43, 57–60, 62, 78, 164, 182, 212, 240, 245, 248, 252, 262, 274; Scotland 212; South Carolina 79, 85; Southwestern University, Texas 195; Vanderbilt 195; University of Virginia 20, 75, 117, 173, 240; Washington (Baltimore) 57–60
Memphis, Tennessee 150, 181, 243
Memphis Conference Female Institute 21, 197, 198, 282
Merchant's National Bank 184, 214, 256
Merritt, Embry 281
Merritt, John B. 151, 239
Merritt, William T. 252, 281
Merriweather, Amelia Marks (Emily) 38
Merriweather County, Georgia 103
Methodist Conference 2, 3, 7, 11, 68, 222, 223, 224; British 31; Memphis 21,

Index

198, 253; Missouri 208; South Carolina 14, 31; Virginia/North Carolina 8, 32, 41, 50, 218, 256, 311
Mettauer, E.M. 58
Mettauer, Dr. Francis Joseph 57
Mettauer, Dr. Francis Joseph, Jr. 40, 57, 58, 210, 284
Mettauer, H.A. 58
Mettauer, Dr. Henry Archer 57, 59, 274, 284
Mettauer, Dr. John Peter 57–59, 284
Mettauer, Margaret E. Carter 57
Mettauer, Mary Woodward 57
Middlebury College 27, 28
Milam, Henry D. 273, 281
Milam, Nathan 273
Miller, Daniel 78
Miller, Elizabeth Ann 78
Miller, Frank X. 273, 281
Miller, Lewis 251
Miller, Dr. W.G. 273
Missouri 4, 33, 57, 59, 75–77, 84, 93, 105, 158, 167–169, 176, 178, 180, 194, 204, 208, 243, 264, 299, 304
Mitchell, E.R. 149
Mitchell, J.R. 149
Mitchell, Margaret 239
Mitchell, Mary 165
Mocksville, North Carolina 102
Mocksville Academy 102, 109
Montgomery, Henry T. 107, 281
Montgomery, Martha 109
Montgomery, Mary 109
Montgomery, Alabama 169, 176
Montgomery County 271
Montgomery "True Blues" 251
Moody, Alice 247
Moody, John 247, 280
Moody, Martha 247
Moore, Edwin G. 273, 281
Moore, Elizabeth 259
Moore, Elizabeth Simmons 110
Moore, Governor 251
Moore, John S. 259, 281, 284
Moore, John Simmons 110
Moore, Munsey 287
Moore, Robert 110
Moore, Robert T. 267, 281
Moore, Samuel 281

Moore, Sarah 259
Moore, Sarah Speight 272
Moore, Smith W. 281
Moores, Julia 116
Moores, Thomas 117
Moran, Rev. Robert S. 281
Morrill Act 236
Morris, Richard G. 281
Morton, Elizabeth D. 75
Mosby, Lt. Col. John Singleton 142, 252
Moses, Peter A. 248, 271, 281
Moses, S.F. 248
Moss, Henry 126
Mullen, Francis N. 281
Mundy, J.C. 149
Mundy, Jesse Charles 239
Mundy, Vicie Louisa Render 239
Murray, John 69
Muse, Edward H. 263
Muse, Mr. 204
Myers, Edward H. 281
Myrick, Ann 239
Myrick, Benjamin 239
Myrick, Walter 149, 151, 152, 239

Napoleon 102, 173
Nashville Christian Advocate 47, 87, 114
Nashville University 103
National Bank of Thurmond 143
Navy: British 48; Confederate States 108, 251, 266; United States 76
negro 31, 76, 130, 155, 164, 171, 209, 219, 221, 228, 298
Nelson, Catherine Isabella 102
Nelson, F.W. 121
Nelson, Lt. Frank W. 122, 271
Nelson, Dr. John, Jr. 16
Nelson, Martha 122
Nelson, Martha Lewis 121
Nelson, Robert C. 24
Nelson, Sally 102
Nelson, Thomas H. 13
Nelson, William 102, 121
New Jersey 8, 12, 52, 258
New York 8, 14, 22, 27, 30, 38, 40, 47, 82, 83, 103, 114, 115, 134, 190, 214, 228, 239, 247, 257, 258, 270, 285
Newton, Rev. Robert 281
Ney, Catherine Isabella 102
Ney, Peter Stuart "Marshall" 102, 173
9th Virginia Cavalry 163, 268

9th Virginia Infantry 269
Noah, John R. 245
Nolley, Rev. George W. 74
Nolley, Rev. James 74
Normal School 33, 74, 109, 168, 176, 177, 209
North Carolina Medical Society 57
Northington, James 101, 102, 267

Oakbowery (Oak Bowery) College 103, 108
O'Brien, Francis 60
O'Brien, Dr. John 51, 52
O'Brien, Junius 52
Ogburn, Benjamin Watkins 132–134, 281
Ogburn, Charles 76, 133
Ogburn, Rev. Charles 133
Ogburn, Charles Wesley 133, 134, 261
Ogburn, Flourney Gill 134
Ogburn, John F. 133, 281
Ogburn, Lucy Rebecca Harrison Harwell 133
Ogburn, Martha Rebecca "Queen" Walker 134
Oglethorpe University 108
O'Hanlon, James 281
Old Brunswick Circuit Foundation 10, 309, 313
Olin, Henry 27
Olin, Louisa Richardson 27
Olin, Stephen Henry 30
Olin, Dr. Stephen P. 27–30, 56, 90, 185, 284, 308
Olin and Preston Institute 30
Olin High School 30, 78, 83
Olive Branch 11
146th North Carolina Militia 252
Oregon 3, 36, 105, 195, 232, 236, 237, 302
Orgain, John 101, 281
Orgain, John, Jr. 101
Overby, Thomas J. 89, 273, 281
Overton, Edward 96
Oxford, England 8, 199
Oxford, Georgia 103, 110
Oxford, North Carolina 7, 74, 132, 250, 305
Oxford Baptist Female College 165
Oxford "Station" 295

Palmer, Elizabeth Frances Rodwell 271
Palmer, Harriett Oliver 73

326 Index

Palmer, Horace, Jr. 73, 271, 273, 282
Palmer, Horace, Sr. 73, 271
Palmer, Gen. I.N. 258
Palmer, Jacob 73, 271, 281
Palmer, Jeff Davis 73
Palmer, Reuben 73, 281
Palmer, Sarah Emily Milan 73
Palmer, Sarah Fitzhenry 49
Palmer, Sophie George Finley 271
Parham, Edward E. 87, 101, 113, 281
Parham, Richard S. 281
Paris Artillery 60, 235
Parks, M.P. 56
Parks, Prof. Rev. Martin P. 90, 284
Parks, Martin T. 27
Parks, N.P. 27, 31
Patrick, Jeanie (Jane) Erwin 137
Patrick, Martha 138
Pattillo, Dr. William 16
Paul, D'Arcey 43, 44, 50, 97, 191, 211, 214, 227, 228, 256
Paul, D'Arcey, Jr. 44
Paul, Mary J. Rainey 44
Paul, Samuel B. 44, 281
Payne-Howard Female College 95, 177
Peace Institute 55
Pearson, Rev. Charles C. 285
Peay, James T. 269, 281
Peete, Catherine Ann Nicholson 248
Peete, Charles Henry 248
Peete, Richard Samuel Fennell 248, 281
Pegram, Capt. Richard G. 265
Penn, G. 149
Penny, William W. 282
Peques, Jane 196
Peques, Martha J. 196
Peques, Rev. 196
Peques, Rufus R. 196, 275, 282
Person, P. 274
Person, Willie M. 274, 282
Petersburg, Virginia 14, 14, 18, 43, 44, 49, 50, 62, 68, 71, 76, 81, 88, 89, 97, 113, 115, 124, 126, 129, 136, 146, 147, 150-154, 187, 189, 192, 203, 214, 242, 244, 245, 249, 255-260, 265
Petersburg Artillery 265
Petersburg City Battalion Reserves 254
Petersburg CSA Hospital 18

Petersburg Express 81, 258
Petersburg Female College 35, 127, 134, 138, 161, 162, 174, 179, 257
Petersburg Home Guard 154
Petersburg Index 211, 238
Pettus, Eliza Puryear 309
Pettus, John 74
Phillips, Amelia 55
Phillips, Claudius G. 269, 282
Phillips, H.B. 149
Phillips, Hunter B. 239
Phillips, Mr. 114
physician 11, 12, 53, 57, 75, 79, 97, 106, 196, 239, 252
Pierce, Alexander B. 282
Pierce, Rev. George F. 282, 284
Pierce, James L. 103, 282
Pierce, Rev. Dr. Lovick 103, 282
Pierce, T.A. 105
Pinckard, Elizabeth Campbell 240
Pinckard, F.A. 149
Pinckard, Francis Ashbury 240
Pinckney, Charles C. 31
plantations 14, 111, 114, 115, 146, 147, 158, 164, 182, 194, 197, 221; Bellgrade 7; Berry Hill 126; Black Walnut 125, 135; Blue Rock 13; Bull-Head Head Swamp 21; "Canaan" 11; Cedar Crest 13; Columbian Grove (NC) 123; Cuscowilla 131; Dromgoole's 10; Eureka 55; Green 14; Greensborough 117; Inglewood 13; Louisiana 242; Mount Airy 61; North Bend 122, 131; Oakville 124; Occoneechee 70; Park Forest 98, 99; Poplar Hill 81; Prestwood 102; Roanoke 8; Rose Hill (SC) 141, 155; Rosemont 120; Sutherlin 136, 138, 311; Tranquility 123; Virginia 32; Wheatland 13, 115; Woodburn 60
Plummer, Dr. Henry L. 85
Plummer, William 85
Poemond (Piedmont), Virginia N. 54
Point Lookout, Maryland (prison) 108, 142, 206, 233, 242, 254, 258, 260, 271
Poisal, Rev. John 211, 282

Poplar Springs Meeting House 7
Powell, Albert Theodore 252
Powell, Elizabeth 251
Powell, Elizabeth Holmes 252
Powell, Louisa Jones Thweatt 252
Powell, Mary Ann Polk 252
Powell, Norberne Berkeley 252
Powell, Richard H., Esq. 114, 267, 282
Powell, Capt. Richard Holmes 252
Presbyterian 110
Presbyterian cemetery 38, 41, 99, 128
Presbyterian church 102, 106, 132, 212, 213, 223
Presbyterian Church, New Jersey 32
Presbyterian minister 83
Pretlow, Jennie D. 253
Pride, Capt. Henry 122
Prince Edward Medical Institute 57, 59
principal (school) 15, 20, 21, 32, 35, 39, 48, 51-54, 74, 75, 94, 102, 118, 120, 127, 154, 163, 177, 196, 236, 238, 254, 266, 273, 285
Proctor, John (James) 268, 282
Providence Church 101, 163, 228, 247, 267
Puryear, Alexander 117
Puryear, Alice P. 174
Puryear, Bennett 70, 71, 88, 90, 94, 117, 125, 126, 150, 159-162, 170-173, 187, 189, 190, 230, 282, 284, 302
Puryear, Bennett, Jr. 117, 300
Puryear, Charles 117, 170, 300
Puryear, Eliza 31
Puryear, Elizabeth Leroy 174
Puryear, Elizabeth Marshall 70
Puryear, Elizabeth Pettus 295
Puryear, Ella Marion Wiles 117, 159
Puryear, Frank 117, 159, 174
Puryear, John 174
Puryear, John L. 127, 268
Puryear, Lewis 71, 174
Puryear, Lucy Goode 174
Puryear, Polly 117
Puryear, Sgt. Reuban A. 125-127, 268
Puryear, Richard C. 25, 70, 74, 117, 126, 127, 187
Puryear, Dr. Richard R. 25

Index

Puryear, Sallie 117
Puryear, Virginia 117, 122
Puryear, Virginia C. 159
Puryear, Virginia Catherine Ragland 70, 117
Puryear, William R. 174

railroad bonds 50, 51
railroad depot 121
railroad spur to Clarksville 95
railroads: Confederate Virginia Central 64; Danville & New River 138; Iron Mountain 168; Milton & Sutherlin 139; Norfolk and Great Western 226; Ohio & Northwestern 36; Petersburg 26; Raleigh 176, 210; Raleigh to Gaston 53; Richmond & Mecklenburg 121; Richmond to Danville 40, 170; Roanoke Valley 43, 64, 72, 124, 126, 128, 186; Southside 50, 206; Union Pacific 43, 168; Virginia Central 64
Rainey, A.F. 41, 144
Rainey, J. Phillip 44, 144
Rainey, Mary J. 44
Randolph, John 8, 32, 181, 182, 224
Randolph, William 7
Randolph Circuit 56, 105, 132
Randolph County, North Carolina 30, 32, 74, 83, 109, 126, 232
Randolph Macon academies 184
Randolph Macon Academy 98, 123
Randolph Macon Cemetery 197, 287
Randolph Macon College: A Southern History—1825 to 1967 1, 292
Randolph-Macon farm (map) 63
Randolph Macon Institute 133
Randolph Macon magazine 77
Randolph Macon Samford 103
Randolph Macon Post Office 64
Randolph Macon Women's College 3, 133, 184
Ravenscroft, Bishop Right Reverend John Stark 16, 18
Rawlins, E.A. 219, 220

Ray, Elizabeth 136
Ray, Enos 136
Ray, Rev. George Henry 30, 135, 150, 153, 240, 253, 268, 285
Reed, James C. 151, 240
Reekes, Capt. Thomas 64, 65, 189
Reekes, Thomas C. 64
Reekes, Thomas E. 188, 189
Reekes, Thomas R., Jr. 188, 189
Reese, Dr. 114
Reese, Joseph T. 282
Reeves, Mary Wyche 115
Register, Rev. Samuel S. 211, 282
Reid, Rev. N.F. 28
Reid, Panthea 3
Revolutionary War 9, 12, 31, 57, 123, 170, 260, 292
Reynolds, J. Stanley 151, 152
Rhodes scholarship 199
Rich Mountain 126, 132
Richards, Adolphus E. 142, 149, 150, 152, 240
Richards, William 66
Richardson, William C. 151, 152, 240
Richmond Advocate 48, 82, 220, 221
Riddick, Rev. Jams A. 163
Ridgeway Depot 170, 208
Rives, James (John) F. 282
Rives, Leonidas O. 275, 282
Roanoke, Virginia 246
Roanoke Circuit 81
Roanoke Colt Show 22
Roanoke Guard 125
Roanoke Mills 64
Roanoke River 63, 64, 65, 70, 95, 122, 161, 187, 192, 299
Roanoke River Navigation Company 63
Roanoke Station 170, 210
Roanoke Valley (newspaper) 126, 128, 132, 159, 160, 167
Roanoke Valley Railroad 43, 64, 72, 124, 186
Robbins, Ahi 109
Robbins, Martha Montgomery 109
Robbins, Mary Brown 109
Robbins, Mary Montgomery 109
Robbins, William McKendree 109, 253, 282
Rogers, Col. George 21, 22, 24–26, 43
Rogers, George, Jr. 25, 58

Rogers, Indiana E. 165
Rogers, Rebecca S.B. 25
Rogers, Thomas H. 25, 45, 58, 252, 286
Rolfe, Elizabeth 99
Rolfe, Pauline 78
Rose, Anne S. 293
Rose, Dr. L. I. 3, 101, 120, 188, 300
Rowzie, William D. 224
Rozel, Rev. S.S. 211
Russell, Charles 122, 133
Russell, Richard 74, 175
Russell, Rev. Thomas B. 113, 282
Russell County, Alabama 196

Sadler, Sallie F. 154
St. Andrew, J.A.H. 128
St. Augustine 82, 83
St. Tammany 18, 19, 59, 60, 120, 161, 192, 19
St. Tammany's Ferry 24, 123
Samford, Randolph Macon 103
Samford, Susan Lewis Dowdell 103
Samford, Prof. Dr. William Flewellen 103, 274, 282
Samford, William Hodges 103
Samford, William James 103
Sanders, Prof. Albert G. 199
Sanders, Harriett 196
Sanders, John 195
Sanders, John Randolph 199
Sanders, Martha J. Peques 196–198
Sanders, Martha P. 199
Sanders, Mary 198, 202
Sanders, Mary J. 196, 197
Sanders, Mary Shipp 202
Sanders, Nannie 199, 202
Sanders, S.G. 201
Sanders, Capt. Dr. Samuel D. 155, 195–198, 201, 202
Sanders, Samuel D., Jr. 198
Sanders, Samuel G. 155, 196, 198, 199, 201, 202
Sanders, Prof. Shipp G. 199
Sangster, James 137, 269, 282
Santa Anna River railroad bridge 250
Sargent, Rev. T.B. 282
Scanlon, James Edward 1, 2, 65, 215, 216, 276, 292, 302, 306, 309; *see also Randolph-Macon College: A Southern History—1825 to 1967*
Schell, Augustus 214

Index

Scoggins, Capt. James L. 22, 69, 73
Scott, Benjamin Irby 204, 213, 282
Scott, Capt. 99
Scott, Dred 76, 77, 84
Scott, H.B. 168
Scott, Martha R. 168
Scott, Pattie B. 168
Scott, Rev. Robert 168
Scott, Samuel B. 282
Scott, Thomas 66
Scott, Virginia Chambers 136
Sebrell, James E. 266, 282
Sebrell, William J. 266
Sebrell, Virginia 266
Sebrell School 266
Sehon, Edward W. 282
Semmes, Admiral Raphael 137
Senate: Missouri 114, 168, 169; North Carolina 110, 112; Virginia 3, 45, 125, 132, 215, 256; United States 8, 120
Shay, Henry 209
Shay, Mrs. J.W. Brent 269
Shay, William H. 78, 269, 282
Shelton, Ann McKinney 4
Shelton, Dr. David 26, 27, 102
Shelton, J.A. 58
Shelton, J. Harper 27
Shelton, John W. 282
Shelton, Roberta 17, 312
Shelton, Dr. William 17, 312
Shepard, William A. 88, 94, 161, 248, 282, 284, 286
Shepherd, E.A. 240
Shepherd, William 240
Sheridan, Gen. Phillip H. 191, 274, 292
Shipp, Prof. Dr. Alfred Micajah 141, 176, 282
Shipp, Elizabeth Oglesby 141
Shipp, John 141
Shipp, Mary Gillespie 141
Shipp, Gen. Scott 32
Silliman, Prof. Benjamin 175
Simmons, Benjamin F. 273, 282
Simmons, Bettie A. 60
Sims, Edward Dromgoole 27, 28, 39, 56, 90, 284, 306, 310
16th North Carolina Infantry 273
6th North Carolina Infantry 81, 273
61st North Carolina Infantry 273

67th North Carolina Militia 80
Skidmore, L. 248
slaves 8, 21, 25, 31, 32, 42, 43, 55, 63, 65, 66, 70, 127, 129, 137, 146, 147, 154–156, 158, 162, 163, 182–184, 189, 192, 195, 207, 242, 290
Slayton, Professor 103
Sledd, Robert W. 282
Slingo, Ireland 10, 11
Small, William F. 130, 268
Small, William T. 128
Smiley, Rebecca 101
Smith, Charles Foster 29
Smith, Dallas 275, 282
Smith, Daniel 74
Smith, Elizabeth V. 54, 78, 177
Smith, Francis W. 265
Smith, Dr. George J. 51, 53, 187
Smith, Gerritt 214
Smith, Hampden S. 28
Smith, J.P. 214
Smith, James 76
Smith, Rev. James Francis 29, 282
Smith, James H. 275
Smith, James Perrin 29
Smith, Gen. Kirby 242
Smith, Laura 54
Smith, Mary Susan 18
Smith, Molly 54
Smith, Oliver G. 282
Smith, R.M. 44, 214, 227
Smith, Susan 54
Smith, William A(ndrew) 12, 50–54, 62, 64, 68, 69, 71, 76, 78, 81–84, 86, 88, 90–94, 113, 116, 125, 134–136, 147, 159–161, 165, 167, 169, 172, 176, 178, 180, 186, 191, 194, 203, 208–210, 244, 264, 282, 287
Smith, William S. 273
Smith, William W. 74, 184, 227
Smith Boarding House 53
Snead, G. 125
Sneed, Henry H. 149–151, 240
Society of Medical Alumni 58
Somerville Female Institute 35
Sons of Liberty 85
Soule, Bishop 47
Soule Female College 21
Soule University 199, 200, 202
South Carolina College 31, 160
South Lowell Academy 102

Southall, J.D. 136
Southern Christian Advocate 32, 114
Southern Cross of Honor 237
Southern Historical Collection 11
Southern Methodist colleges (mother of) 89
Southern Rifles 252
Southern Virginia Historical Society 3
Southern University 95, 103, 110, 141, 174, 178
Southern Female College *see* Petersburg Female College
The Southern Literary Magazine 77
Southern Literary Messenger 252
Southwestern University 3, 76, 155, 195, 197–199, 201
Spainhauer, Mary 73
Spartanburg Female College 80
Speaker of the House 12, 13, 32, 107, 200
Speed, Maria 65
Speed, Rev. Richard A. 64, 287, 289
spy detachment 98
spy ring 30
"spy scope" 264
stagecoach 26, 55, 62, 69, 73, 162, 236
Stainback, Belle West 241, 242
Stainback, George 242
Stainback, Robert 242
Stainback, Robert Alexander 149, 152, 240, 255
Stallard, Kathryn 3, 202
Stamford, William F. 282
Stanley, Marcellus 256, 281
Stanton, Battle of 75, 121, 122, 125, 260, 265
Stanton River Bridge 122
Starr, William F. 89, 113, 159, 160, 248, 282, 310
Staubly, Godfrey Esq. 94, 153, 159, 245
Stevens, Alexander H. 234
Steward Hall 16, 17, 30, 37, 69, 71, 194, 211, 288–290, 312
Stewart, Charles 282
Stewart, J.R. 96
Stewart, Theophilus S. 29, 282
Stone, Dr. DeWitt, Jr. 3
Stone, Dr. Phillip 3
Stone, Miss Suky 70
Stoneman, Gen., 1st U.S. Dis-

Index

trict, Virginia 213, 214, 216, 222, 224, 227, 228
Stratford Women's College 133
Stuart, Judge Charles Bingley 52, 53
Stuart, Prof. Rev. Dr. Charles S. 51, 52, 90, 275, 282, 285
Stuart, Gen. J.E.B. 246
Stuart, John R. 51–53
Stuart, John W. 285
Stuart's Horse Artillery 265
Styron, Oscar M. 150–153, 241, 282
Supreme Court 77, 104, 109, 237
Sutherlin, George S. 136
Sutherlin, Jamie L. 138
Sutherlin, Jeanie (Jane) Erwin Patrick 137
Sutherlin, Polly S. Norman 136, 137
Sutherlin, Maj. William Thomas 136–139, 215
Sutphin, Dr. John T. 124, 125
Sutphin, Martha Ann Singleton 125
Sutton, Joseph 282
"Swamp Fox" 31
Sydnor, Alex 96, 97, 267
Sydnor, Capt. Beverly 7, 13, 14, 16, 24, 65, 85, 97, 98, 130, 175, 310
Sydnor, Lucy Beverly 85

Talbot, Allen 144, 151, 241, 248
Tallifarer, Henry 71
Tally, W.G. 259
Tally, Young 126
Tanner's house 24
Tanner's Store 59, 120
Tarry, Edward 16
Taylor, Elizabeth 24
Taylor, Felix F. (H.G.) 274, 282
Taylor, Howell 7, 12
Taylor, John M. 185, 189
Taylor, John W. 248, 283
Taylor, Judge John W. 274
Taylor, Thomas V. 171
Taylor family 7
Taylor Meeting House 7
Taylor's Ferry 7, 12, 20, 64, 65, 71, 119, 128, 181, 189
Taylor's Ferry Road 17, 30, 78, 119, 128, 161
Tazewell 13, 239
Telefrue, R.C. 90
"Texas Hall" 16
Thackston, Benjamin H. 265, 283

Thackston, R.D. 149
Thackston, Richard D. 242
Thackston, Thomas C. 77, 78, 121, 128, 283
3rd Virginia Brigade 48
3rd Virginia Cavalry 30, 75, 97–99, 118, 127, 128, 130, 153, 157, 167, 179, 207, 231–233, 239, 246, 248, 267
3rd Virginia Local Defense 265
3rd Virginia Regiment 211
3rd Virginia Reserves 265
38th Virginia Infantry 18, 99, 131, 231, 233–235, 240, 263–265, 270
Thomas, F.G. 275
Thomas, I.I. 56
Thomas, James R. 283
Thomas Branch Dormitories 256
Thompson, Edwin A. 253, 283
Thompson, John 76
Thrower, Christopher 88, 275, 283
Thrower, Samuel P. 78
Thurmond, Lt. Elias 144
Thurmond, Lt. John Dudley 143
Thurmond, Capt. John W. 143, 255
Thurmond, P. 140
Thurmond, Maj. Phillip (Peyton) James 143, 253
Thurmond, R.J. 140
Thurmond, R.W. 140
Thurmond, Richard C. 143, 269
Thurmond, Richard Claiborne 269
Thurmond, Richard W. 283
Thurmond, Robert Given 143
Thurmond, Sarah Pauline Jones 143
Thurmond, William Dabney 143, 255
Thurmond, William T. 143, 255
Thurmond County, West Virginia 143
Thurmond's Battalion 142
Thurmond's Partisan Rangers 142, 143, 269
Tillet, John 283
Tolefree, Amelia Marks (Emily) Merriweather 38
Tolefree, Catherine Brand 38
Tolefree, Robert 38
Tolefree (Tolfree), Dr. Robert C. 38, 285

"Torpedo Bureau" 30
Townes, Col. 131
Townes, Isabella 7, 25
Townes, Capt. William 131, 132
Townes, Col. William 7, 13, 25, 42, 50, 70, 220
Townes, William, Jr. 96, 160, 209, 255, 299, 309
Townsend, Amelia 47
Trinity College 33, 74, 80, 83, 84, 199, 272
Trinity Episcopal Church 27
Trinity "Guard" 33, 83
trustees: Boydton Academy 15; Boydton Methodist Church 118; Christiansville Academy 74, 220; Corvallis College 232; Eastern Alabama College 106, 107; Easter's Church 61; Ebenezer Academy 11; Merchant's National Bank 184; Normal School 33, 83; Oak Bowery Female College 112; Olin High School 83; Ridgeway Academy 49; School of Military Tactics 159; Southwestern College 199; Trinity College 83; University of Alabama 103; University of North Carolina 112; Virginia Normal School Board of the State 251; William & Mary 223; Wofford College 49, 50, 175
Tucker, Frank G. 296
Tucker, Lucy Goode 41
Tucker, John M. 96, 99, 268
Tucker, Rev. William 105
Turner, Henrietta Kemp 143
Turner, Lewis 160, 162, 175, 185
Turner, William of Halifax 175
12th North Carolina Infantry 73, 124
20th Virginia Infantry 126, 256, 270
21st North Carolina Infantry 273
21st Virginia 167
22nd Virginia Battalion 98
22nd Virginia Infantry 61, 143
Twitty, James Turnbull 49
Twitty, Robert Cheek 49, 61
Twitty, Sallie 49
Tyler, President John 32

330　Index

Union Courthouse 247
Union Hall 96
Union Institute 32
Union Level, Virginia 37, 118, 221, 235, 236, 238, 276
Union Springs, Alabama 114, 252
Union Springs Herald 252
Union Theological Seminary 75, 212
University of North Carolina 20, 33, 35, 39, 46, 61, 81, 83, 98, 111, 112, 125, 141
University of Southern California, School of Law 79

Vaden, Catherine Rowlett 154, 241
Vaden, Kate Lockett 155, 199
Vaden, Michael 80, 154, 241
Vaden, Sallie F. Sadler 154, 241
Vaden, Wesley Carroll 155, 199
Vaden, Prof. the Rev. Wesley Childs 36, 132, 150–154, 191, 199, 241, 285
Valentines, Virginia 11
Vanderbilt, Commodore Cornelius 47, 83, 214
Vanderbilt, Frank Crawford 47, 83
Vanderbilt Divinity School 76, 141
Vanderbilt University 29, 47, 174, 175, 195, 199, 245, 287
Vanlandingham, Clement L. 85
Vanlandingham, John 85
Venable, Jacob 20
Venable, Nancy 20, 52
Venable, Pittman R. 270, 283
Virginia Baptist Historical Society 160, 173, 189, 302, 311
Virginia Bible Society 184
Virginia Board of Medical Examiners 256
Virginia Medical Society 234, 256
Virginia Military Institute 36

Waddill, Nathaniel R. 283
Wade, Dr. W.R. 192
Wadsworth, Edward 102, 283
Wadsworth, Rev. Edward S. 102, 203, 283
Walker, John C. 283
Walker, Julia Hicks 180

Walker, Martha Rebecca "Queen" 134
Walker, Robert 150, 153
Waller, Caroline 241
Waller, Dabney J., Jr. 149, 151, 241, 242
Waller, Thomas Conway 241
Waller, William I. 13
Waller's Battalion 241
Waller's War: Reminisces—Wingfield 242
Walton, John 11
Walton, Rebecca Mary 11
Ware, Albert G. 242
Ware, Dabney 253
Ware, Elizabeth 253
Ware, Jennie D. Pretlow 253
Ware, Joe 312, 319
Ware, Jordan P. 150–153, 242, 283
Ware, Judith T. 242
Ware, Martha 312, 319
Ware, Rev. Thomas A. 253, 285
Ware Bottom Church 111
warehouse 22, 134, 185, 225
Warrenton, North Carolina 12, 53, 55, 57, 72, 123, 189, 248
Warrenton, Virginia 245
Warrenton Baptist Church 123
Warrenton Female Academy 87, 101, 13
Warrenton Male Academy 12, 20, 35
Warrenton Military Academy 248
Warrenton "Rifles" 73
Washington, George 12
Washington, James R. 288
Washington, D.C. 12, 18, 19, 30, 76, 77, 107, 108, 136, 162, 174, 192, 236, 247, 269, 300
Washington and Lee University 136
Washington City 114, 136
Washington College 35, 38
Washington County, Arkansas 175
Washington County, Georgia 246
Washington County, Missouri 168
Washington Hospital 142
Washington Literary Society 5, 87, 95, 114, 140
Washington Medical School 57, 59, 60

Washington Street M.E. Church 211
Washington Tavern 69, 130, 131
Watts, James Dillard 248
Watts, Dr. James J. 180
Watts, John Wesley 140, 150–153, 180, 242
Watts, Lucy Ann Simmons 240
Weatherford, Hugh 69
Weatherford, Mary Frances Bugg 69
Weldon, North Carolina 23, 116, 161
Weldon Ordnance Depot 73
Wesley, John 8, 9, 10, 11, 78, 79
Wesleyan College 28–30, 115
Wesleyan Journal 31
Wesleyan Female College 34, 162
West, Belle 241
West, T.S. 149
West, Thomas Scott 242
West Tennessee College 21, 194, 232, 236
West Virginia 126, 142–144, 148
Wheatley, William Arthur 149, 150, 242
Wheelwright, Margaret Keerfoot 163, 164
Wheelwright, Thomas Stuart 164
Wheelwright, Rev. Prof. Maj. William Henry 163, 247, 253, 285
White, Emma Gray 243
White, Francis 184
White, Henrietta Kemp Turner 243
White, Lucy 184
White, Lucy Carter Minor 243
White, Mary 111
White, Mary E. 243
White, Minnie M. 232
White, Rev. T.B. 232
White, Col. William 243
White, William Henry 243
White, William W. 151–153, 243
White River, Arkansas 175
Whitice, James 21, 23, 37, 38, 61, 62, 64, 66, 69
Wightman, James W. 95
Wightman, Rev. Dr. William May 90, 94, 140, 141, 174, 196, 283, 285, 296

Index

Wiles, Ella Marion 117, 174
Wiles, Leroy W. 71, 117
Wiles, Lucy L. 159
Wilkerson, Howell 66
William and Mary Center for Archeology 311
William and Mary College 11, 13, 37, 123, 227
William and Mary Seminary 7
Williams, Benjamin J. 258
Williams, Charles E. 255, 283
Williams, E.A. 164
Williams, Henry H. 283
Williams, John 283
Williams, John B. 273, 283
Williams, Oliver P. 255, 283
Williams, Richard H. 262, 283
Williams, Robert 11
Williams, William S. (Missouri) 150, 152, 159, 243, 283
Williams, William S. (South Carolina) 255
Williams, William S. (Virginia) 262
Williams College 106
Williamson, Benjamin R. 96, 268
Williamson, James J. 99
Williamston, South Carolina 29, 80
Williamston Female College 79, 80
Williamston Hotel 50, 80
Wills, Catherine 61
Wills, Edwin V. 95
Wills, George M.D. 95
Wills, Hall 178, 185
Wills, "J. & K.W." 289
Wills, Prof. John C. 43, 53, 61, 88, 90, 94, 95, 113, 114, 178, 275, 283, 285, 289, 296
Wills, John C., Jr. 95, 296
Wills, John H. 95
Wills, Kate 95
Wills, Louisa 95
Wills, Martha Martin 95
Wills, Rosaline 61, 289
Wills, Rose (infant) 289
Wills, Rosine M.D. 95

Wills, Wyllie 61
Wilmington, North Carolina 27, 60, 197, 249
Wilson, Bishop A.W. 227
Wilson, Rev. John O. 79, 80
Wilson, Leroy M. 118, 128, 248, 268, 283
Wilson, North Carolina 82
Wilson-Kautz Raid 75, 121, 191
Winans, William 283
Winckler, W.M. 61
Winfield, John O. 283
Winfield, Robert H. 283
Winfield, West Virginia 143, 144
Wingfield, Henry W. 255, 283
Wingfield, I.O. 56
Wingfield, Joseph B. 255
Witcher, Lt. Col. William A., 142, 143
Wofford, Benjamin 49, 141
Wofford College 29, 48-50, 86, 87, 95, 113, 114, 140-142, 175, 197, 198, 282
Wood, Benjamin 214
Wood, David 76
Wood, Henry 77
Wood, Jack 197
Wood, Jackie 3, 292
Woodson, Judge John 119
Woodson, Mary 119
Woodson, W.K. 149
Woodson, William K. 243
Woodward, Rev. M. 211
Wooten, Frank 120
Wooten, Dr. Lucius T. 60
Wooten, Mary Ellen (Etta) Walton 60
Wooten, Hon. Taylor 60
Wootten family 67
Wootton, A.J. (Andrew Jackson) 165
Wootton, Annie N. 165
Wootton, Arlene McKinney 4, 168
Wootton, C.N. 96
Wootton, George 147
Wootton, Glenda 4
Wootton, John 65, 66, 147, 166

Wootton, John C. 65, 66, 96, 165
Wootton, John P. 165
Wootton, John T. 66, 67, 96, 164, 165, 188
Wootton, John W. 62, 65, 70, 96, 98, 146, 158, 164, 165, 186-188, 295
Wootton, Joseph L. 66, 69, 96, 164, 165
Wootton, N.J. 165
Wootton, Nancy J. 165
Wootton, Norfleet 165
Wootton, P.S. 165
Wootton, Samuel, Sr. 165
Wootton, Sandy Herndon 63
Wootton family 3, 63, 66, 67, 188, 189, 295
Wright, James T. 283
Wright, Luther 89, 253, 283
Wright, Virginia Moody 3, 158, 166, 186
Wright and Rogers, Ltd. 24
Wright brothers 24
Wyatt (slave) 147
Wyatt, Richard O. 283
Wyche, Cyril C. 13
Wyche, George E. 13, 283
Wyche, James 13
Wynne, Arthur Lee 150, 152, 153
Wynne, C.H. 243

Yale University 30, 155, 161, 175
Yancey, Elizabeth 37, 53, 287, 289
Yancey, Ellen 53, 113
Yancey, Helen 133
Yancey, John 37
Yancey, Rosanna 53
Yancey, Thomas 37
Yancey Boarding House 53
York, Brantley 32, 33
York, Virginia 136
Young, R.F. 201
Young, Thaddeus H.L. 62, 283, 286

Zion Church 66, 69, 118, 226
Zion Hill Academy 238

www.ingramcontent.com/pod-product-compliance
Lightning Source LLC
Chambersburg PA
CBHW051208300426
44116CB00006B/469